Organization Charts

Highlights

Overview

One of the largest collections of its kind, this third edition of *Organization Charts* contains structural diagrams and general profiles of 230 corporations, nonprofit organizations, and government agencies. Including a special set of reorganization profiles for selected companies (see below), this volume integrates more than 240 separate diagrams.

Diverse Coverage

Geographically, these organizations represent more than 30 countries on four continents, and their activities span all the major sectors of the world economy, excluding agriculture. In many cases multiple companies in a given industry are listed, enabling organizational comparisons of competing firms. For example, three or more companies are listed in such industries as automobiles and automotive parts, computer programming services, commercial banking, insurance, and telecommunications services.

Detailed Information

Each listing includes general contact information such as the mailing address, telephone and fax numbers, Web site address, general e-mail address, primary industry classifications, and a short description of the organization. Charts also list the source and date of the structure information.

Profiles of Major Companies

Approximately 40 percent of the organizations are major national or international for-profit companies with annual revenues exceeding $1 billion. Many of these large enterprises appear on well-known rankings lists such as the *Fortune* 500™, the *Fortune* Global 500™, and the *Business Week* 1000™.

Some of the major corporations appearing in this edition include the following:

- Bell & Howell Company
- DaimlerChrysler AG
- Edison International
- France Telecom
- General Motors Corporation
- Lockheed Martin Corporation
- Novartis AG
- Toshiba Corporation
- Warner-Lambert Company
- Xerox Corporation

Reorganization Profiles

A special feature to this edition is a set of reorganization profiles of nine major corporations that have undergone various kinds of restructurings in recent years. These profiles display the organization charts from before and after the restructuring, and include a few paragraphs about what was changed and why (see the preface for more details).

Convenient Indexes

In addition, this book contains several access points for locating particular organizations or types of organizations: Standard Industrial Classification (SIC) index, North American Industry Classification System (NAICS) index, country index, and the general index (including company and major subsidiary names).

Organization CHARTS

3rd Edition

Structures of 230 businesses, government agencies, and non-profit organizations

Edited by Nick Sternberg and Scott Heil

GALE GROUP

Detroit
San Francisco
London
Boston
Woodbridge, CT

Nick Sternberg and Scott Heil, Editors

Jennifer Carman, Assistant Graphics Editor

Graphics and page layout by Frontline Design, Ltd.

The Gale Group Staff

Terry Peck, Coordinating Editor
Erin Braun, Managing Editor

Mary Beth Trimper, Composition Manager
Wendy Blurton, Senior Buyer

Gary Leach, Artist
Cindy Baldwin, Product Design Manager

Library of Congress Catalog Card Number 96-8231
ISBN 0-7876-2452-7
ISSN 1526-0879
Printed in the United States of America

Contents

Preface

This volume provides a rare glimpse into the management structures and inner workings of some 230 large and small companies, nonprofit organizations, and government agencies. Included are organizations heralding from more than two dozen countries and representing approximately 100 separate industry classifications. A fair number of the companies are household names, and 29 of them appeared on the 1999 *Fortune* 500 list. A much larger share of the companies featured in this third edition of *Organization Charts* have revenues of $1 billion or more, including many of the non-U.S. firms.

Highlighting Corporate Restructuring

Mergers, acquisitions, downsizings, reorganizations, and other forms of restructuring are common to the modern business vocabulary and experience. But what exactly changes when a company reorganizes? To help answer this question, we've assembled in this edition a set of nine special profiles of major international corporations that have undertaken reorganizations over the past decade or so. Most of these events, whether triggered by mergers or by market changes, occurred in the latter half of the 1990s. The featured companies are listed in Table 1.

Table 1. Reorganizations Profiled in This Volume
DaimlerChrysler AG
General Motors Corporation
International Business Machines Corporation
Mitsubishi Corporation
Motorola Inc.
PPG Industries, Inc.
Siemens AG
The Tokai Bank, Limited
Xerox Corporation

In each profile, we present one chart of the company's structure from before the reorganization followed by a view from afterwards. At the back of the book we provide for each a short narrative summary of the major structural changes, the reasons they happened, and the intended outcomes.

Understanding Different Organizational Models

On the surface many of the charts in this book look the same, and indeed some from unlike companies have striking similarity. However, in many cases there are subtleties that a quick glance may not reveal, and it is often no coincidence that organizations end up with their particular structure. The field of organization theory and design provides us with a number of concepts that are useful for describing, understanding, and interpreting these differences and their ramifications for organizational effectiveness.

Management scholars have long identified three basic models for large organizations: the functional structure, the divisional structure, and the matrix structure. To this list a number of writers have added a variety of special categories or emergent models that aren't quite captured under these three headings. Many of these newer models focus on highly diversified and geographically dispersed companies, and particular attention has been paid to how multinational corporations are organized. Below we summarize the features of the three well-known models and briefly survey a few of the nontraditional models.

FUNCTIONAL STRUCTURE. The functional structure is the traditional hierarchical organization familiar to most people. Under a functional structure, departments are established based on their particular specialties, e.g., marketing, finance, production, and generally each department performs its specialized tasks across all or most of the organization, wherever those duties are required. Functional structures tend to be centralized and emphasize authority. Their departments are often divided conceptually between line and staff authority. Line authority is exercised in departments that are directly

Figure 1. The Functional Structure

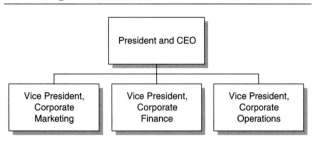

related to the company's operations, such as manufacturing, whereas staff authority is given to departments that consult or advise the management, such as accounting and human resources. Figure 1 illustrates a simple functional set-up.

DIVISIONAL STRUCTURE. By contrast, a divisional structure cleaves the corporation into several semi-autonomous business units. These units may be organized by product or service line, geography, or customer focus (e.g., business customers, private individuals), among other formats. Each division may have a functional structure or some other configuration, but generally there is minimal overlap of resources across different divisions. This means that areas like human resources, marketing, and finance may be duplicated in each division, creating redundancies and potential inefficiencies.

At the same time, in the true divisional structure, division leadership is able, ideally at least, to implement corporate strategy as it sees fit and to respond to the market conditions that concern it directly. In the pure divisional model, top management only intervenes in division affairs on major strategy and corporate governance issues. Unit autonomy is a harbinger of a divisional structure, and thus companies that use the word "division" to describe their departments may or may

Figure 2. The Divisional Structure

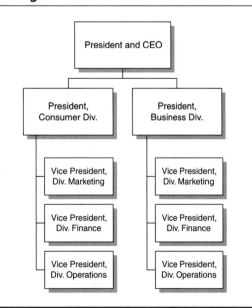

not actually have a divisional structure. General Motors is the most famous example of the division structure, which it helped pioneer in the 1920s. Companies like General Electric and Lockheed Martin, both appearing in this book, are associated with a variation on divisional structure known as the sector structure. A simple example of a divisional structure is shown in Figure 2.

MATRIX STRUCTURE. Matrix structures are characterized by decentralized and cross-functional relationships among employees and, in some cases, management. In effect, matrix structures borrow elements from both functional and divisional structures, stitching the two together through multiple reporting relationships. Often matrix organizations have a project or product leadership structure that is separate from the departmental/supervisory structure. As the example in Figure 3 indicates, when these various roles intersect it forms a matrix-like grid in the visual representation. The different relations in the matrix may be highly formalized or fairly ad hoc. A matrix approach benefits business activities that are highly collaborative or interactive, such as R&D, product design, or regional sales management. Aerospace companies were some of the first to use matrix structures.

INTERNATIONAL STRUCTURES. The fast growth of international trade, and specifically the rapid expansion by large companies to tap into foreign markets, has drawn a good deal of attention to how companies organize their business concerns internationally. For example, Christopher Bartlett and Sumantra Ghoshal in their book Managing Across Borders (Harvard Business School Press, 1989) make fine distinctions between businesses that have "global" structures versus a "multinational" or "transnational" structure. A global organization, according to the authors, has a centralized command-and-control structure rooted in the home country, and its headquarters closely dictates the policies and practices of the international operating units. The result is a rather monolithic marketing organization that behaves essentially the same in each country it does business in.

Bartlett and Ghoshal identified what they termed the transnational structure as the most recent and most advantageous approach to managing international businesses. Developing this concept more fully in the 1998 update of their book, the two business professors characterize the transnational business as a complex structure that adapts to local strengths and differences and weaves them into the international fabric of the organization. As a result, manufacturing may be distributed across several countries, but new research might be centered in one country where the company has strong access to technical skills, and none of these activities may take place in the home country.

MIXED OR HYBRID STRUCTURES. In practice, most large companies mix elements of several of these conceptual models for different areas of their operations. In recent years, for instance, it isn't uncommon for a business to profess having

Figure 3.   The Matrix Structure

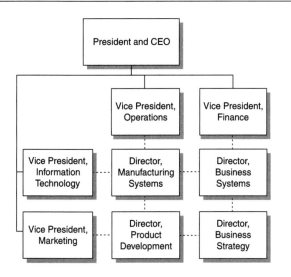

decentralized, autonomous, market-oriented operating units—each responsible for its own profitability—while functions like marketing, R&D, and human resources are still carried out primarily at the corporate level. Similarly, within international companies various regional units may have differing degrees of autonomy, local focus, and centralization.

Significance of Structure

If the jargon and semantics of organization theory seem inconsequential, the implications for the business world are often taken quite seriously. Executives at many large corporations associate organizational structure directly with, among other things, market responsiveness, employee motivation, economies of scale and scope, and ultimately, the bottom line.

When management is cognizant of the effects of organizational design, it usually seeks to align the business structure with the corporate strategy. Over the past decade or so, for example, a high premium has been placed on an enterprise's ability to quickly adapt to changes it perceives in the marketplace. Decentralized, flatter structures tend to facilitate faster decision making, and this is in part why reorganizations to this effect have been popular. Central also to many business strategies has been cost containment, which provides additional rationale for removing layers of hierarchy.

Still, decentralization doesn't always mean a more efficient organization. If it creates redundancies or erects barriers between centers (or individuals) of operational expertise and knowledge, the result can be worse than leaving a more hierarchical or centralized system in place.

Because so much is perceived to be riding on organizational design, in fact, many companies labor tirelessly over devising the exact configuration of persons and resources that best matches their business strategies. Indeed, some even regard the visual representation of their structure—the organization chart—as a trade secret and will not release the information to a publication such as this.

Charting the Uncharted

Such fears about competitive intelligence leaks as well as other factors mean that finding information on recent, real-life corporate structures can be a hit-or-miss proposition. Interestingly, in compiling this volume, one of the most common explanations we heard for why a company didn't wish to release its chart was that too much was changing on it. This was not entirely surprising given how frequently we learn of ever newer and bigger stock-financed mergers and acquisitions, and it is perhaps revealing commentary when dozens of major companies' structures are changing so quickly that no one has time to record them.

Somewhat more perplexing are the large companies, particularly in the high-tech industries, that claim not to have organization charts at all. Surely they have departments and executives and various techniques of specialization and collaboration like other companies, right?

One such company is Apple Computer, Inc. Entering the mid-1990s, Apple was reportedly a fragmented, decentralized company with 15 product lines and as many as 22 marketing groups. In a series of layoffs and restructurings extending from 1996 to 1998, the company dramatically reduced its product lines to four main segments and centralized marketing in one organization-wide department. By 1998 the company's product and marketing realignment, along with a successful new product launch, had reversed its losses and set Apple off on a new course.

But the question remains, what would Apple's chart look like? Simply put, Apple is organized along functional lines—the company admits as much. Sales, marketing, hardware design, software design, and worldwide manufacturing operations are all overseen on a company-wide basis by senior executives reporting to the CEO. The sales area includes four international sales divisions for various regions of the world, and the operations center manages three computer assembly plants, one each in Asia, Europe, and the United States.

We leave the visual representation of this structure to the reader's imagination.

Introduction and User's Guide

Compilation

Charts for this volume were obtained by a variety of means. In many cases information was provided directly by the companies in response to a phone call or letter from us. In a large number of cases the organizations already provided the information to the public through annual reports, Internet sites, or company literature. In addition, in a few instances, when more current information was not available, the editors revised older charts using published information from company reports and disclosures and other sources. Each chart contains a note identifying its source, including whether it was revised by the editors.

Presentation

All the charts in this book were drawn expressly for this publication based on the information we compiled. Whenever possible, we tried to retain the general feel of the original presentation, but space, standardization, and other considerations meant that some were altered and look quite a bit different from how the individual organizations represent them. In extremely detailed charts, occasionally we omitted fine detail at the bottom of the hierarchy. Personal names are also omitted. Of course, all structural relationships remain intact.

Parts of the Book

MAIN BODY. The main body is organized alphabetically by organization name, ignoring leading articles. For non-English names, we generally spelled them as the organization did in its official literature. If the company provided an English translation of its name, we used that version. Most, however, are left in the original language.

Each chart includes a summary box with basic contact information, such as mailing address, telephone number, and Internet address, as well as industry classification codes and a short description of the organization.

Industry classification is based on the U.S. Standard Industrial Classification (SIC) and the newer North American Industry Classification System (NAICS). These codes are intended to portray the organization's primary activity, but for highly diversified firms a single industry code does not indicate the full array of business activities they may participate in. The industry codes were assigned by the editors and may differ from the organization's classification listed elsewhere.

SIC INDEX. All organizations in the book are indexed numerically by their primary four-digit SIC codes as described above. The NAICS equivalent of each SIC appearing in the book is also listed. If there were no companies for a particular SIC, the heading does not appear in the index; hence, this is not a comprehensive table of all SIC codes.

NAICS INDEX. This index follows the same format as the SIC Index, only it is organized by five- or six-digit NAICS codes.

COUNTRY INDEX. This section lists all organizations alphabetically by their country of origin.

GENERAL INDEX. All companies, nonprofit organizations, and government entities whose charts we list are indexed here. In addition, when significant and distinct corporate subsidiaries (i.e., well-known companies that don't share their parent company's name) are referenced on the parent's chart, they are also indexed here. We don't, however, index subagencies of government or nonprofit entities.

Acknowledgements

The editors sincerely thank all the individuals who assisted in bringing this publication together, including the company officials who provided us their charts. Special appreciation goes to Lynn Laufenberg and Tom Rajt for their unwavering support and patience throughout the process.

Comments and Suggestions

Comments and questions about this publication are welcome and may be directed to the publisher at: Editor, *Organization Charts,* The Gale Group, 27500 Drake Rd., Farmington Hills, MI 48331, tel. 1-800-347-GALE.

Abbott Laboratories

One of the world's largest drug and nutritional product makers

100 Abbott Park Rd.
Abbott Park, IL 60064-3500
Phone: (847) 937-6100
Web: www.abbott.com

Primary SIC: 2834—Pharmaceutical Preparations
Primary NAICS: 325412—Pharmaceutical Preparation Mfg

Board of Directors

- Audit Committee
- Compensation Committee
- Executive Committee
- Nominations and Board Affairs Committee

Chief Executive Officer

Operations Committee

President and Chief Operating Officer

Senior Vice President, Finance Chief Financial Officer

Senior Vice President, Secretary, and General Counsel

Senior Vice President Human Resources

Vice President, Corporate Quality Assurance and Regulatory Affairs

Vice President Corporate Engineering

Vice President Abbott Health Systems

President TAP Holdings, Inc.

Senior Vice President Diagnostics Operations

Senior Vice President Chemical & Agricultural Products

Senior Vice President Pharmaceutical Operations

Senior Vice President Hospital Products

Senior Vice President Ross Products

Senior Vice President International Operations

Source: Company and revisions by the editors, 1998

Agfa-Gevaert N.V.

This Bayer AG subsidiary is a global manufacturer of film and other photographic imaging products

Septestraat 27
B-2640 Mortsel, Belgium
Phone: +32-3-444-7094 **Fax:** +32-3-444-0094
Web: www.agfa.com

Primary SIC: 3861—Photographic Equipment & Supplies
Primary NAICS: 325992—Photo Film,
Paper, Plate & Chemical Mfg

Board of Management

- Subsidiaries/Sales Organizations
- Finance, Legal, Human Resources, and Logistics

Business Group, Photographic Products (FO)
- Film (FLM)
  Photographic Film, Single Use Cameras, and Cameras
- Finishing (FIN)
  Photographic Paper and Photochemicals
- Lab Equipment (LAB)
  Equipment for Wholesale Finishing Labs, Minilabs, and Commercial Labs

Business Group, Graphic Systems (GS)
- Photographic Pre-Press Systems (PPS)
  Graphic Film and Paper, Processing-and-Proof Systems, and Inkjet Systems
- Offset Printing Systems (OPS)
  Printing Plates
- Electronic Pre-Press Systems (EPS)
  Imagesetters & Plate Imagers, Scanners (mid-range, high end), and Software
- Desktop Publishing (DTP)
  DTP Scanners, Digital Cameras, and Inkjet Consumables
- Digital Printing (DPS)
  Digital Printing Systems

Business Group, Technical Imaging (TI)
- Medical (MED)
  Photographic and Digital Systems for Medical Radiography, and Computer Imaging
- Non-Destructive Testing (NDT)
  Photographic Materials and Processing Equipment for Non-Destructive Testing with Radiography
- Micrographic Systems (MDS)
  Films and Equipment and COM (Computer Output on Microfilm) Systems
- Motion Pictures (CIN)
  Release Print for Cinema
- Specialty Foils (SFC)
  Foils and Semifinished Products

Source: Company web site, 1998

Akron-Summit County Public Library

A 17-branch public library system serving a metropolitan area of more than 530,000 residents

55 Main St.
Akron, OH 44326-0001
Phone: (330) 643-9000
Web: www.ascpl.lib.oh.us

Primary SIC: 8231—Libraries
Primary NAICS: 51412—Libraries & Archives
E-mail: ascpl@acorn.net

Board of Trustees
ASCPL

Librarian-Director
Clerk-Treasurer

Administration Office

Building Maintenance

Marketing Communications Dept.

Human Resources Dept.

Librarian-Assistant Director
Public Service

- Branch & Mobile Services Coordinator
  - Branch Libraries
  - Mobile Services
- Main Library Coordinator
  - Subject Divisions
  - Other Depts.
- Youth Services Coordinator
  - Youth Services Office
  - Assistant Coordinator, Young Adult Services
- Delivery Services

Librarian-Assistant Director
Technical & Automated Services

- Automated Services Librarian
- Computer Room Operations Supervisor
- Technical Services Head
  - Acquisitions
  - Cataloging

Assistant Director
Finance

- Accounting Supervisor Budget
- Accounting Supervisor Payroll
- Business Office

Source: Organization web site, 1999

Allen Daniel Associates, Inc.

A small collection agency specializing in defaulted student loans

77 Franklin Street
Boston, MA 02110-2100 **Fax:** (617) 357-9423
Phone: (800) 882-2100
Web: www.pressenter.com/~rgerdes/

Primary SIC: 7322—Adjustment & Collection Services
Primary NAICS: 56144—Collection Agencies
E-mail: rgerdes@pressenter.com

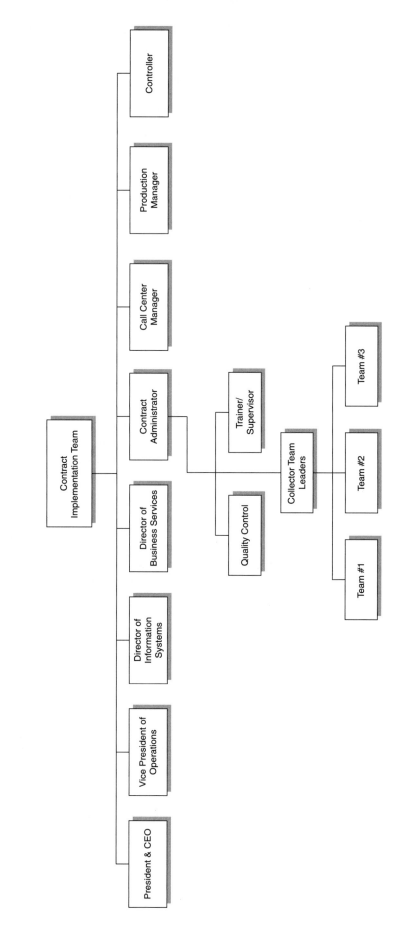

Source: Company web site, 1999

American Cancer Society, Inc.

This famous nonprofit has an annual budget in excess of $500 million and has over 2 million volunteers

1599 Clifton Rd. NE
Atlanta, GA 30329-4251
Phone: (404) 320-3333 **Fax:** (404) 329-5787
Web: www.cancer.org

Primary SIC: 8399—Social Services, NEC
Primary NAICS: 813212—Voluntary Health Organizations

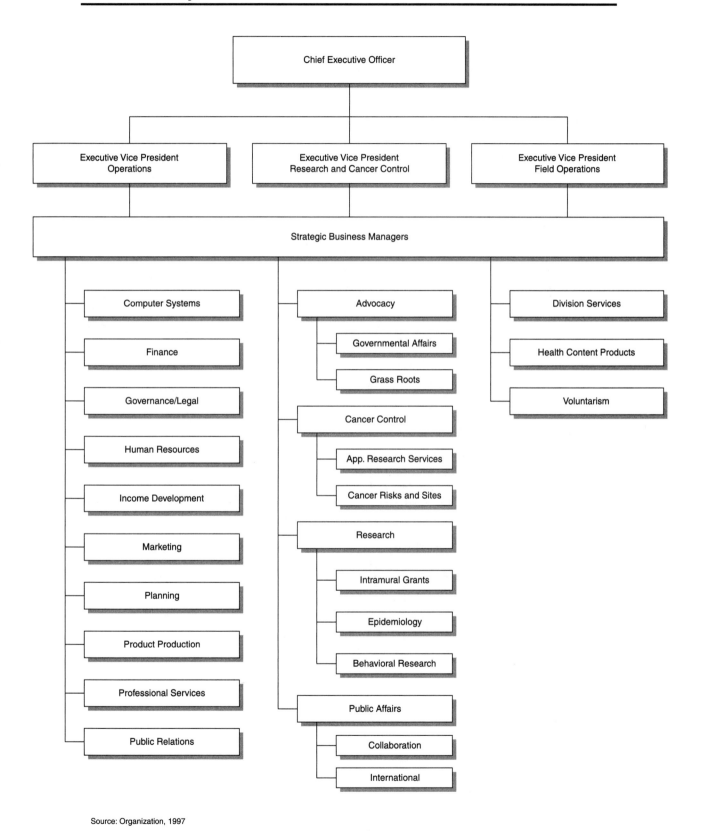

Source: Organization, 1997

American National Standards Institute

A private membership organization that serves as a forum for developing and promoting technical standards

11 W. 42nd St., 13th Fl.
New York, NY 10036
Phone: (212) 642-4900 **Fax:** (212) 398-0023
Web: web.ansi.org

Primary SIC: 8611—Business Associations
Primary NAICS: 81391—Business Associations

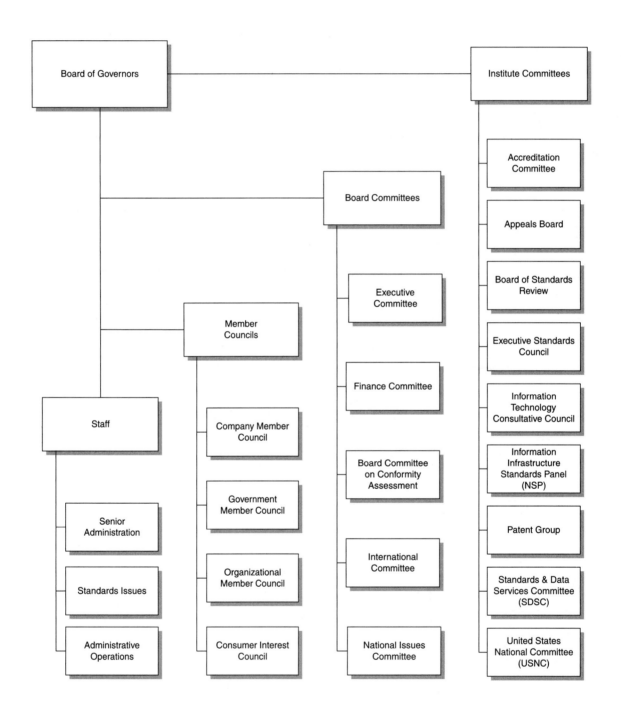

Source: Organization web site, 1999

American Psychological Association

The primary professional association for psychology and related fields

750 First Street, NE
Washington, DC 20002
Phone: (202) 336-5500
Web: www.apa.org

Primary SIC: 8621—Professional
Membership Organizations
Primary NAICS: 81392—Professional Organizations

General Counsel

Executive Office

Governance Affairs
- Board of Directors
- Council of Representatives
- Elections
- APA Awards
- Special Projects
- Presidential Initiatives

Education Directorate
- Governance and Communications
- Education and Training in Psychology
- Professional Education and Training
- Center for Psychology in Schools and Education

Practice Directorate
- Government Relations
- Legal & Regulatory Affairs
- Marketing
- Public Relations/Communications
- State Advocacy
- Professional Development
- Policy and Advocacy in the Schools
- Professional Issues
- College of Professional Psychology

Science Directorate
- Scientific Affairs
- Communications & Member Relations
- Science Education & Informal Learning
- Science Administration
- Testing and Assessment
- Research Ethics
- Animal Research Issues

Public Interest Directorate
- Aging Issues
- Children, Youth, and Families
- Disability Issues
- Ethnic Minority Affairs
- Lesbian, Gay, and Bisexual Concerns
- Public Interest Initiatives
- Office on AIDS
- Urban Initiatives
- Women's Programs

Continued on next page

Source: Organization web site, 1998

American Psychological Association (cont.)

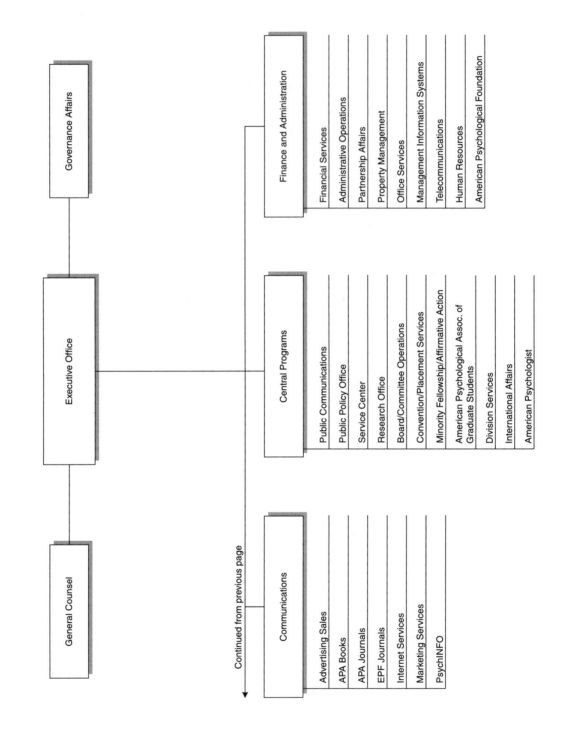

Executive Office

- General Counsel
- Governance Affairs

Communications
- Advertising Sales
- APA Books
- APA Journals
- EPF Journals
- Internet Services
- Marketing Services
- PsychINFO

Continued from previous page

Central Programs
- Public Communications
- Public Policy Office
- Service Center
- Research Office
- Board/Committee Operations
- Convention/Placement Services
- Minority Fellowship/Affirmative Action
- American Psychological Assoc. of Graduate Students
- Division Services
- International Affairs
- American Psychologist

Finance and Administration
- Financial Services
- Administrative Operations
- Partnership Affairs
- Property Management
- Office Services
- Management Information Systems
- Telecommunications
- Human Resources
- American Psychological Foundation

Ammann Group

A mid-size European construction materials and services firm with branches in nine countries

Eisenbahnstrasse 25
CH-4901 Langenthal, Switzerland
Phone: +41-062-916-6775
Web: www.ammann-group.ch

Primary SIC: 2951—Asphalt Paving Mixtures & Blocks
Primary NAICS: 324121—Asphalt Paving
Mixture & Block Mfg

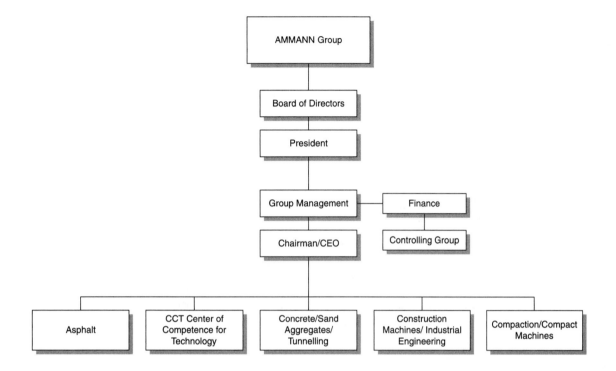

Source: Company web site, 1999

Asahi Chemical Industry Co., Ltd.

In addition to chemicals, this large diversified firm makes building materials, beverages, electronics, and pharmaceuticals

1-2 Yurakucho 1-chome
Chiyoda-ku, Tokyo 100-8440, Japan
Phone: +81 03-3507-2060 **Fax:** +81 03-3507-2495
Web: www.asahi-kasei.co.jp

Primary SIC: 2812—Alkalies & Chlorine
Primary NAICS: 325181—Alkalies & Chlorine Mfg

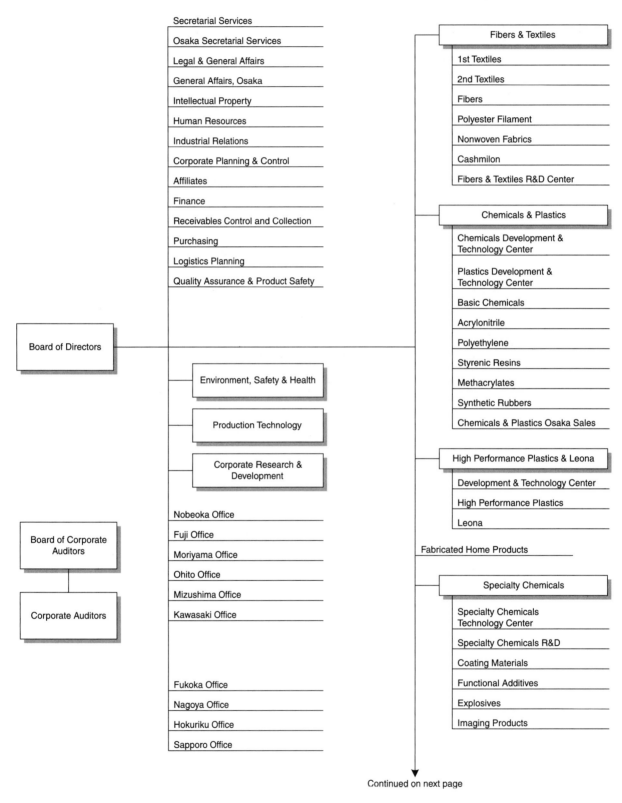

Continued on next page

Source: Annual report, 1998

Continued from previous page

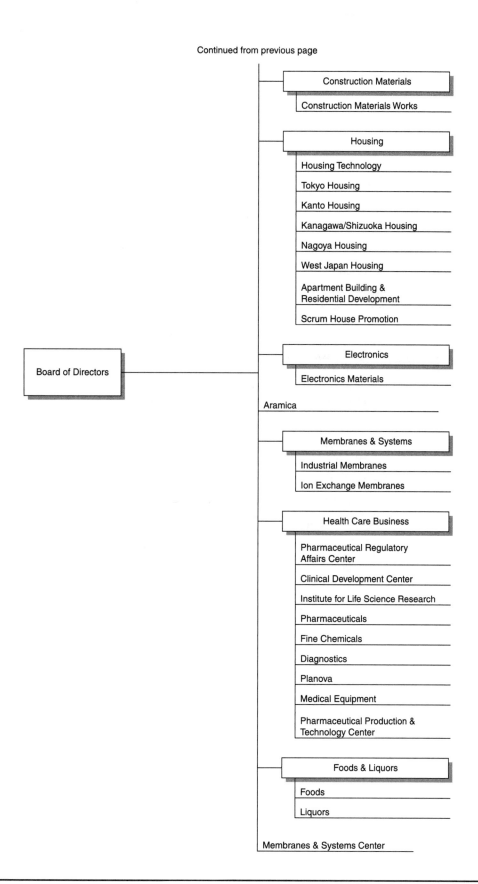

Board of Directors

Construction Materials
- Construction Materials Works

Housing
- Housing Technology
- Tokyo Housing
- Kanto Housing
- Kanagawa/Shizuoka Housing
- Nagoya Housing
- West Japan Housing
- Apartment Building & Residential Development
- Scrum House Promotion

Electronics
- Electronics Materials

Aramica

Membranes & Systems
- Industrial Membranes
- Ion Exchange Membranes

Health Care Business
- Pharmaceutical Regulatory Affairs Center
- Clinical Development Center
- Institute for Life Science Research
- Pharmaceuticals
- Fine Chemicals
- Diagnostics
- Planova
- Medical Equipment
- Pharmaceutical Production & Technology Center

Foods & Liquors
- Foods
- Liquors

Membranes & Systems Center

Autoliv Inc.

One of the world's top manufacturers of automotive safety equipment such as airbags and seatbelts

Box 70381
SE-107 244 Stockholm, Sweden
Phone: +46 8 402 0600 **Fax:** +46 8 244479
Web: www.autoliv.com

Primary SIC: 3714—Motor Vehicle Parts & Accessories
Primary NAICS: 336399—All Other
Motor Vehicle Parts Mfg

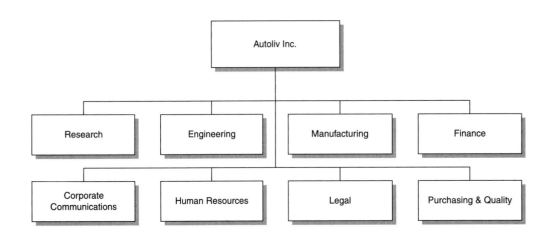

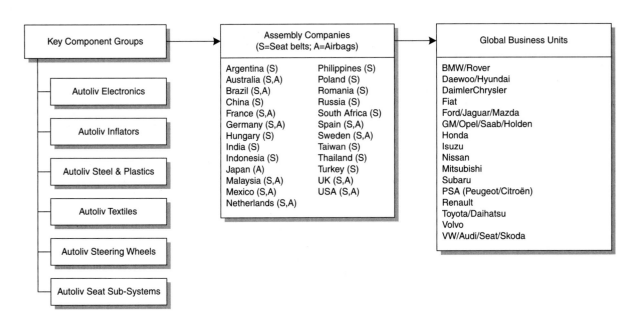

Key Component Groups	Assembly Companies (S=Seat belts; A=Airbags)		Global Business Units
Autoliv Electronics	Argentina (S)	Philippines (S)	BMW/Rover
Autoliv Inflators	Australia (S,A)	Poland (S)	Daewoo/Hyundai
Autoliv Steel & Plastics	Brazil (S,A)	Romania (S)	DaimlerChrysler
Autoliv Textiles	China (S)	Russia (S)	Fiat
Autoliv Steering Wheels	France (S,A)	South Africa (S)	Ford/Jaguar/Mazda
Autoliv Seat Sub-Systems	Germany (S,A)	Spain (S,A)	GM/Opel/Saab/Holden
	Hungary (S)	Sweden (S,A)	Honda
	India (S)	Taiwan (S)	Isuzu
	Indonesia (S)	Thailand (S)	Nissan
	Japan (A)	Turkey (S)	Mitsubishi
	Malaysia (S,A)	UK (S,A)	Subaru
	Mexico (S,A)	USA (S,A)	PSA (Peugeot/Citroën)
	Netherlands (S,A)		Renault
			Toyota/Daihatsu
			Volvo
			VW/Audi/Seat/Skoda

Source: Company, 1999

AverStar, Inc.

An information technology contractor primarily to government agencies, AverStar employs 1,900 people at 30 offices

23 4th Ave.
Burlington, MA 01803
Phone: (781) 221-6990 **Fax:** (781) 221-6991
Web: www.averstar.com

Primary SIC: 7371—Computer Programming Services
Primary NAICS: 541511—Custom Computer
Programming Services

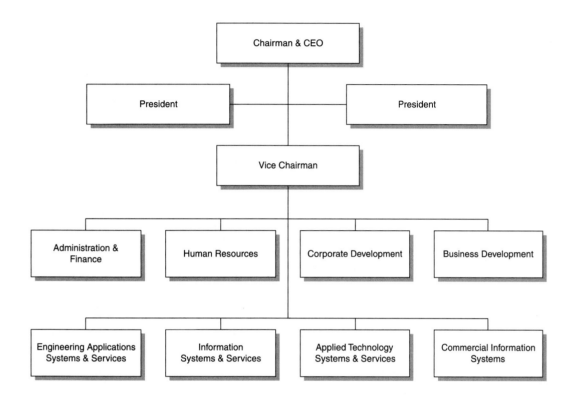

Source: Company web site, 1999

Baker Hughes Inc.

A leading oilfield machinery and services supplier

P.O. Box 4740
Houston, TX 77210-4740
Phone: (713) 439-8600 **Fax:** (713) 843-7964
Web: www.bakerhughes.com

Primary SIC: 3533—Oil & Gas Field
Machinery & Equipment
Primary NAICS: 333132—Oil & Gas Field
Machinery & Equipment Mfg

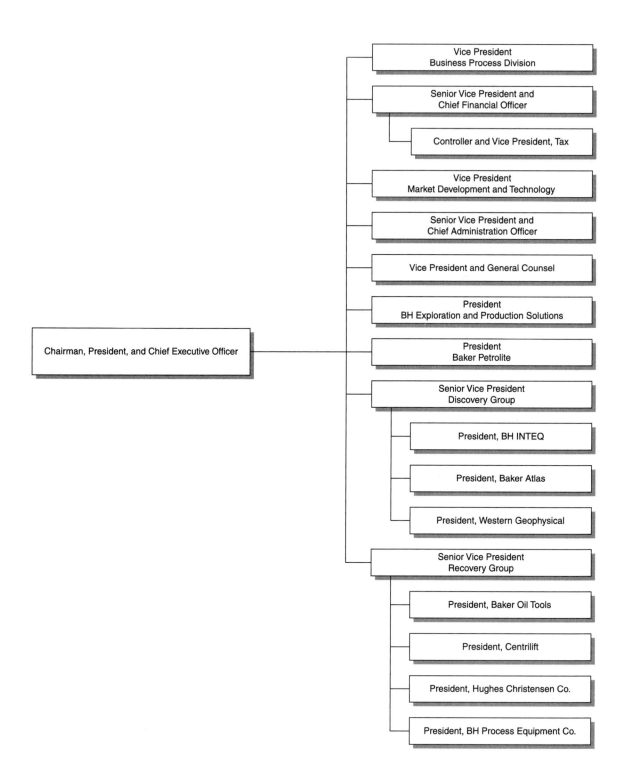

Source: Company and revisions by the editors, 1997

Baltimore Gas and Electric Company

Held by Constellation Energy Group, BGE is the United States' 12th-largest diversified utility by stock market capitalization

39 W. Lexington St.
Baltimore, MD 21201
Phone: (410) 783-5920 **Fax:** (410) 234-5367
Web: www.bge.com

Primary SIC: 4931—Electric & Other Services Combined
Primary NAICS: 221112—Fossil Fuel
Electric Power Generation

```
                    COB, CEO, and President,
                    Baltimore Gas and Electric

    Vice Chairman,
    Baltimore Gas and Electric

                    Executive Vice President,
                    Utility Operations
```

Continued on next page

```
Vice President, Electric                              Vice President, Retail
Transmission and                                     Services
Distribution

Mgr., System Operation and                           Energy Supply and Sales
Maintenance (Transmission                            (Merchant Function)
Operations)

    Supervisor, Maintenance                              Director, Gas Supply
    Management & Support                                 and Bulk Sales Unit

    Supervisor,                    Principal Engineer,      Principal Engineer,
    Training and Safety            Oper. Engineering &      Technical Services Unit
                                   Applications             (Merchant Function)

    General Supervisor,            Engineer/Senior          Senior Engineer/
    System Relay & Control         Engineer                 Engineer

                                   Engineer Technician      Functional Business
                                                            Analyst
    Principal Engineer,            Systems Support Leader
    Transmission &                                          Economic Operations
    Interconnection Planning       Operations Computer      Specialist
                                   Specialist
                                                            Bulk Power Data
    Director, Substation           General Supervisor,      Processor
    Operations &                   System Operations
    Maintenance
                                   Shift Supervisor, Bulk   Director,
                                   Power                    Power Marketing
    Director, Bulk Power                                    (Merchant Function)
    System Operation               System Operator, Bulk
    (Transmission                  Power                    Sr. Bulk Power Business
    Operations)                                             Developer
                                   System Operations
                                   Analyst                  Bulk Power Transaction
                                                            Coordinator
                                   Outage Scheduler
```

Source: Company web site, 1998

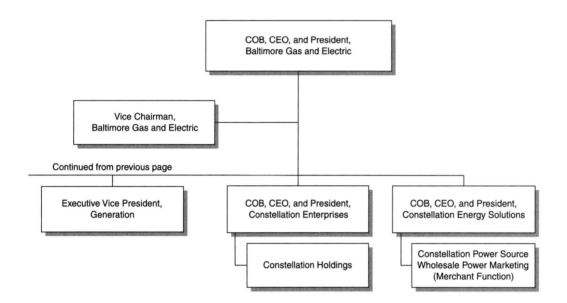

Bank of England

The United Kingdom's central bank

Threadneedle St.
London EC2R 8AH, United Kingdom
Phone: +44 020 7601 4444 **Fax:** +44 020 7601 5460
Web: www.bankofengland.co.uk

Primary SIC: 6011—Federal Reserve Banks
Primary NAICS: 52111—Monetary
Authorities - Central Bank
E-mail: enquiries@bankofengland.co.uk

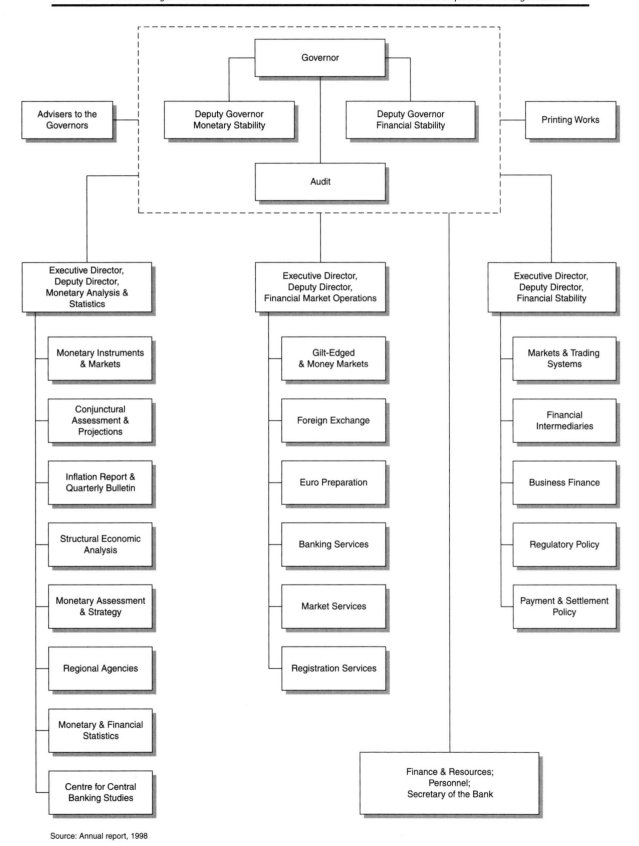

Source: Annual report, 1998

Bank of Japan

Japan's central bank

2-1-1 Hongoku-cho
Chuo-ku, Tokyo, Japan
Phone: +81 03-3279-1111
Web: www.boj.or.jp

Primary SIC: 6011—Federal Reserve Banks
Primary NAICS: 52111—Monetary
Authorities - Central Bank

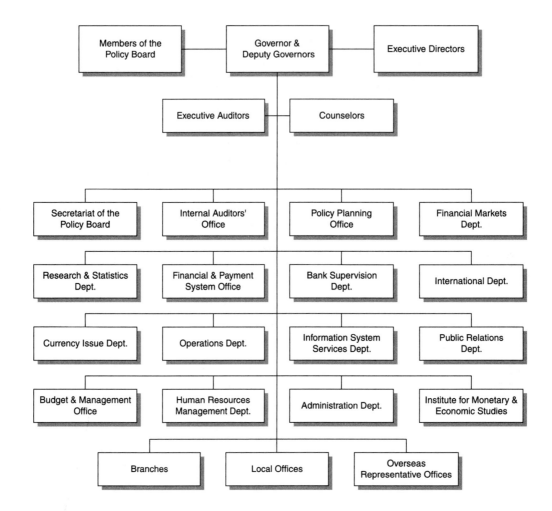

Source: Company web site, 1999

Bechtel Jacobs Company LLC

An environmental clean-up venture between Bechtel National, Inc. (a unit of Bechtel Corp.) and Jacobs Engineering Group

151 Lafayette Dr.
Oak Ridge, TN 37831-0350
Phone: (423) 576-4006
Web: www.bechteljacobs.com

Primary SIC: 4953—Refuse Systems
Primary NAICS: 562211—Hazardous
Waste Treatment & Disposal

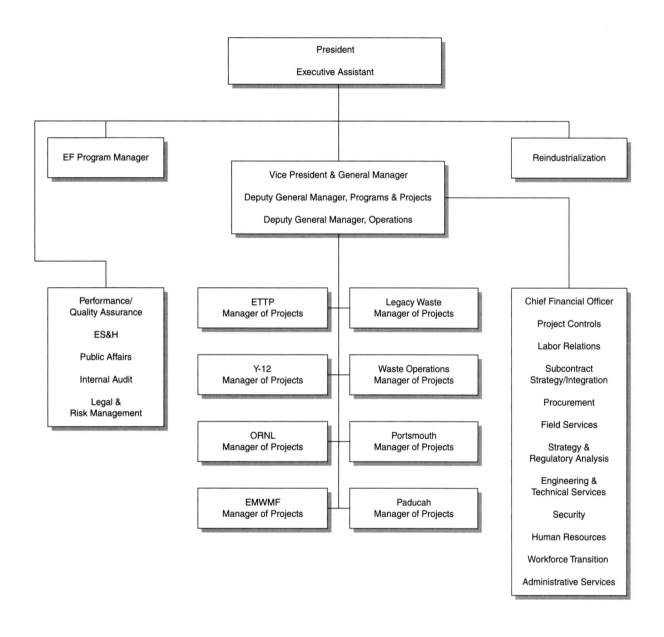

President

Executive Assistant

EF Program Manager

Reindustrialization

Vice President & General Manager

Deputy General Manager, Programs & Projects

Deputy General Manager, Operations

Performance/
Quality Assurance

ES&H

Public Affairs

Internal Audit

Legal &
Risk Management

ETTP
Manager of Projects

Legacy Waste
Manager of Projects

Y-12
Manager of Projects

Waste Operations
Manager of Projects

ORNL
Manager of Projects

Portsmouth
Manager of Projects

EMWMF
Manager of Projects

Paducah
Manager of Projects

Chief Financial Officer

Project Controls

Labor Relations

Subcontract
Strategy/Integration

Procurement

Field Services

Strategy &
Regulatory Analysis

Engineering &
Technical Services

Security

Human Resources

Workforce Transition

Administrative Services

Becton Dickinson and Company

This leading manufacturer of medical devices and supplies yields half of its sales from outside the U.S.

1 Becton Dr.
Franklin Lakes, NJ 07417-1880
Phone: (201) 847-6800
Web: www.bd.com

Primary SIC: 3841—Surgical & Medical
Instruments & Apparatus
Primary NAICS: 339112—Surgical & Medical
Instrument Mfg

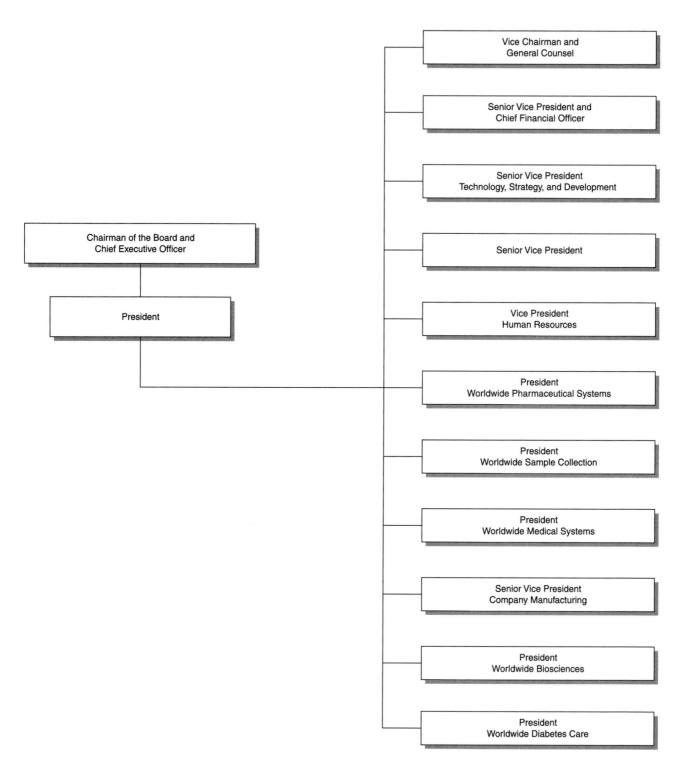

Source: Company and revisions by the editors, 1999

Bell & Howell Company

A publicly traded provider of document imaging equipment and services

5215 Old Orchard Rd.
Skokie, IL 60077-1076
Phone: (847) 470-7100 **Fax:** (847) 470-9425
Web: www.bellhowell.com

Primary SIC: 3861—Photographic Equipment & Supplies
Primary NAICS: 333315—Photographic
& Photocopying Equipment Mfg

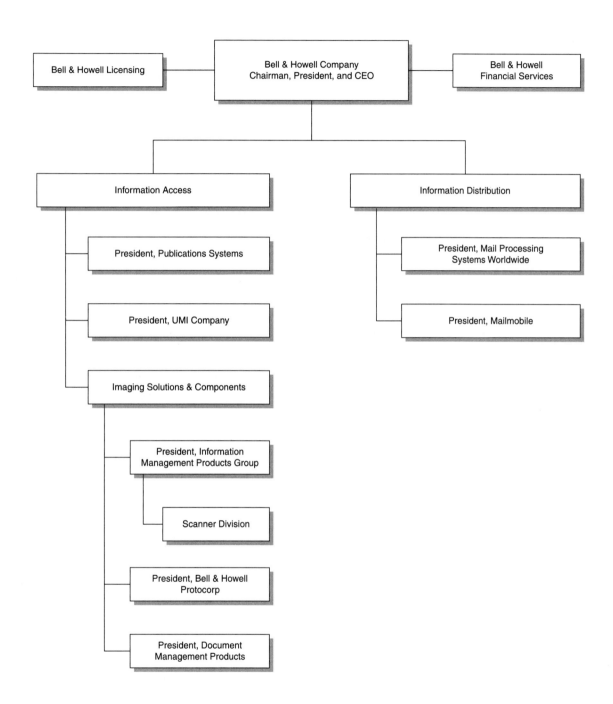

Source: Company web site, 1998

Bethlehem Steel Corp.

The United States' 2nd-largest steel maker

1170 8th Ave.
Bethlehem, PA 18016-7699
Phone: (215) 694-2424
Web: www.bethsteel.com

Primary SIC: 3312—Steel Works, Blast Furnaces
(Including Coke Ovens), & Rolling Mills
Primary NAICS: 331111—Iron & Steel Mills

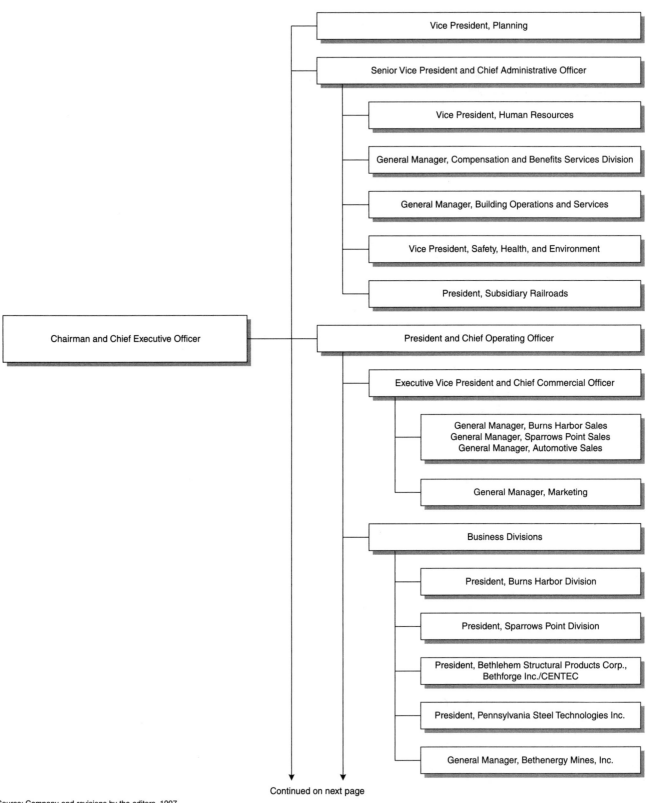

Chairman and Chief Executive Officer

Vice President, Planning

Senior Vice President and Chief Administrative Officer

Vice President, Human Resources

General Manager, Compensation and Benefits Services Division

General Manager, Building Operations and Services

Vice President, Safety, Health, and Environment

President, Subsidiary Railroads

President and Chief Operating Officer

Executive Vice President and Chief Commercial Officer

General Manager, Burns Harbor Sales
General Manager, Sparrows Point Sales
General Manager, Automotive Sales

General Manager, Marketing

Business Divisions

President, Burns Harbor Division

President, Sparrows Point Division

President, Bethlehem Structural Products Corp.,
Bethforge Inc./CENTEC

President, Pennsylvania Steel Technologies Inc.

General Manager, Bethenergy Mines, Inc.

Continued on next page

Source: Company and revisions by the editors, 1997

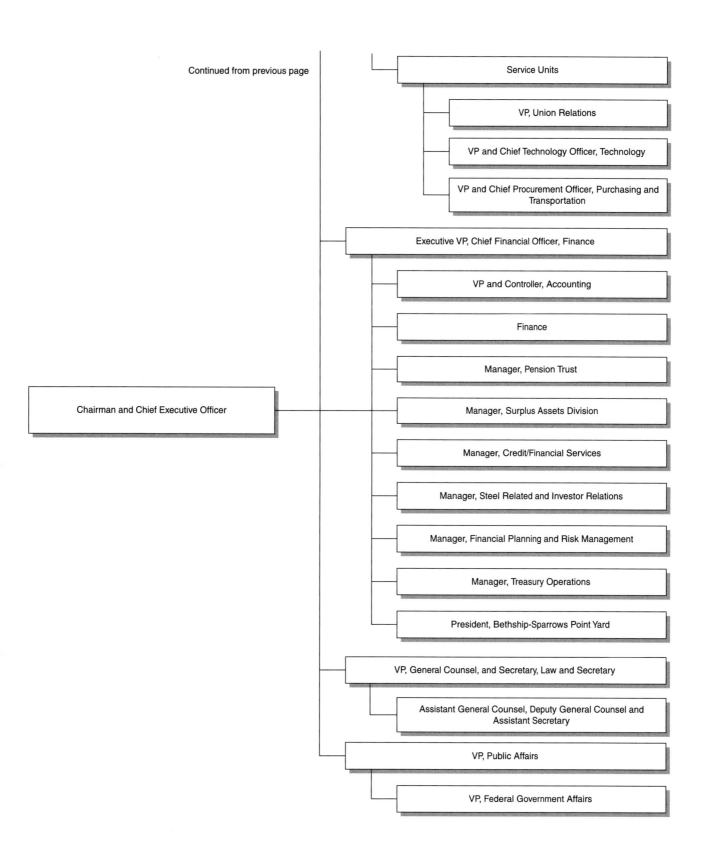

Continued from previous page

Service Units

VP, Union Relations

VP and Chief Technology Officer, Technology

VP and Chief Procurement Officer, Purchasing and Transportation

Executive VP, Chief Financial Officer, Finance

VP and Controller, Accounting

Finance

Manager, Pension Trust

Manager, Surplus Assets Division

Manager, Credit/Financial Services

Manager, Steel Related and Investor Relations

Manager, Financial Planning and Risk Management

Manager, Treasury Operations

President, Bethship-Sparrows Point Yard

Chairman and Chief Executive Officer

VP, General Counsel, and Secretary, Law and Secretary

Assistant General Counsel, Deputy General Counsel and Assistant Secretary

VP, Public Affairs

VP, Federal Government Affairs

Bonneville Pacific Services

A subsidiary of Bonneville Pacific Corp., the firm provides management services for industrial cogeneration plants

50 W. 300 S., Suite 300
Salt Lake City, UT 84101
Phone: (800) 730-2520
Web: www.bpcogen.com

Primary SIC: 8744—Facilities Support
Management Services
Primary NAICS: 56121—Facilities Support Services

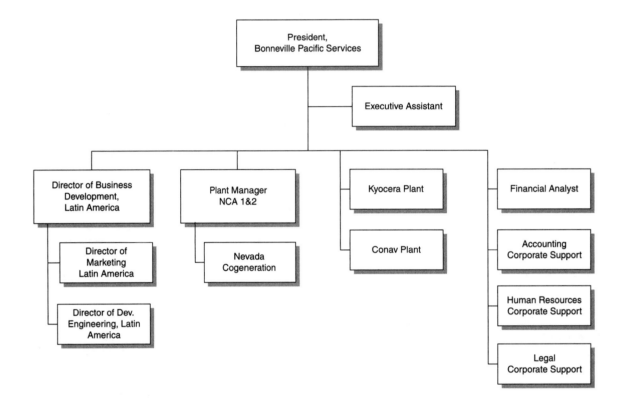

Source: Company web site, 1999

BROKAT Infosystems AG

A publicly traded international provider of business security software for Internet-based electronic commerce

Industriestr. 3
D-70565 Stuttgart, Germany
Phone: +49-711-78844-298 **Fax:** +49-711-78844-773
Web: www.brokat.de

Primary SIC: 7371—Computer Programming Services
Primary NAICS: 541511—Custom Computer
Programming Services

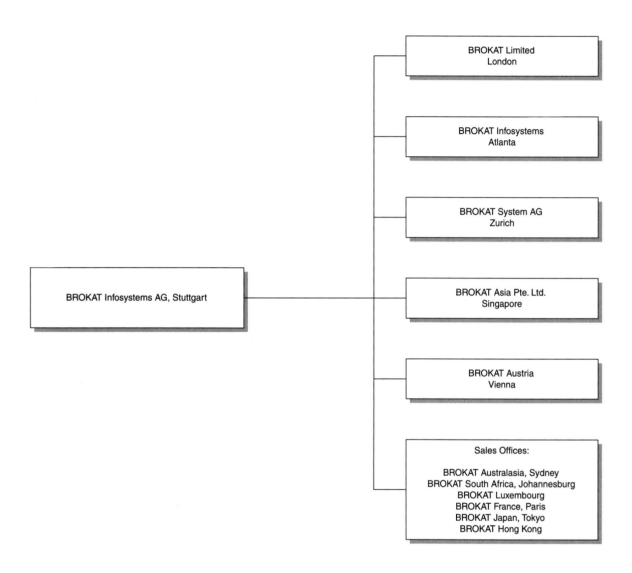

BROKAT Limited
London

BROKAT Infosystems
Atlanta

BROKAT System AG
Zurich

BROKAT Infosystems AG, Stuttgart

BROKAT Asia Pte. Ltd.
Singapore

BROKAT Austria
Vienna

Sales Offices:

BROKAT Australasia, Sydney
BROKAT South Africa, Johannesburg
BROKAT Luxembourg
BROKAT France, Paris
BROKAT Japan, Tokyo
BROKAT Hong Kong

Source: Company web site, 1999

Caterpillar Inc.

Worldwide manufacturer and distributor of heavy machinery for construction, agriculture, and mining

100 N.E. Adams St.
Peoria, IL 61629-7310
Phone: (309) 675-1000
Web: www.caterpillar.com

Primary SIC: 3531—Construction Machinery & Equipment
Primary NAICS: 33312—Construction Machinery Mfg

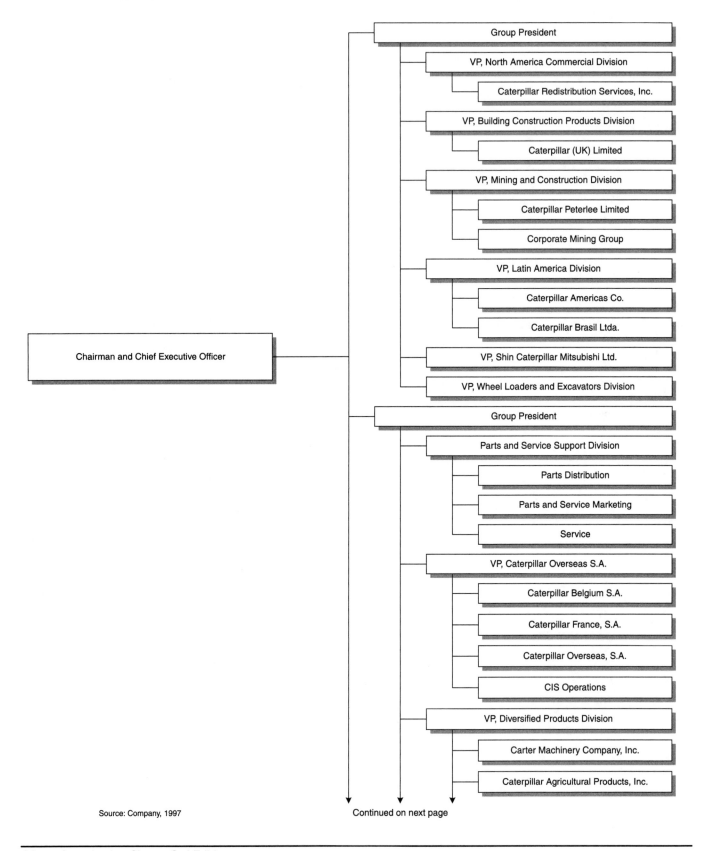

Chairman and Chief Executive Officer

Group President
- VP, North America Commercial Division
  - Caterpillar Redistribution Services, Inc.
- VP, Building Construction Products Division
  - Caterpillar (UK) Limited
- VP, Mining and Construction Division
  - Caterpillar Peterlee Limited
  - Corporate Mining Group
- VP, Latin America Division
  - Caterpillar Americas Co.
  - Caterpillar Brasil Ltda.
- VP, Shin Caterpillar Mitsubishi Ltd.
- VP, Wheel Loaders and Excavators Division

Group President
- Parts and Service Support Division
  - Parts Distribution
  - Parts and Service Marketing
  - Service
- VP, Caterpillar Overseas S.A.
  - Caterpillar Belgium S.A.
  - Caterpillar France, S.A.
  - Caterpillar Overseas, S.A.
  - CIS Operations
- VP, Diversified Products Division
  - Carter Machinery Company, Inc.
  - Caterpillar Agricultural Products, Inc.

Source: Company, 1997

Continued on next page

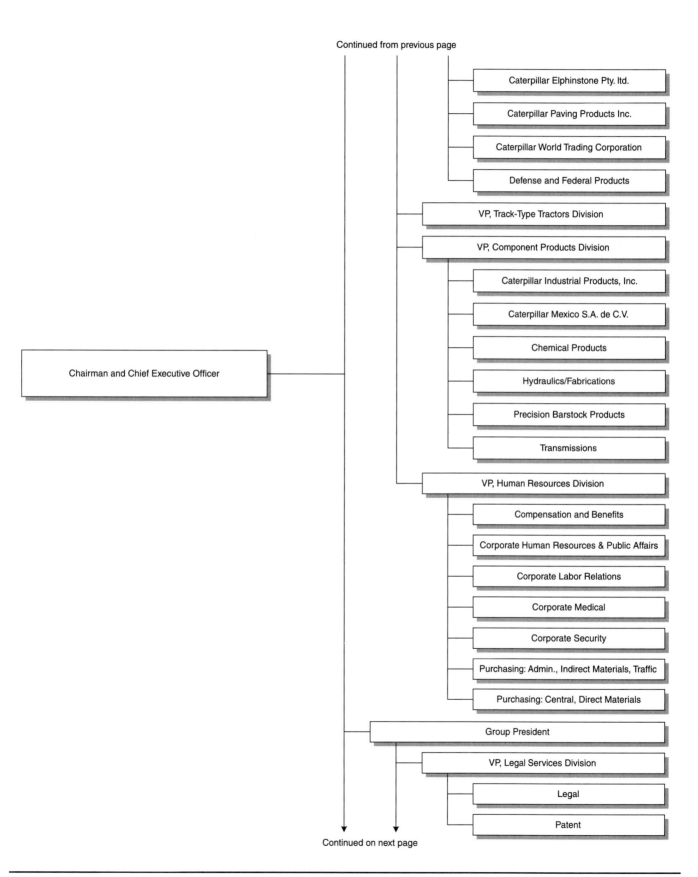

Continued from previous page

Caterpillar Elphinstone Pty. ltd.

Caterpillar Paving Products Inc.

Caterpillar World Trading Corporation

Defense and Federal Products

VP, Track-Type Tractors Division

VP, Component Products Division

Caterpillar Industrial Products, Inc.

Caterpillar Mexico S.A. de C.V.

Chemical Products

Hydraulics/Fabrications

Precision Barstock Products

Transmissions

Chairman and Chief Executive Officer

VP, Human Resources Division

Compensation and Benefits

Corporate Human Resources & Public Affairs

Corporate Labor Relations

Corporate Medical

Corporate Security

Purchasing: Admin., Indirect Materials, Traffic

Purchasing: Central, Direct Materials

Group President

VP, Legal Services Division

Legal

Patent

Continued on next page

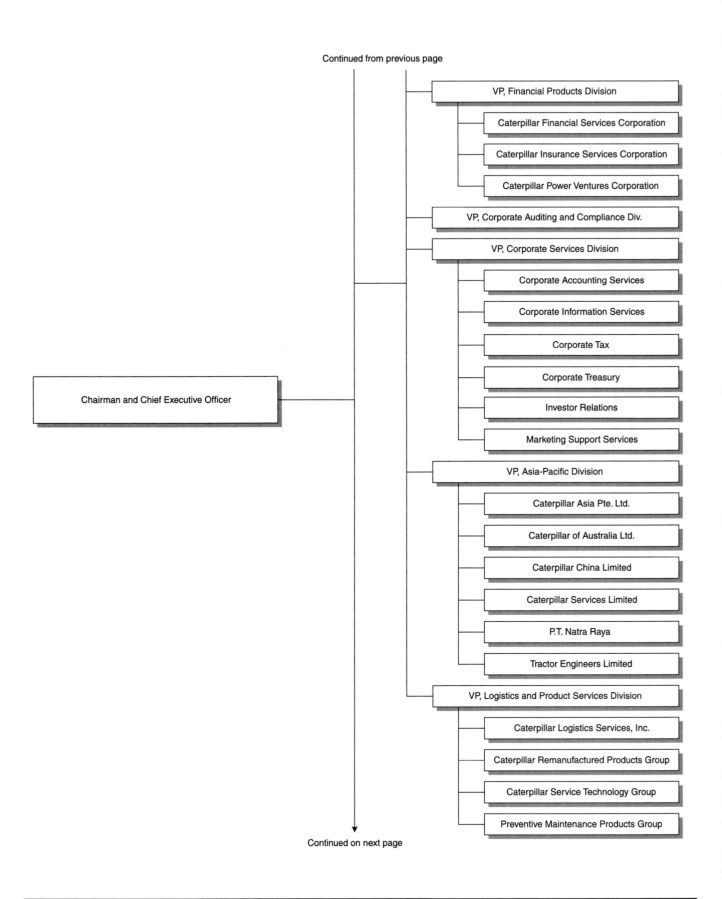

Continued from previous page

Chairman and Chief Executive Officer

VP, Financial Products Division

Caterpillar Financial Services Corporation

Caterpillar Insurance Services Corporation

Caterpillar Power Ventures Corporation

VP, Corporate Auditing and Compliance Div.

VP, Corporate Services Division

Corporate Accounting Services

Corporate Information Services

Corporate Tax

Corporate Treasury

Investor Relations

Marketing Support Services

VP, Asia-Pacific Division

Caterpillar Asia Pte. Ltd.

Caterpillar of Australia Ltd.

Caterpillar China Limited

Caterpillar Services Limited

P.T. Natra Raya

Tractor Engineers Limited

VP, Logistics and Product Services Division

Caterpillar Logistics Services, Inc.

Caterpillar Remanufactured Products Group

Caterpillar Service Technology Group

Preventive Maintenance Products Group

Continued on next page

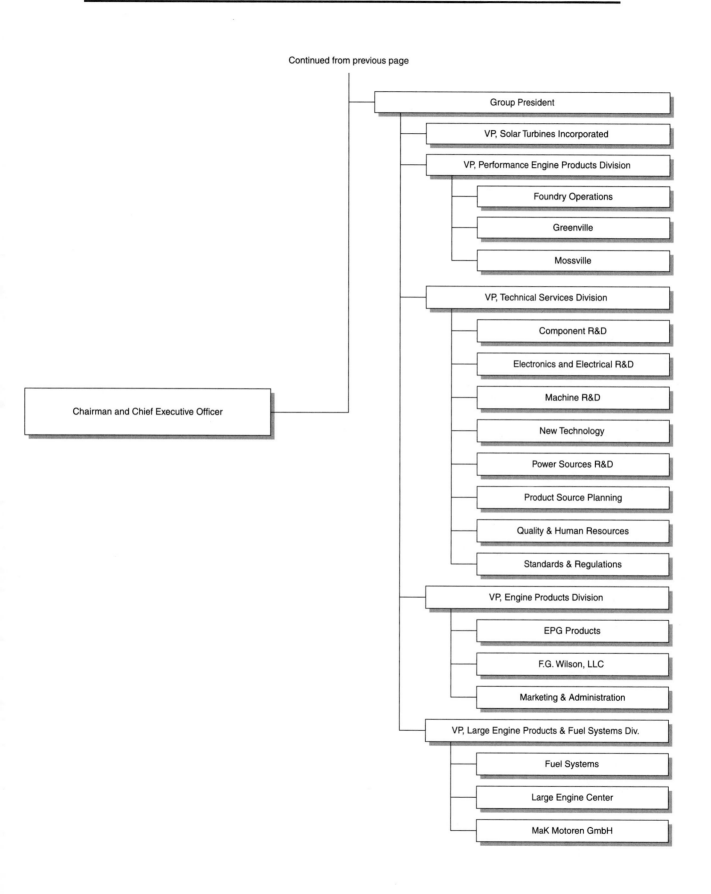

Continued from previous page

Chairman and Chief Executive Officer

Group President

VP, Solar Turbines Incorporated

VP, Performance Engine Products Division
- Foundry Operations
- Greenville
- Mossville

VP, Technical Services Division
- Component R&D
- Electronics and Electrical R&D
- Machine R&D
- New Technology
- Power Sources R&D
- Product Source Planning
- Quality & Human Resources
- Standards & Regulations

VP, Engine Products Division
- EPG Products
- F.G. Wilson, LLC
- Marketing & Administration

VP, Large Engine Products & Fuel Systems Div.
- Fuel Systems
- Large Engine Center
- MaK Motoren GmbH

Catholic Diocese of Pittsburgh

The regional Roman Catholic administrative unit containing 218 parishes and over 100 parochial schools

111 Blvd. of the Allies
Pittsburgh, PA 15222
Phone: (412) 456-3021
Web: www.diopitt.org

Primary SIC: 8661—Religious Organizations
Primary NAICS: 81311—Religious Organizations

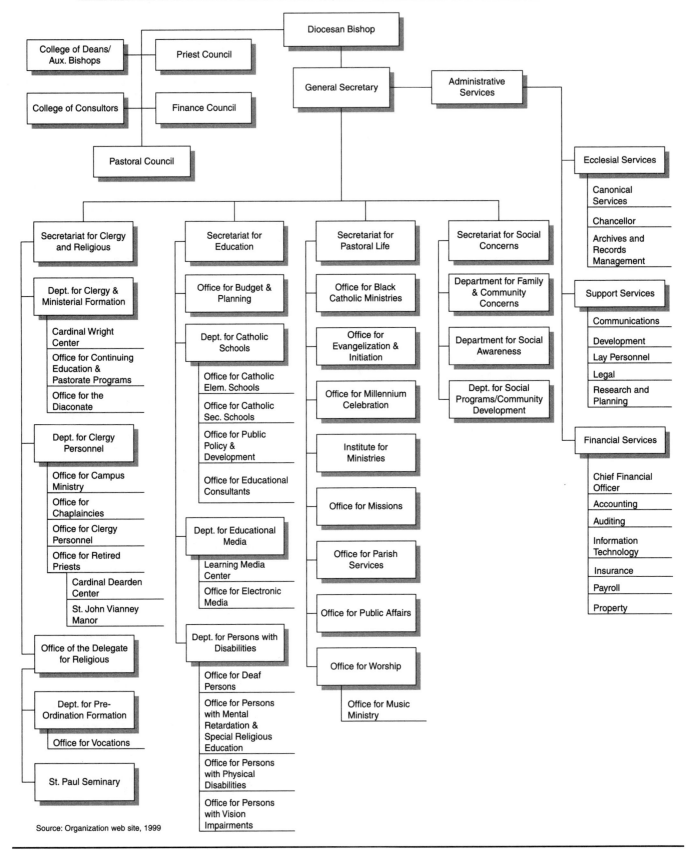

Source: Organization web site, 1999

Cemex S.A. de C.V.

The world's 3rd-largest cement manufacturer and one of Mexico's largest conglomerates

Av. Constitución 444 Pte.
C.P. 64000 Apdo. Postal 392, Monterrey, NL Mexico
Phone: +52-8 328-3000 **Fax:** +52-8 328-3188
Web: www.cemex.com

Primary SIC: 3241—Cement, Hydraulic
Primary NAICS: 32731—Cement Mfg

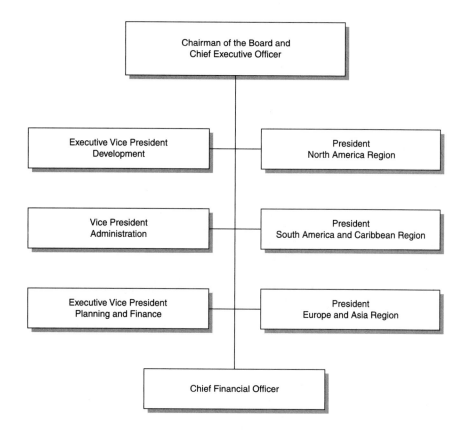

Source: Company and revisions by the editors, 1999

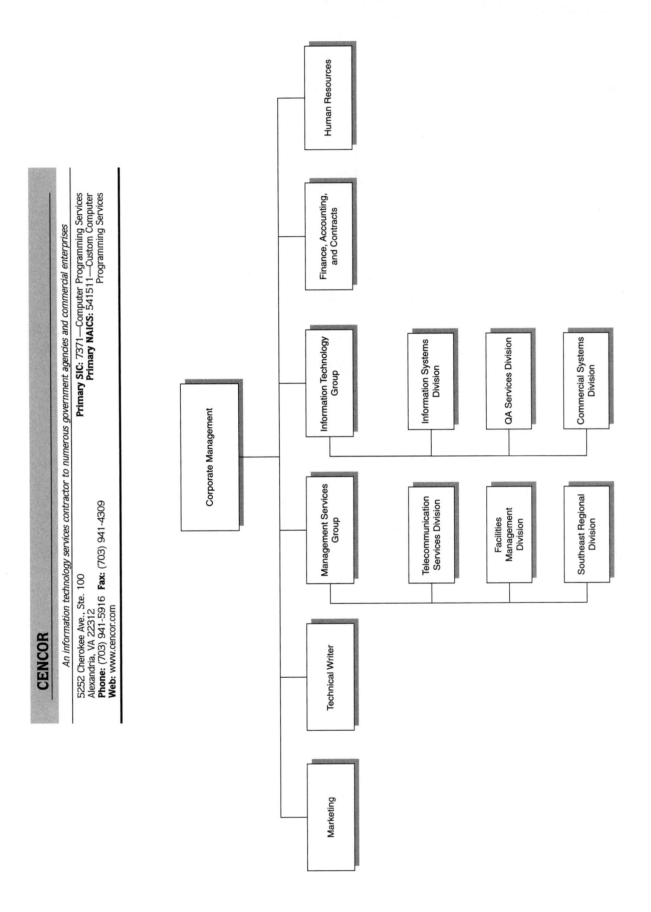

CENCOR

An information technology services contractor to numerous government agencies and commercial enterprises

5252 Cherokee Ave., Ste. 100
Alexandria, VA 22312
Phone: (703) 941-5916 **Fax:** (703) 941-4309
Web: www.cencor.com

Primary SIC: 7371—Computer Programming Services
Primary NAICS: 541511—Custom Computer Programming Services

Corporate Management

Marketing

Technical Writer

Management Services Group

Telecommunication Services Division

Facilities Management Division

Southeast Regional Division

Information Technology Group

Information Systems Division

QA Services Division

Commercial Systems Division

Finance, Accounting, and Contracts

Human Resources

Source: Company web site, 1999

Center for African & African-American Art & Culture

A local-oriented nonprofit organization promoting cultural events and education centering around African themes

762 Fulton St.
San Francisco, CA 94102
Phone: (415) 928-8546
Web: www.caaac.org

Primary SIC: 8399—Social Services, NEC
Primary NAICS: 813319—Other
Social Advocacy Organizations
E-mail: contacts@caaac.org

Source: Organization web site, 1999

Champion International Corporation

One of the top ten U.S. forest products companies

1 Champion Plaza
Stamford, CT 06921
Phone: (203) 358-7000
Web: www.championinternational.com

Primary SIC: 2621—Paper Mills
Primary NAICS: 322121—Paper
(except Newsprint) Mills

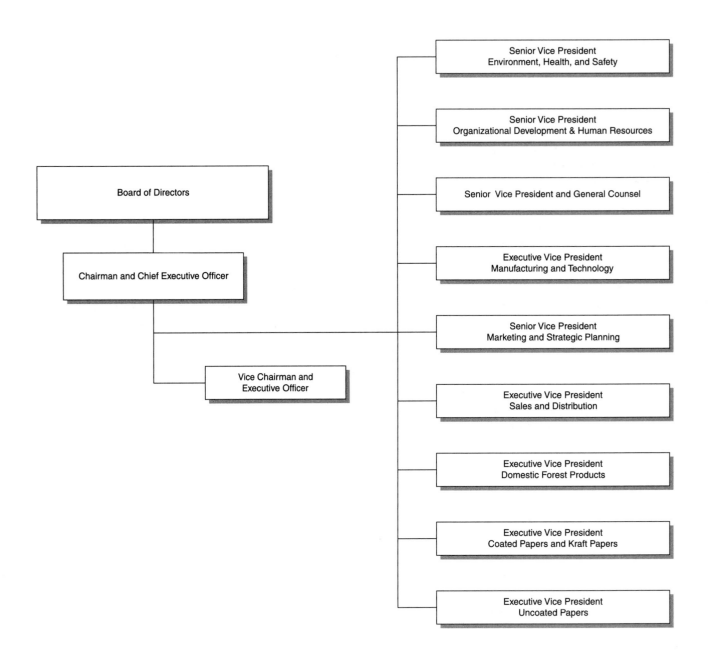

Source: Company and revisions by the editors, 1998

Citicorp

The parent of Citibank and partner in the 1998 merger with the Travelers Group that formed Citigroup Inc.

153 E. 53rd St.
New York, NY 10043
Phone: (212) 559-1000 **Fax:** (212) 714-5794
Web: www.citicorp.com

Primary SIC: 6021—National Commercial Banks
Primary NAICS: 52211—Commercial Banking

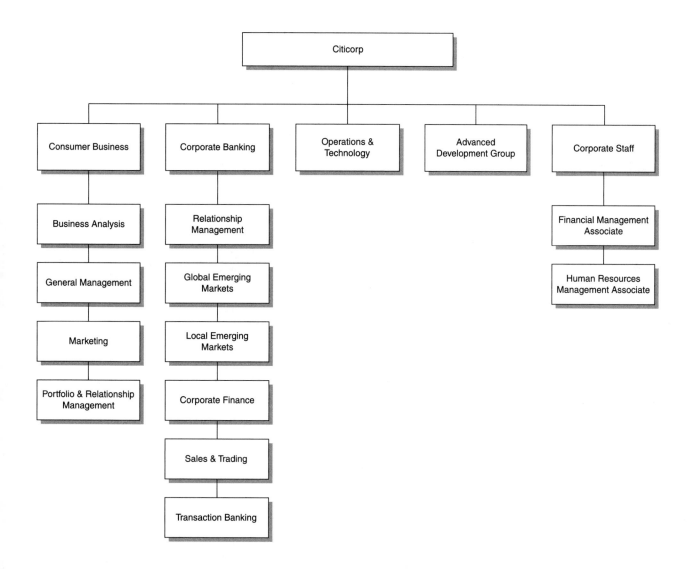

* Structure does not reflect Citicorp's 1998 merger with
  The Travelers Group, which created Citigroup Inc.

Source: Company web site, 1998

City of Vancouver

With approximately 2 million residents, Vancouver is Canada's 3rd-largest city, behind Toronto and Montreal

City Hall, 453 W. 12th Ave.
Vancouver, BC V5Y 1V4 Canada
Phone: (604) 873-7011
Web: www.city.vancouver.bc.ca

Primary SIC: 9111—Executive Offices
Primary NAICS: 92111—Executive Offices

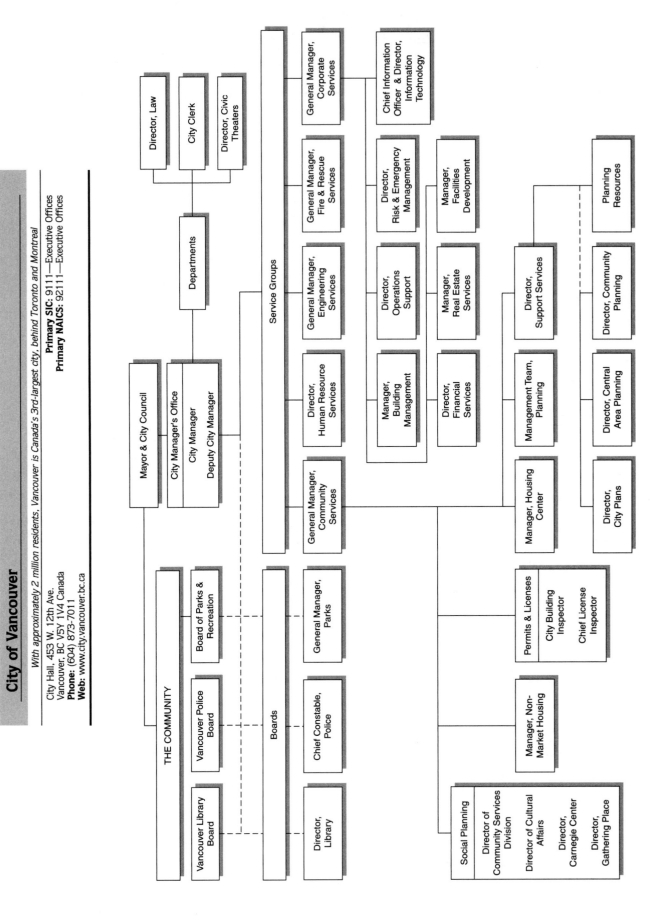

Source: Agency web site, 1998

CMP Group, Inc.

A publicly traded holding company for Central Maine Power Company and other New England utilities

83 Edison Drive
Augusta, ME 04336
Phone: (207) 621-3985
Web: www.cmpco.com

Primary SIC: 4911—Electric Services
Primary NAICS: 221119—Other Electric
Power Generation

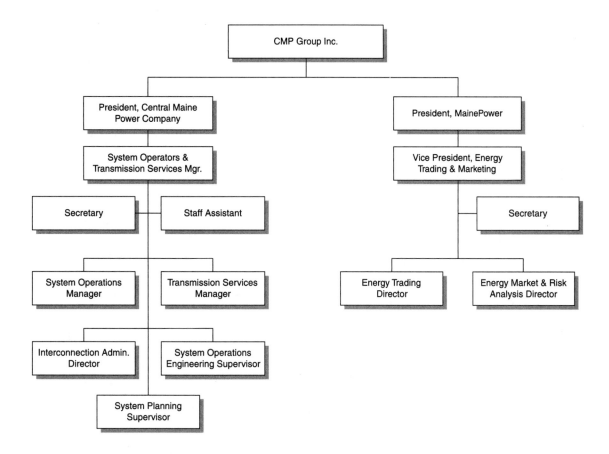

Source: Company web site, 1998

Commonwealth of Virginia

Virginia's state government administers public affairs for the 12th-largest state

Office of the Secretary of the Commonwealth
Old Finance Building, 1st Floor, Capitol Square
Richmond, VA 23219
Phone: (804) 786-2441

Primary SIC: 9111—Executive Offices
Primary NAICS: 92111—Executive Offices
Web: www.soc.state.va.us

Executive Branch

- Governor
  - Chief of Staff
  - Virginia Liaison Office
  - Lieutenant Governor
  - Secretary of the Commonwealth

- Attorney General
  - Department of Law

- Secretary of Administration
  - Charitable Gaming Commission
  - Commission on Local Government
  - Compensation Board
  - Department of General Services
  - Department of Personnel and Training
  - Department of Employee Relations Counselors
  - State Board of Elections
  - Council on Human Rights
  - Department of Veteran's Affairs
  - Board of Trustees, Virginia Veterans Care Center

- Secretary of Commerce & Trade
  - Virginia Housing Development Authority
  - Department of Professional & Occupational Regulation
  - Department of Labor & Industry
  - Department of Mines, Minerals & Energy
  - Virginia Economic Development Partnership
  - Virginia Employment Commission
  - Milk Commission
  - Department of Agriculture & Consumer Services
  - Department of Business Assistance
  - Department of Housing and Community Development
  - Department of Forestry
  - Virginia Racing Commission
  - Virginia Resources Authority
  - Department of Minority Business Enterprise

- Secretary of Education
  - Department of Education
  - Gunston Hall
  - Jamestown-Yorktown Foundation
  - The Library of Virginia
  - Frontier Culture Museum of Virginia
  - The Science Museum of Virginia
  - Virginia Museum of Fine Arts
  - Southwest Virginia Higher Education Center
  - Virginia Community College System
  - Virginia Commission for the Arts
  - State Council of Higher Education
  - Christopher Newport University
  - George Mason University
  - James Madison University
  - Longwood College
  - Mary Washington College
  - Norfolk State University
  - Old Dominion University
  - Radford University
  - University of Virginia
  - Virginia Commonwealth University
  - Virginia Military Institute
  - Virginia Polytechnic Institute and State University
  - Virginia State University
  - The College of William and Mary

Continued on next page

Source: Agency web site, 1999

Commonwealth of Virginia (cont.)

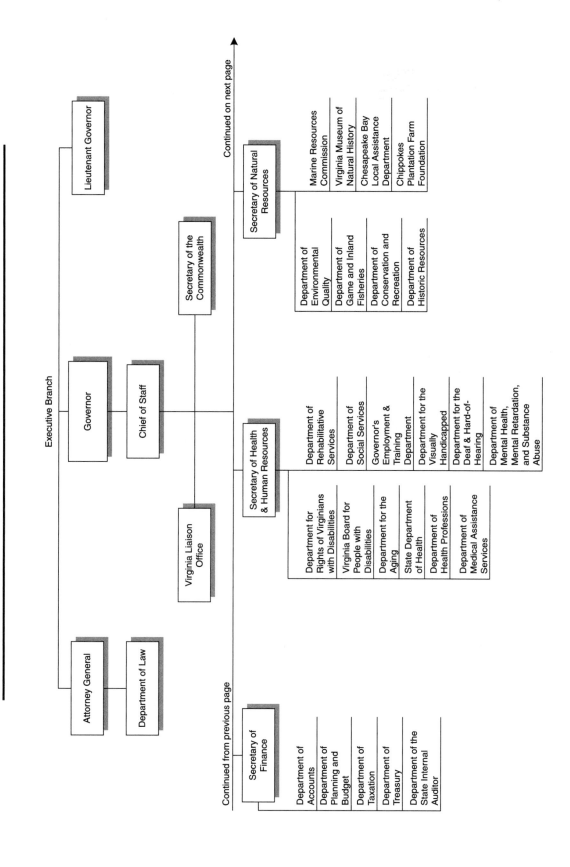

Executive Branch

- Attorney General
  - Department of Law

- Lieutenant Governor

- Governor
  - Chief of Staff
  - Virginia Liaison Office

- Secretary of the Commonwealth

Continued from previous page

Secretary of Finance
- Department of Accounts
- Department of Planning and Budget
- Department of Taxation
- Department of Treasury
- Department of the State Internal Auditor

Secretary of Health & Human Resources
- Department for Rights of Virginians with Disabilities
- Virginia Board for People with Disabilities
- Department for the Aging
- State Department of Health
- Department of Health Professions
- Department of Medical Assistance Services
- Department of Rehabilitative Services
- Department of Social Services
- Governor's Employment & Training Department
- Department for the Visually Handicapped
- Department for the Deaf & Hard-of-Hearing
- Department of Mental Health, Mental Retardation, and Substance Abuse

Secretary of Natural Resources
- Department of Environmental Quality
- Department of Game and Inland Fisheries
- Department of Conservation and Recreation
- Department of Historic Resources
- Marine Resources Commission
- Virginia Museum of Natural History
- Chesapeake Bay Local Assistance Department
- Chippokes Plantation Farm Foundation

Continued on next page

Commonwealth of Virginia (cont.)

Executive Branch

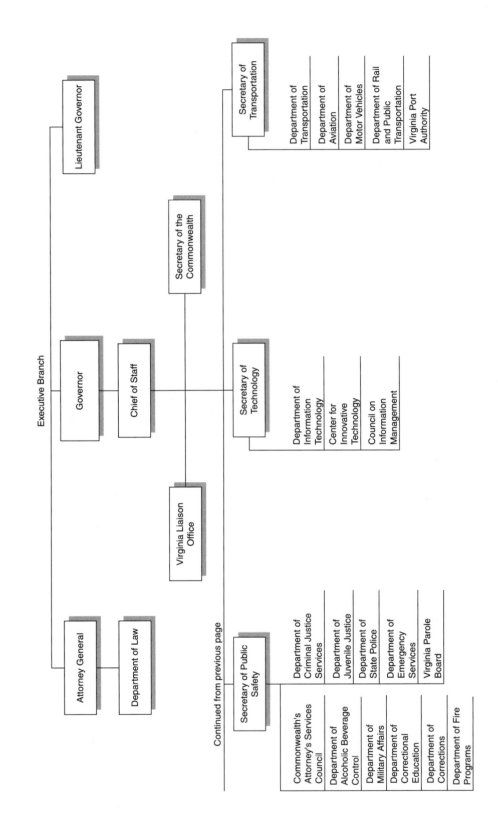

Governor

- Lieutenant Governor
- Attorney General
  - Department of Law
- Chief of Staff
- Secretary of the Commonwealth
- Virginia Liaison Office
- Secretary of Technology
  - Department of Information Technology
  - Center for Innovative Technology
  - Council on Information Management
- Secretary of Transportation
  - Department of Transportation
  - Department of Aviation
  - Department of Motor Vehicles
  - Department of Rail and Public Transportation
  - Virginia Port Authority

Continued from previous page

- Secretary of Public Safety
  - Department of Criminal Justice Services
  - Department of Juvenile Justice
  - Department of State Police
  - Department of Emergency Services
  - Virginia Parole Board
  - Commonwealth's Attorney's Services Council
  - Department of Alcoholic Beverage Control
  - Department of Military Affairs
  - Department of Correctional Education
  - Department of Corrections
  - Department of Fire Programs

Companhia Vale do Rio Doce

Part state-owned, CVRD is Brazil's largest minerals company and the world's top producer and exporter of iron ore

Av. Graça Aranha, 26 - 17th floor
Castelo, Rio de Janeiro, Brazil
Phone: +55-21-814-4088 **Fax:** +55-21-814-4571
Web: ironside.cvrd.com.br

Primary SIC: 1011—Iron Ores
Primary NAICS: 21221—Iron Ore Mining

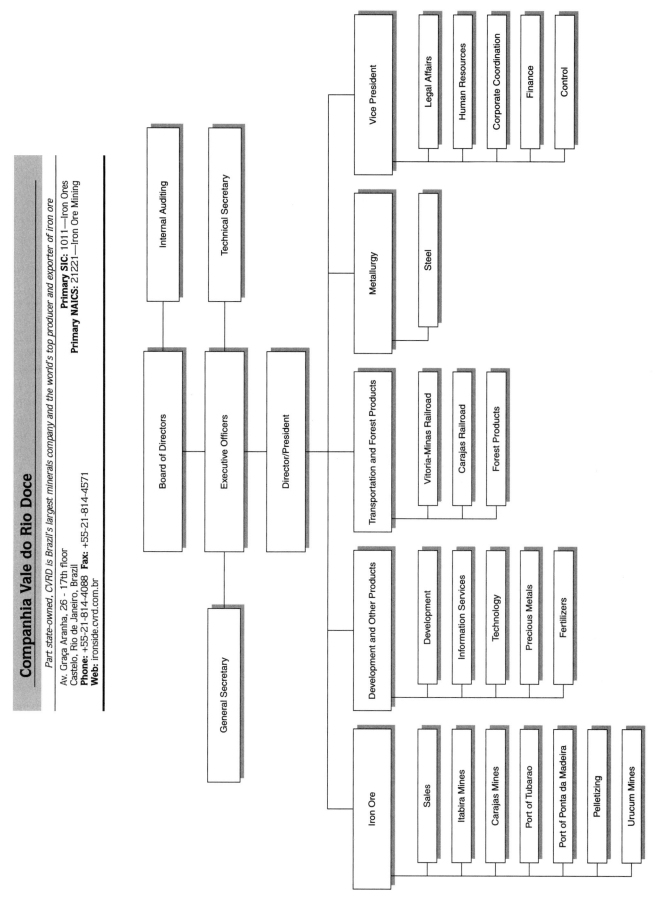

Source: Company web site, 1999

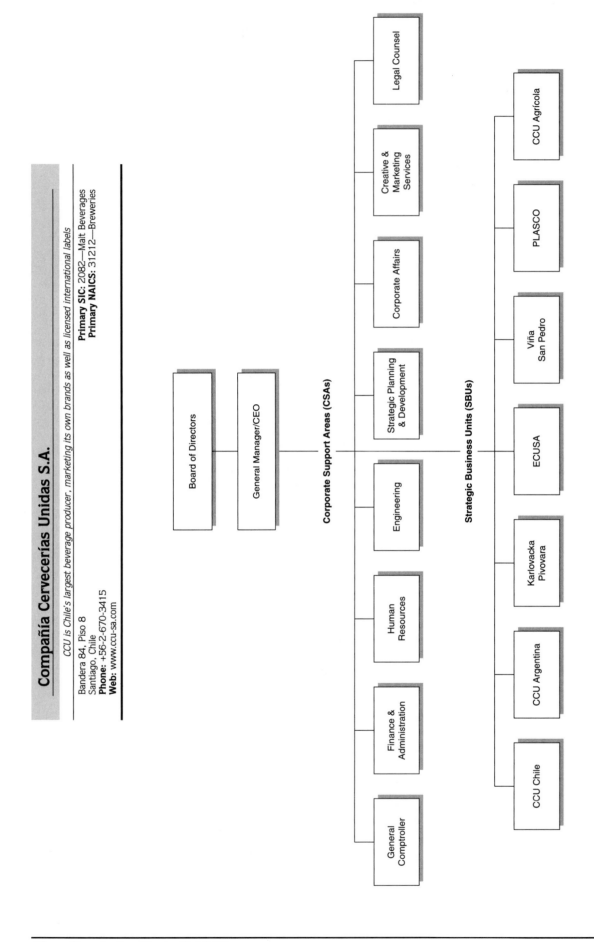

Compañía Cervecerías Unidas S.A.

CCU is Chile's largest beverage producer, marketing its own brands as well as licensed international labels

Bandera 84, Piso 8
Santiago, Chile
Phone: +56-2-670-3415
Web: www.ccu-sa.com

Primary SIC: 2082—Malt Beverages
Primary NAICS: 31212—A—Breweries

Board of Directors

General Manager/CEO

Corporate Support Areas (CSAs)

General Comptroller

Finance & Administration

Human Resources

Engineering

Strategic Planning & Development

Corporate Affairs

Creative & Marketing Services

Legal Counsel

Strategic Business Units (SBUs)

CCU Chile

CCU Argentina

Karlovacka Pivovara

ECUSA

Viña San Pedro

PLASCO

CCU Agricola

Source: Annual report, 1997

Composites Atlantic Limited

A subsidiary of France's Aerospatiale group, the company manufactures composite materials for aerospace applications

71 Hall Street
Lunenburg, NS B0J 2C0 Canada
Phone: (902) 634-4475 **Fax:** (902) 634-3993
Web: www.compositesatlantic.com

Primary SIC: 3728—Aircraft
Parts & Auxiliary Equipment, NEC
Primary NAICS: 336413—Other
Aircraft Part & Auxiliary Equipment Mfg

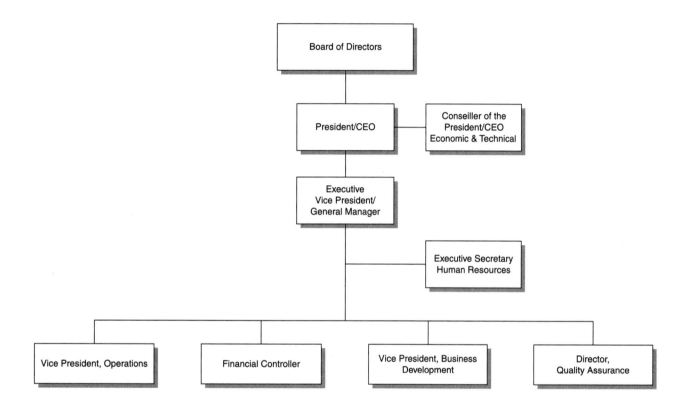

Source: Company web site, 1998

COMSAT Corporation

A government-created private-sector provider of satellite-based telecommunications and networking services to businesses

6560 Rock Spring Dr.
Bethesda, MD 20817
Phone: (301) 214-3000
Web: www.comsat.com

Primary SIC: 4899—Communications Services, NEC
Primary NAICS: 51334—Satellite Telecommunications

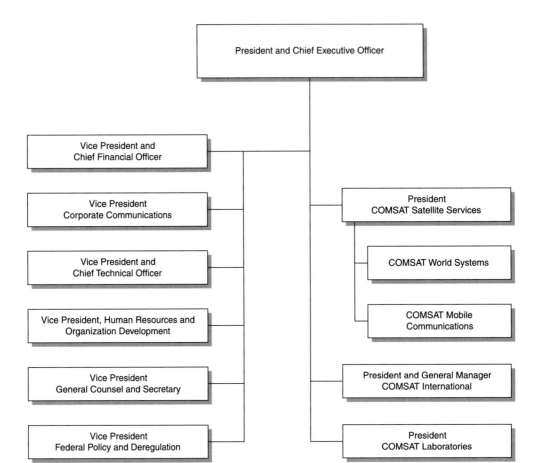

Source: Company and revisions by the editors, 1998

Credit Suisse Group

Switzerland's 2nd-largest bank and a major world investment bank

Paradeplatz 8
CH-8070 Zürich, Switzerland
Phone: +41-1-333-1111 **Fax:** +41-1-332-5555
Web: www.csg.ch

Primary SIC: 6021—National
Commercial Banks
Primary NAICS: 52211—Commercial Banking

```
                         ┌─────────────────────┐
                         │ Credit Suisse Group │
                         └─────────────────────┘
        ┌────────────────────────┼────────────────────────┐
┌─────────────────┐   ┌──────────────────────────┐   ┌──────────────┐
│  Credit Suisse  │   │ Credit Suisse First Boston│   │  Winterthur  │
└─────────────────┘   └──────────────────────────┘   └──────────────┘
```

Credit Suisse	Private Banking	First Boston	Asset Management	Winterthur
Subsidiaries:	Subsidiaries:	Subsidiaries:	Subsidiaries:	Subsidiaries:
Neue Aargauer Bank	Bank Leu*	Credit Suisse Financial Products	BEA Associates	Winterthur Life
Credit Suisse Leasing	Affida Bank*		Credit Suisse Trust and Banking	Winterthur-Columna
Credit Suisse Immobilien Leasing	Bank Heusser*			Winterthur International
	Credit Suisse Fides*			DBV-Winterthur Holding
	Clariden Bank*			Winterthur Holding Italia
	Bank Hoffman*			Hispanowin S.A. (Spain)
	Bank für Handel & Effekten			Winterthur-Europe Assurances
	Credit Suisse Trust*			Winterthur (UK) Holdings
				Winterthur U.S. Holdings
				HIH Winterthur (Australia)

* direct holding of Credit Suisse Corp.

Source: Annual report, 1998

CTI Engineering Co., Ltd

This large publicly traded engineering and consulting firm obtains most of its business from public sector projects

4-9-11, Nihonbashi-Honcho
Chuo-ku, Tokyo, Japan
Phone: +81 03-3668-0451
Web: www.ctie.co.jp

Primary SIC: 1623—Water, Sewer, Pipeline,
& Communications & Power Line Construction
Primary NAICS: 23491—Water,
Sewer & Pipeline Construction

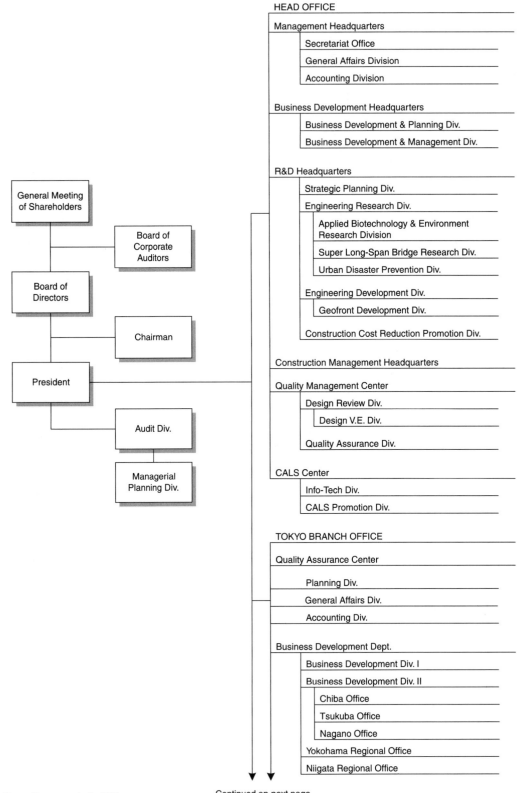

Source: Company web site, 1997

Continued on next page

Continued from previous page

Dam & Waterworks Dept.
- Dam Div.
- River Structure Div.
- Geotechnical Div.

Road & Traffic Dept.
- Highway Div.
  - Road Planning & ITS
- Traffic Structure Div. I
- Traffic Structure Div. II

Water Resources Dept.
- Water Resources Div. I
- Water Resources Div. II
- Coast & Ocean Development Div.

Human Intelligence Dept.
- Environmental Div.
  - Environmental Conservation Div.
- Urban & Regional Div.
- Sewerage Div.
- Water Environment Div.

General Meeting of Shareholders

Board of Directors

President

Information & CM Dept.
- Information Technology Div.
  - Information Research Div.
- Information Planning Div.
  - Construction Management Div.

Sendai Region Dept.
- Sales & Management Div.
  - Morioka Office
- River Engineering Div.
- Highway & Bridges Div.

Nagoya Region Dept.
- Sales & Management Div.
- Engineering Div.
- Shizuoka Regional Office

Sapporo Regional Office

Tokyo CALS Center

OSAKA BRANCH OFFICE

Quality Assurance Center
- Planning Div.
- General Affairs Div.

Business Development Dept.
- Business Development Div.
- Fukui Regional Office
- Takamatsu Regional Office
  - Matsuyama Office
- Kobe Regional Office

Dam & Waterworks Dept.
- Dam & River Structure Div.
- Environmental Assessment & Engineering Div.
- Geotechnical Div.

Road & Traffic Dept.
- Highway & Bridge Div. I
- Highway & Bridge Div. II
  - Road Planning Div.

Water Resources Dept.
- Water Resources Div.
- River Planning Div.
- Environmental & Systems Engineering Div.
  - Riverbasin Management Planning Div.

Hiroshima Region Center
- Sales & Management Div.
  - Yamaguchi Office
- Engineering Div.
  - River Engineering Div.
  - Road Div.

Osaka CALS Center

Continued on next page

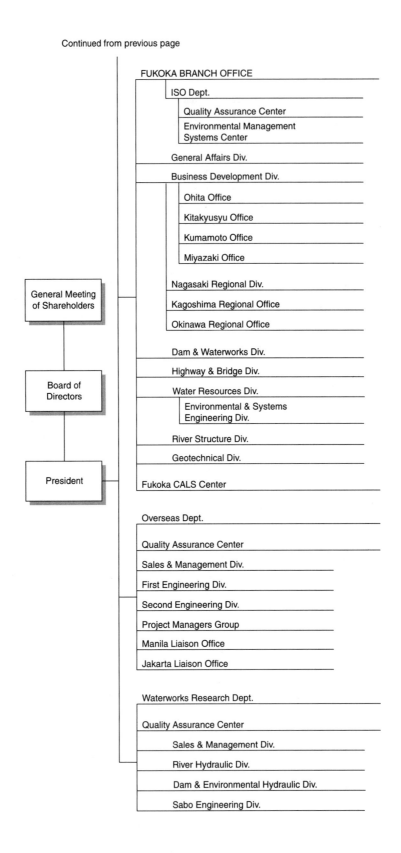

Continued from previous page

FUKOKA BRANCH OFFICE

ISO Dept.

Quality Assurance Center

Environmental Management Systems Center

General Affairs Div.

Business Development Div.

Ohita Office

Kitakyusyu Office

Kumamoto Office

Miyazaki Office

Nagasaki Regional Div.

Kagoshima Regional Office

Okinawa Regional Office

Dam & Waterworks Div.

Highway & Bridge Div.

Water Resources Div.

Environmental & Systems Engineering Div.

River Structure Div.

Geotechnical Div.

Fukoka CALS Center

Overseas Dept.

Quality Assurance Center

Sales & Management Div.

First Engineering Div.

Second Engineering Div.

Project Managers Group

Manila Liaison Office

Jakarta Liaison Office

Waterworks Research Dept.

Quality Assurance Center

Sales & Management Div.

River Hydraulic Div.

Dam & Environmental Hydraulic Div.

Sabo Engineering Div.

General Meeting of Shareholders

Board of Directors

President

Daiichi Jitsugyo Co., Ltd.

This $800 million-a-year public company imports, exports, and distributes specialized machinery for diverse industries

Kowa Nibancho Building 11-19 Nibancho
Chiyoda-ku, Tokyo 102-0084, Japan
Phone: +81 03-5214-8500 **Fax:** +81 03-5214-8501
Web: www.djk.co.jp

Primary SIC: 5084—Industrial
Machinery & Equipment
Primary NAICS: 42183—Industrial
Machinery & Equipment Whsle

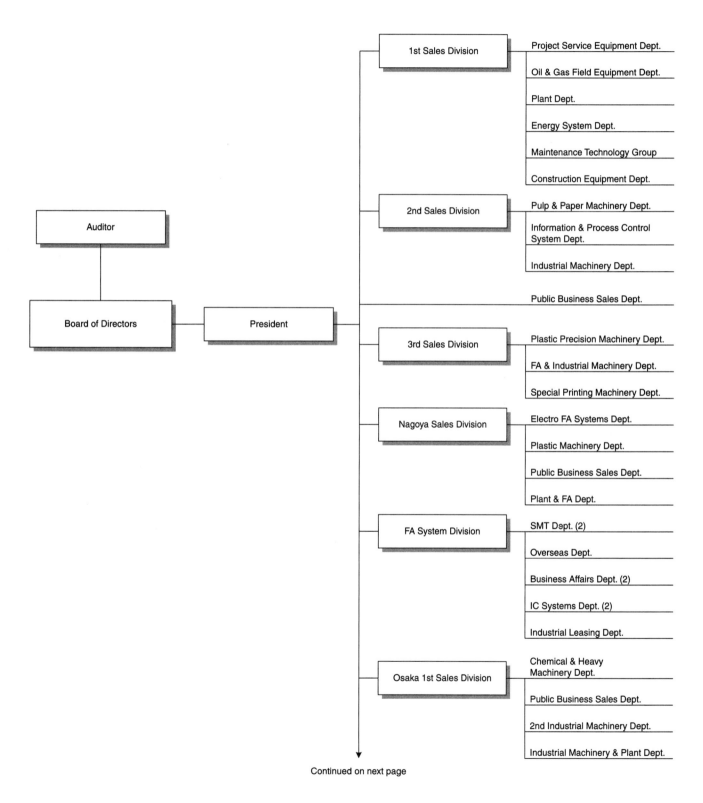

Continued on next page

Source: Company web site, 1999

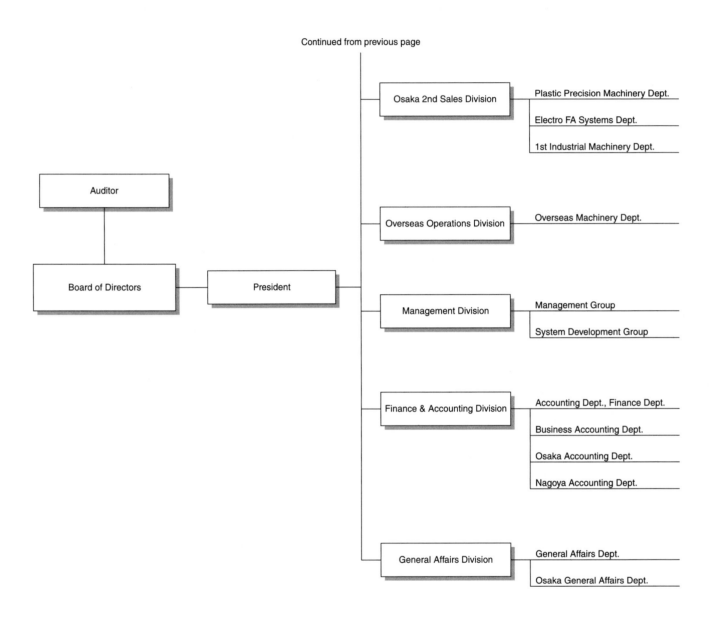

Continued from previous page

Osaka 2nd Sales Division
- Plastic Precision Machinery Dept.
- Electro FA Systems Dept.
- 1st Industrial Machinery Dept.

Overseas Operations Division
- Overseas Machinery Dept.

Management Division
- Management Group
- System Development Group

Finance & Accounting Division
- Accounting Dept., Finance Dept.
- Business Accounting Dept.
- Osaka Accounting Dept.
- Nagoya Accounting Dept.

General Affairs Division
- General Affairs Dept.
- Osaka General Affairs Dept.

Auditor

Board of Directors

President

DaimlerChrysler AG

Formed by the 1998 merger of the automotive giants Daimler-Benz AG and Chrysler Corp.

Epplestrasse 225
D-70546 Stuttgart, Germany
Phone: +49 711 17 1 **Fax:** +49 711 17 94022
Web: www.daimlerchrysler.com

Primary SIC: 3711—Motor
Vehicles & Passenger Car Bodies
Primary NAICS: 336111—Automobile Mfg

▶ **REORGANIZATION Part 1 (1996)**
For additional details on the restructuring
see profiles starting on page 331

Chrysler Corporation (1996)

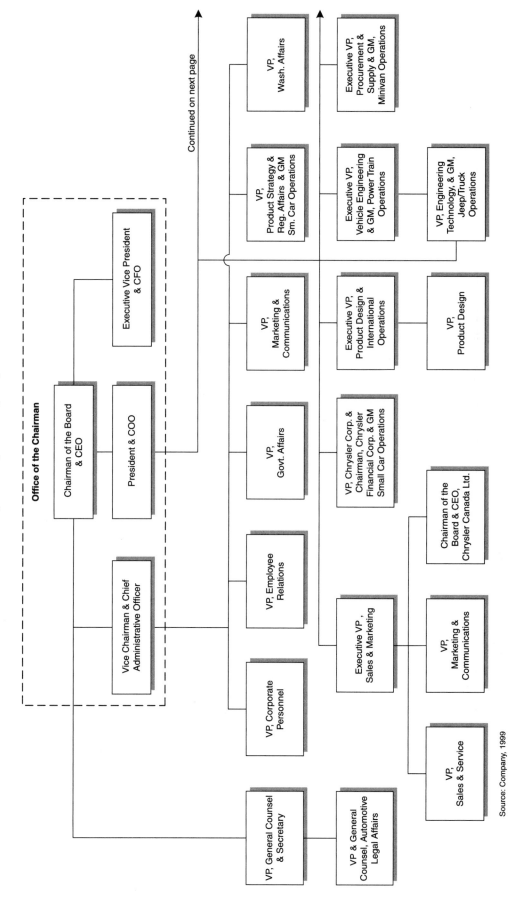

Continued on next page

Source: Company, 1999

Chrysler Corporation (1996) cont.

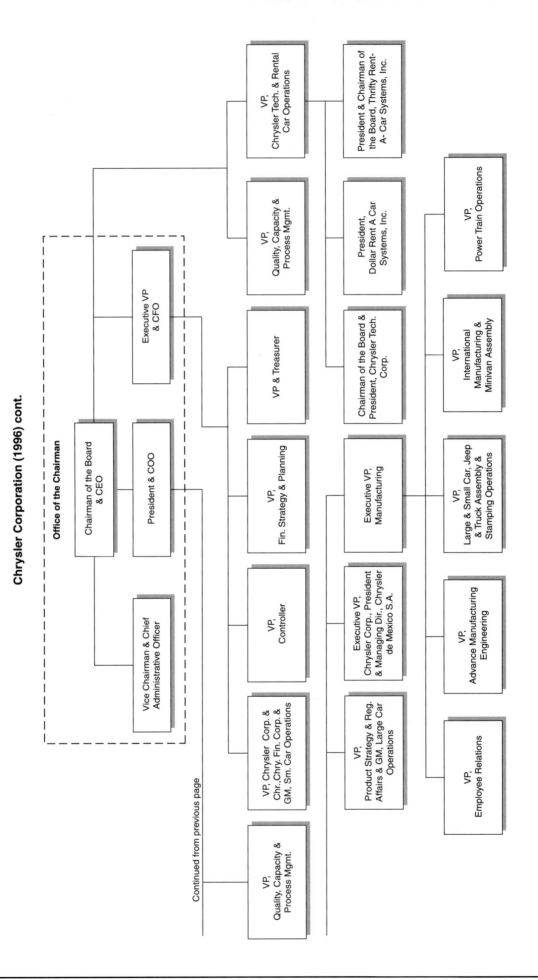

DaimlerChrysler AG (cont.)

▶ **REORGANIZATION Part 1 (1996)**
For additional details on the restructuring see profiles starting on page 331

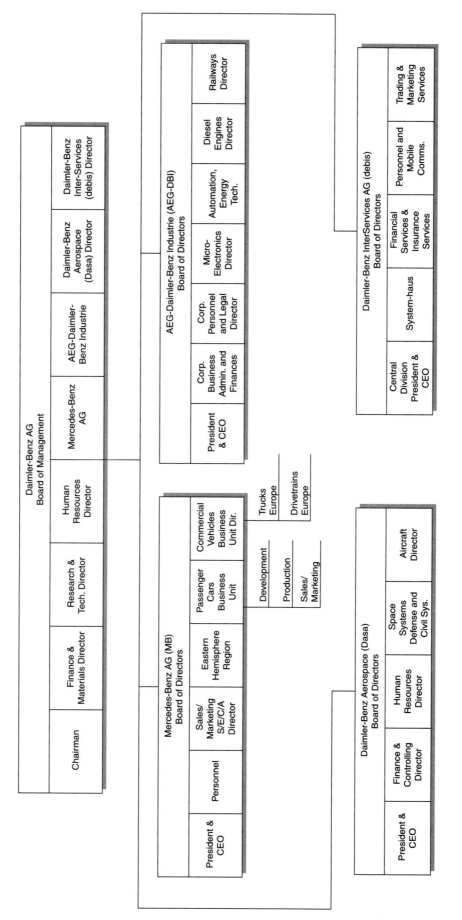

Daimler-Benz AG (1996)

Daimler-Benz AG
Board of Management

| Chairman | Finance & Materials Director | Research & Tech. Director | Human Resources Director | Mercedes-Benz AG | AEG-Daimler-Benz Industrie | Daimler-Benz Aerospace (Dasa) Director | Daimler-Benz Inter-Services (debis) Director |

Mercedes-Benz AG (MB)
Board of Directors

| President & CEO | Personnel | Sales/Marketing S/E/C/A Director | Eastern Hemisphere Region | Passenger Cars Business Unit | Commercial Vehicles Business Unit Dir. |

- Development
- Production
- Sales/Marketing
- Trucks Europe
- Drivetrains Europe

AEG-Daimler-Benz Industrie (AEG-DBI)
Board of Directors

| President & CEO | Corp. Business Admin. and Finances | Corp. Personnel and Legal Director | Micro-Electronics Director | Automation, Energy Tech. | Diesel Engines Director | Railways Director |

Daimler-Benz Aerospace (Dasa)
Board of Directors

| President & CEO | Finance & Controlling Director | Human Resources Director | Space Systems Defense and Civil Sys. | Aircraft Director |

Daimler-Benz InterServices AG (debis)
Board of Directors

| Central Division President & CEO | System-haus | Financial Services & Insurance Services | Personnel and Mobile Comms. | Trading & Marketing Services |

DaimlerChrysler AG (cont.)

REORGANIZATION Part 2 (1999)

For additional details on the restructuring see profiles starting on page 331

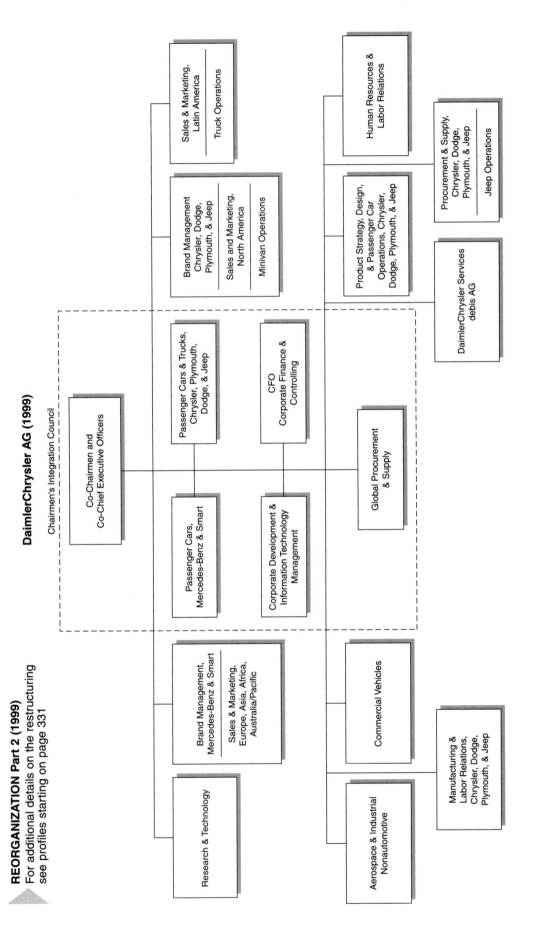

Darma Bajatra Aditunggal, PT

General contractor and construction materials exporter

Pulo Mas Jaya Bldg. 3rd Fl.
1 Jalan Pulo Mas Jaya, Jakarta,13210 Indonesia
Phone: (021) 478-64952 **Fax:** (021) 478-64953
Web: www.darma-group.co.id

Primary SIC: 1541—General Contractors-Industrial
Buildings & Warehouses
Primary NAICS: 23331—Mfg
& Industrial Building Construction

Principals
Local Partners

Managing Director

Continued on next page

General Manager
Commercial

Manager
Product Support

Manager
Oil & Lubricants Business

Manager
Product Development

Project Operational

Office Operational

General Manager
Business Development

Manager
Advertising and Exhibitions

Manager
Oil & Gas Services

Manager
Mining Services

Manager
Transportation and Materials Handling

Manager
Steel & Products Export

Supervisor
Business Administration

General Operational

General Manager
Technical and Engineering

Maintenance Manager
Utility Equipment

Manager
Workshop

Project Installation &
Commissioning Manager

Technical and
Engineering Administration

Project Operational

Darma Bajatra Aditunggal, PT (cont.)

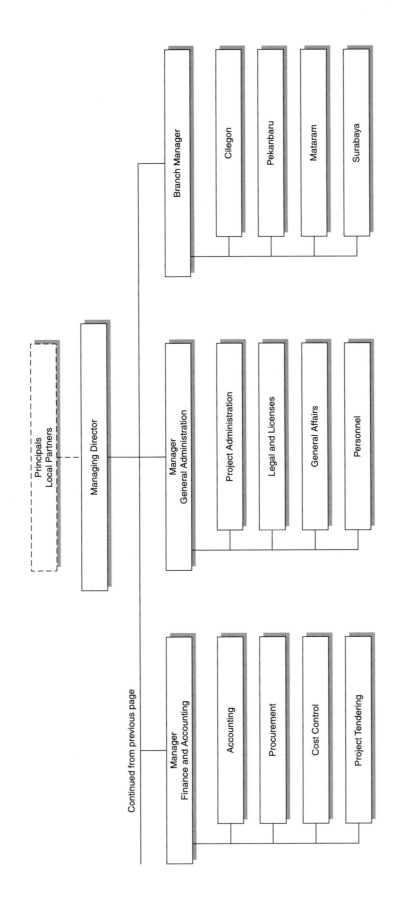

Delphi Automotive Systems Corporation

This former General Motors unit is the world's largest auto parts supplier

5725 Delphi Dr.
Troy, MI 48098
Phone: (248) 813-2000 **Fax:** (248) 813-2523
Web: www.delphiauto.com

Primary SIC: 3714—Motor
Vehicle Parts & Accessories
Primary NAICS: 336322—Other Motor
Vehicle Electrical & Electronic Equip Mfg

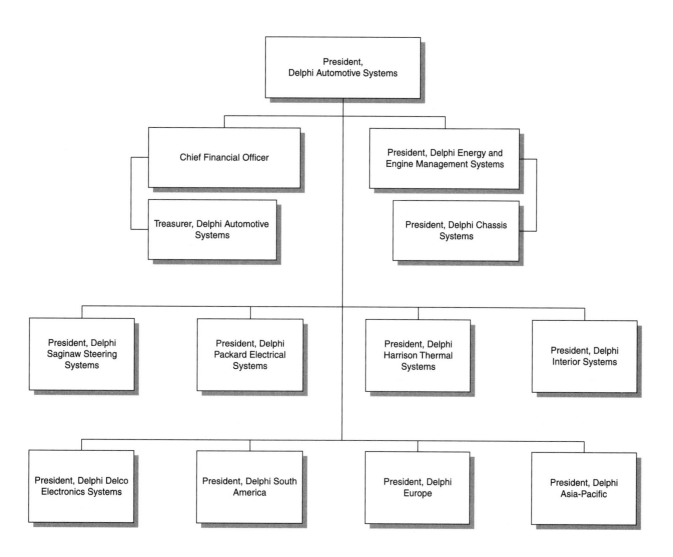

Source: Company web site, 1999

Dentsu Inc.

This century-old closely held advertising agency is Japan's largest and the 4th-largest in the world

1-11-10, Tsukiji
Chuo-ku, Tokyo 104-0045, Japan
Phone: +81-3-5551-5111 **Fax:** +81-3-5551-2013
Web: www.dentsu.co.jp

Primary SIC: 7311—Advertising Agencies
Primary NAICS: 54181—Advertising Agencies

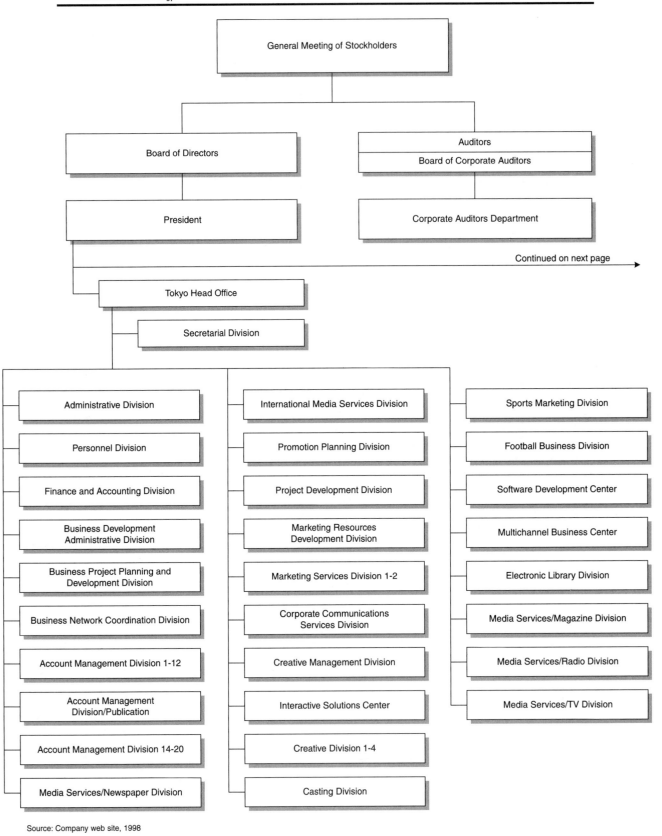

Continued on next page

Source: Company web site, 1998

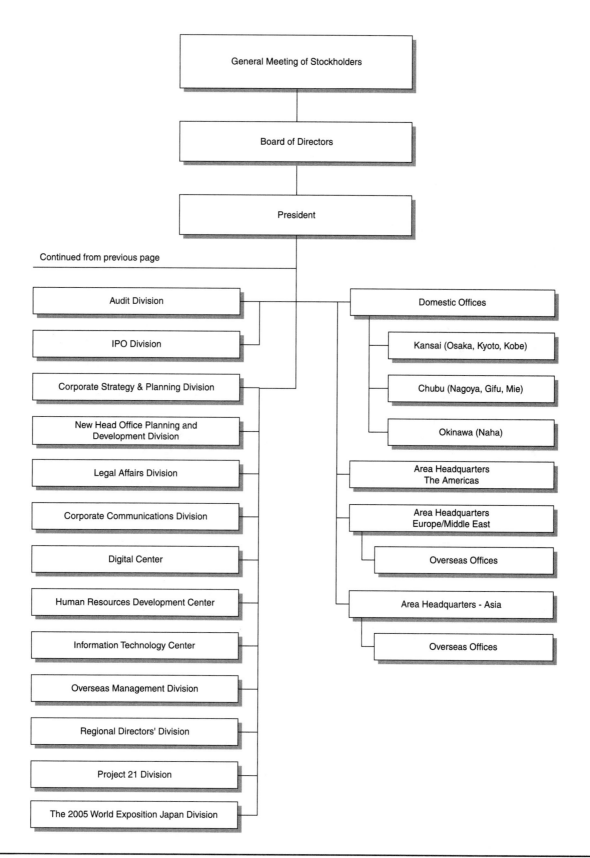

General Meeting of Stockholders

Board of Directors

President

Continued from previous page

Audit Division

IPO Division

Corporate Strategy & Planning Division

New Head Office Planning and Development Division

Legal Affairs Division

Corporate Communications Division

Digital Center

Human Resources Development Center

Information Technology Center

Overseas Management Division

Regional Directors' Division

Project 21 Division

The 2005 World Exposition Japan Division

Domestic Offices

Kansai (Osaka, Kyoto, Kobe)

Chubu (Nagoya, Gifu, Mie)

Okinawa (Naha)

Area Headquarters The Americas

Area Headquarters Europe/Middle East

Overseas Offices

Area Headquarters - Asia

Overseas Offices

Desco de Schultess Ltd.

A diversified textiles and consumer luxury products company with an extensive international presence

Brandschenkestrasse 5
CH-8039 Zürich, Switzerland
Phone: +41 1 209-1111 **Fax:** +41 1 209-1290
Web: www.desco-group.com

Primary SIC: 2337—Women's
Suits, Skirts, & Coats
Primary NAICS: 315212—Women's
Cut & Sew Apparel Contractors

Organization chart:

- Board of Administration
  - Head of the Board
  - Committee of the Board of Administration
- General Management
  - Foreign Exchange
    - Bristle Group
      - Zürich
  - Finances
    - Silk
      - Tokyo
      - Hong Kong
      - JFM Therwil
  - Informatics EDP
    - Textiles
      - Englewood Cliffs
      - Lyon
      - Milan
  - Human Resources
    - Watches Agencies
      - Australia
      - Singapore
      - Kuala Lumpur
      - Bangkok
      - Korea
    - ML Watches
      - ML Saignelégier
      - ML Pforzheim
      - Queloz SL
      - Los Angeles ML
      - ML Paris UTI
  - Administrative Services
    - Financial Services
      - Tunbridge Wells
      - Appenzell
      - Stuttgart
      - Amsterdam

Source: Company web site, 1998

Deutsche Ges. für Technische Zusammmenarbeit

A government-owned technical cooperation consultancy that promotes economic development in 142 countries

Dag-Hammerskjöld-Weg 1-5
D-65760 Eschborn, Germany
Phone: +49 61 96 79 0 **Fax:** +49 61 96 79 11 15
Web: www.gtz.de

Primary SIC: 8399—Social Services, NEC
Primary NAICS: 813319—Other
Social Advocacy Organizations

Office of the Directors General

- Corporate Communication
- Auditing
- Strategic Corporate Development
- Saudi Arabia/GCC Countries
- Centrum für Internationale Migration und Entwicklung (CIM)

Country Departments

Sub-Saharan Africa
- Sahel, Sudan, Western Africa I
- Central Africa, Western Africa II
- Eastern Africa
- Southern Africa

Asia
- South Asia
- Southeast Asia & the Pacific
- East Asia

Latin America, Near East, Maghreb
- Regional Contracting & Offers
- Eastern Latin America
- Andean Countries
- Northern Latin America, Caribbean
- Near & Middle East

Europe, Caucasian & Central Asian Countries
- Southeastern Europe, Caucasian & Central Asian Countries
- Central & Eastern Europe, Special Programs
- International Program Support

Continued on next page

Source: Organization web site, 1999

Deutsche Ges. für Technische Zusammenarbeit (cont.)

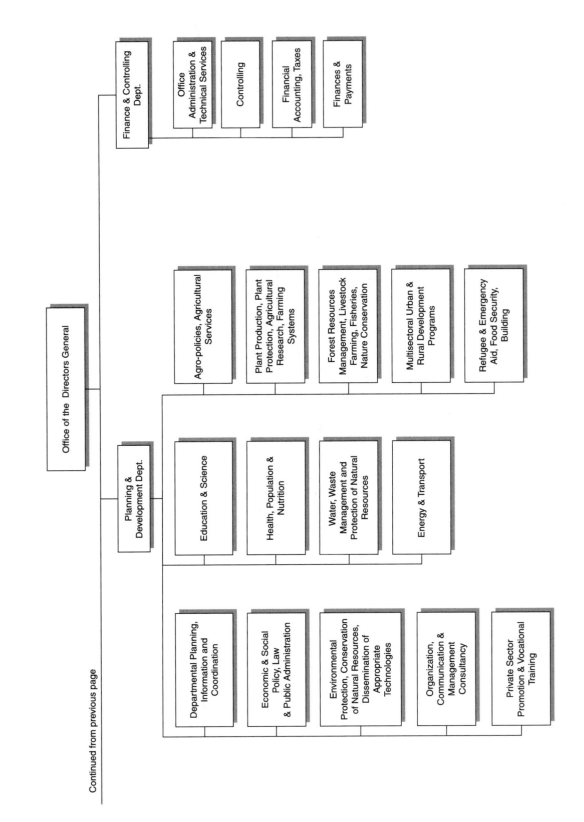

Continued from previous page

Office of the Directors General

Finance & Controlling Dept.

- Office Administration & Technical Services
- Controlling
- Financial Accounting, Taxes
- Finances & Payments

Planning & Development Dept.

- Agro-policies, Agricultural Services
- Plant Production, Plant Protection, Agricultural Research, Farming Systems
- Forest Resources Management, Livestock Farming, Fisheries, Nature Conservation
- Multisectoral Urban & Rural Development Programs
- Refugee & Emergency Aid, Food Security, Building

- Education & Science
- Health, Population & Nutrition
- Water, Waste Management and Protection of Natural Resources
- Energy & Transport

- Departmental Planning, Information and Coordination
- Economic & Social Policy, Law & Public Administration
- Environmental Protection, Conservation of Natural Resources, Dissemination of Appropriate Technologies
- Organization, Communication & Management Consultancy
- Private Sector Promotion & Vocational Training

DFI Inc.

A mid-size manufacturer of PC circuit board components and accessories for computer manufacturers and the aftermarket

100 Huan-Ho St.
Hsi-Chih Town, Taipei Hsien, Taiwan
Phone: +886 2 2694-2986 **Fax:** +886 2 2694-3226
Web: www.dfi.com

Primary SIC: 3679—Electronic
Components, NEC
Primary NAICS: 334419—Other
Electronic Component Mfg

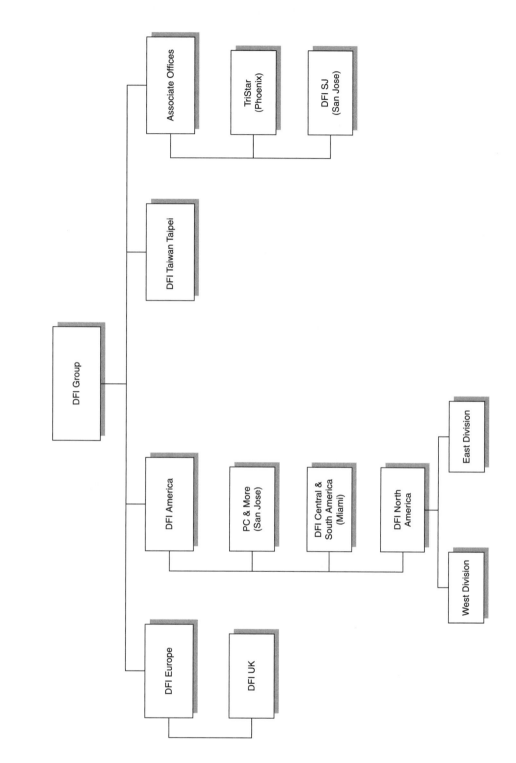

Digital Systems International Corporation

A mid-size systems integrator for defense and industrial clients

4301 N. Fairfax Dr., Ste. 725
Arlington, VA 22203
Phone: (703) 522-6067 **Fax:** (703) 522-6367
Web: www.dsint.com

Primary SIC: 7373—Computer
Integrated Systems Design
Primary NAICS: 541512—Computer
Systems Design Services

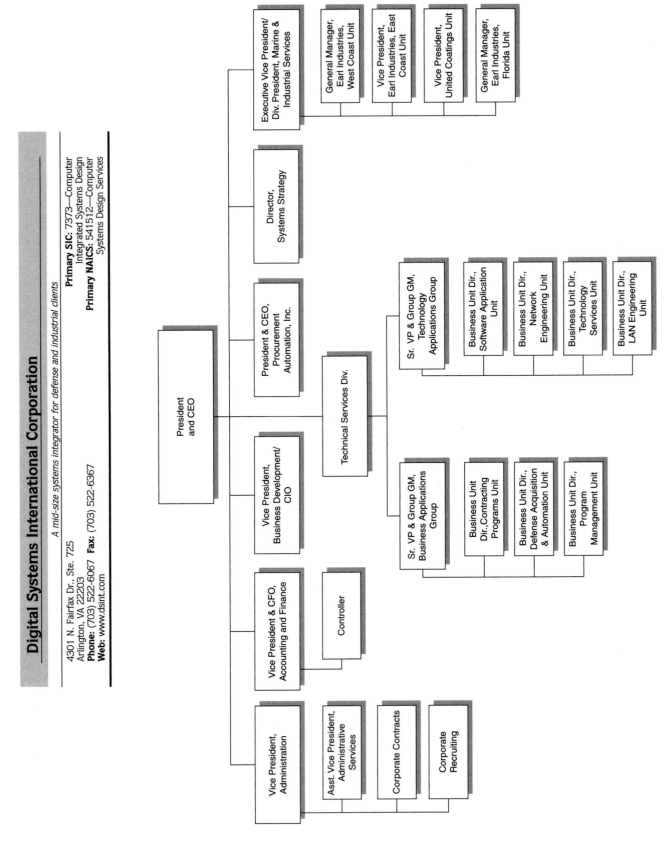

Source: Company web site, 1999

Domino's Pizza Inc.

One of the world's largest pizza chains, Domino's operates 6,200 franchises and corporate stores worldwide

P.O. Box 997
Ann Arbor, MI 48106-0997
Phone: (313) 930-3030 **Fax:** (313) 668-4614
Web: www.dominos.com

Primary SIC: 5812—Eating & Drinking Places
Primary NAICS: 722211—Limited-Service Restaurants

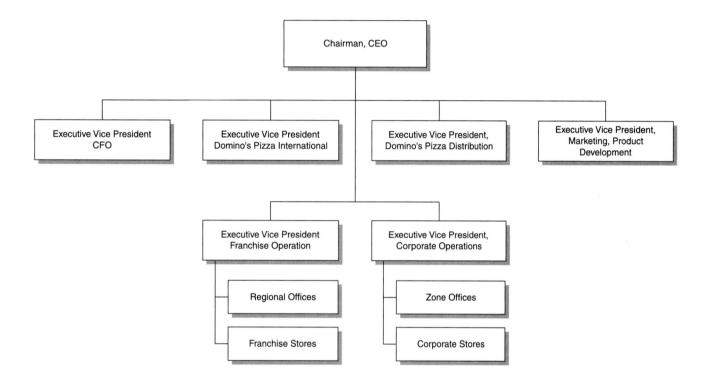

Source: Company, 1999

DTE Energy Company

Holding company for the Detroit Edison electric utility and a number of energy-related subsidiaries

Primary SIC: 4911—Electric Services
Primary NAICS: 221122—Electric Power Distribution

2000 Second Ave.
Detroit, MI 48226-1279
Phone: (313) 235-4000 **Fax:** (313) 235-0223
Web: www.dteenergy.com

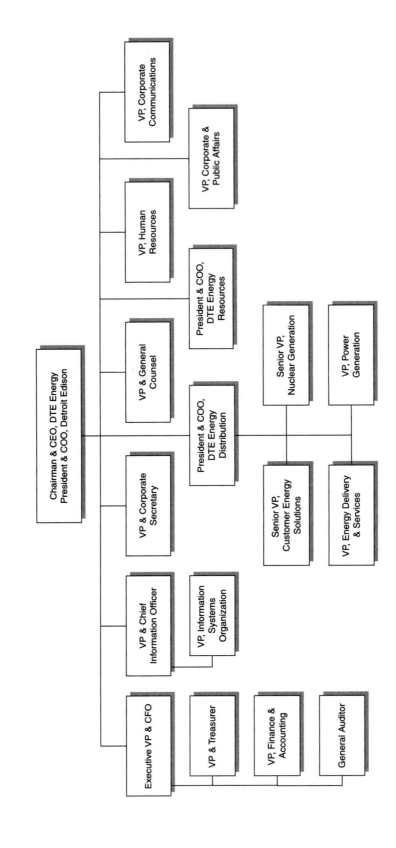

Source: Company and revisions by the editors, 1999

Durham Public Schools

Serving North Carolina's 5th-largest city, the Durham system supports a student population of 29,000 at 43 schools

511 Cleveland St.
P.O. Box 30002
Durham, NC 27702
Phone: (919) 560-2000

Primary SIC: 8211—Elementary & Secondary Schools
Primary NAICS: 61111—Elementary & Secondary Schools
Web: www.dpsnc.com

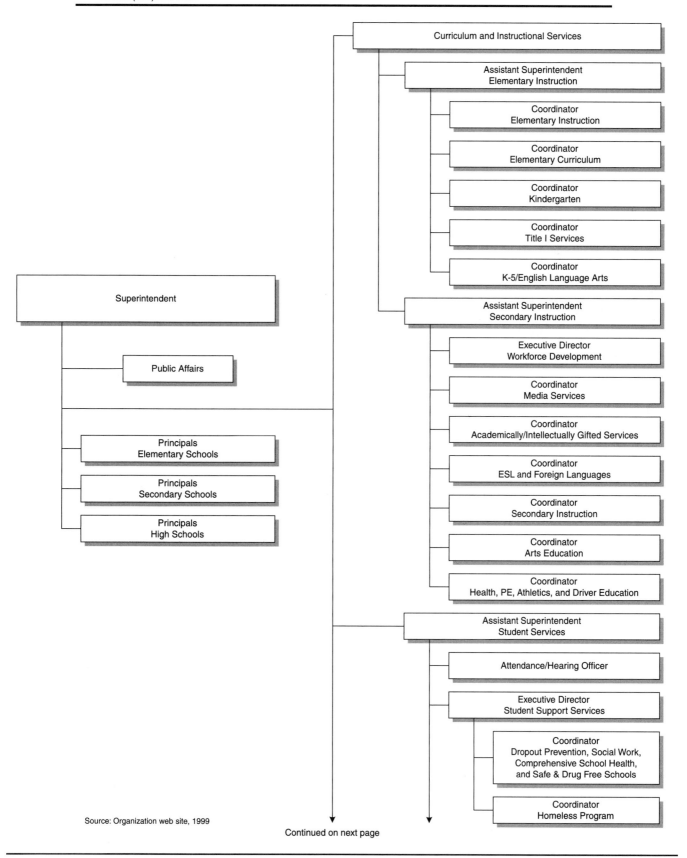

Source: Organization web site, 1999

Continued on next page

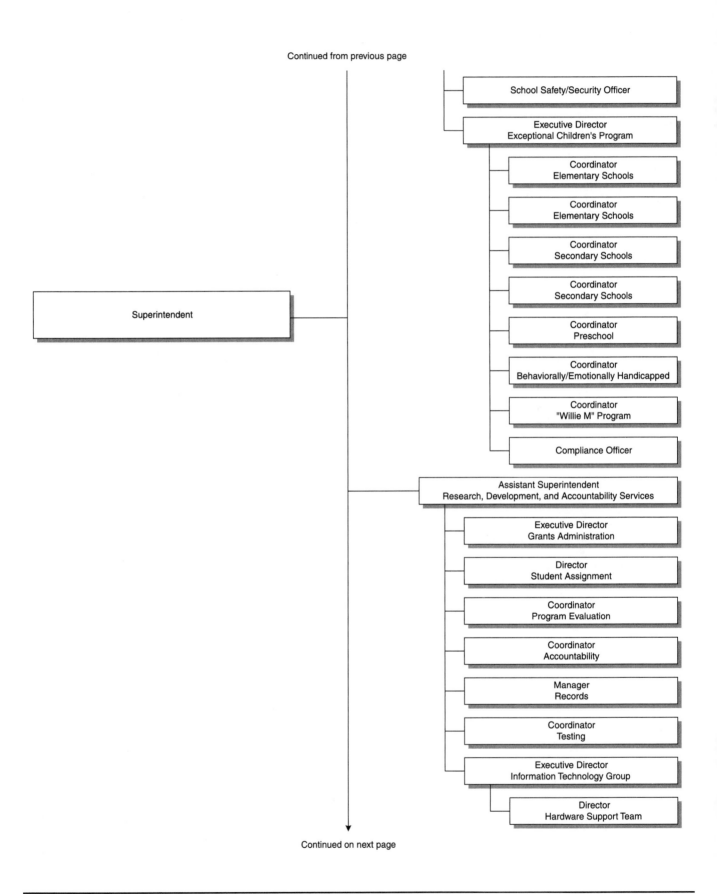

Continued from previous page

School Safety/Security Officer

Executive Director
Exceptional Children's Program

Coordinator
Elementary Schools

Coordinator
Elementary Schools

Coordinator
Secondary Schools

Coordinator
Secondary Schools

Coordinator
Preschool

Coordinator
Behaviorally/Emotionally Handicapped

Coordinator
"Willie M" Program

Compliance Officer

Superintendent

Assistant Superintendent
Research, Development, and Accountability Services

Executive Director
Grants Administration

Director
Student Assignment

Coordinator
Program Evaluation

Coordinator
Accountability

Manager
Records

Coordinator
Testing

Executive Director
Information Technology Group

Director
Hardware Support Team

Continued on next page

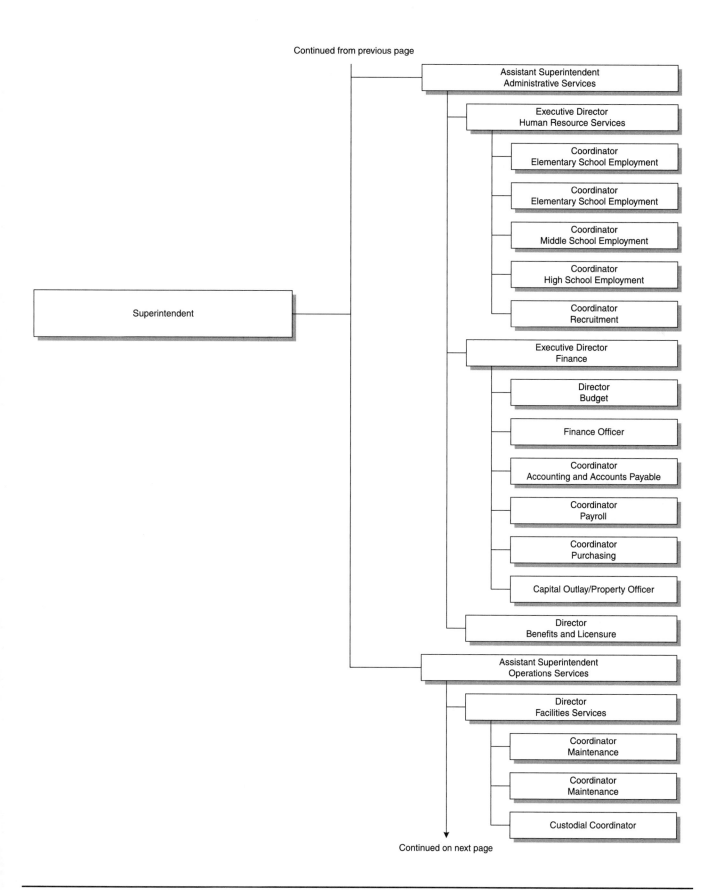

Continued from previous page

Superintendent

Assistant Superintendent
Administrative Services

Executive Director
Human Resource Services

Coordinator
Elementary School Employment

Coordinator
Elementary School Employment

Coordinator
Middle School Employment

Coordinator
High School Employment

Coordinator
Recruitment

Executive Director
Finance

Director
Budget

Finance Officer

Coordinator
Accounting and Accounts Payable

Coordinator
Payroll

Coordinator
Purchasing

Capital Outlay/Property Officer

Director
Benefits and Licensure

Assistant Superintendent
Operations Services

Director
Facilities Services

Coordinator
Maintenance

Coordinator
Maintenance

Custodial Coordinator

Continued on next page

Continued from previous page

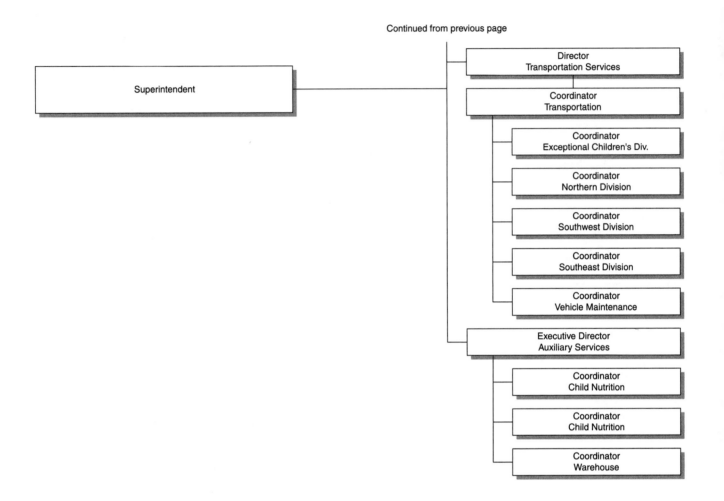

Edinburgh University Library

Founded in the 16th century, the library system serves one of the world's most prestigious universities

George Square
Edinburgh EH8 9LJ, United Kingdom
Phone: +44 0131 650 3384 **Fax:** +44 0131 667 9780
Web: www.lib.ed.ac.uk

Primary SIC: 8231—Libraries
Primary NAICS: 51412—Libraries & Archives
E-mail: library@ed.ac.uk

Librarian

Deputy Librarian
(Oversight of Main Library)

Continued on next page

Sellic Director

Information Strategy
(Senior Sub-Librarian)

- Systems
- Information Services

Special Collections
(Sub-Librarian)

- Special Collections
- University Archives
- Medical Archives
- Photographic Service
- Binding, Conservation & Processing
- SHEFC Projects

Bibliographic Services
(Sub-Librarian)

- Acquisitions Support
- Book Orders (Main Library)
- Serials
- Database Management
- Editing
- Subject Classification
- Donations & Exchanges

Administration
(Sub-Librarian)

- General Office
- Buildings & Security
- Accounts
- Reader Services
- Lending Services (ML)

Source: Organization web site, 1999

Edinburgh University Library (cont.)

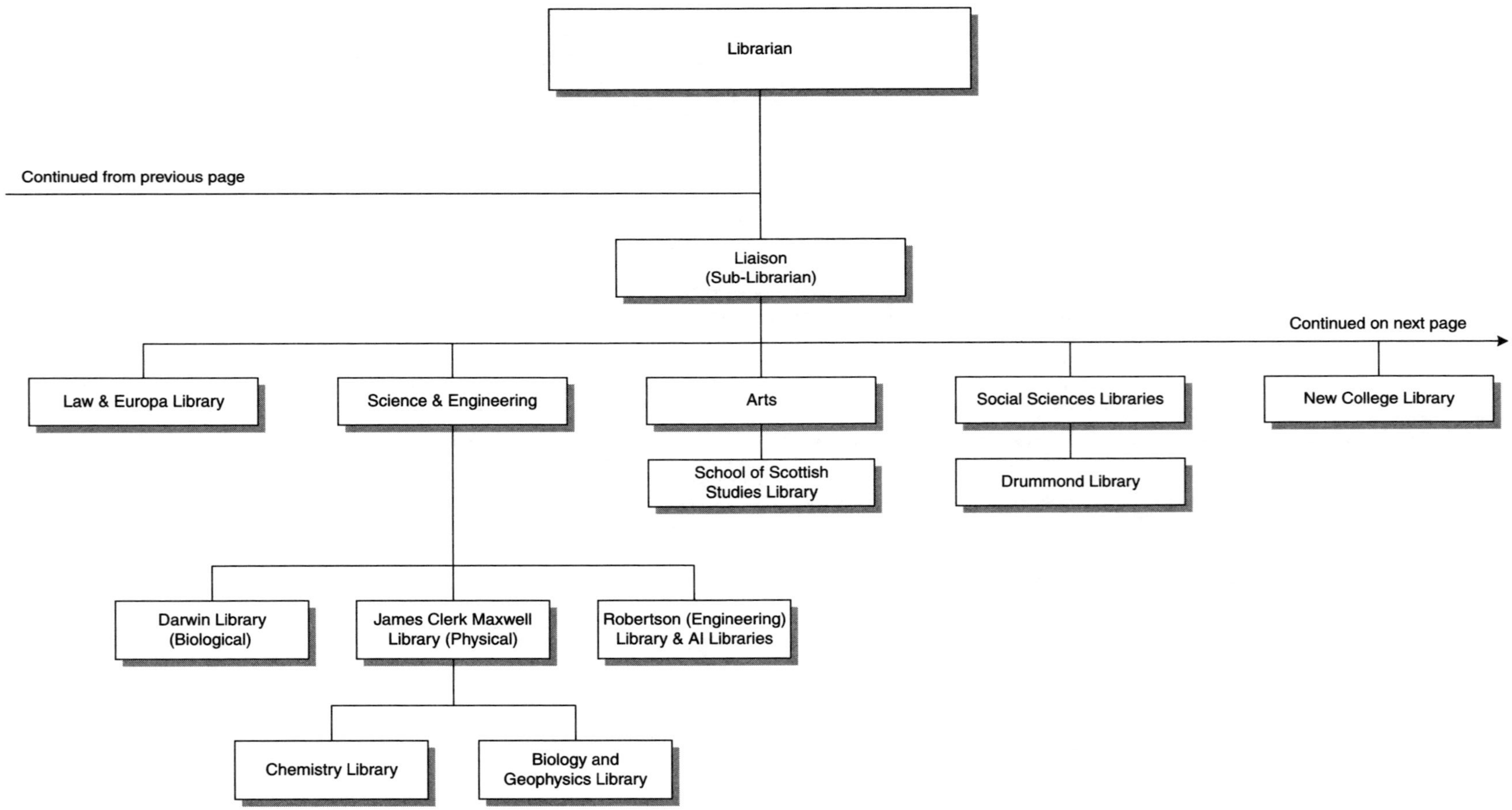

Continued on next page

Continued from previous page

Librarian

Liaison (Sub-Librarian)

Arts

School of Scottish Studies Library

Social Sciences Libraries

Drummond Library

New College Library

Science & Engineering

Law & Europa Library

Robertson (Engineering) Library & AI Libraries

Darwin Library (Biological)

James Clerk Maxwell Library (Physical)

Chemistry Library

Biology and Geophysics Library

Edinburgh University Library (cont.)

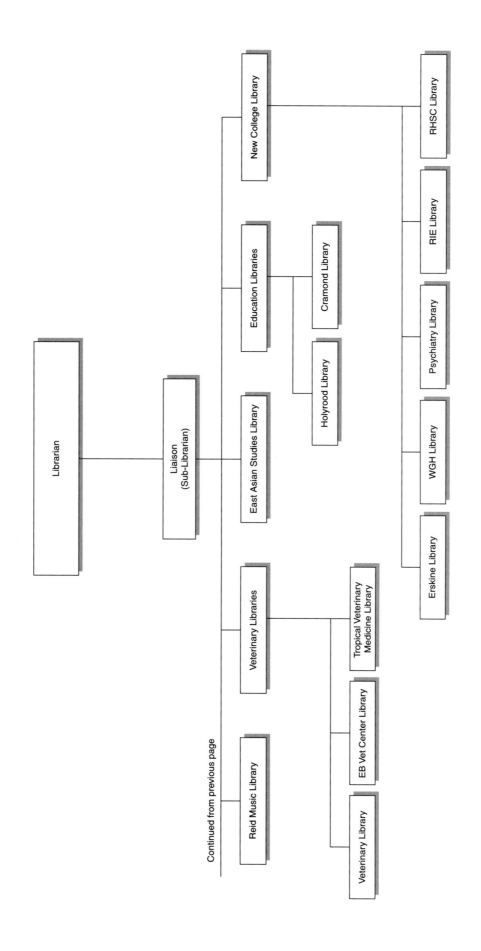

Continued from previous page

Librarian

Liaison (Sub-Librarian)

Reid Music Library

Veterinary Libraries

East Asian Studies Library

Education Libraries

New College Library

Veterinary Library

EB Vet Center Library

Tropical Veterinary Medicine Library

Holyrood Library

Cramond Library

Erskine Library

WGH Library

Psychiatry Library

RIE Library

RHSC Library

Edison International

The holding company for Southern California Edison and a variety of international energy ventures

P.O. Box 400
Rosemead, CA 91770
Phone: (626) 302-1212
Web: www.edison.com

Primary SIC: 4911—Electric Services
Primary NAICS: 221122—Electric Power Distribution

Chairman & Chief Executive Officer
Edison International

Special Assistant to the Chairman and CEO

Edison International Companies

President and Chief Operating Officer
Southern California Edison

President and Chief Executive Officer
Edison Mission Energy

President and Chief Executive Officer
Edison Capital

President and Chief Executive Officer
Edison Enterprises

President & Chief Operating Officer
Edison Source

President & Chief Operating Officer
Edison Select

Senior VP & General Manager
Edison Utilities Services

Edison International and Southern California Edison Corporate Center

Executive Vice President
Chief Financial Officer

Senior Vice President, Treasurer

Vice President, Chief Information Officer

Vice President, Controller

Vice President, Tax

General Auditor

Executive Vice President
General Counsel

Senior Vice President
Human Resources

Senior Vice President
Public Affairs

Vice President
Corporate Communications

Corporate Secretary

Senior Vice President
Strategic Planning & New Business Dev.

Source: Company, 1999

Ekono Energy Ltd.

Finland's largest energy consulting and engineering firm

Tekniikantie 4A
P.O. Box 93
FIN-02151 Espoo, Finland **Fax:** +358 9 469 1981
Phone: +358 9 469 11

Primary SIC: 8711—Engineering Services
Primary NAICS: 54133—Engineering Services
E-mail: ekono.energy@poyry.fi
Web: www.ekonoenergy.fi

President

- Quality Management
- Marketing Communications
- Information Technology
- Human Resources
- Finance & General Administration

Consulting
- Energy Strategies
- Regional Energy Planning
- Restructuring & Financial Planning
- Environmental Consulting

Project Development
- Russia and Eastern Europe
- Nordic Countries/ Western Europe
  - Development Managers
- Asia
- Finland (community) & Baltic Countries
  - Energy Studies
- Finland (industry)

Projects
- Project Management
- Process Engineering
- Boilers & Turbines
- Plant Design
- Electrical and C&I
- District Heating Systems
- O&M Services

El Paso Energy Corporation

This New York Stock Exchange listee is a major natural gas processor, pipeline operator, and distributor

1001 Louisiana St.
Houston, TX 77002-5083
Phone: (713) 757-2131 **Fax:** (713) 420-4417
Web: www.epng.com

Primary SIC: 4925—Mixed, Manufactured, or Liquefied
Petroleum Gas Production and/or Distribution
Primary NAICS: 22121—Natural Gas Distribution

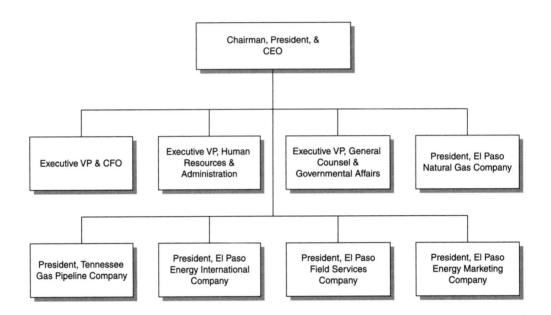

Source: Company web site, 1999

Elf Aquitaine

This oil and chemical producer and marketer is France's largest industrial company

2 place de la Coupole
Tour Elf, F-92078 Paris La Défense Cedex, France
Phone: +33 1 47 44 45 46 **Fax:** +33 1 47 44 78 78
Web: www.elf.fr

Primary SIC: 1311—Crude Petroleum & Natural Gas
Primary NAICS: 211111—Crude Petroleum
& Natural Gas Extraction

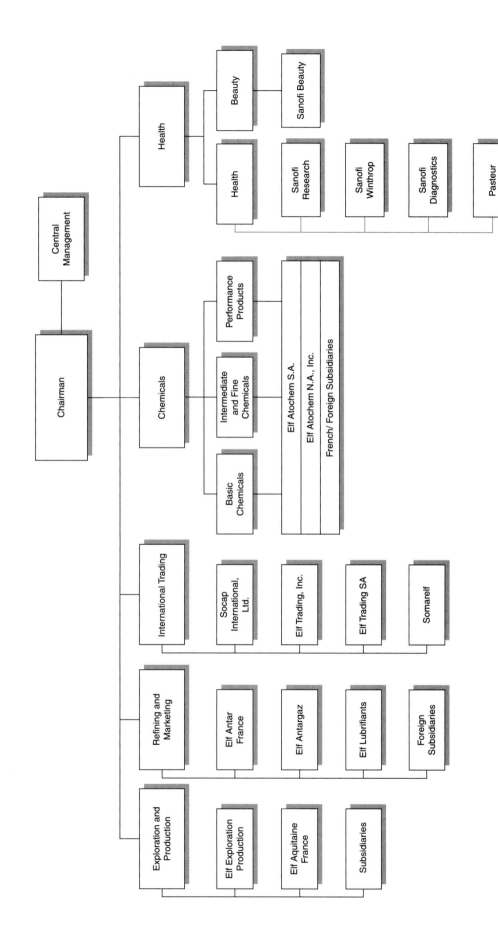

Source: Annual report, 1998

This drug maker markets mostly over-the-counter preparations such as contraceptives, skin treatments, and pain relievers

Birahane Sokak No. 40 Bomonti
Istanbul, Turkey
Phone: (212) 248 48 32 **Fax:** (212) 230 99 32
Web: www.embil.com

Primary SIC: 2834—Pharmaceutical Preparations
Primary NAICS: 325412—Pharmaceutical
Preparation Mfg

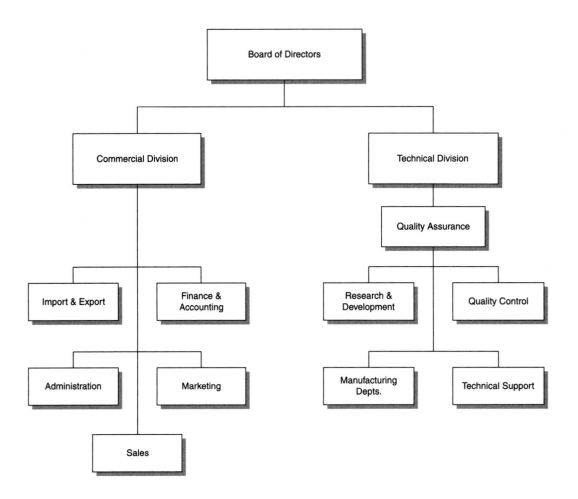

Source: Company web site, 1998

Empresa Colombiana de Petróleos (Ecopetrol)

Colombia's state-run petroleum company is involved in exploration, production, refining, and marketing

Cra 13 No. 36-24
Santafé de Bogotá, Colombia
Phone: +57-1 2344000 **Fax:** +57-1 2344743
Web: www.ecopetrol.com.co

Primary SIC: 1311—Crude Petroleum & Natural Gas
Primary NAICS: 211111—Crude Petroleum & Natural Gas Extraction

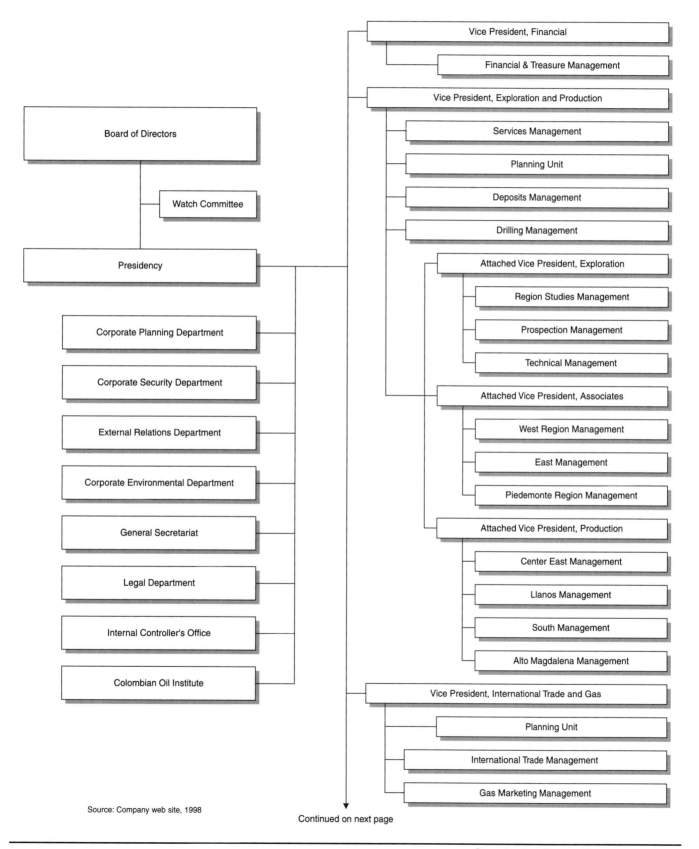

Source: Company web site, 1998

Continued on next page

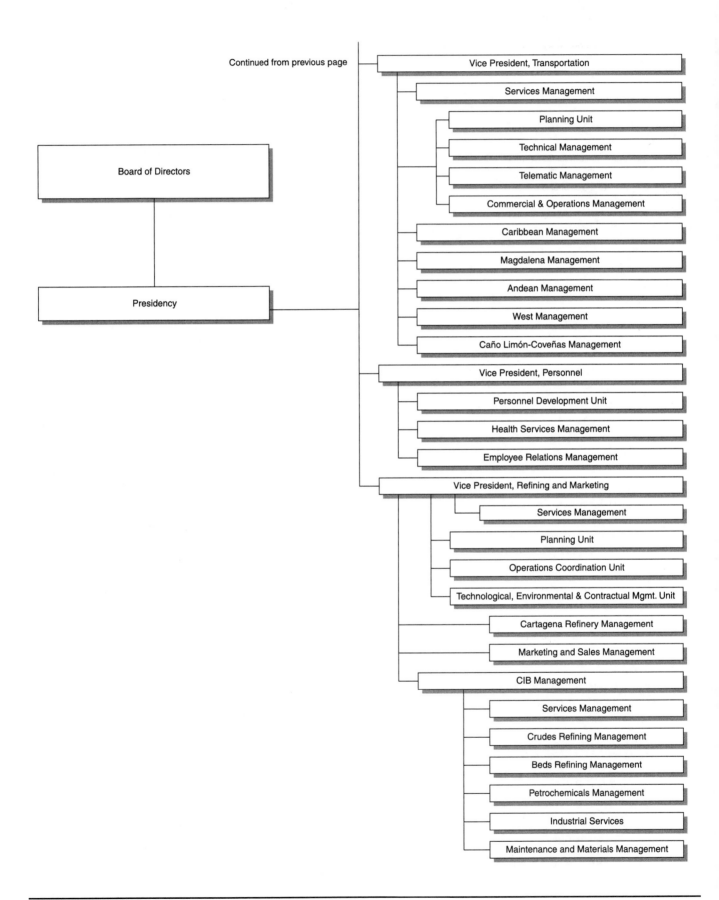

Continued from previous page

Board of Directors

Presidency

Vice President, Transportation

Services Management

Planning Unit

Technical Management

Telematic Management

Commercial & Operations Management

Caribbean Management

Magdalena Management

Andean Management

West Management

Caño Limón-Coveñas Management

Vice President, Personnel

Personnel Development Unit

Health Services Management

Employee Relations Management

Vice President, Refining and Marketing

Services Management

Planning Unit

Operations Coordination Unit

Technological, Environmental & Contractual Mgmt. Unit

Cartagena Refinery Management

Marketing and Sales Management

CIB Management

Services Management

Crudes Refining Management

Beds Refining Management

Petrochemicals Management

Industrial Services

Maintenance and Materials Management

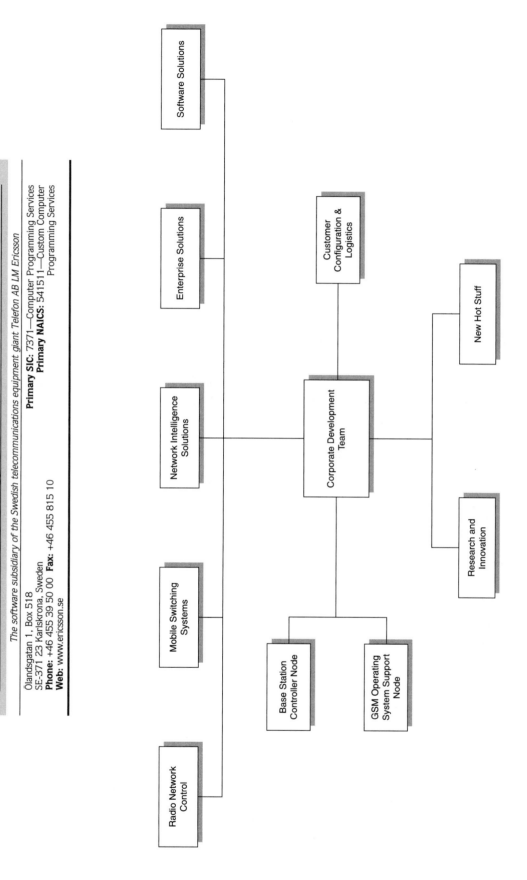

Ericsson Software Technology AB

The software subsidiary of the Swedish telecommunications equipment giant Telefon AB LM Ericsson

Ölandsgatan 1, Box 518
SE-371 23 Karlskrona, Sweden
Phone: +46 455 39 50 00 **Fax:** +46 455 815 10
Web: www.ericsson.se

Primary SIC: 7371—Computer Programing Services
Primary NAICS: 541511—Custom Computer
Programming Services

- Radio Network Control
- Mobile Switching Systems
- Network Intelligence Solutions
  - Corporate Development Team
    - Base Station Controller Node
    - GSM Operating System Support Node
    - Research and Innovation
    - Customer Configuration & Logistics
    - New Hot Stuff
- Enterprise Solutions
- Software Solutions

Source: Company web site, 1999

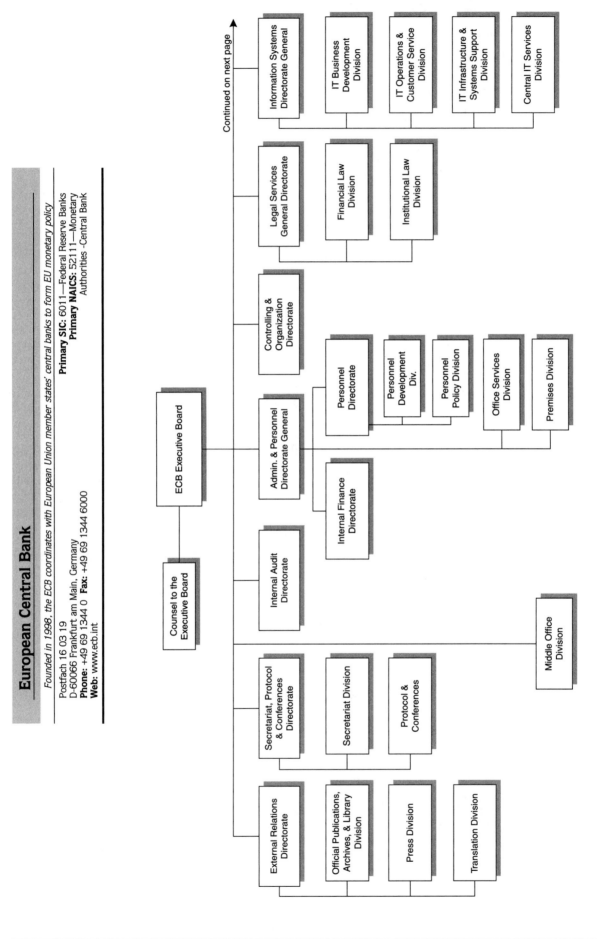

European Central Bank

Founded in 1998, the ECB coordinates with European Union member states' central banks to form EU monetary policy

Postfach 16 03 19
D-60066 Frankfurt am Main, Germany
Phone: +49 69 1344 0 **Fax:** +49 69 1344 6000
Web: www.ecb.int

Primary SIC: 6011—Federal Reserve Banks
Primary NAICS: 52111—Monetary Authorities -Central Bank

Continued on next page

Source: Organization web site, 1999

European Central Bank (cont.)

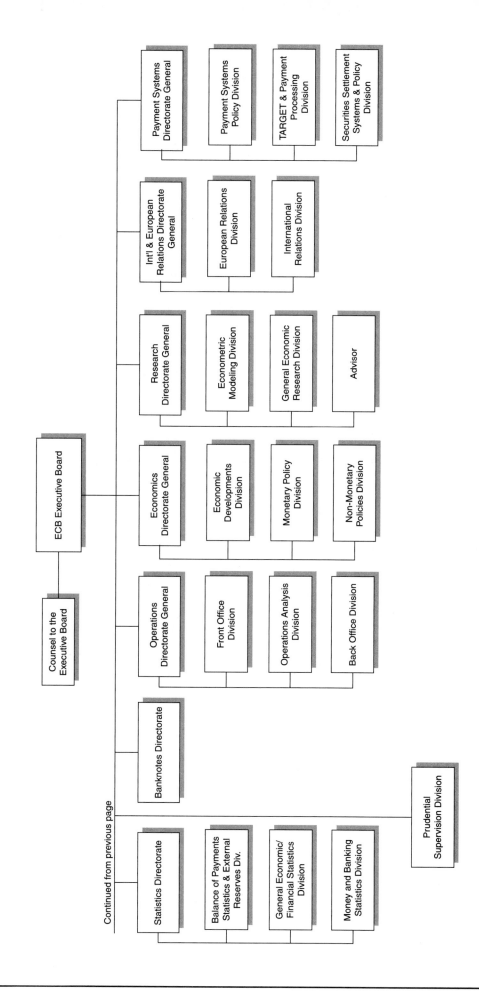

European Union

A 15-member economic bloc of some of the largest and most advanced European countries

Primary SIC: 9721—International Affairs
Primary NAICS: 92812—International Affairs

20 rue de la Lois
B-1049 Brussels, Belgium
Phone: +32-2-299-1111   **Fax:** +32-2-295-0138
Web: www.europa.eu.int

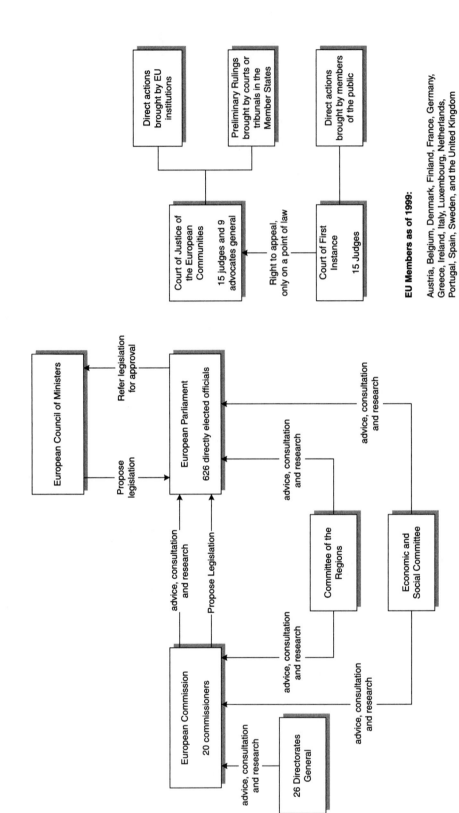

EU Members as of 1999:

Austria, Belgium, Denmark, Finland, France, Germany, Greece, Ireland, Italy, Luxembourg, Netherlands, Portugal, Spain, Sweden, and the United Kingdom

Source: Organization web site, 1998

Federal Communications Commission

The overseer of U.S. communications companies and practices

445 12th St., SW
Washington, DC 20554
Phone: (202) 418-0200 **Fax:** (202) 418-0232
Web: www.fcc.gov

Primary SIC: 9631—Regulation & Administration
of Communications, Electric, Gas, & Other Utilities
Primary NAICS: 92613—Regulation
& Administration of Utilities

Commissioners

- Office of Inspector General

- Office of Engineering & Technology
- Office of General Counsel
- Office of Managing Director
- Office of Public Affairs
- Office of Legislative & Intergovernmental Affairs

- Office of Administrative Law Judges
- Office of Plans & Policy
- Office of Communications Business Opportunities
- Office of Workplace Diversity

- Common Carrier Bureau
- Wireless Telecommunications Bureau
- Mass Media Bureau
- Compliance & Information Bureau
- International Bureau
- Cable Services Bureau

Source: Agency web site, 1999

Federal Deposit Insurance Corporation

The federally chartered insurer of some types of bank deposits with responsibility for some areas of bank regulation

550 17th St., N.W.
Washington, DC 20429-9990
Phone: (202) 393-8400
Web: www.fdic.gov

Primary SIC: 6399—Insurance Carriers, NEC
Primary NAICS: 524128—All Other Direct
Insurance Carriers

Deputy for Policy

Chairman
Office of the Chairman

General Counsel
Legal Division

Inspector General
Office of the Inspector General

Deputy to the Chairman and
Chief Operating Officer

Chief Financial Officer

Director
Finance Division

Director, Office of Internal
Control Management

Director
Insurance Division

Director, Research and
Statistics Division

Director
Supervision Division

Director, Office of Diversity &
Economic Opportunity

Director
Administration Division

Director, Compliance &
Consumer Affairs Div.

Director, Resolutions &
Receiverships Division

Director, Information
Resources Management Div.

Executive Secretary, Office of
the Executive Secretary

Director, Corporate
Communications Office

Director, Legislative
Affairs Office

Director
Ombudsman Office

Director, Policy
Development Office

Federal Reserve System

As the U.S. central bank, the Fed is responsible for monetary policy & partial oversight of the commercial banking industry

20th St. and Constitution Ave., N.W.
Washington, DC 20551
Phone: (202) 452-3000
Web: www.federalreserve.gov

Primary SIC: 6011—Federal Reserve Banks
Primary NAICS: 52111—Monetary
Authorities - Central Bank

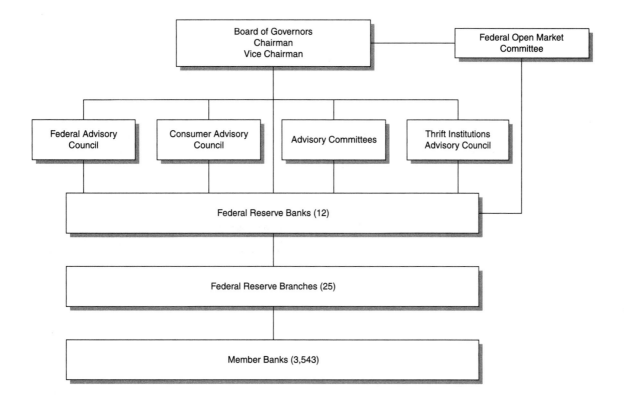

Source: Compiled from various, 1999

Fiat Auto S.p.A.

Part of the broader Fiat Group, the firm sells nearly 3 million cars a year under the Fiat and Alfa Romeo nameplates

Corso Agnelli, 200
I-10135 Turin, Italy
Phone: +39-011-68-31111 **Fax:** +39-011-68-37591
Web: www.fiat.com

Primary SIC: 3711—Motor Vehicles &
Passenger Car Bodies
Primary NAICS: 336111—Automobile Mfg

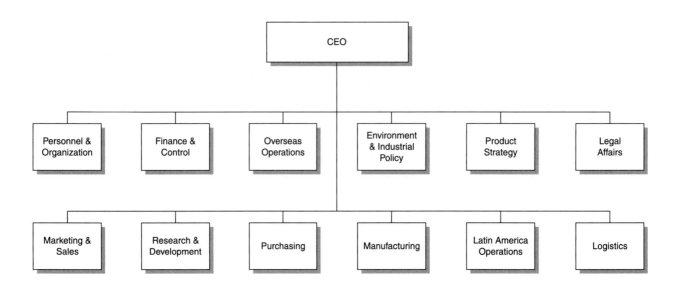

Source: Company, 1997

Finance and Trade Bank (FinComBank)

One of only 23 national commercial banks in this former Soviet republic

26, Pushkin Str.
MD-2012 Chisinau, Republic of Moldova
Phone: +373-2-22 74 35 **Fax:** +373-2-22 82 53
Web: www.fincombank.com

Primary SIC: 6021—National Commercial Banks
Primary NAICS: 52211—Commercial Banking

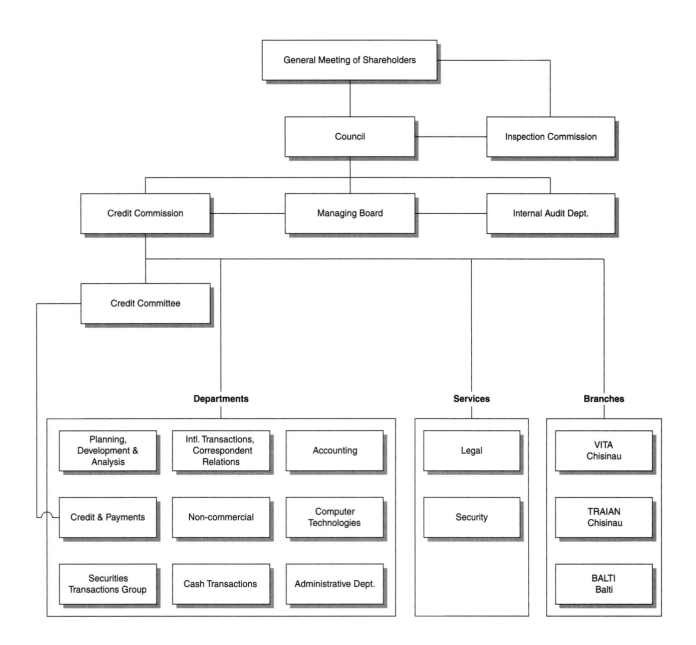

Fleet Financial Group Inc.

One of the top 10 U.S. bank holding companies, Fleet in 1999 agreed to merge with BankBoston to form Fleet Boston

1 Federal St.
Boston, MA 02211-2010
Phone: (617) 346-4000
Web: www.fleet.com

Primary SIC: 6021—National Commercial Banks
Primary NAICS: 52211—Commercial Banking

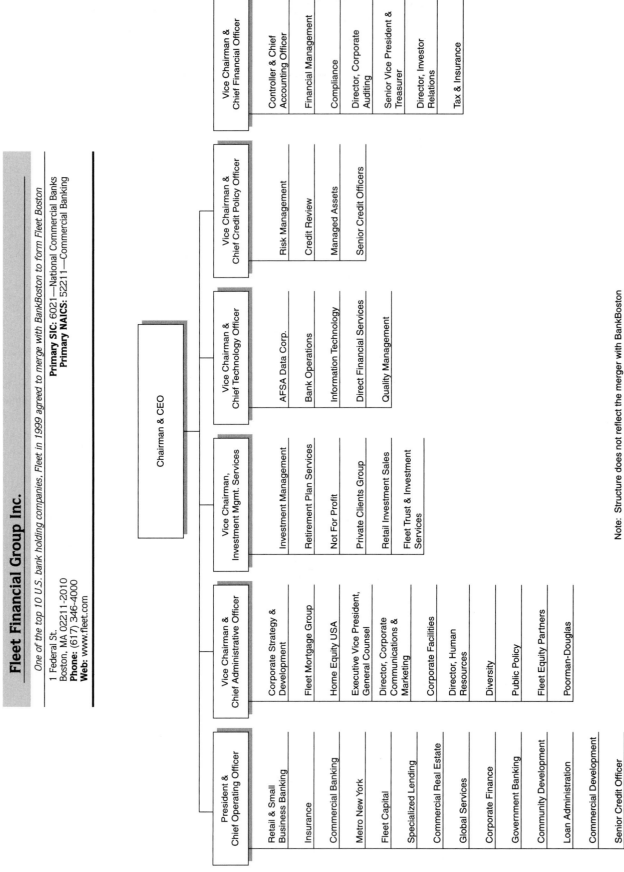

Note: Structure does not reflect the merger with BankBoston

Source: Company and revisions by the editors, 1998

Floyd Oil Company

A mid-size operator of 168 oil wells in four states.

777 Walker St., Ste. 2400
Houston, TX 77002-5314
Phone: (713) 222-6275 **Fax:** (713) 222-6418
Web: floydoil.com

Primary SIC: 1382—Oil & Gas Field Exploration Services
Primary NAICS: 213112—Oil & Gas
Operations Support Activities

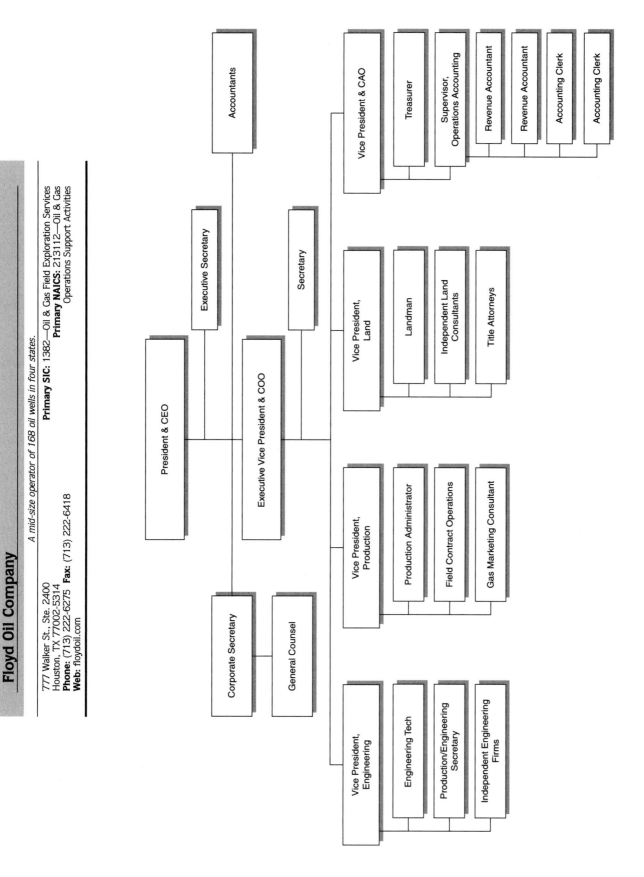

Ford Motor Company

The No. 2 U.S. automaker produces 7 million vehicles a year and boasts one of the industry's strongest profit margins

P.O. Box 1899
The American Rd.
Dearborn, MI 48121-1899
Phone: (313) 322-3000

Primary SIC: 3711—Motor Vehicles &
Passenger Car Bodies
Primary NAICS: 336111—Automobile Mfg
Web: www.ford.com

- Stockholders
- Board of Directors
- Chairman
- President & Chief Executive Officer

President, Ford Automotive Operations

Continued on next page

Vice Chairman
- Executive Director, New Markets Development

Vice Chairman & Chief of Staff
- Corporate Relations
- VP, Washington Affairs
- VP, Governmental Affairs
- VP, Environmental & Safety Engineering
- VP, General Counsel
  - Secretary
- VP, Public Affairs
- VP, Human Resources

President, Ford Financial Services Group
- Chairman & CEO President & CEO Ford Credit
- Chairman & CEO, USL Capital

Executive Vice President & Chief Financial Officer
- VP, Finance
- VP & Treasurer
- Chairman & CEO, The Hertz Corporation
- VP, Business Development Office
- General Auditor
- VP & Chief Tax Officer
- Chairman of the Board, Ford Motor Land Development Corp.

Source: Company and revisions by the editors, 1998

Ford Motor Company (cont.)

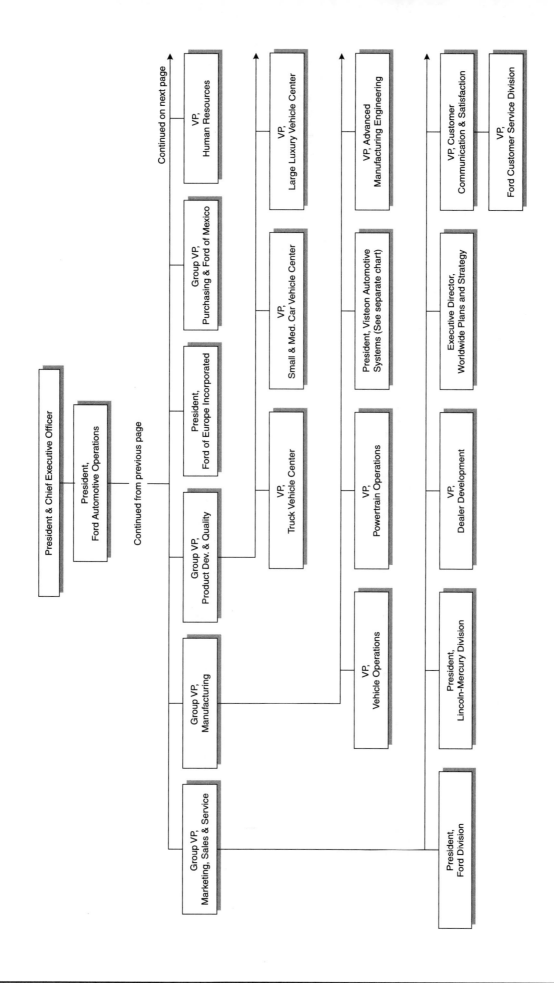

President & Chief Executive Officer

President, Ford Automotive Operations

Continued from previous page

Continued on next page

Group VP, Marketing, Sales & Service

Group VP, Manufacturing

Group VP, Product Dev. & Quality

President, Ford of Europe Incorporated

Group VP, Purchasing & Ford of Mexico

VP, Human Resources

VP, Vehicle Operations

VP, Truck Vehicle Center

VP, Small & Med. Car Vehicle Center

VP, Large Luxury Vehicle Center

President, Lincoln-Mercury Division

VP, Powertrain Operations

President, Visteon Automotive Systems (See separate chart)

VP, Advanced Manufacturing Engineering

President, Ford Division

VP, Dealer Development

Executive Director, Worldwide Plans and Strategy

VP, Customer Communication & Satisfaction

VP, Ford Customer Service Division

Ford Motor Company (cont.)

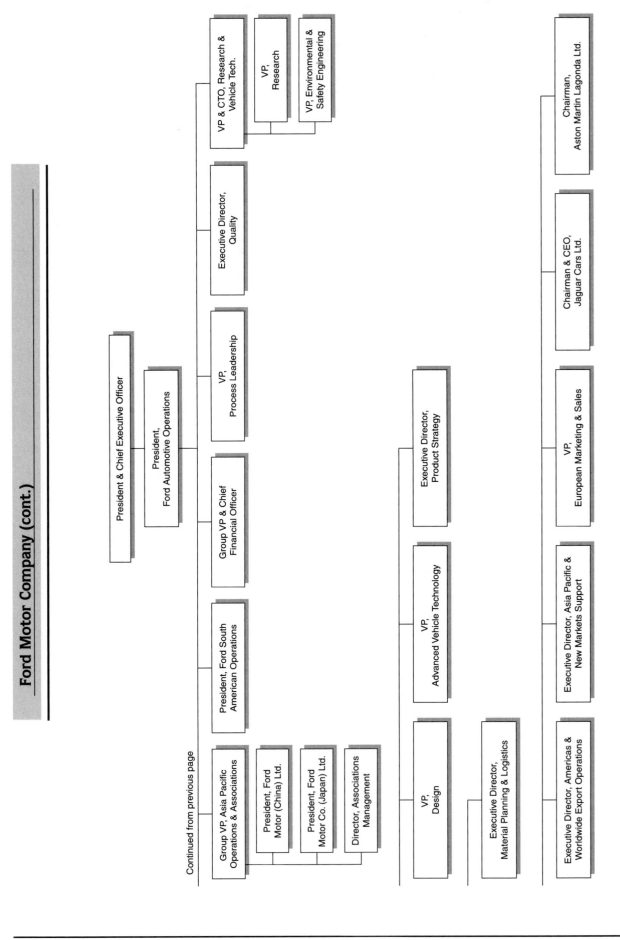

France Telecom

France Telecom remains France's largest telecommunications provider and one of the world's top five

6 place d'Alleray
F-75505 Paris Cedex 15, France
Phone: +33 1 44 44 22 22 **Fax:** +33 1 44 44 21 20
Web: www.francetelecom.fr

Primary SIC: 4813—Telephone Communications,
Except Radiotelephone
Primary NAICS: 51331—Wired
Telecommunications Carriers

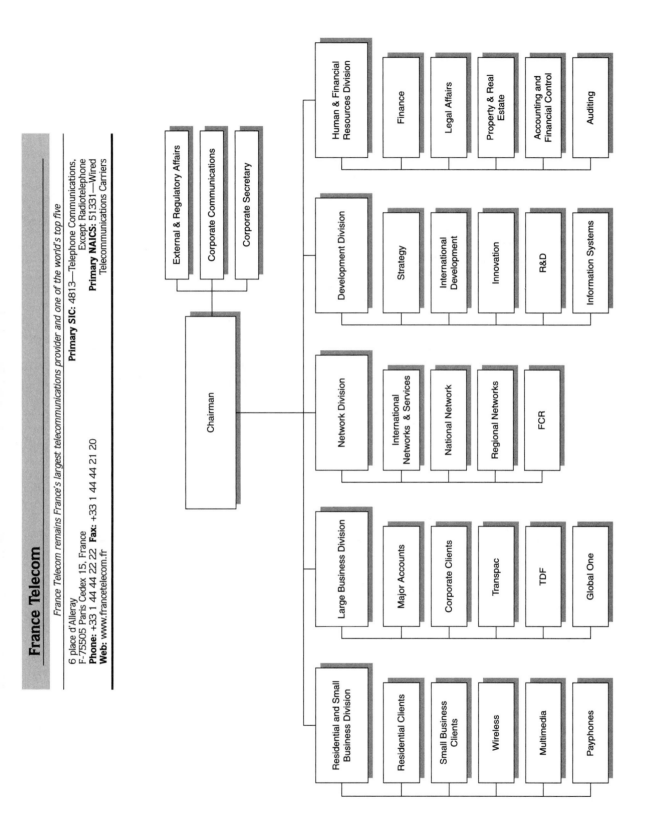

A mid-size research institute developing biotechnology solutions for environmental remediation and general industry

Nobelstrasse 12
D-70569 Stuttgart, Germany
Phone: +49 (0) 7 11 9 70-00
Fax: +49 (0) 7 11 9 70-42 00   **Web:** www.igb.fhg.de

Primary SIC: 8731—Commercial Physical
& Biological Research
Primary NAICS: 54171—R&D in Physical,
Engineering & Life Sciences

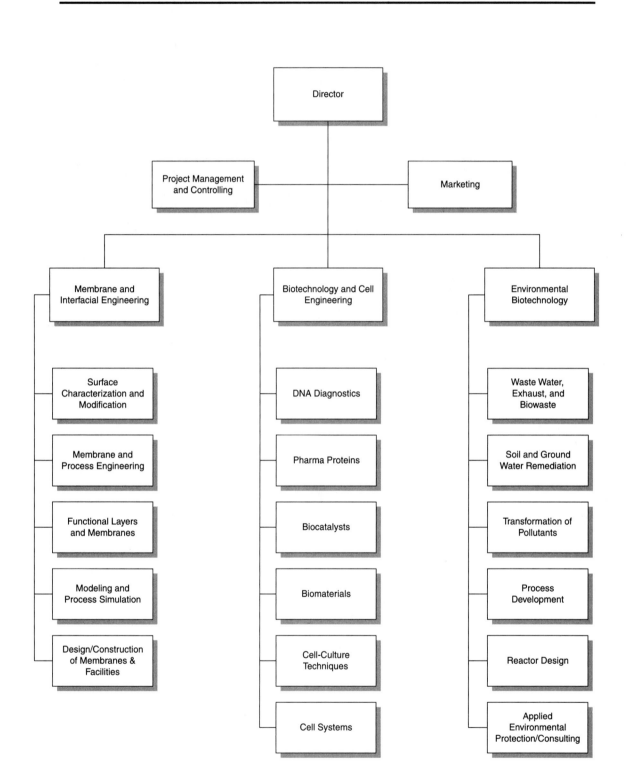

Source: Organization web site, 1999

Fuller Company

Subsidiary of the Danish industrial engineering firm F.L. Smidth-Fuller Engineering A/S

2040 Avenue C
Bethlehem, PA 18017-2188
Phone: (610) 264-6011 **Fax:** (610) 264-6170
Web: www.fullerco.com

Primary SIC: 8711—Engineering Services
Primary NAICS: 54133—Engineering Services

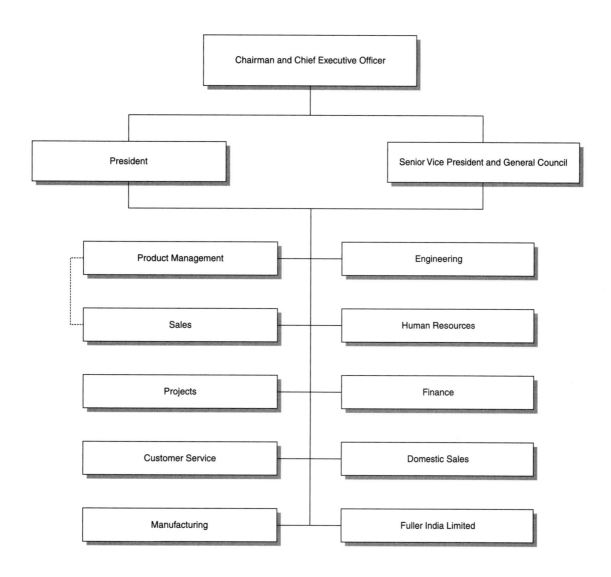

Source: Company web site, 1999

Gasmin Limited

A large Bangladeshi engineering and construction firm specializing in heavy construction and commercial buildings

741 CDA Ave. E. Nasirabad
Chittagong, Bangladesh
Phone: +880-31-619850 **Fax:** +880-31-610123
Web: www.gasmin.com

Primary SIC: 1629—Heavy Construction, NEC
Primary NAICS: 23491—Water, Sewer &
Pipeline Construction

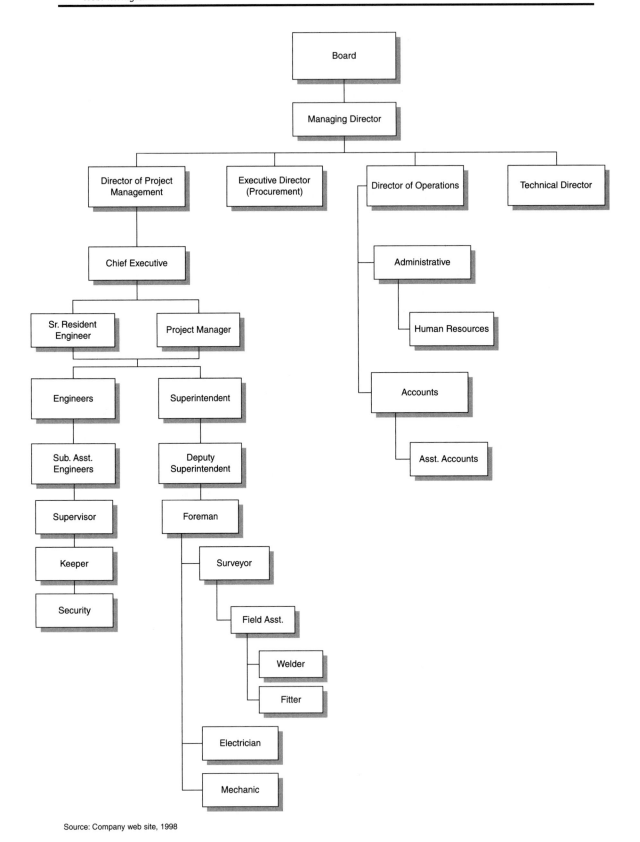

Source: Company web site, 1998

Gener S.A.

This privatized electricity generator and distributor serves markets in four Latin American countries

Miraflores 222, Piso 7
Santiago, Chile
Phone: +56-2-686-8000 **Fax:** +56-2-686-8668
Web: www.gener.com

Primary SIC: 4911—Electric Services
Primary NAICS: 221112—Fossil Fuel
Electric Power Generation
E-mail: gener@gener.com

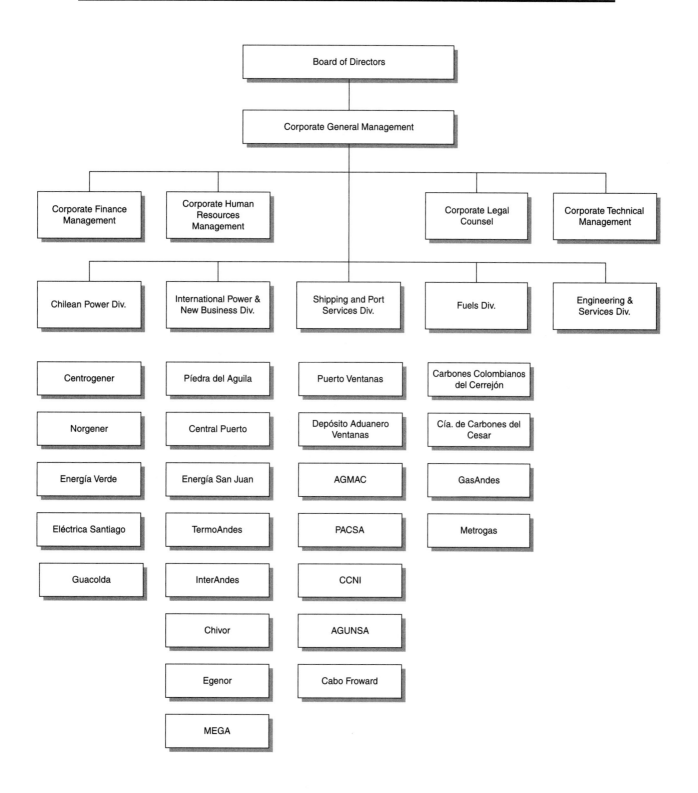

Source: Annual report, 1997

General Electric Company

One of the world's largest companies, GE brought in nearly half its $100 billion in 1998 revenues from financing activities

3135 Easton Tpke.
Fairfield, CT 06431-0001
Phone: (203) 373-2211 **Fax:** (203) 373-2884
Web: www.ge.com

Primary SIC: 6159—Miscellaneous Business
Credit Institutions
Primary NAICS: 52222—Sales Financing

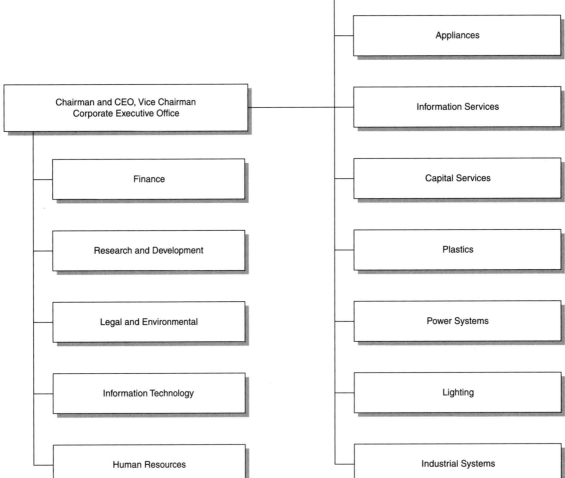

Source: Company, 1999

General Motors Corporation

The world's largest automotive firm produces some 8 million vehicles a year and has a 29% share of the U.S. market

100 Renaissance Center
Detroit, MI 48243-7301
Phone: (313) 556-5000 **Fax:** (313) 556-5108
Web: www.gm.com

Primary SIC: 3711—Motor Vehicles &
Passenger Car Bodies
Primary NAICS: 336111—Automobile Mfg

REORGANIZATION Part 1 (1996)

For additional details on the restructuring
see profiles starting on page 331

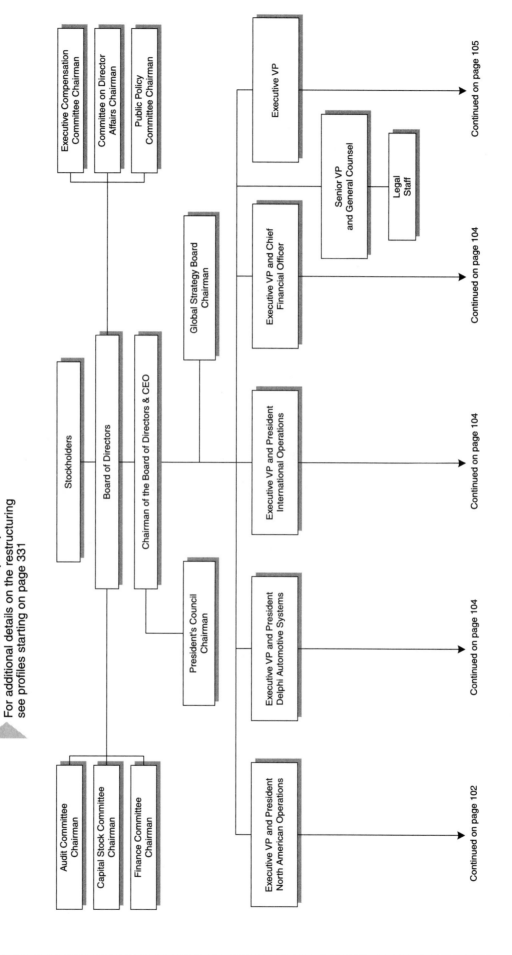

Continued on page 105

Continued on page 104

Continued on page 104

Continued on page 104

Continued on page 102

Source: Company, 1999

General Motors Corporation (cont.)

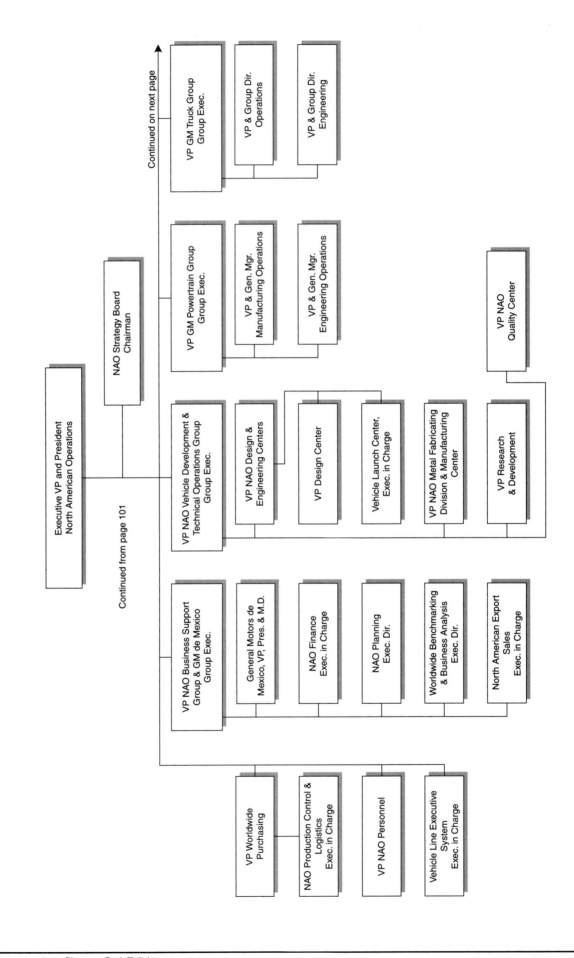

Continued on next page

Continued from page 101

Executive VP and President
North American Operations

NAO Strategy Board
Chairman

VP GM Truck Group
Group Exec.

VP & Group Dir.
Operations

VP & Group Dir.
Engineering

VP GM Powertrain Group
Group Exec.

VP & Gen. Mgr.
Manufacturing Operations

VP & Gen. Mgr.
Engineering Operations

VP NAO
Quality Center

VP NAO Vehicle Development &
Technical Operations Group
Group Exec.

VP NAO Design &
Engineering Centers

VP Design Center

Vehicle Launch Center,
Exec. in Charge

VP NAO Metal Fabricating
Division & Manufacturing
Center

VP Research
& Development

VP NAO Business Support
Group & GM de Mexico
Group Exec.

General Motors de
Mexico, VP, Pres. & M.D.

NAO Finance
Exec. in Charge

NAO Planning
Exec. Dir.

Worldwide Benchmarking
& Business Analysis
Exec. Dir.

North American Export
Sales
Exec. in Charge

VP Worldwide
Purchasing

NAO Production Control &
Logistics
Exec. in Charge

VP NAO Personnel

Vehicle Line Executive
System
Exec. in Charge

General Motors Corporation (cont.)

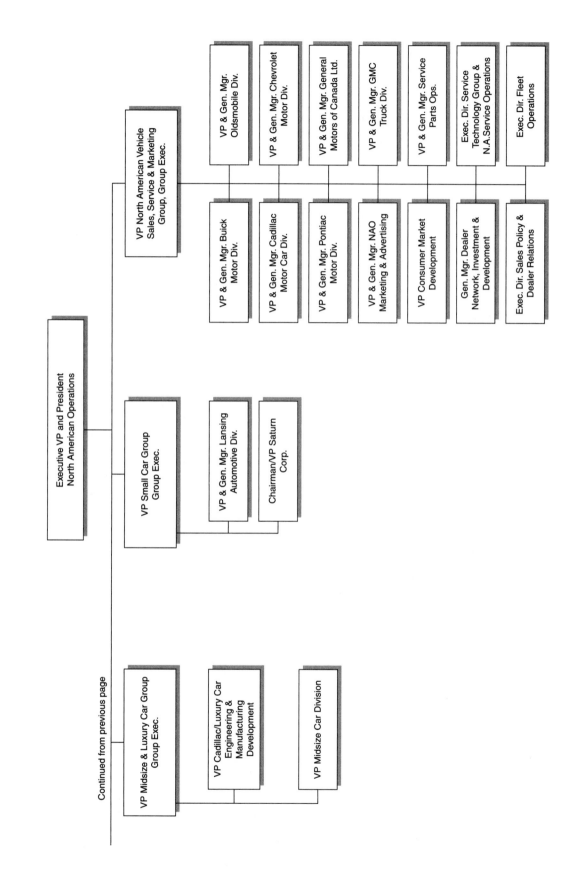

Executive VP and President North American Operations

VP Midsize & Luxury Car Group Group Exec.
- VP Cadillac/Luxury Car Engineering & Manufacturing Development
- VP Midsize Car Division

Continued from previous page

VP Small Car Group Group Exec.
- VP & Gen. Mgr. Lansing Automotive Div.
- Chairman/VP Saturn Corp.

VP North American Vehicle Sales, Service & Marketing Group, Group Exec.
- VP & Gen. Mgr. Oldsmobile Div.
- VP & Gen. Mgr. Chevrolet Motor Div.
- VP & Gen. Mgr. General Motors of Canada Ltd.
- VP & Gen. Mgr. GMC Truck Div.
- VP & Gen. Mgr. Service Parts Ops.
- Exec. Dir. Service Technology Group & N.A.Service Operations
- Exec. Dir. Fleet Operations
- VP & Gen. Mgr. Buick Motor Div.
- VP & Gen. Mgr. Cadillac Motor Car Div.
- VP & Gen. Mgr. Pontiac Motor Div.
- VP & Gen. Mgr. NAO Marketing & Advertising
- VP Consumer Market Development
- Gen. Mgr. Dealer Network, Investment & Development
- Exec. Dir. Sales Policy & Dealer Relations

General Motors Corporation (cont.)

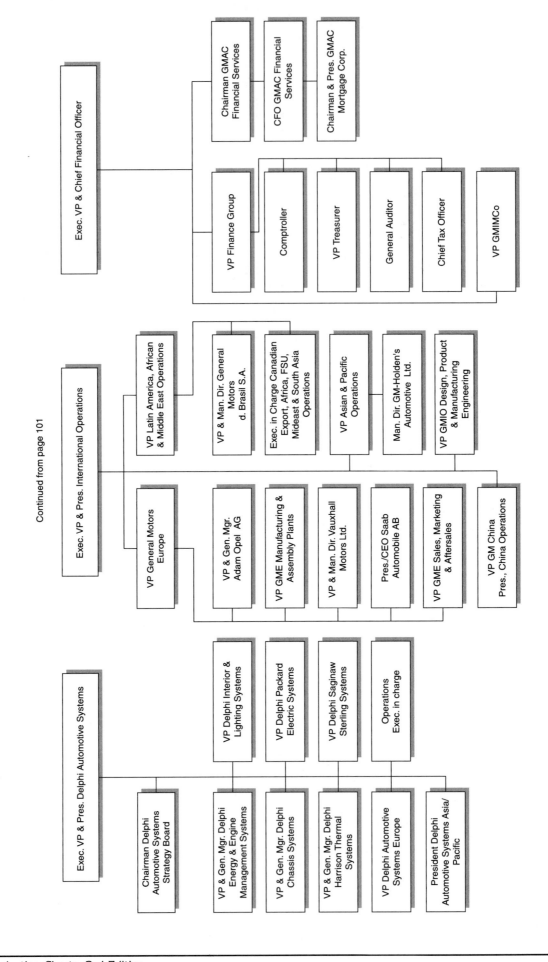

Continued from page 101

Exec. VP & Chief Financial Officer
- VP Finance Group
  - Comptroller
  - VP Treasurer
  - General Auditor
  - Chief Tax Officer
  - VP GMIMCo
- Chairman GMAC Financial Services
- CFO GMAC Financial Services
- Chairman & Pres. GMAC Mortgage Corp.

Exec. VP & Pres. International Operations
- VP General Motors Europe
  - VP & Gen. Mgr. Adam Opel AG
  - VP GME Manufacturing & Assembly Plants
  - VP & Man. Dir. Vauxhall Motors Ltd.
  - Pres./CEO Saab Automobile AB
  - VP GME Sales, Marketing & Aftersales
  - VP GM China Pres., China Operations
- VP Latin America, African & Middle East Operations
  - VP & Man. Dir. General Motors d. Brasil S.A.
  - Exec. in Charge Canadian Export, Africa, FSU, Mideast & South Asia Operations
  - VP Asian & Pacific Operations
  - Man. Dir. GM-Holden's Automotive Ltd.
  - VP GMIO Design, Product & Manufacturing Engineering

Exec. VP & Pres. Delphi Automotive Systems
- Chairman Delphi Automotive Systems Strategy Board
- VP Delphi Interior & Lighting Systems
  - VP & Gen. Mgr. Delphi Energy & Engine Management Systems
- VP Delphi Packard Electric Systems
  - VP & Gen. Mgr. Delphi Chassis Systems
- VP Delphi Saginaw Sterling Systems
  - VP & Gen. Mgr. Delphi Harrison Thermal Systems
- Operations Exec. in charge
  - VP Delphi Automotive Systems Europe
  - President Delphi Automotive Systems Asia/Pacific

General Motors Corporation (cont.)

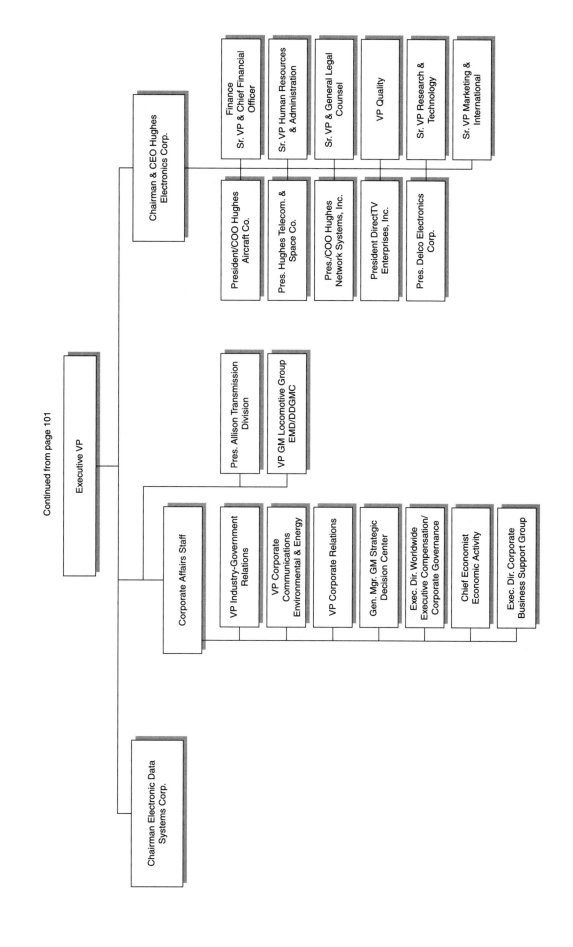

Continued from page 101

Executive VP

Chairman & CEO Hughes Electronics Corp.

Chairman Electronic Data Systems Corp.

Corporate Affairs Staff

Pres. Allison Transmission Division

VP GM Locomotive Group EMD/DDGMC

VP Industry-Government Relations

VP Corporate Communications Environmental & Energy

VP Corporate Relations

Gen. Mgr. GM Strategic Decision Center

Exec. Dir. Worldwide Executive Compensation/ Corporate Governance

Chief Economist Economic Activity

Exec. Dir. Corporate Business Support Group

Finance Sr. VP & Chief Financial Officer

Sr. VP Human Resources & Administration

Sr. VP & General Legal Counsel

VP Quality

Sr. VP Research & Technology

Sr. VP Marketing & International

President/COO Hughes Aircraft Co.

Pres. Hughes Telecom. & Space Co.

Pres./COO Hughes Network Systems, Inc.

President DirectTV Enterprises, Inc.

Pres. Delco Electronics Corp.

General Motors Corporation (cont.)

REORGANIZATION Part 2 (1999)
For additional details on the restructuring
see profiles starting on page 331

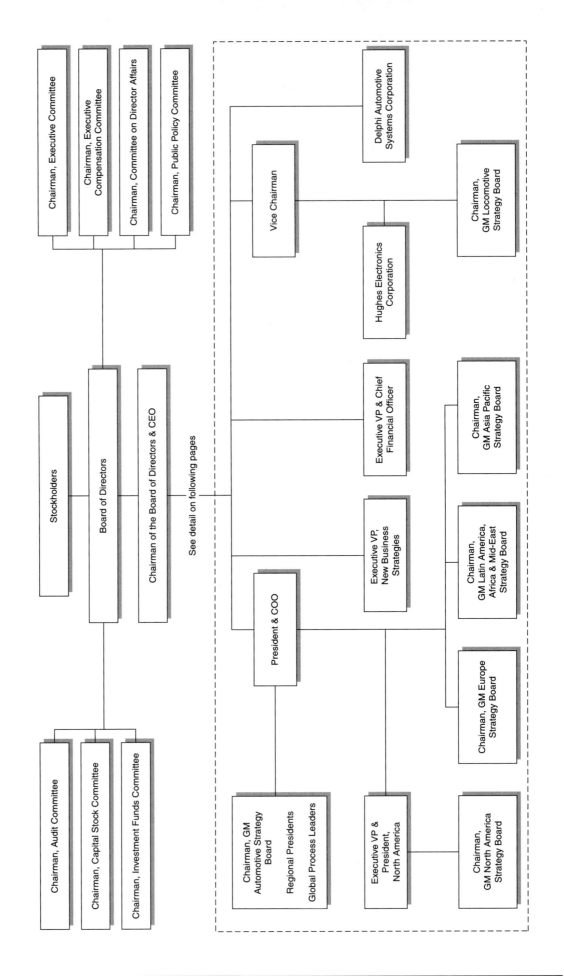

General Motors Corporation (cont.)

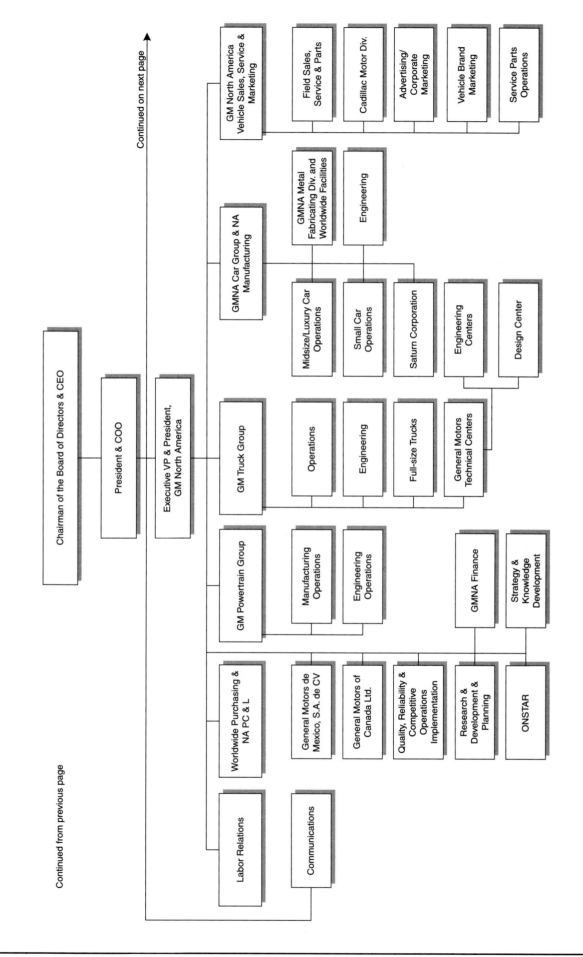

Continued from previous page

Continued on next page

Chairman of the Board of Directors & CEO

President & COO

Executive VP & President, GM North America

GM North America Vehicle Sales, Service & Marketing
- Field Sales, Service & Parts
- Cadillac Motor Div.
- Advertising/ Corporate Marketing
- Vehicle Brand Marketing
- Service Parts Operations

GMNA Car Group & NA Manufacturing
- GMNA Metal Fabricating Div. and Worldwide Facilities
- Engineering
- Midsize/Luxury Car Operations
- Small Car Operations
- Saturn Corporation
- Engineering Centers
- Design Center

GM Truck Group
- Operations
- Engineering
- Full-size Trucks
- General Motors Technical Centers

GM Powertrain Group
- Manufacturing Operations
- Engineering Operations

GMNA Finance

Strategy & Knowledge Development

Worldwide Purchasing & NA PC & L

General Motors de Mexico, S.A. de CV

General Motors of Canada Ltd.

Quality, Reliability & Competitive Operations Implementation

Research & Development & Planning

ONSTAR

Labor Relations

Communications

General Motors Corporation (cont.)

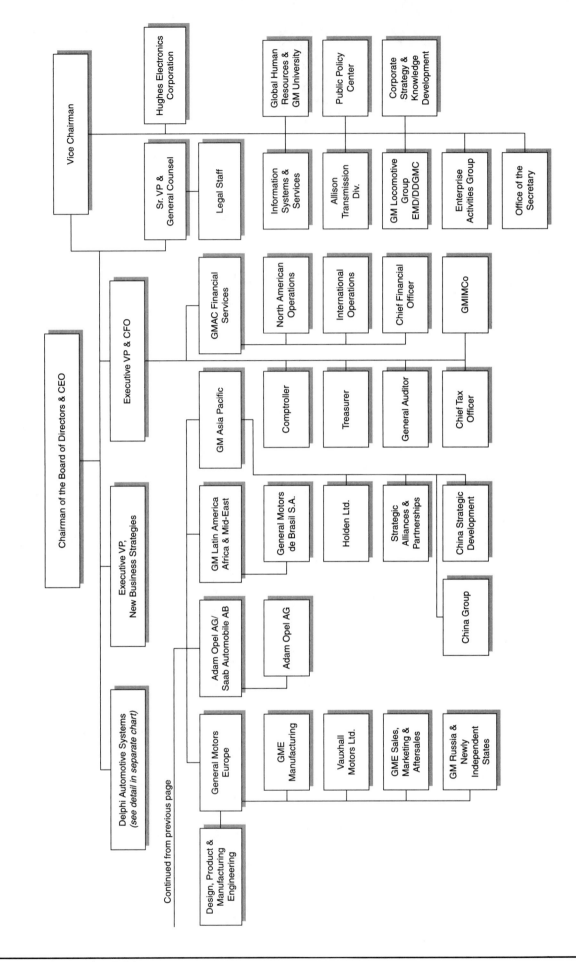

A top publisher of books and entertainment products for young children

888 7th Ave.
New York, NY 10106
Phone: (212) 547-6700
Web: www.goldenbooks.com

Primary SIC: 2731—Books: Publishing
Primary NAICS: 51113—Book Publishers

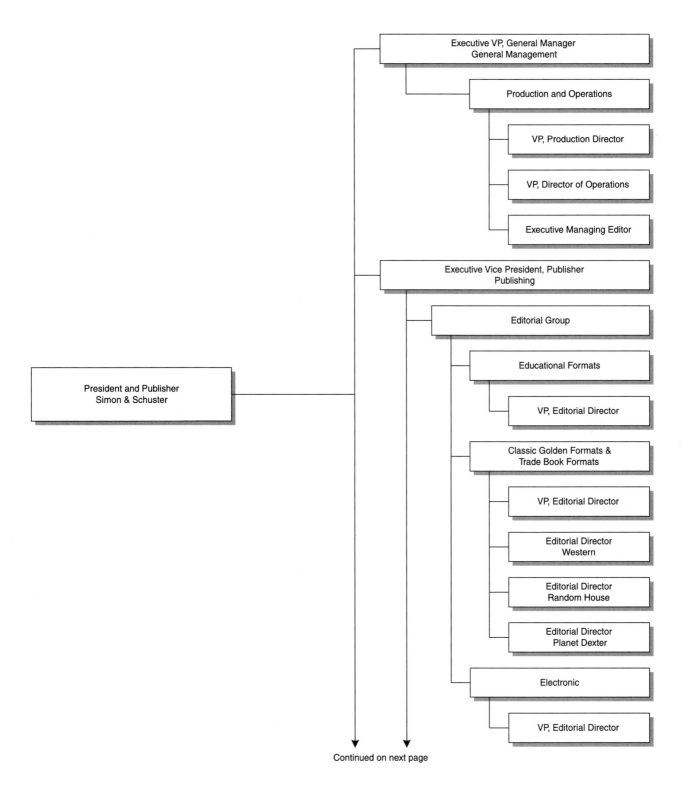

President and Publisher
Simon & Schuster

Executive VP, General Manager
General Management

Production and Operations

VP, Production Director

VP, Director of Operations

Executive Managing Editor

Executive Vice President, Publisher
Publishing

Editorial Group

Educational Formats

VP, Editorial Director

Classic Golden Formats &
Trade Book Formats

VP, Editorial Director

Editorial Director
Western

Editorial Director
Random House

Editorial Director
Planet Dexter

Electronic

VP, Editorial Director

Continued on next page

Source: Publishers Weekly, 1998

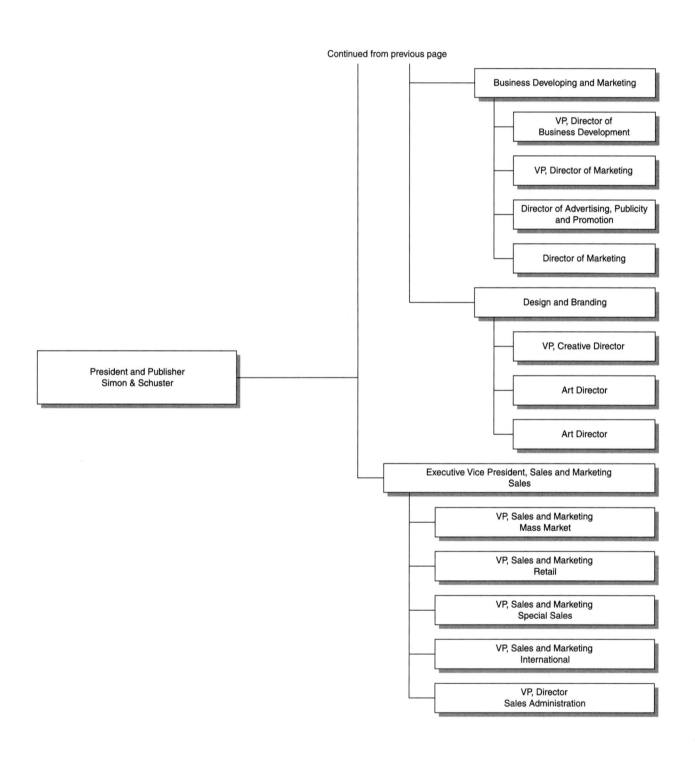

Continued from previous page

Business Developing and Marketing

VP, Director of Business Development

VP, Director of Marketing

Director of Advertising, Publicity and Promotion

Director of Marketing

Design and Branding

VP, Creative Director

Art Director

Art Director

President and Publisher
Simon & Schuster

Executive Vice President, Sales and Marketing
Sales

VP, Sales and Marketing
Mass Market

VP, Sales and Marketing
Retail

VP, Sales and Marketing
Special Sales

VP, Sales and Marketing
International

VP, Director
Sales Administration

Government of Canada

Major institutions in the Canadian national government

Prime Minister's Office
Ottawa, ON K1A 0A6 Canada
Phone: (613) 992-4211 **Fax:** (613) 941-6900
Web: canada.gc.ca

Primary SIC: 9131—Executive & Legislative
Offices, Combined
Primary NAICS: 92111—Executive Offices

Source: Agency web site, 1998

GTS Duratek Inc.

A publicly traded hazardous waste processing and consulting firm

10100 Old Columbia Rd.
Columbia, MD 21046
Phone: (410) 312-5100 **Fax:** (410) 290-9112
Web: www.gtsduratek.com

Primary SIC: 4953—Refuse Systems
Primary NAICS: 562211—Hazardous Waste
Treatment & Disposal

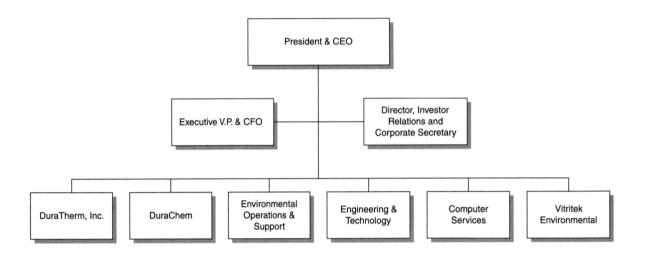

Source: Company web site, 1999

H.J. Pertzborn Plumbing & Fire Protection Corp.

A general plumbing contractor and sprinkler system designer

Primary SIC: 1711—Plumbing, Heating, & Air-Conditioning
Primary NAICS: 23511—Plumbing, Heating & AC Contractor

802 John Nolen Dr.
Madison, WI 53791
Web: www.hjpertzborn.com

Source: Company web site, 1999

Harbin Power Engineering Company Limited

With both domestic and international contracts, HPE is China's largest power plant engineering firm

95 Daqing Road
Harbin 150040, China
Phone: (0451) 2136688 **Fax:** (0451) 2135566
Web: www.chinahpe.com

Primary SIC: 8711—Engineering Services
Primary NAICS: 54133—Engineering Services
E-mail: hpe@chinahpe.com

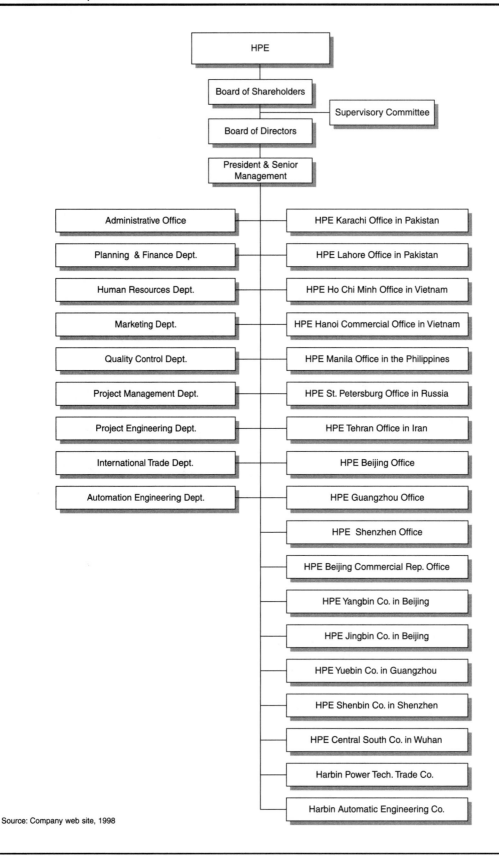

Source: Company web site, 1998

Henry Ford Health System

This nonprofit metropolitan health system employs 17,000 full-time workers and takes in $1.75 billion in annual receipts

One Ford Place
Detroit, MI 48202-3450
Phone: (313) 872-8100
Web: www.henryfordhealth.org

Primary SIC: 8011—Offices & Clinics
of Doctors of Medicine
Primary NAICS: 621491—HMO Medical Centers

Office of the President & Chief Executive Officer
Henry Ford Health System

Senior Vice President and Chief Financial Officer
- Financial Services
- Financial Operations
- Information Services
- Insurance & Legal Services
- Corporate Support Services
- Diversified Services

Senior Vice President Planning & Strategic Development
- Planning and Marketing
- Public Affairs
- Management Services
- Quality Improvement Education and Research
- Government Relations
- Business and Labor Relations
- Center for Health System Studies

Senior Vice President for Managed Care
- HAP
- Joint Venture Insurance Programs
- Other Prepaid Contracts
- Senior Services

Senior Vice President for Hospital Affairs
- Henry Ford Hospital
- Cottage Hospital
- Wyandotte Hospital and Medical Center
- Henry Ford Mercy Health Network
- Regional Coordination
- Urban Health Programs

Senior Vice President Medical Affairs
Chairman, Board of Governors
- System Medical Council
- Henry Ford Medical Group
- Detroit Campus Leadership
- Suburban Ambulatory Health System
- Behavioral Services
- Kingswood Hospital
- Health Sciences Center

Corporate Vice President and Secretary
- Governance
- Board Development

Corporate Vice President
- Staff Assistant to President
- Detroit Campus Plan Project Oversight
- Health Sciences Center Support

Corporate Vice President Human Resources
- Employment
- Compensation and Benefits
- Organizational Development
- Minority Development

Corporate Vice President Philanthropy
- Philanthropy
- Capital Campaign
- Planned Giving
- Alumni Relations

Source: Company, 1999

Hewlett-Packard Company

One of the world's largest producers of computer equipment and other electronic components

3800 Hanover St.
Palo Alto, CA 94304-1185
Phone: (650) 857-1501 **Fax:** (650) 857-5518
Web: www.hp.com

Primary SIC: 3571—Electronic Computers
Primary NAICS: 334111—Electronic Computer Mfg

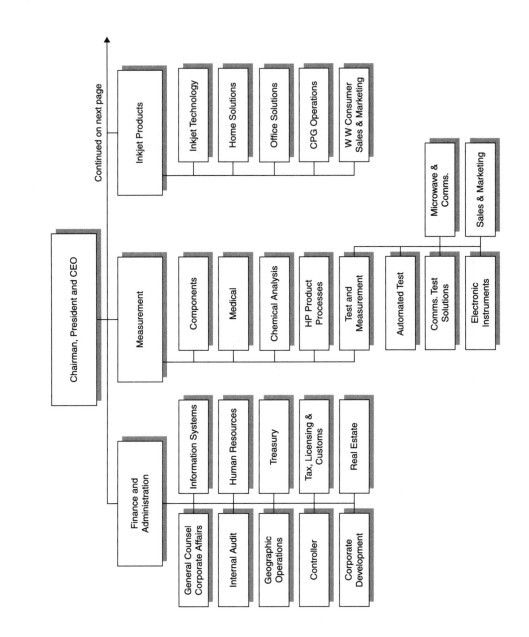

Continued on next page

Chairman, President and CEO

Finance and Administration
- Information Systems
- Human Resources
- Treasury
- Tax, Licensing & Customs
- Real Estate
- General Counsel Corporate Affairs
- Internal Audit
- Geographic Operations
- Controller
- Corporate Development

Measurement
- Components
- Medical
- Chemical Analysis
- HP Product Processes
- Test and Measurement
  - Automated Test
  - Comms. Test Solutions
  - Electronic Instruments
  - Microwave & Comms.
  - Sales & Marketing

Inkjet Products
- Inkjet Technology
- Home Solutions
- Office Solutions
- CPG Operations
- W W Consumer Sales & Marketing

Source: Company web site, 1999

Hewlett-Packard Company (cont.)

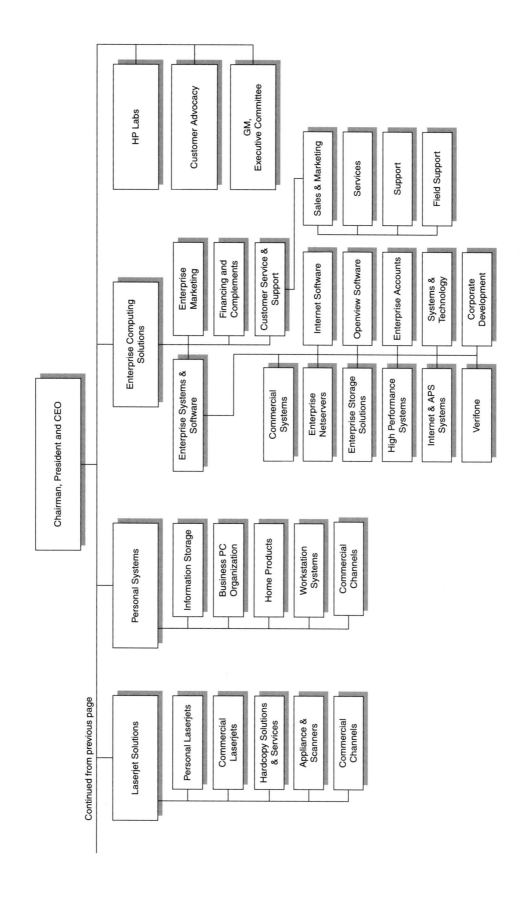

Continued from previous page

Hitachi Construction Machinery Co., Ltd.

Hydraulic shovels are this manufacturer's biggest product line, contributing a large share of its $2.8 billion in 1998 sales

Nippon Building, 6-2, 2-chome, Otemachi
Chiyoda-ku, Tokyo, Japan
Web: www.hitachi-kenki.co.jp

Primary SIC: 3531—Construction Machinery & Equipment
Primary NAICS: 33312—Construction Machinery Mfg
E-mail: general@ho.hitachi-kenki.co.jp

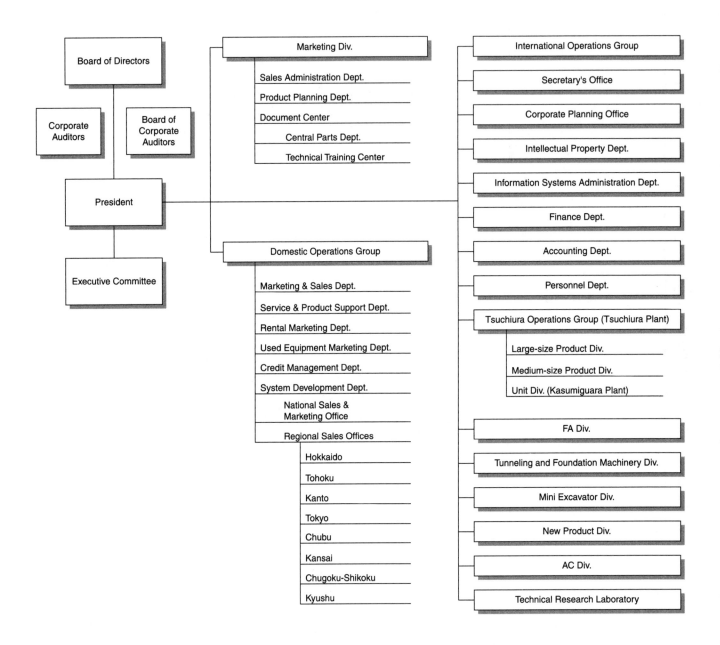

Source: Company web site, 1999

The Hokkaido Takushoku Bank, Limited

Better known by its nickname Takugin, this commercial lender is one of Japan's 10 city banks

7, Odori-nishi 3
Chuo-ku, Sapporo 060, Japan
Phone: +81 011 (271) 2111

Primary SIC: 6021—National Commercial Banks
Primary NAICS: 52211—Commercial Banking

Continued on next page

Source: Annual report, 1997

Continued from previous page

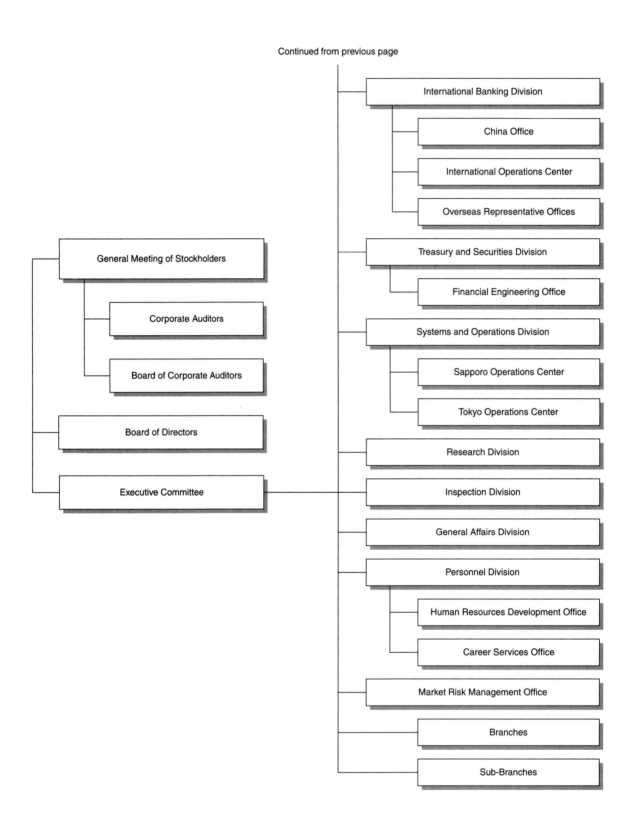

General Meeting of Stockholders

Corporate Auditors

Board of Corporate Auditors

Board of Directors

Executive Committee

International Banking Division

China Office

International Operations Center

Overseas Representative Offices

Treasury and Securities Division

Financial Engineering Office

Systems and Operations Division

Sapporo Operations Center

Tokyo Operations Center

Research Division

Inspection Division

General Affairs Division

Personnel Division

Human Resources Development Office

Career Services Office

Market Risk Management Office

Branches

Sub-Branches

IFS Financial Corporation

Also known as Pueblo Holdings, this mortgage and insurance company is one of the top 10 U.S. Hispanic-owned businesses

10055 Grogan's Mill Rd., Ste. 200
The Woodlands, TX 77380
Phone: (281) 363-4001 **Fax:** (281) 298-7460
Web: www.ifsfinancial.com

Primary SIC: 6311—Life Insurance
Primary NAICS: 524113—Direct Life
Insurance Carriers

IFS Financial Corporation
(DE Corp.)

Interstar Investment Corp.
(DE Corp.)

AccuBanc Mortgage Corp.
(TX Corp.)

SFMC, Inc.
(TX Corp.)

Colorado Express Mortgage
Corporation, Ltd.
(TX Partnership)

SFMC
No. 2, Inc.
(TX Corp.)

Enterprise First
Mortgage, Inc.
(TX Corp.)

Enterprise First
Mortgage, Ltd.
(TX Partnership)

Southeast Mortgage
Funding, Inc. (TX Corp.)

Southeast Mortgage
Funding, Ltd.
(TX Partnership)

IFS Insurance Holdings Corporation
(DE Corp.)

Bradford Brokerage, Inc.
(DE Corp.)

Bradford National Life
Insurance Company
(LA Corp.)

IFS Money
Services, Inc.
(DE Corp.)

IFS Management Corp.
(DE Corp.)

Continued on next page

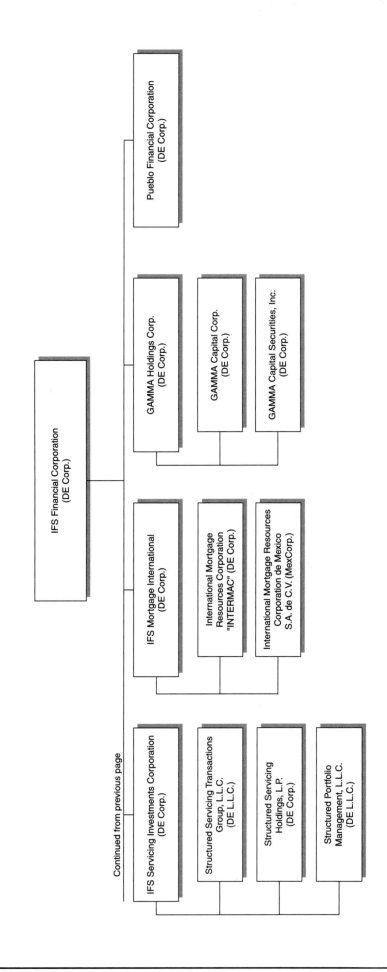

IFS Financial Corporation
(DE Corp.)

GAMMA Holdings Corp.
(DE Corp.)

GAMMA Capital Corp.
(DE Corp.)

GAMMA Capital Securities, Inc.
(DE Corp.)

Pueblo Financial Corporation
(DE Corp.)

IFS Mortgage International
(DE Corp.)

International Mortgage
Resources Corporation
"INTERMAC" (DE Corp.)

International Mortgage Resources
Corporation de Mexico
S.A. de C.V. (MexCorp.)

Continued from previous page

IFS Servicing Investments Corporation
(DE Corp.)

Structured Servicing Transactions
Group, L.L.C.
(DE L.L.C.)

Structured Servicing
Holdings, L.P.
(DE Corp.)

Structured Portfolio
Management, L.L.C.
(DE L.L.C.)

IKKO Corporation

A leading Japanese lender to domestic small and medium-size businesses

Minami Hommachi IK Building
1-3-17, Minami Hommachi, Chuo-ku
Osaka 541-0054, Japan
Phone: +81 06-263-1500 **Fax:** +81 06-268-1541

Primary SIC: 6159—Miscellaneous Business Credit Institutions
Primary NAICS: 522298—All Other Nondepository Credit Intermediation

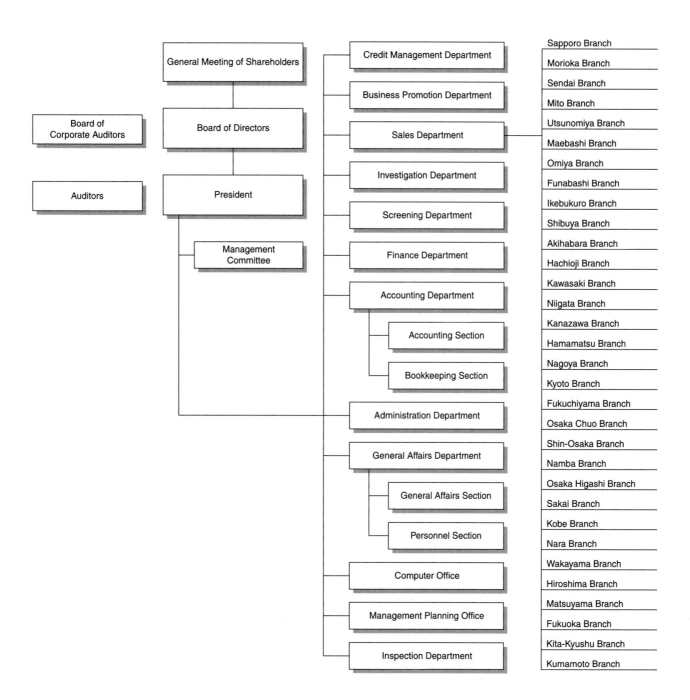

Imation Corp.

The multibillion-dollar spin-off of 3M Corp.'s data storage and imaging businesses

1 Imation Place
Oakdale, MN 55128
Phone: (612) 704-4000
Web: www.imation.com

Primary SIC: 3572—Computer Storage Devices
Primary NAICS: 334112—Computer Storage Device Mfg

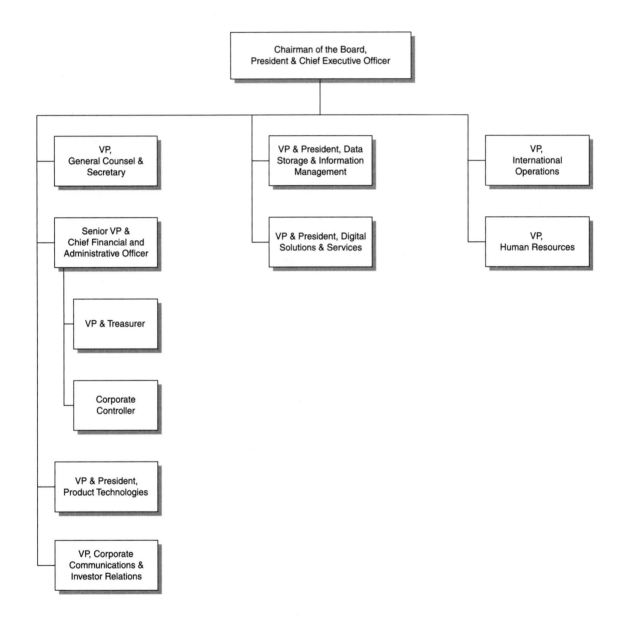

Source: Company and revisions by the editors, 1997

The Industrial Bank of Japan, Limited

Commercial bank specializing in asset management and finance for institutional customers

3-3, Marunouchi 1-chome
Chiyoda-ku, Tokyo 100-8210, Japan
Phone: +81-3-3214-1111 **Fax:** +81-3-3201-7643
Web: www.ibjbank.co.jp

Primary SIC: 6021—National Commercial Banks
Primary NAICS: 52211—Commercial Banking

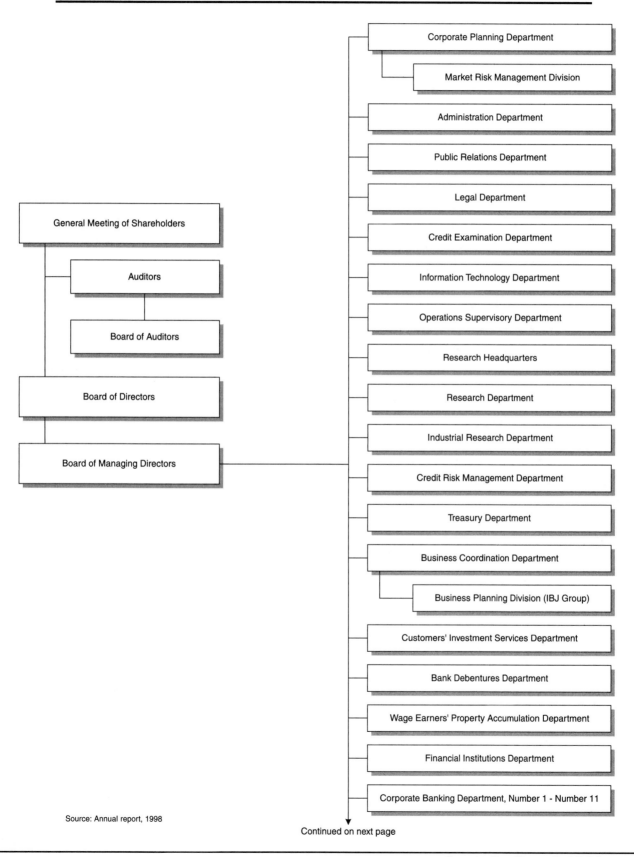

Source: Annual report, 1998

Continued on next page

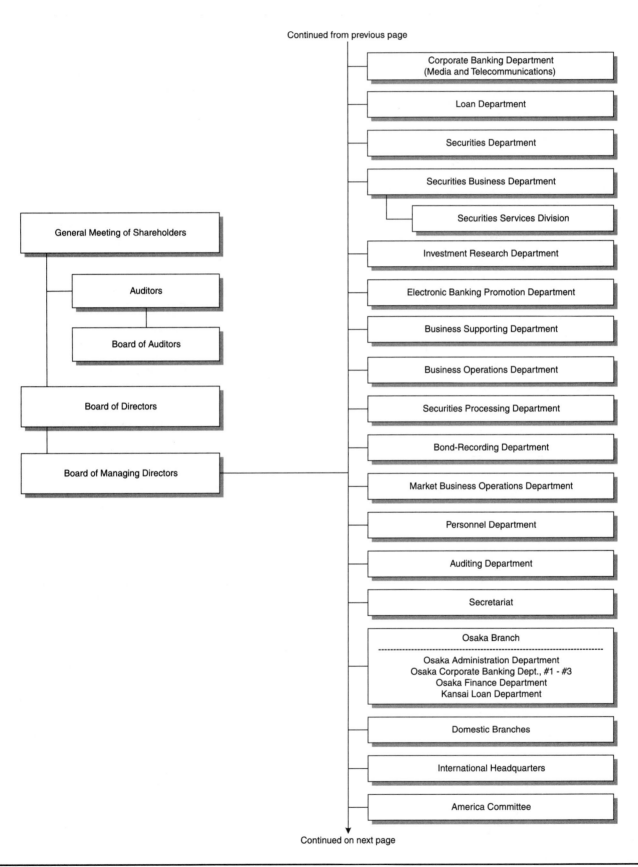

Continued from previous page

Corporate Banking Department
(Media and Telecommunications)

Loan Department

Securities Department

Securities Business Department

Securities Services Division

Investment Research Department

Electronic Banking Promotion Department

Business Supporting Department

Business Operations Department

Securities Processing Department

Bond-Recording Department

Market Business Operations Department

Personnel Department

Auditing Department

Secretariat

Osaka Branch

Osaka Administration Department
Osaka Corporate Banking Dept., #1 - #3
Osaka Finance Department
Kansai Loan Department

Domestic Branches

International Headquarters

America Committee

Continued on next page

General Meeting of Shareholders

Auditors

Board of Auditors

Board of Directors

Board of Managing Directors

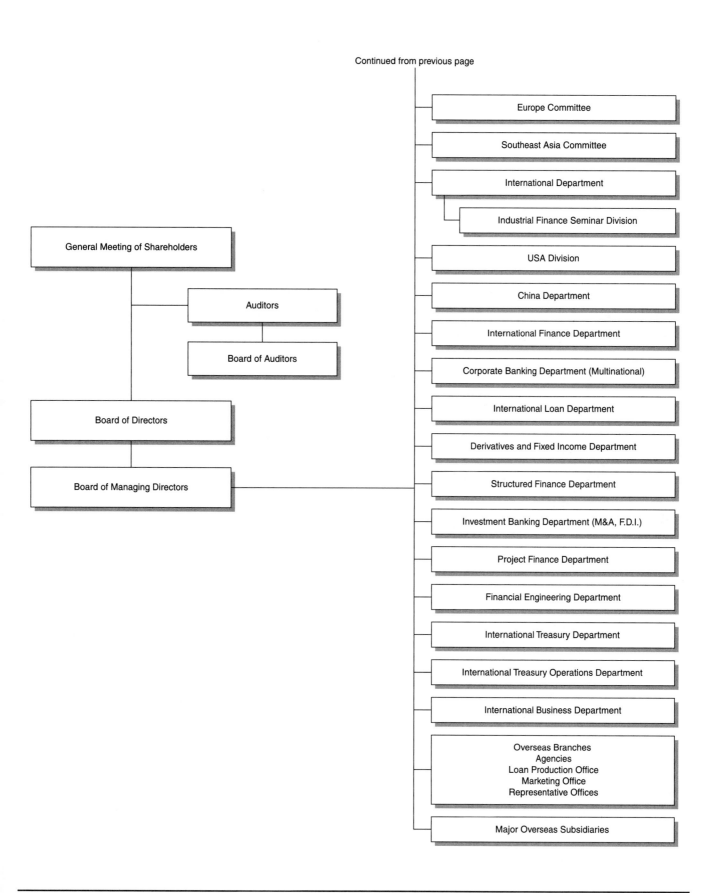

Continued from previous page

Europe Committee

Southeast Asia Committee

International Department

Industrial Finance Seminar Division

USA Division

China Department

International Finance Department

Corporate Banking Department (Multinational)

International Loan Department

Derivatives and Fixed Income Department

Structured Finance Department

Investment Banking Department (M&A, F.D.I.)

Project Finance Department

Financial Engineering Department

International Treasury Department

International Treasury Operations Department

International Business Department

Overseas Branches
Agencies
Loan Production Office
Marketing Office
Representative Offices

Major Overseas Subsidiaries

General Meeting of Shareholders

Auditors

Board of Auditors

Board of Directors

Board of Managing Directors

Ingra Engineering and Construction Co.

A large Croatian construction firm with international presence specializing in energy and industrial projects

Alexandera von Humboldta 4B
10000 Zagreb, Croatia
Phone: +385 1 611 53 55
Web: www.ingra.com

Primary SIC: 1629—Heavy Construction, NEC
Primary NAICS: 23492—Pwr/Communication
Transmission Line Construction
E-mail: ingra@ingra.com

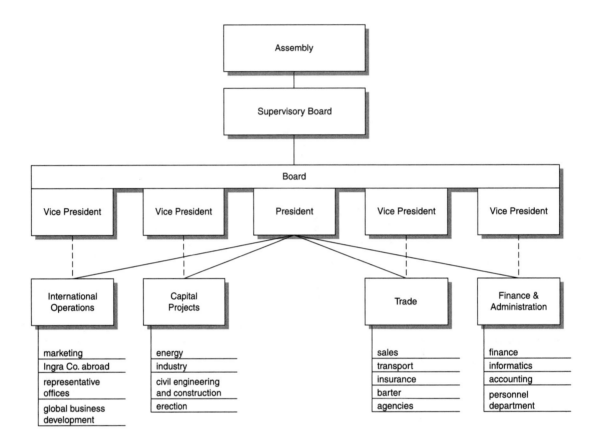

Source: Company web site, 1998

Institut Français du Pétrole

With a staff of nearly 2,000, IFP is a major world research and development organization for the petroleum industry

1 & 4, Avenue de Bois-Préau
F-92852 Rueil-Malmaison Cedex, France
Phone: +33 1 47 52 60 00 **Fax:** +33 1 47 52 70 00
Web: www.ifp.fr

Primary SIC: 8731—Commercial Physical
& Biological Research
Primary NAICS: 54171—R&D in Physical,
Engineering & Life Sciences

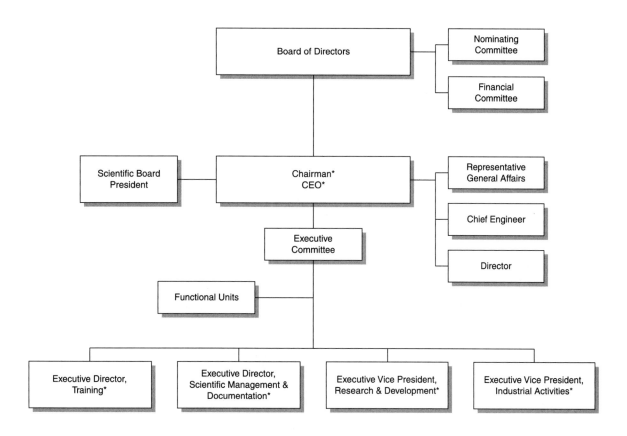

* Member of the Executive Committee

Source: Organization web site, 1999

Institution of Structural Engineers

A professional organization of some 22,000 engineers from around the world

11 Upper Belgrave St.
London SW1X 8BH, United Kingdom
Web: www.istructe.org.uk

Primary SIC: 8621—Professional
Membership Organizations
Primary NAICS: 81392—Professional Organizations

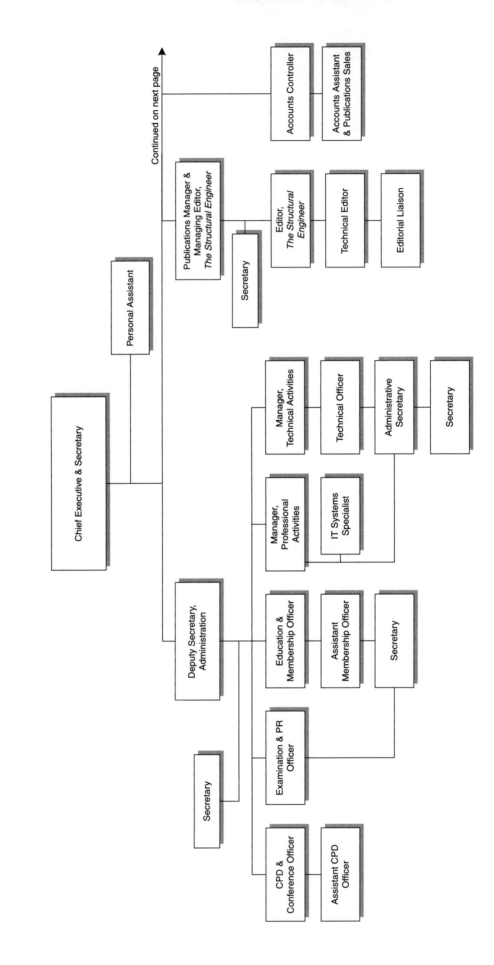

Continued on next page

Chief Executive & Secretary

Personal Assistant

Publications Manager & Managing Editor, *The Structural Engineer*

Secretary

Editor, *The Structural Engineer*

Technical Editor

Editorial Liaison

Accounts Controller

Accounts Assistant & Publications Sales

Deputy Secretary, Administration

Secretary

CPD & Conference Officer

Assistant CPD Officer

Examination & PR Officer

Education & Membership Officer

Assistant Membership Officer

Secretary

Manager, Professional Activities

IT Systems Specialist

Manager, Technical Activities

Technical Officer

Administrative Secretary

Secretary

Source: Organization web site, 1999

Institution of Structural Engineers (cont.)

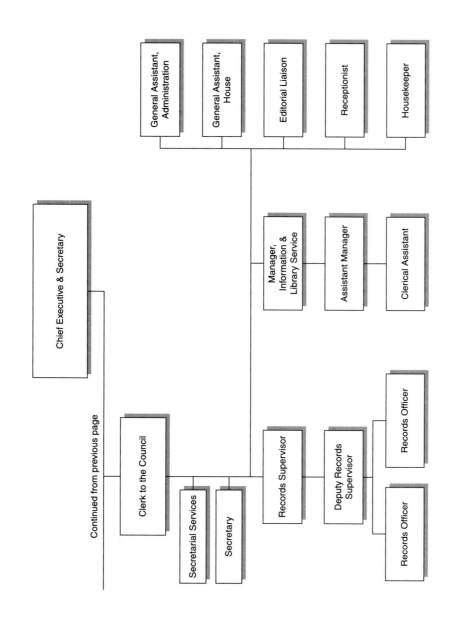

International Business Machines Corporation

This $80 billion behemoth earns 44% of its sales from computer hardware and 35% from computer-related services

Old Orchard Rd.
Armonk, NY 10504
Phone: (914) 765-1900 **Fax:** (914) 765-4190
Web: www.ibm.com

Primary SIC: 3571—Electronic Computers
Primary NAICS: 334111—Electronic Computer Mfg

▶ **REORGANIZATION Part 1 (1996)**
For additional details on the restructuring see profiles starting on page 331

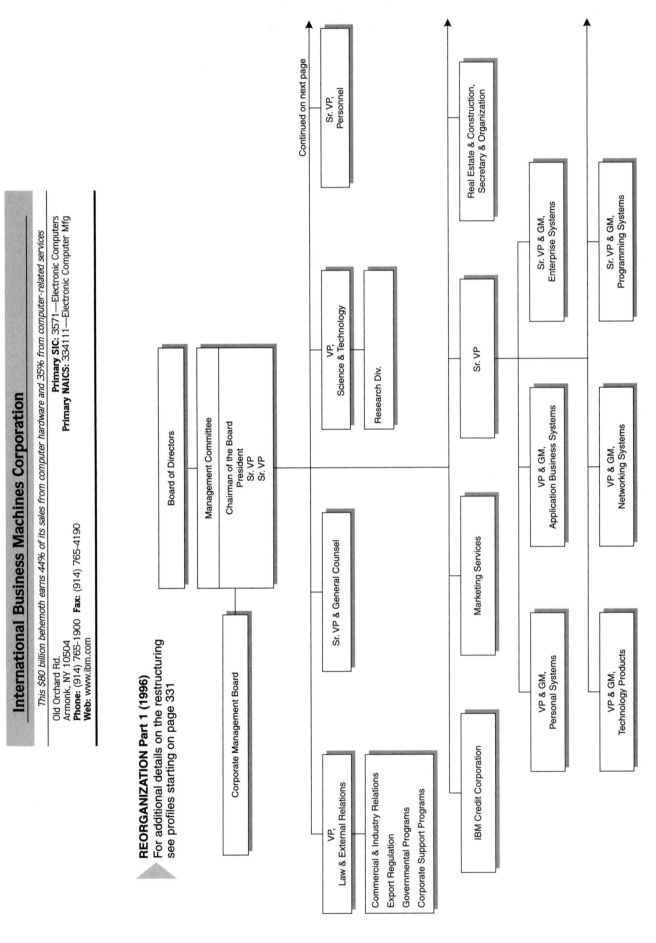

Continued on next page

Source: Company and revisions by the editors, 1998

International Business Machines Corporation (cont.)

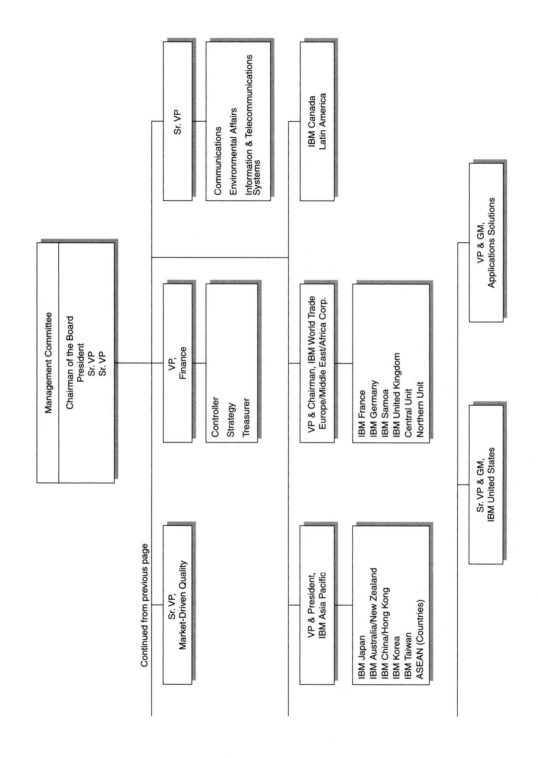

Continued from previous page

Management Committee

Chairman of the Board
President
Sr. VP
Sr. VP

**Sr. VP,
Market-Driven Quality**

**VP,
Finance**

Controller
Strategy
Treasurer

Sr. VP

Communications
Environmental Affairs
Information & Telecommunications Systems

**VP & President,
IBM Asia Pacific**

IBM Japan
IBM Australia/New Zealand
IBM China/Hong Kong
IBM Korea
IBM Taiwan
ASEAN (Countries)

**VP & Chairman, IBM World Trade
Europe/Middle East/Africa Corp.**

IBM France
IBM Germany
IBM Samoa
IBM United Kingdom
Central Unit
Northern Unit

**IBM Canada
Latin America**

**Sr. VP & GM,
IBM United States**

**VP & GM,
Applications Solutions**

International Business Machines Corporation (cont.)

REORGANIZATION Part 2 (1999)
For additional details on the restructuring
see profiles starting on page 331

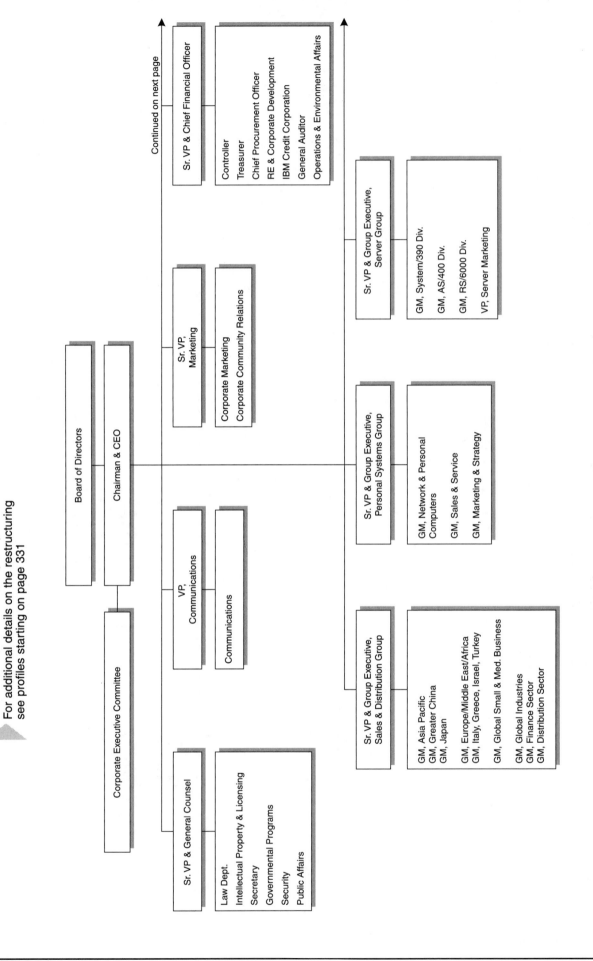

Continued on next page

Board of Directors

Chairman & CEO

Corporate Executive Committee

Sr. VP & General Counsel
- Law Dept.
- Intellectual Property & Licensing
- Secretary
- Governmental Programs
- Security
- Public Affairs

VP, Communications
- Communications

Sr. VP, Marketing
- Corporate Marketing
- Corporate Community Relations

Sr. VP & Chief Financial Officer
- Controller
- Treasurer
- Chief Procurement Officer
- RE & Corporate Development
- IBM Credit Corporation
- General Auditor
- Operations & Environmental Affairs

Sr. VP & Group Executive, Sales & Distribution Group
- GM, Asia Pacific
- GM, Greater China
- GM, Japan
- GM, Europe/Middle East/Africa
- GM, Italy, Greece, Israel, Turkey
- GM, Global Small & Med. Business
- GM, Global Industries
- GM, Finance Sector
- GM, Distribution Sector

Sr. VP & Group Executive, Personal Systems Group
- GM, Network & Personal Computers
- GM, Sales & Service
- GM, Marketing & Strategy

Sr. VP & Group Executive, Server Group
- GM, System/390 Div.
- GM, AS/400 Div.
- GM, RS/6000 Div.
- VP, Server Marketing

International Business Machines Corporation (cont.)

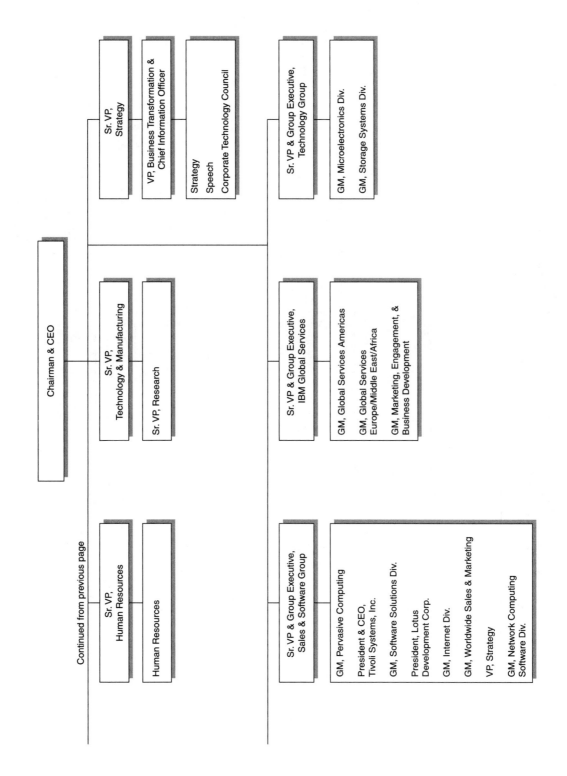

Continued from previous page

Chairman & CEO

Sr. VP, Human Resources
- Human Resources

Sr. VP, Technology & Manufacturing
- Sr. VP, Research

Sr. VP, Strategy
- VP, Business Transformation & Chief Information Officer
- Strategy
- Speech
- Corporate Technology Council

Sr. VP & Group Executive, Sales & Software Group
- GM, Pervasive Computing
- President & CEO, Tivoli Systems, Inc.
- GM, Software Solutions Div.
- President, Lotus Development Corp.
- GM, Internet Div.
- GM, Worldwide Sales & Marketing
- VP, Strategy
- GM, Network Computing Software Div.

Sr. VP & Group Executive, IBM Global Services
- GM, Global Services Americas
- GM, Global Services Europe/Middle East/Africa
- GM, Marketing, Engagement, & Business Development

Sr. VP & Group Executive, Technology Group
- GM, Microelectronics Div.
- GM, Storage Systems Div.

International Labour Organization

A United Nations agency that monitors labor practices worldwide and advocates for basic worker rights

4, route des Morillons
CH-1211 Geneva 22, Switzerland
Phone: +41-22-799-6111 **Fax:** +41-22-798-8685
Web: www.ilo.org

Primary SIC: 9721—International Affairs
Primary NAICS: 92812—International Affairs
E-mail: doscom@hq1.ilo.ch

International Labour Conference

Governing Body

Director General, International Labour Office

Deputy Director General, Relations
- Relations with Intergovernmental and Non-Governmental Organizations
- Publications
- Library & Documentation

Assistant Director General, Technical Programs
- Employment & Training
- Industrial Relations and Labour Administration
- Social Security
- Working Conditions & Environment
- Development Policies
- Statistics

Assistant Director General, Promotion and Coordination of ILO Enterprise Activities
- Enterprise and Cooperative Development

- Legal Advisor
- Employers' Activities
- Workers' Activities
- Personnel
- Programming & Management
- Public Information
- Multinational Enterprises and Social Policy

Assistant Director General, International Institute for Labour Studies

Continued on next page

International Labour Organization (cont.)

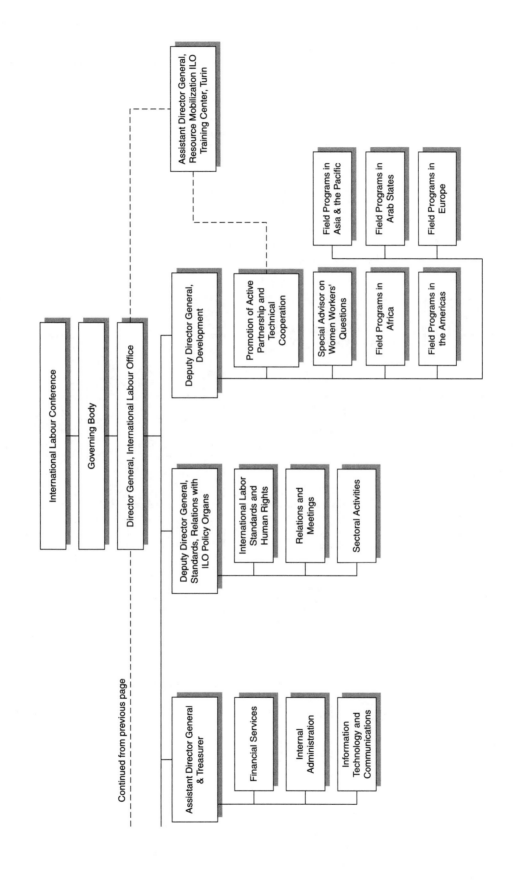

International Labour Conference

Governing Body

Director General, International Labour Office

Continued from previous page

Assistant Director General, Resource Mobilization ILO Training Center, Turin

Deputy Director General, Development

Promotion of Active Partnership and Technical Cooperation

Special Advisor on Women Workers' Questions

Field Programs in Africa

Field Programs in the Americas

Field Programs in Asia & the Pacific

Field Programs in Arab States

Field Programs in Europe

Deputy Director General, Standards, Relations with ILO Policy Organs

International Labor Standards and Human Rights

Relations and Meetings

Sectoral Activities

Assistant Director General & Treasurer

Financial Services

Internal Administration

Information Technology and Communications

International Monetary Fund

With over $80 billion in outstanding loans on its books, the UN-affiliated agency works to promote world monetary stability

1700 19th St. NW
Washington, DC 20431
Web: www.imf.org

Primary SIC: 9721—International Affairs
Primary NAICS: 92812—International Affairs

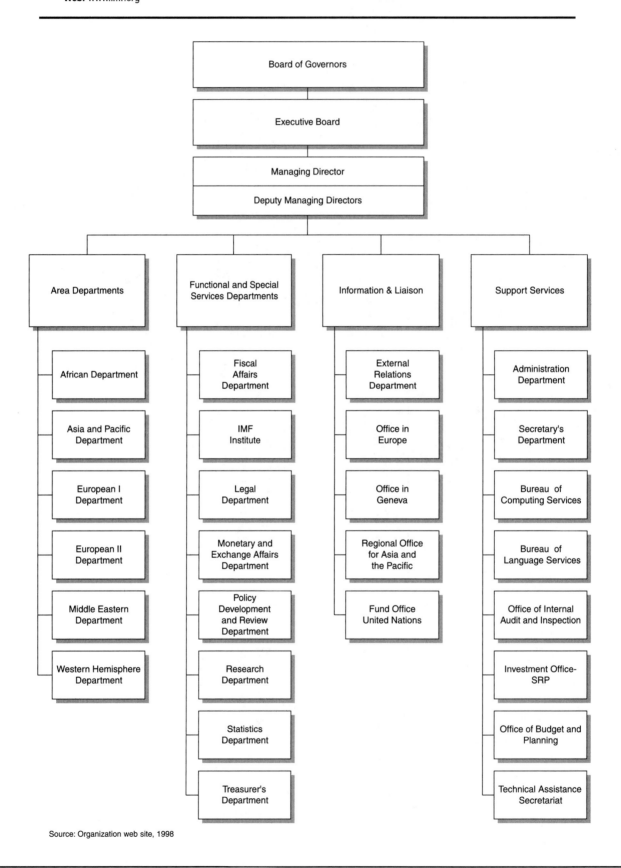

Source: Organization web site, 1998

ITD Associates

A technology and management consulting firm for the engineering field

2 Westwoods Dr.
Liberty, MO 64068
Phone: (816) 415-9150 **Fax:** (816) 415-9148
Web: www.itd.com

Primary SIC: 8741—Management Services
Primary NAICS: 541611—Admin & Gen Management
Consulting Services

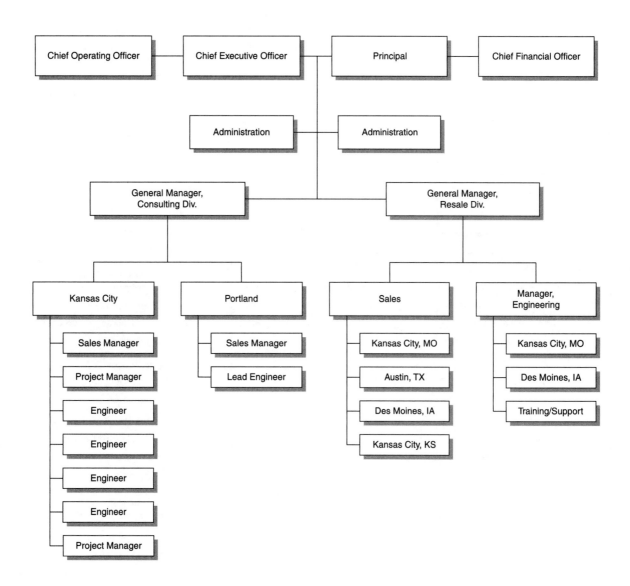

Source: Company web site, 1999

ITOCHU Corporation

One of Japan's top 3 trading companies, ITOCHU distributes everything from oil and chemicals to machinery and foods

5-1, Kita-Aoyama 2-chome
Minato-ku, Tokyo 107-8077, Japan
Phone: +81-6-3-3497-7295 **Fax:** +81-6-3-3497-7296
Web: www.itochu.co.jp

Primary SIC: 5172—Petroleum & Petroleum
Products Wholesalers, Except Bulk Stations & Terminals
Primary NAICS: 42272—Petroleum
Prod Whsle (exc Bulk Sta/Terminals)

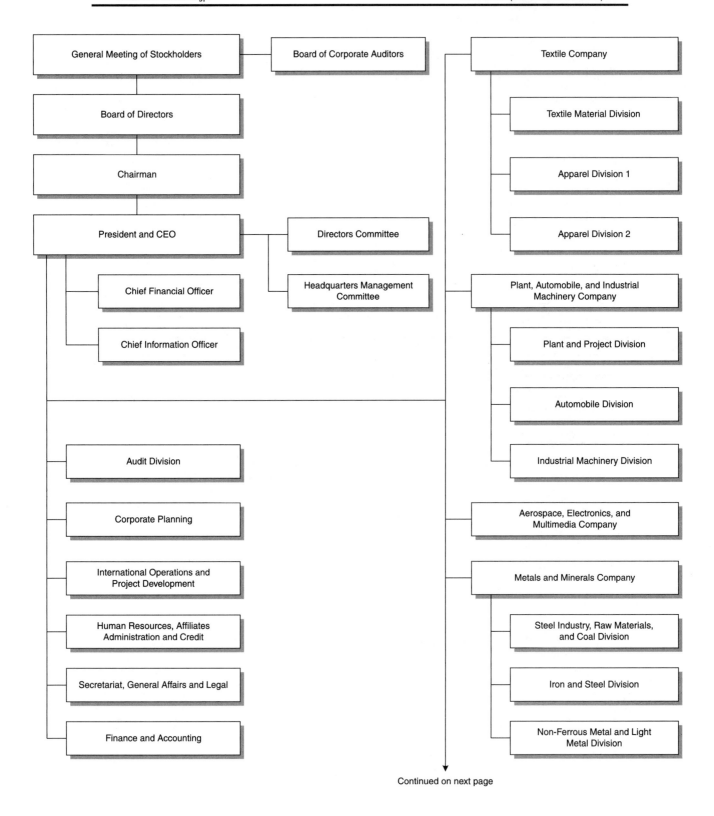

Continued on next page

Source: Annual report, 1998

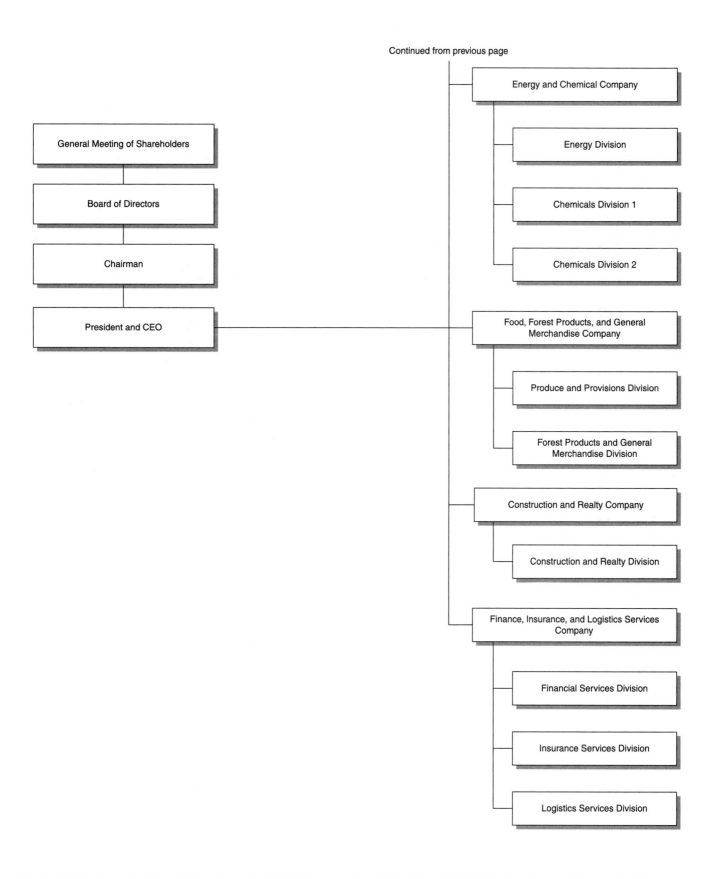

Continued from previous page

General Meeting of Shareholders

Board of Directors

Chairman

President and CEO

Energy and Chemical Company

Energy Division

Chemicals Division 1

Chemicals Division 2

Food, Forest Products, and General Merchandise Company

Produce and Provisions Division

Forest Products and General Merchandise Division

Construction and Realty Company

Construction and Realty Division

Finance, Insurance, and Logistics Services Company

Financial Services Division

Insurance Services Division

Logistics Services Division

J. Ray McDermott S.A.

A major marine engineering and construction contractor to the oil industry

1450 Paydras St.
New Orleans, LA 70112-6050
Phone: (504) 587-5300
Web: www.jrayncdermott.com

Primary SIC: 1389—Oil & Gas
Field Services, NEC
Primary NAICS: 213112—Oil & Gas
Operations Support Activities

Source: Company web site, 1999

JACCS Co., Ltd.

One of Japan's largest consumer credit firms, JACCS offers credit cards, loans, and other financial services

Ebisu Neonato Bldg.
1-18, Ebisu 4-chome
Shibuya-ku, Tokyo 150-8932, Japan
Phone: +81 03 5448-1311 **Fax:** +81 03 5448-9514

Primary SIC: 6141—Personal Credit Institutions
Primary NAICS: 52221—Credit Card Issuing

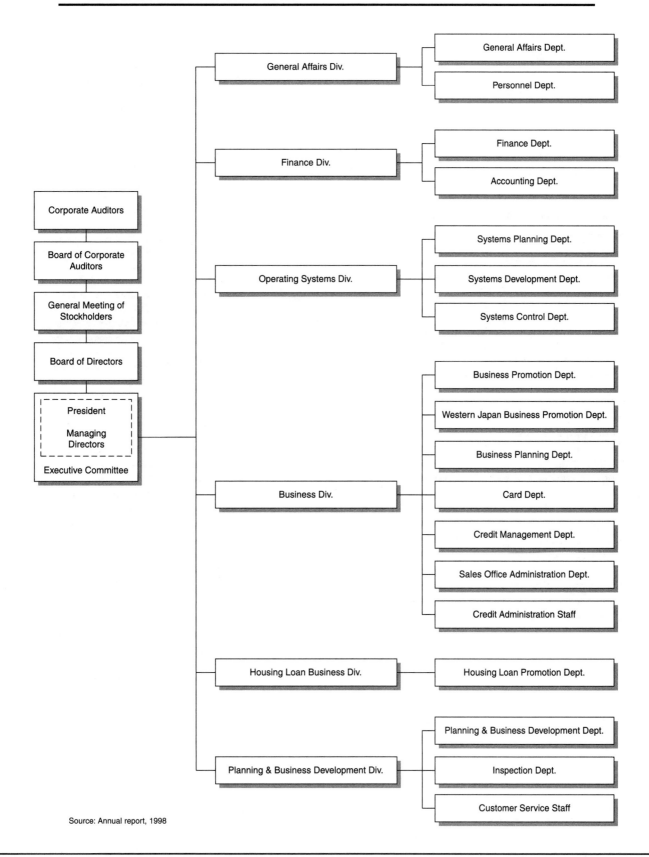

Source: Annual report, 1998

Japan Airlines Company, Ltd.

Japan's largest airline and a major international carrier

4-11, Higashi-shinagawa 2-chome
Shinagawa-ku, Tokyo 140-8637, Japan
Phone: +81-3-5460-3191 **Fax:** +81-3-5460-5929
Web: www.jal.co.jp

Primary SIC: 4512—Air Transportation, Scheduled
Primary NAICS: 481111—Scheduled Passenger
Air Transportation

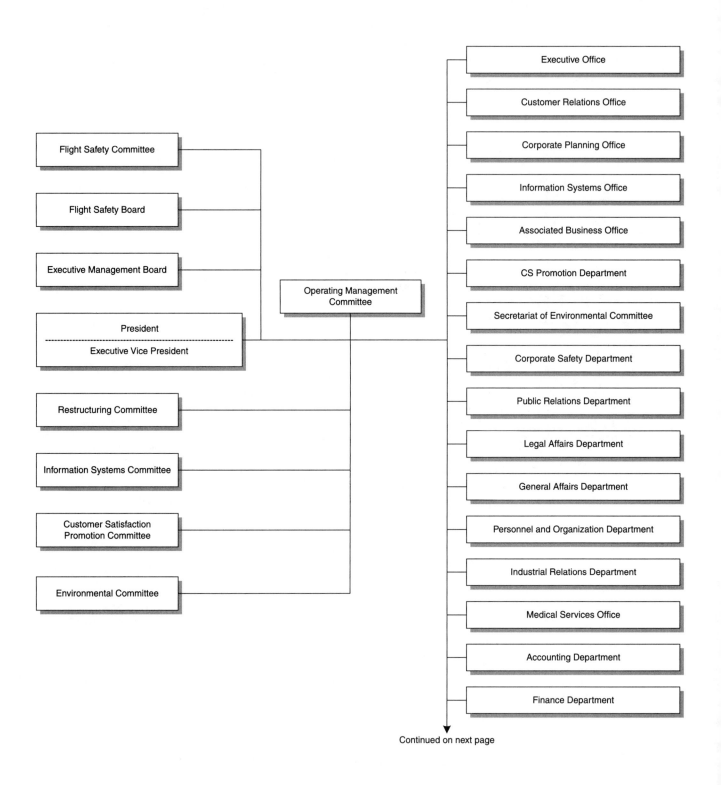

Continued on next page

Source: Annual report, 1998

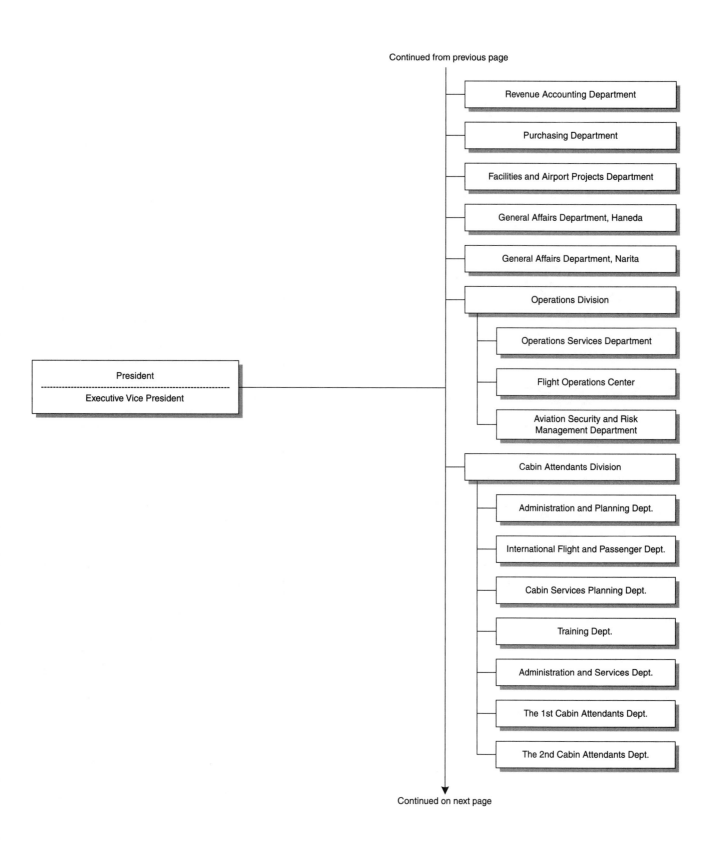

Continued from previous page

- Revenue Accounting Department
- Purchasing Department
- Facilities and Airport Projects Department
- General Affairs Department, Haneda
- General Affairs Department, Narita
- Operations Division
  - Operations Services Department
  - Flight Operations Center
  - Aviation Security and Risk Management Department

President
- -
Executive Vice President

- Cabin Attendants Division
  - Administration and Planning Dept.
  - International Flight and Passenger Dept.
  - Cabin Services Planning Dept.
  - Training Dept.
  - Administration and Services Dept.
  - The 1st Cabin Attendants Dept.
  - The 2nd Cabin Attendants Dept.

Continued on next page

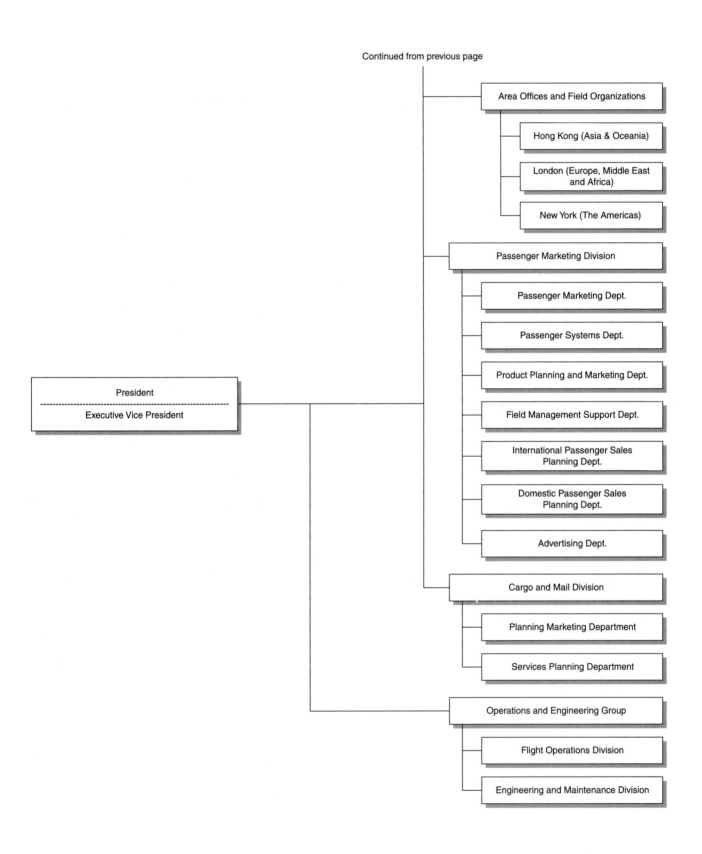

Continued from previous page

- Area Offices and Field Organizations
  - Hong Kong (Asia & Oceania)
  - London (Europe, Middle East and Africa)
  - New York (The Americas)
- Passenger Marketing Division
  - Passenger Marketing Dept.
  - Passenger Systems Dept.
  - Product Planning and Marketing Dept.
  - Field Management Support Dept.
  - International Passenger Sales Planning Dept.
  - Domestic Passenger Sales Planning Dept.
  - Advertising Dept.
- Cargo and Mail Division
  - Planning Marketing Department
  - Services Planning Department
- Operations and Engineering Group
  - Flight Operations Division
  - Engineering and Maintenance Division

President

Executive Vice President

Japan Automobile Federation

This 13 million-member organization is similar, though unrelated, to the American Automobile Association

3-5-8 Shiba-koen
Minato-ku, Tokyo, Japan
Phone: +81 03-3436-2811
Web: www.jaf.or.jp

Primary SIC: 8699—Membership Organizations, NEC
Primary NAICS: 81341—Civic & Social Organizations

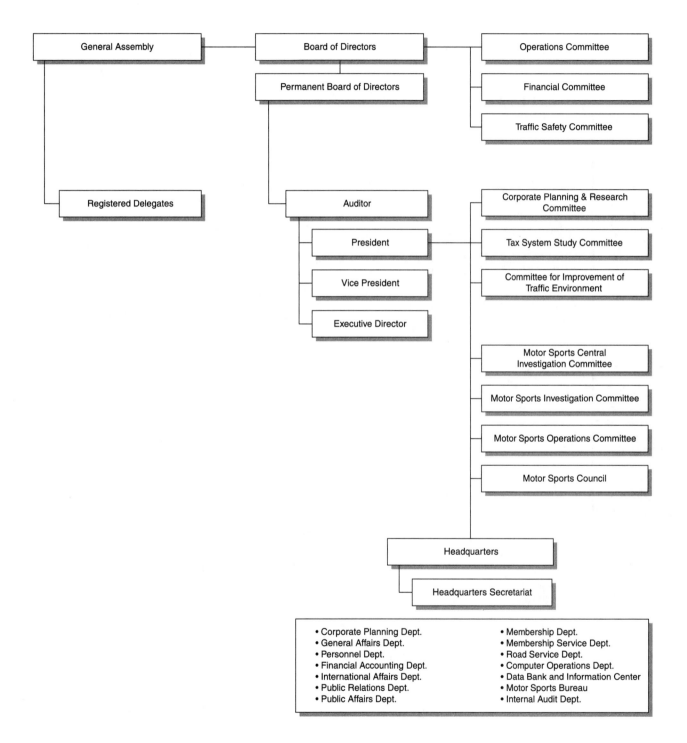

Source: Organization web site, 1998

Japan Institute of Energy

Founded in 1922 as the Fuel Society of Japan, the JIE has 1,600 members, mostly academics in energy-related fields

Kairaku Bldg, (Sotokanda) 6F, 6-5-4 Sotokanda
Chiyoda-ku, Tokyo 101-0021, Japan
Phone: +81-3-3834-6456 **Fax:** +81-3-3834-6458
Web: www.jie.or.jp

Primary SIC: 8621—Professional
Membership Organizations
Primary NAICS: 81392—Professional
Organizations

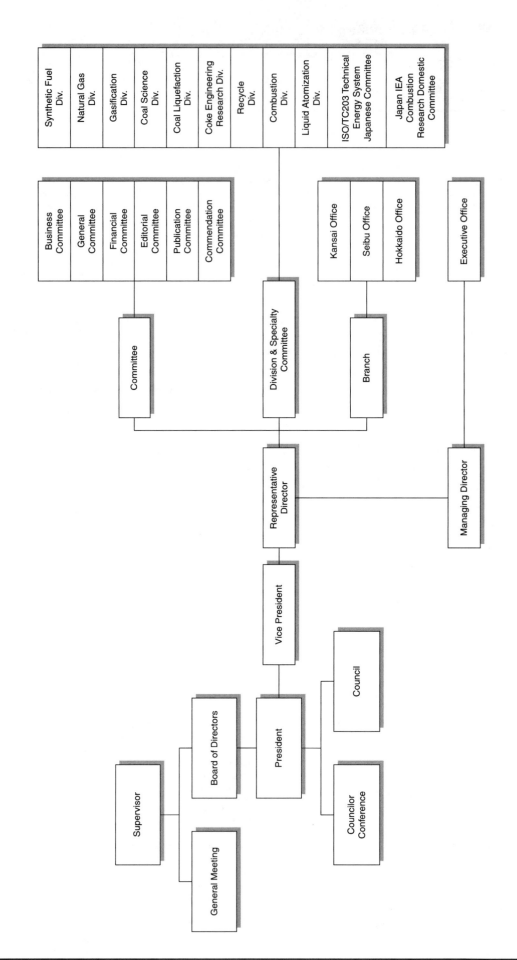

Japan Telecom Co., Ltd.

A key competitor in Japan's long-distance market, Japan Telecom brings in well over $3 billion a year in revenue

4-7-1, Hatchobori, 4-chome
Chuo-ku, Tokyo 104, Japan
Phone: +81 3 5540-8020
Web: www.japan-telecom.co.jp

Primary SIC: 4813—Telephone Communications, Except Radiotelephone
Primary NAICS: 51331—Wired Telecommunications Carriers

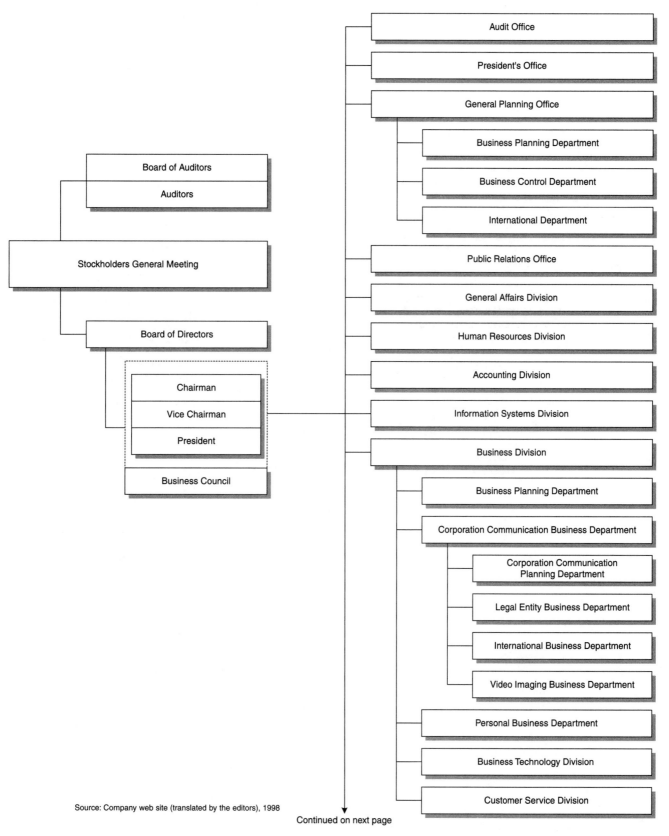

Board of Auditors
Auditors

Stockholders General Meeting

Board of Directors

Chairman
Vice Chairman
President

Business Council

Audit Office

President's Office

General Planning Office

Business Planning Department

Business Control Department

International Department

Public Relations Office

General Affairs Division

Human Resources Division

Accounting Division

Information Systems Division

Business Division

Business Planning Department

Corporation Communication Business Department

Corporation Communication Planning Department

Legal Entity Business Department

International Business Department

Video Imaging Business Department

Personal Business Department

Business Technology Division

Customer Service Division

Source: Company web site (translated by the editors), 1998

Continued on next page

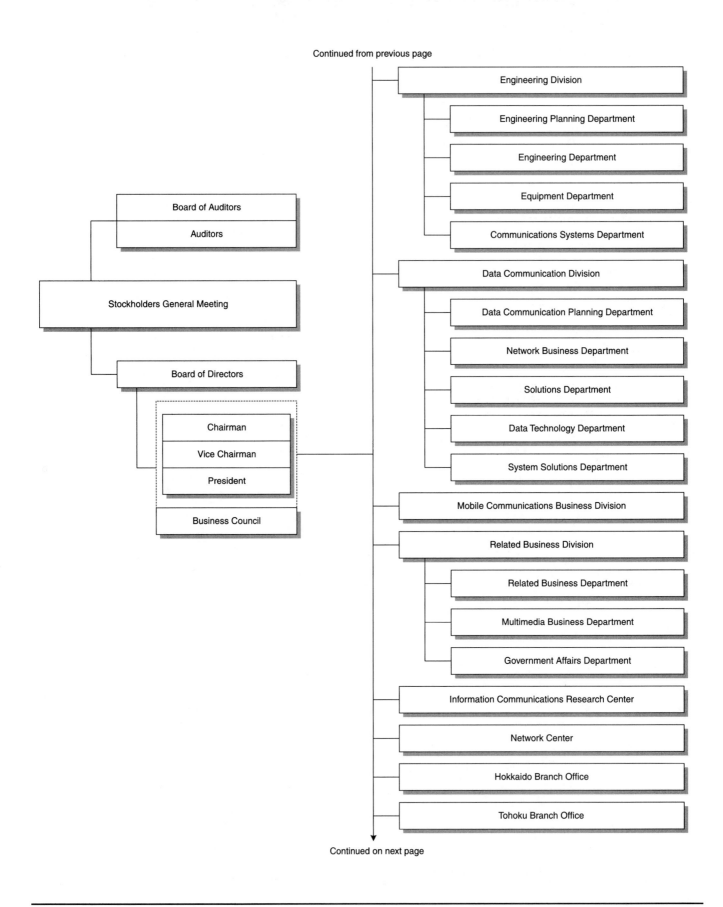

Continued from previous page

Engineering Division

Engineering Planning Department

Engineering Department

Equipment Department

Communications Systems Department

Data Communication Division

Data Communication Planning Department

Network Business Department

Solutions Department

Data Technology Department

System Solutions Department

Mobile Communications Business Division

Related Business Division

Related Business Department

Multimedia Business Department

Government Affairs Department

Information Communications Research Center

Network Center

Hokkaido Branch Office

Tohoku Branch Office

Board of Auditors

Auditors

Stockholders General Meeting

Board of Directors

Chairman

Vice Chairman

President

Business Council

Continued on next page

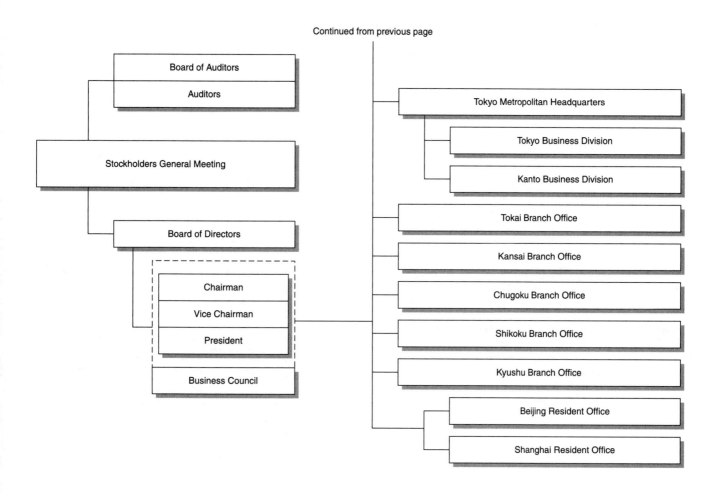

Continued from previous page

Board of Auditors

Auditors

Stockholders General Meeting

Board of Directors

Chairman

Vice Chairman

President

Business Council

Tokyo Metropolitan Headquarters

Tokyo Business Division

Kanto Business Division

Tokai Branch Office

Kansai Branch Office

Chugoku Branch Office

Shikoku Branch Office

Kyushu Branch Office

Beijing Resident Office

Shanghai Resident Office

John Hancock Mutual Life Insurance Company

This major insurance carrier is converting from a mutual ownership company to a publicly traded stock corporation

200 Clarendon St.
Boston, MA 02117
Phone: (617) 572-6000 **Fax:** (617) 572-6451
Web: www.johnhancock.com

Primary SIC: 6311—Life Insurance
Primary NAICS: 524113—Direct Life
Insurance Carriers

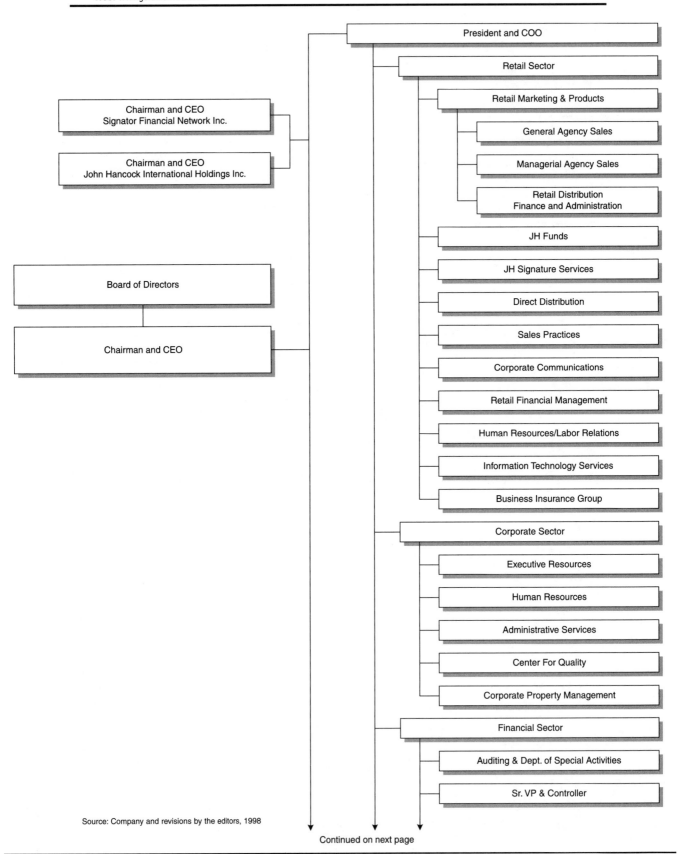

Source: Company and revisions by the editors, 1998

Continued on next page

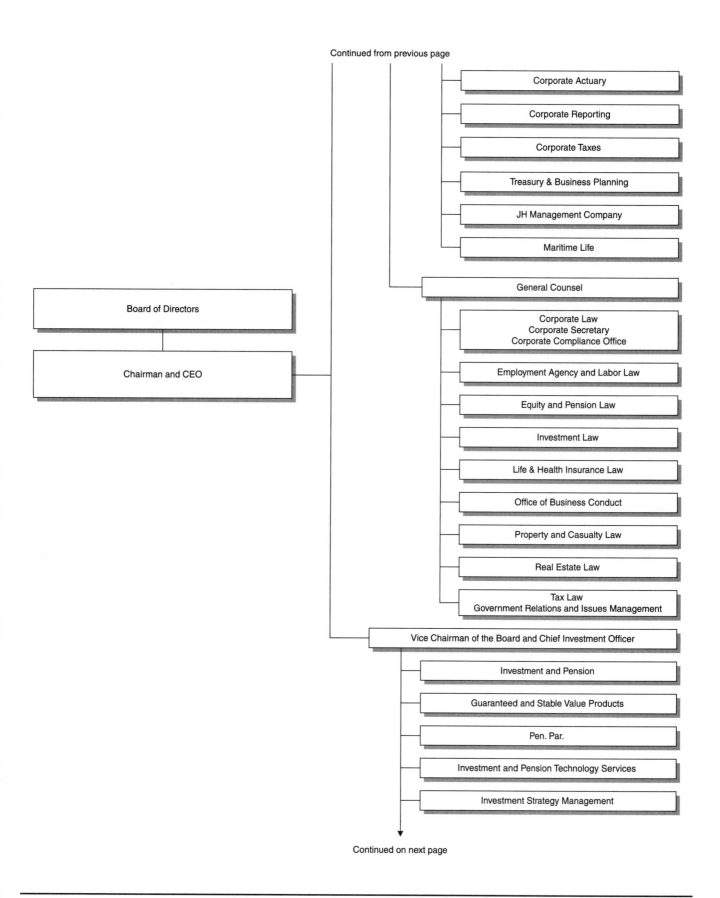

Continued from previous page

Corporate Actuary

Corporate Reporting

Corporate Taxes

Treasury & Business Planning

JH Management Company

Maritime Life

General Counsel

Corporate Law
Corporate Secretary
Corporate Compliance Office

Employment Agency and Labor Law

Equity and Pension Law

Investment Law

Life & Health Insurance Law

Office of Business Conduct

Property and Casualty Law

Real Estate Law

Tax Law
Government Relations and Issues Management

Board of Directors

Chairman and CEO

Vice Chairman of the Board and Chief Investment Officer

Investment and Pension

Guaranteed and Stable Value Products

Pen. Par.

Investment and Pension Technology Services

Investment Strategy Management

Continued on next page

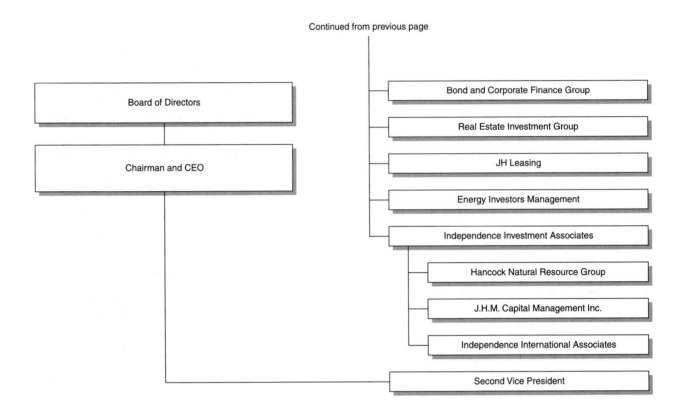

Continued from previous page

Board of Directors

Chairman and CEO

Bond and Corporate Finance Group

Real Estate Investment Group

JH Leasing

Energy Investors Management

Independence Investment Associates

Hancock Natural Resource Group

J.H.M. Capital Management Inc.

Independence International Associates

Second Vice President

Johnson & Johnson

The famed maker of numerous consumer, pharmaceutical, and medical products had sales approaching $24 billion in 1998

1 Johnson and Johnson Plz.
New Brunswick, NJ 08933
Phone: (732) 524-0400 **Fax:** (732) 214-0332
Web: www.johnsonjohnson.com

Primary SIC: 2844—Perfumes, Cosmetics, &
Other Toilet Preparations
Primary NAICS: 32562—Toilet Preparation Mfg

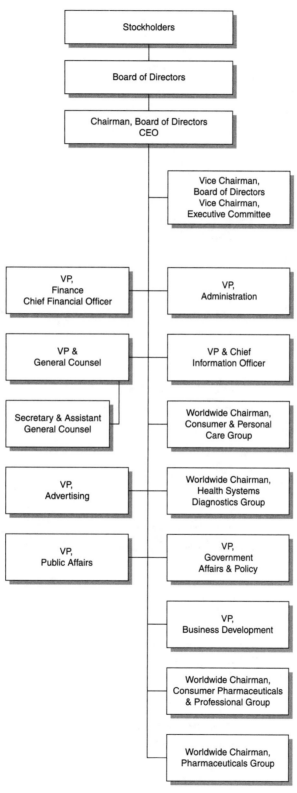

Source: Company and revisions by the editors, 1997

The Kansai Electric Power Co., Inc.

Kansai is Japan's 2nd-largest electric utility

3-22 Nakanoshima 3-chome
Kita-ku, Osaka 530-8270, Japan
Phone: +81 06 441-8821 **Fax:** +81 06 441-8598

Primary SIC: 4911—Electric Services
Primary NAICS: 221112—Fossil Fuel
Electric Power Generation

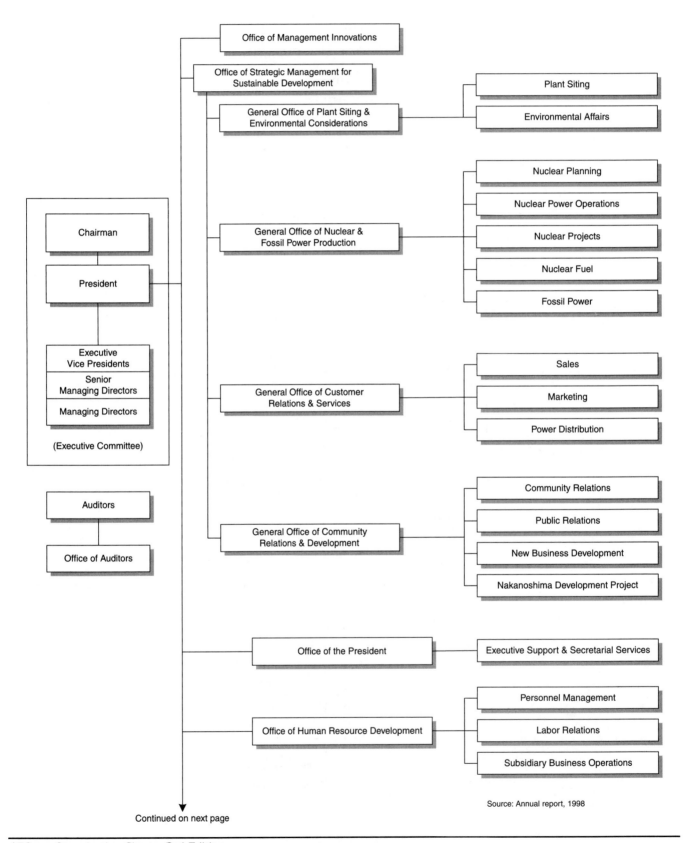

Source: Annual report, 1998

Continued on next page

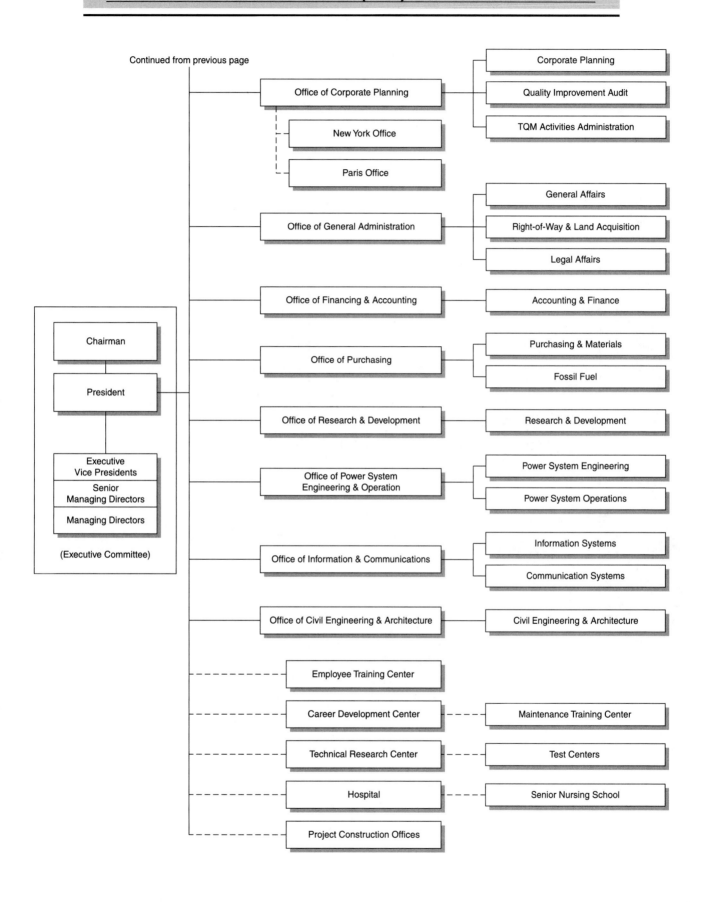

Continued from previous page

Chairman

President

Executive Vice Presidents
Senior Managing Directors
Managing Directors

(Executive Committee)

Office of Corporate Planning
- Corporate Planning
- Quality Improvement Audit
- TQM Activities Administration

New York Office

Paris Office

Office of General Administration
- General Affairs
- Right-of-Way & Land Acquisition
- Legal Affairs

Office of Financing & Accounting
- Accounting & Finance

Office of Purchasing
- Purchasing & Materials
- Fossil Fuel

Office of Research & Development
- Research & Development

Office of Power System Engineering & Operation
- Power System Engineering
- Power System Operations

Office of Information & Communications
- Information Systems
- Communication Systems

Office of Civil Engineering & Architecture
- Civil Engineering & Architecture

Employee Training Center

Career Development Center — Maintenance Training Center

Technical Research Center — Test Centers

Hospital — Senior Nursing School

Project Construction Offices

Kawasaki Steel Corp.

One of Japan's top steelmakers, Kawasaki is also involved in chemicals, engineering, and construction

2-3 Uchisaiwaicho, 2-chome
Chiyoda-ku, Tokyo 100, Japan
Phone: +81 3-3597-3111 **Fax:** +81 3-3597-4860
Web: www.kawasaki-steel.co.jp

Primary SIC: 3312—Steel Works, Blast Furnaces
(Including Coke Ovens), & Rolling Mills
Primary NAICS: 331111—Iron & Steel Mills

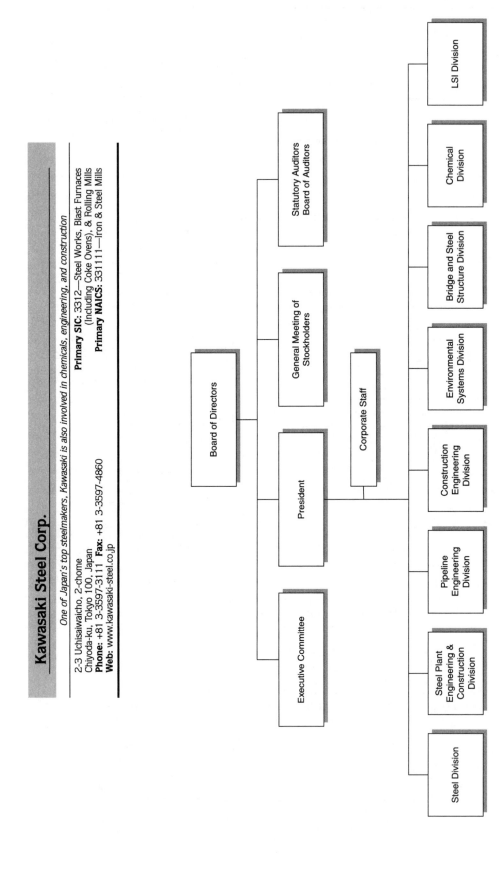

Kirin Brewery Co., Ltd.

One of the world's top breweries, Kirin also has holdings in pharmaceuticals, restaurants, and a host of other fields

10-1 Shinkawa 2-chome
Chou-ku, Tokyo 104, Japan
Phone: +81 03 55403424 **Fax:** +81 03 55403550
Web: 210.169.167.31/index.html

Primary SIC: 2082—Malt Beverages
Primary NAICS: 31212—Breweries

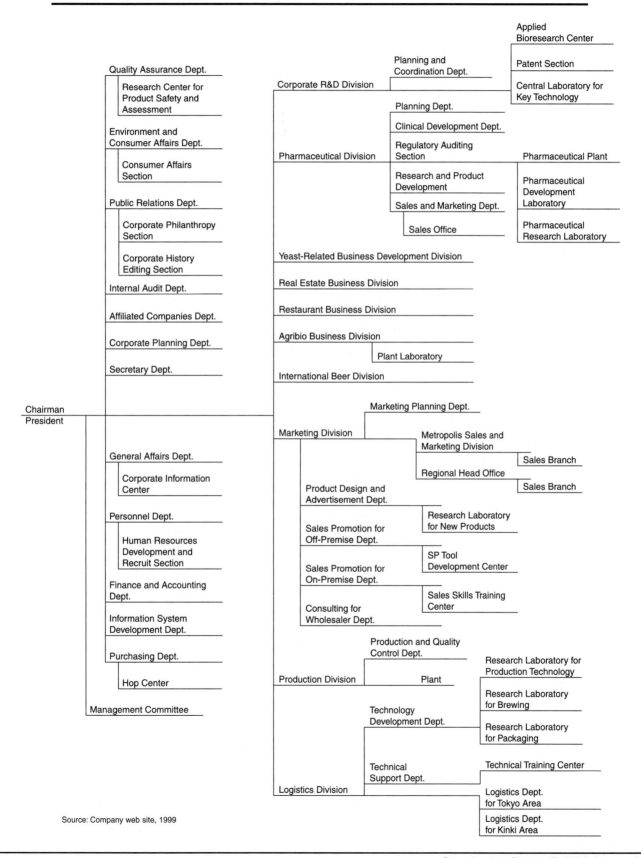

Source: Company web site, 1999

Kobelco Systems Corporation

This mid-sized systems integrator is a spin-off from Japan's Kobe Steel

Shinko Building Neoest 4F, Wakinohama-cho
Chuo-ku, Kobe 651, Japan
Phone: +81-78-261-6132 **Fax:** +81-78-261-6106
Web: www.kobelcosys.co.jp

Primary SIC: 7373—Computer Integrated
Systems Design
Primary NAICS: 541512—Computer Systems
Design Services

Head Office

- General administration, personnel, corporate, midrange strategy planning
- Promotion of quality assurance activities
- Information Systems Technology R&D
- Procurement

TS Group

- System planning, analysis, development, improvement and operation for Kobe steel

IS Group

- Computer Center operation
- Promotion of remote computing services
- Sales of online services and communication equipment
- Providing EUC (End User Computing)

SS Group

- ERP, CIM, sales & distribution, construction work, system consulting & development for governmental organizations
- Designing and development of information systems such as DataWarehouse, Groupware, RDB, etc.

NS Group

- Design consulting and network integration for LANs, WANs, and open systems
- System engineering support for multimedia
- Internet/Intranet promotion

ES Group

- Design and VAR activities employing CAD, CAM and CAE
- Design and VAR activities for numerical analysis, CG and measurement
- Consulting & development of factory automated control systems

Board of Directors

President

Executive Committee

Source: Company web site, 1998

Kubota Corporation

A diversified manufacturer of industrial machinery, metal castings, engines, and building materials

1-2-47, Shikitsu-higashi 1-chome
Naniwa-ku, Osaka 556-8601, Japan
Phone: +81 06 648-2622
Web: www.kubota.co.jp

Primary SIC: 3321—Gray & Ductile Iron Foundries
Primary NAICS: 331511—Iron Foundries

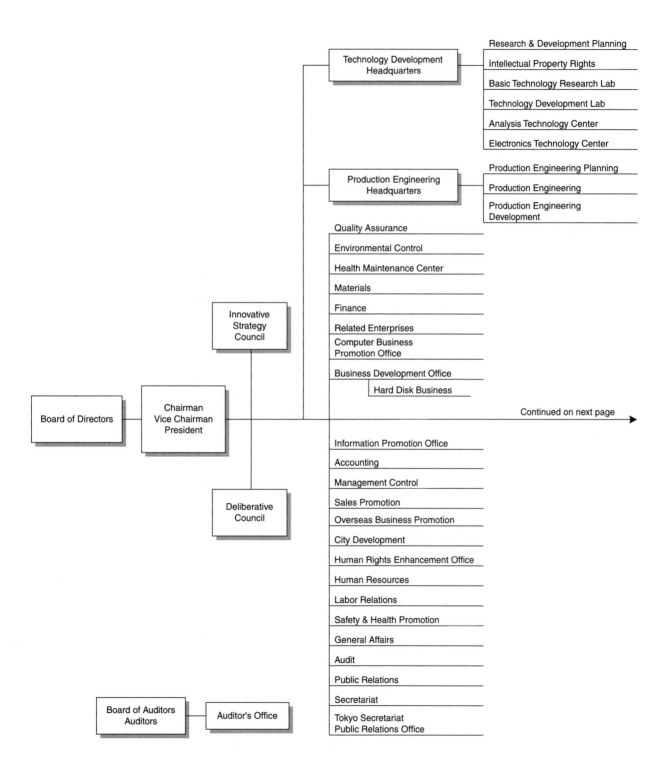

Technology Development Headquarters
- Research & Development Planning
- Intellectual Property Rights
- Basic Technology Research Lab
- Technology Development Lab
- Analysis Technology Center
- Electronics Technology Center

Production Engineering Headquarters
- Production Engineering Planning
- Production Engineering
- Production Engineering Development

Quality Assurance
Environmental Control
Health Maintenance Center
Materials
Finance
Related Enterprises
Computer Business Promotion Office
Business Development Office
- Hard Disk Business

Board of Directors

Chairman
Vice Chairman
President

Innovative Strategy Council

Deliberative Council

Continued on next page ➤

Information Promotion Office
Accounting
Management Control
Sales Promotion
Overseas Business Promotion
City Development
Human Rights Enhancement Office
Human Resources
Labor Relations
Safety & Health Promotion
General Affairs
Audit
Public Relations
Secretariat
Tokyo Secretariat
Public Relations Office

Board of Auditors
Auditors

Auditor's Office

Source: Company web site (translated by the editors), 1998

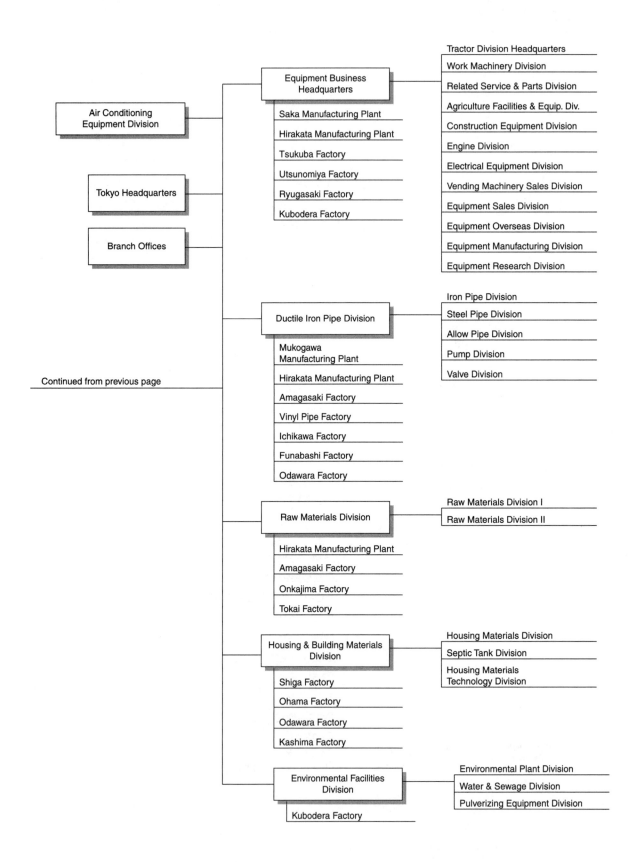

Air Conditioning Equipment Division

Tokyo Headquarters

Branch Offices

Continued from previous page

Equipment Business Headquarters
- Saka Manufacturing Plant
- Hirakata Manufacturing Plant
- Tsukuba Factory
- Utsunomiya Factory
- Ryugasaki Factory
- Kubodera Factory

- Tractor Division Headquarters
- Work Machinery Division
- Related Service & Parts Division
- Agriculture Facilities & Equip. Div.
- Construction Equipment Division
- Engine Division
- Electrical Equipment Division
- Vending Machinery Sales Division
- Equipment Sales Division
- Equipment Overseas Division
- Equipment Manufacturing Division
- Equipment Research Division

Ductile Iron Pipe Division
- Mukogawa Manufacturing Plant
- Hirakata Manufacturing Plant
- Amagasaki Factory
- Vinyl Pipe Factory
- Ichikawa Factory
- Funabashi Factory
- Odawara Factory

- Iron Pipe Division
- Steel Pipe Division
- Allow Pipe Division
- Pump Division
- Valve Division

Raw Materials Division
- Hirakata Manufacturing Plant
- Amagasaki Factory
- Onkajima Factory
- Tokai Factory

- Raw Materials Division I
- Raw Materials Division II

Housing & Building Materials Division
- Shiga Factory
- Ohama Factory
- Odawara Factory
- Kashima Factory

- Housing Materials Division
- Septic Tank Division
- Housing Materials Technology Division

Environmental Facilities Division
- Kubodera Factory

- Environmental Plant Division
- Water & Sewage Division
- Pulverizing Equipment Division

Kuraray Co., Ltd.

A publicly traded manufacturer of chemicals, fibers, and resins and diversified services firm

Shin-Hankyu Bldg., 1-12-39, Umeda
Kita-ku, Osaka 530, Japan
Phone: +81 06 348-2111 **Fax:** +81 06 348-2165
Web: www.kuraray.co.jp

Primary SIC: 2821—Plastics Material
& Synthetic Resins
Primary NAICS: 325211—Plastics Material
& Resins Mfg

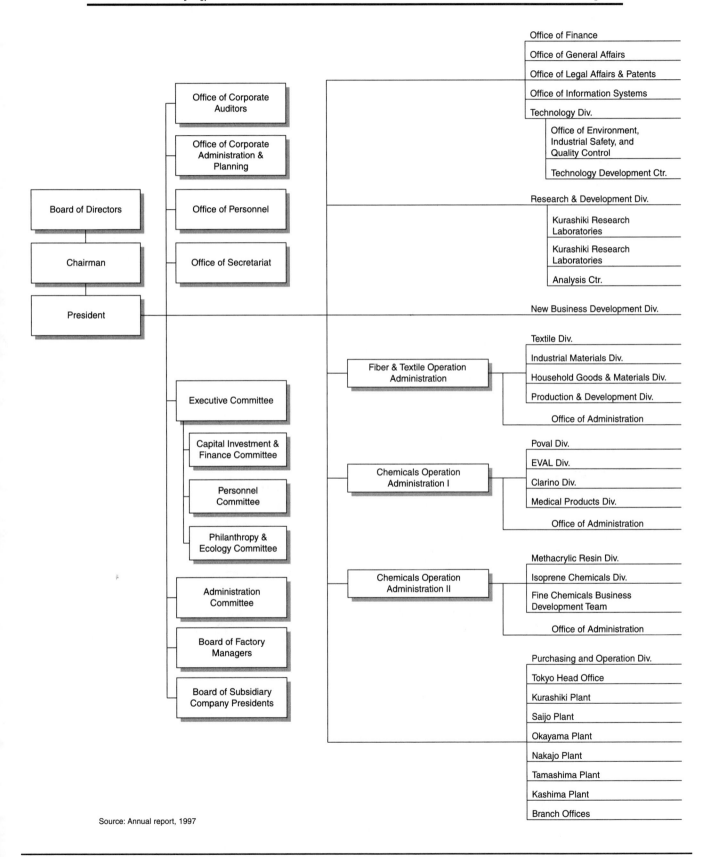

Source: Annual report, 1997

Lawrence Livermore National Laboratory

Run by the University of California, the laboratory performs scientific research for the U.S. Department of Energy

7000 East Ave.
Livermore, CA 94550-9234
Phone: (925) 422-1100 **Fax:** (925) 422-1370
Web: www.llnl.gov

Primary SIC: 8733—Noncommercial
Research Organizations
Primary NAICS: 54171—R&D in Physical,
Engineering & Life Sciences

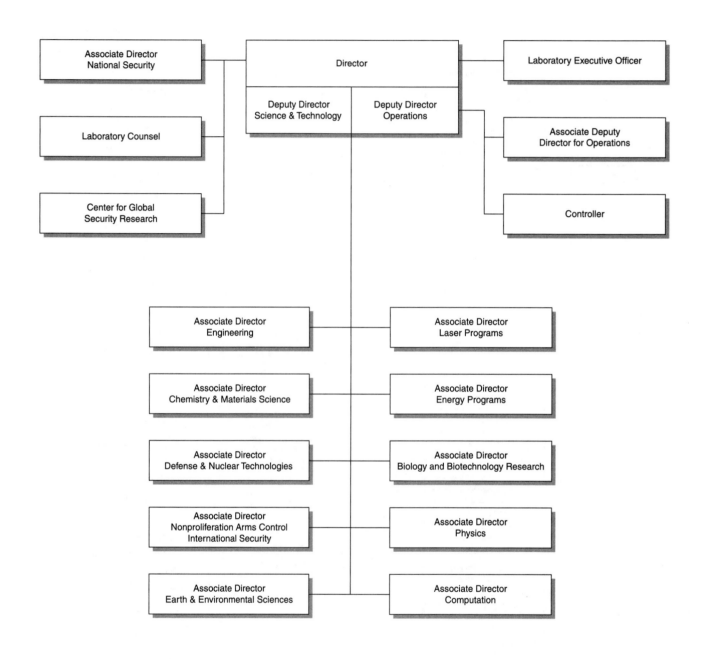

Source: Organization web site, 1999

Lockheed Martin Corporation

The U.S. government's largest contractor. Lockheed designs and makes missiles, aircraft, and related technology

6801 Rockledge Dr.
Bethesda, MD 20817
Phone: (301) 897-6000
Web: www.lockheedmartin.com

Primary SIC: 3761—Guided Missiles & Space Vehicles
Primary NAICS: 336414—Guided Missile & Space Vehicle Mfg

- VP & Chief Financial Officer
- VP & Treasurer
- VP & Controller

- Chairman & Chief Executive Officer
- President & Chief Operating Officer

- Sr. VP & General Counsel
- Corporate Staff
- President & Chief Operating Officer, Energy & Environment Sector
- President & Chief Operating Officer, Aeronautics Sector
- President & Chief Operating Officer, Information & Services Sector*; VP, Strategic Development
- President & Chief Operating Officer, Electronics Sector*
- President & Chief Operating Officer, Space & Strategic Missiles Sector

* See separate chart

Source: Annual report, 1999

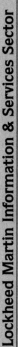

Lockheed Martin Information & Services Sector

One of Lockheed Martin's core business units, the I&S Sector employs some 46,000 people in 17 companies

6801 Rockledge Dr.
Bethesda, MD 20817
Phone: (301) 897-6000
Web: www.it.lmco.com

Primary SIC: 7371—Computer Programming Services
Primary NAICS: 541511—Custom Computer Programming Services

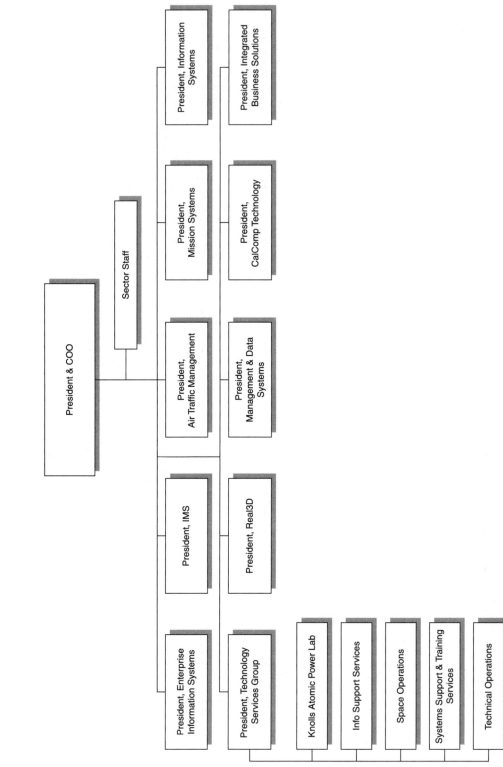

- President & COO
  - Sector Staff
  - President, IMS
  - President, Real3D
  - President, Enterprise Information Systems
  - President, Technology Services Group
    - Knolls Atomic Power Lab
    - Info Support Services
    - Space Operations
    - Systems Support & Training Services
    - Technical Operations
  - President, Air Traffic Management
  - President, Management & Data Systems
  - President, Mission Systems
  - President, CalComp Technology
  - President, Information Systems
  - President, Integrated Business Solutions

Source: Company web site, 1999

Lockheed Martin Tactical Defense Systems

A sub-unit of Lockheed Martin's electronics sector, LMTDS develops military information and communications systems

3333 Pilot Knob Road
Eagan, MN 55121
Phone: (651) 456-2222
Web: www.lmco.com/minn/index.htm

Primary SIC: 3663—Radio & Television
Broadcasting & Communications Equipment
Primary NAICS: 33422—Radio/TV
Broadcast & Wireless Comm Equip Mfg

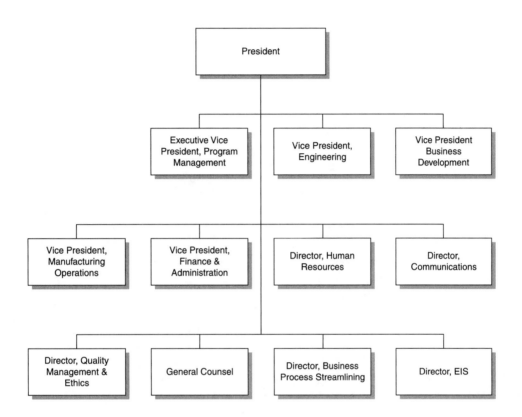

Maine Electric Power Company

A small electrical power transmission company owned jointly by Central Maine Power Co. and other state utilities

83 Edison Drive
Augusta, ME 04336
Phone: (207) 629-1000 **Fax:** (207) 621-4778
Web: www.cmpco.com/OASIS/mepc/index.html

Primary SIC: 4911—Electric Services
Primary NAICS: 221122—Electric
Power Distribution

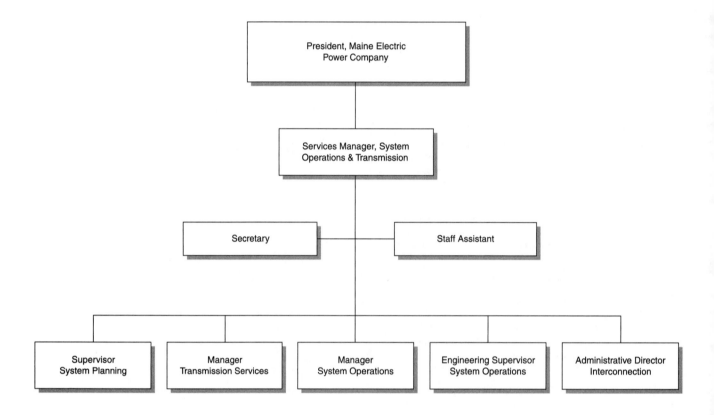

Source: Company web site, 1999

Masisa S.A.

With nearly 1,000 employees, Masisa is Latin America's top maker of particle and fiber board construction materials

Los Conquistadores 1700, 12th & 13th Fl.
Santiago, Chile
Phone: +56-2-707 8800 **Fax:** +56-2-234-2666
Web: www.masisa.com

Primary SIC: 2493—Reconstituted Wood Products
Primary NAICS: 321219—Reconstituted Wood
Product Mfg

Board of Directors

Chief Executive Officer

Planning & Development Deputy Manager

Chief Engineering Officer

Chief Financial Officer
- Finance Deputy Manager
- Administration Deputy Manager
- Procurement Deputy Manager
- Information Systems Deputy Manager

Chief Sales & Marketing Officer
- Domestic Market Deputy Manager
- Export Market Deputy Manager
- Marketing Deputy Manager

Chief Operating Officer
- Operations Manager Concepción

Human Resources Officer

Maderas y Sintéticos del Perú S.A.C.

Source: Annual report, 1997

Matsushita Communication Industrial Co., Ltd.

This Matsushita group unit produces communications equipment, audio/video products, and automotive electronics

3-1, Tsunashima-Higashi 4-chome
Kohoku-ku, Yokohama 223-8639, Japan
Phone: +81 45 531-1231
Web: www.mci.panasonic.co.jp

Primary SIC: 3669—Communications Equipment, NEC
Primary NAICS: 33429—Other Communications Equipment Mfg

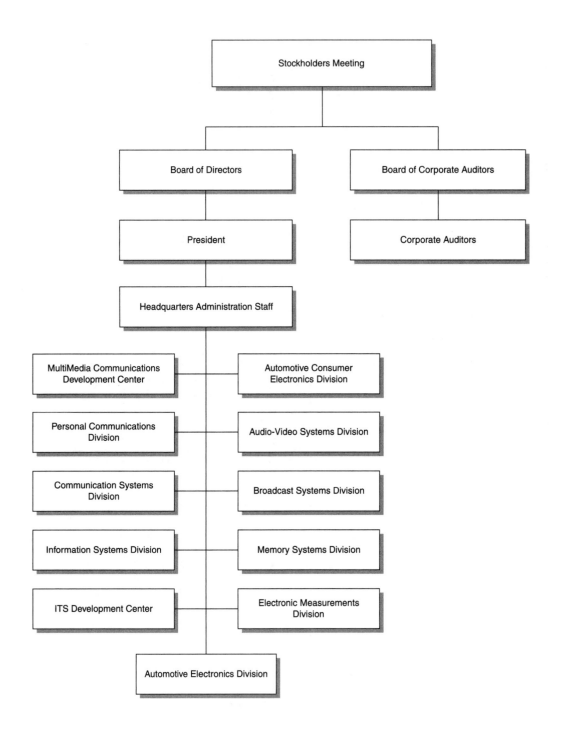

Source: Company web site, 1999

McDermott International Inc.

A large industrial equipment and services supplier to energy-related industries

1450 Poydras St.
New Orleans, LA 70112-6050
Phone: (504) 587-5400
Web: www.mcdermott.com

Primary SIC: 3621—Motors & Generators
Primary NAICS: 335312—Motor & Generator Mfg

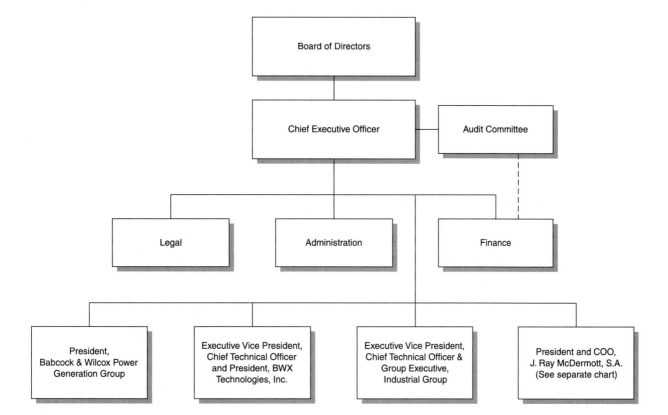

Source: Company web site, 1999

Micro Craft, Inc.

Provides services to manufacturing and industrial engineering customers, including facilities management

726 Arcadia Circle
Huntsville, AL 35801
Phone: (205) 533-7929 **Fax:** (205) 534-6555
Web: www.microcraft.com

Primary SIC: 8744—Facilities Support
Management Services
Primary NAICS: 56121—Facilities Support Services

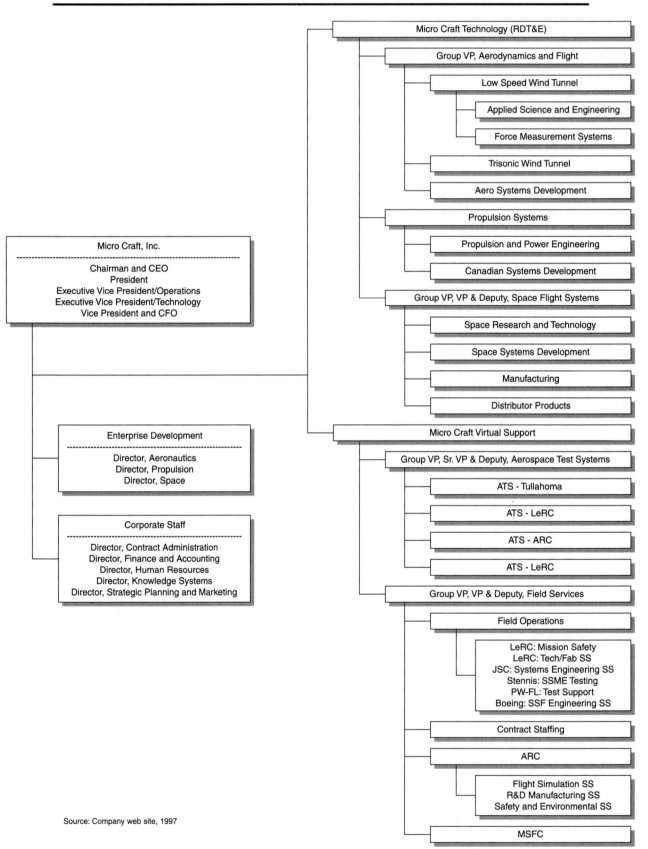

Source: Company web site, 1997

Micron Technology Inc.

Provides products and services related to memory chips and circuit boards for computers and other electronic devices

8000 S. Federal Way
Boise, ID 83707-0006
Phone: (208) 368-4000 **Fax:** (208) 368-2536
Web: www.micron.com

Primary SIC: 3674—Semiconductors & Related Devices
Primary NAICS: 334413—Semiconductor &
Related Device Mfg

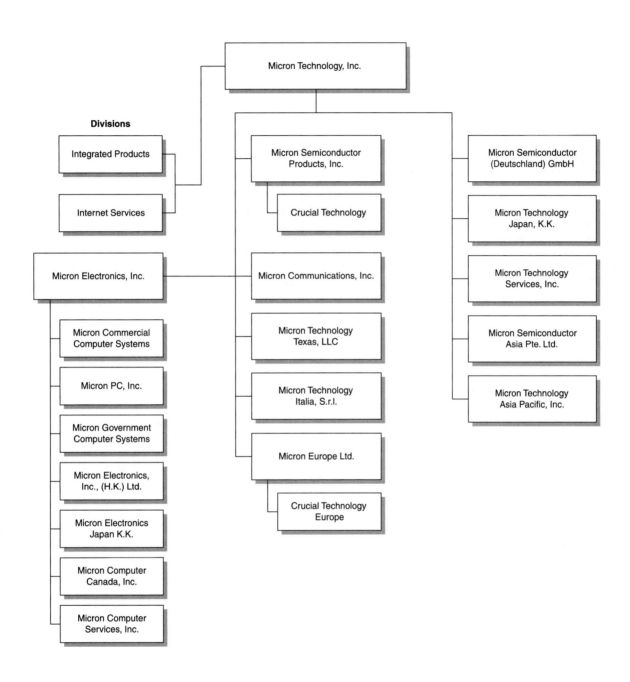

Divisions

Integrated Products

Internet Services

Micron Electronics, Inc.

- Micron Commercial Computer Systems
- Micron PC, Inc.
- Micron Government Computer Systems
- Micron Electronics, Inc., (H.K.) Ltd.
- Micron Electronics Japan K.K.
- Micron Computer Canada, Inc.
- Micron Computer Services, Inc.

Micron Technology, Inc.

Micron Semiconductor Products, Inc.

- Crucial Technology

Micron Communications, Inc.

Micron Technology Texas, LLC

Micron Technology Italia, S.r.l.

Micron Europe Ltd.

- Crucial Technology Europe

Micron Semiconductor (Deutschland) GmbH

Micron Technology Japan, K.K.

Micron Technology Services, Inc.

Micron Semiconductor Asia Pte. Ltd.

Micron Technology Asia Pacific, Inc.

Source: Company web site, 1999

Minnesota Mining and Manufacturing Company

Adhesives and abrasives for consumer and industrial products are 3M's top lines, accounting for half of its sales

3M Center
St. Paul, MN 55144-1000
Phone: (612) 733-1110 **Fax:** (612) 733-9973
Web: www.mmm.com

Primary SIC: 3291—Abrasive Products
Primary NAICS: 32791—Abrasive Product Mfg

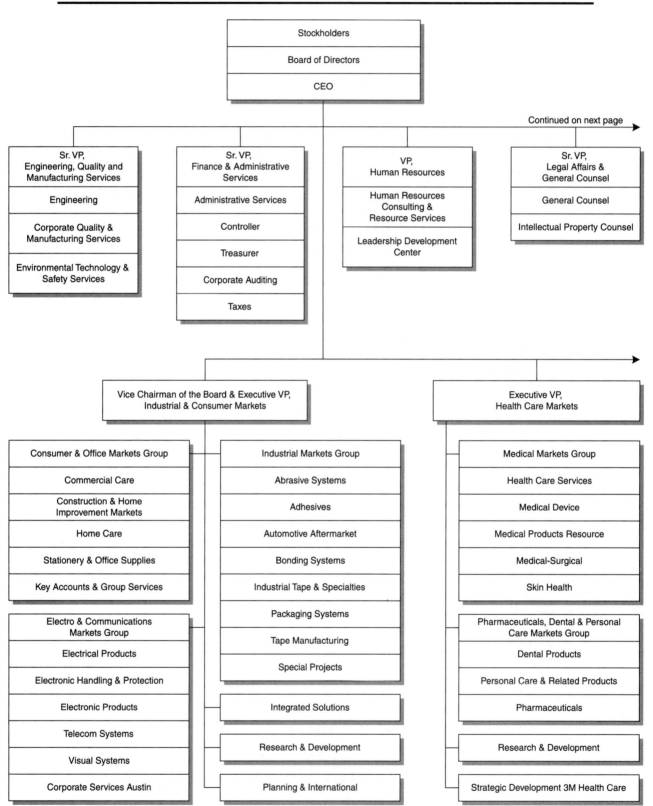

Stockholders

Board of Directors

CEO

Continued on next page

Sr. VP, Engineering, Quality and Manufacturing Services
- Engineering
- Corporate Quality & Manufacturing Services
- Environmental Technology & Safety Services

Sr. VP, Finance & Administrative Services
- Administrative Services
- Controller
- Treasurer
- Corporate Auditing
- Taxes

VP, Human Resources
- Human Resources Consulting & Resource Services
- Leadership Development Center

Sr. VP, Legal Affairs & General Counsel
- General Counsel
- Intellectual Property Counsel

Vice Chairman of the Board & Executive VP, Industrial & Consumer Markets

Executive VP, Health Care Markets

Consumer & Office Markets Group
- Commercial Care
- Construction & Home Improvement Markets
- Home Care
- Stationery & Office Supplies
- Key Accounts & Group Services

Electro & Communications Markets Group
- Electrical Products
- Electronic Handling & Protection
- Electronic Products
- Telecom Systems
- Visual Systems
- Corporate Services Austin

Industrial Markets Group
- Abrasive Systems
- Adhesives
- Automotive Aftermarket
- Bonding Systems
- Industrial Tape & Specialties
- Packaging Systems
- Tape Manufacturing
- Special Projects

Integrated Solutions

Research & Development

Planning & International

Medical Markets Group
- Health Care Services
- Medical Device
- Medical Products Resource
- Medical-Surgical
- Skin Health

Pharmaceuticals, Dental & Personal Care Markets Group
- Dental Products
- Personal Care & Related Products
- Pharmaceuticals

Research & Development

Strategic Development 3M Health Care

Source: Company and revisions by the editors, 1998

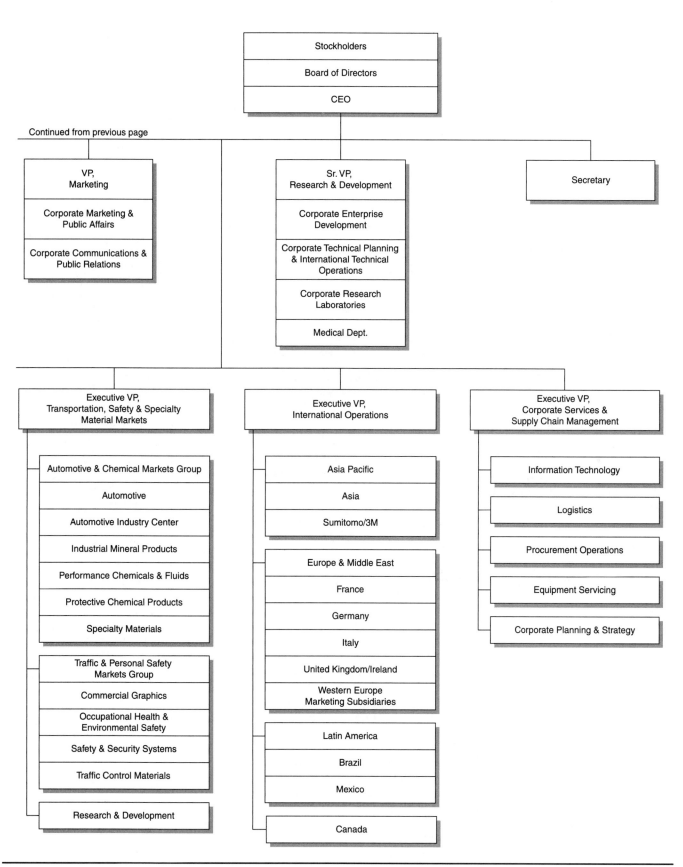

Continued from previous page

Stockholders

Board of Directors

CEO

VP, Marketing
- Corporate Marketing & Public Affairs
- Corporate Communications & Public Relations

Sr. VP, Research & Development
- Corporate Enterprise Development
- Corporate Technical Planning & International Technical Operations
- Corporate Research Laboratories
- Medical Dept.

Secretary

Executive VP, Transportation, Safety & Specialty Material Markets
- Automotive & Chemical Markets Group
- Automotive
- Automotive Industry Center
- Industrial Mineral Products
- Performance Chemicals & Fluids
- Protective Chemical Products
- Specialty Materials
- Traffic & Personal Safety Markets Group
- Commercial Graphics
- Occupational Health & Environmental Safety
- Safety & Security Systems
- Traffic Control Materials
- Research & Development

Executive VP, International Operations
- Asia Pacific
- Asia
- Sumitomo/3M
- Europe & Middle East
- France
- Germany
- Italy
- United Kingdom/Ireland
- Western Europe Marketing Subsidiaries
- Latin America
- Brazil
- Mexico
- Canada

Executive VP, Corporate Services & Supply Chain Management
- Information Technology
- Logistics
- Procurement Operations
- Equipment Servicing
- Corporate Planning & Strategy

Mitsubishi Corporation

This firm's largest business line is industrial equipment wholesaling, but it has affiliates in many other industries

6-3, Marunouchi 2-chome
Chiyoda-ku, Tokyo 100-8086, Japan
Phone: +81 03 3210-2121 **Fax:** +81 03 3210-8935
Web: www.mitsubishi.co.jp

Primary SIC: 5084—Industrial Machinery & Equipment
Primary NAICS: 42183—Industrial Machinery & Equipment Whsle

REORGANIZATION Part 1 (1996)
For additional details on the restructuring see profiles starting on page 331

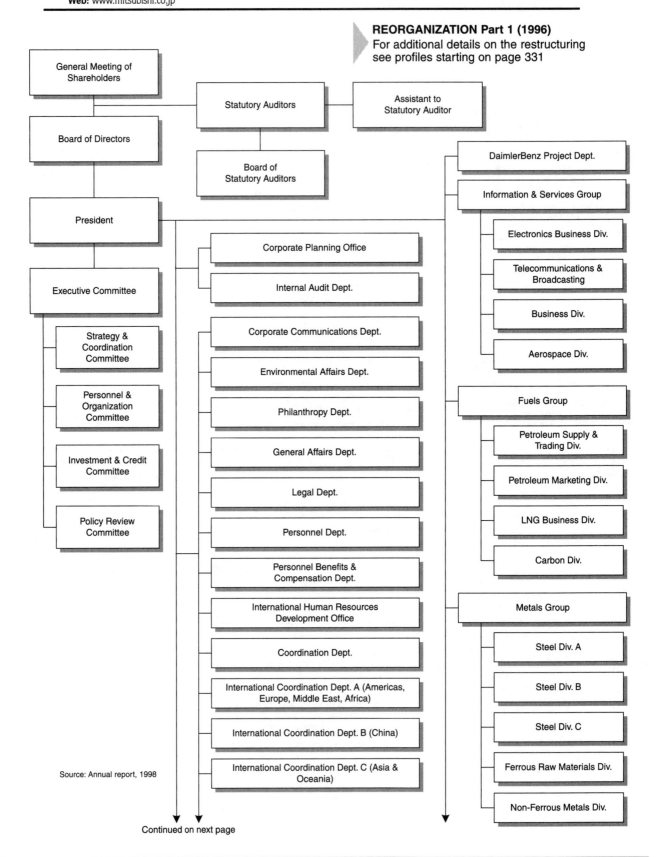

Source: Annual report, 1998

General Meeting of Shareholders

Statutory Auditors

Assistant to Statutory Auditor

Board of Directors

Board of Statutory Auditors

President

Executive Committee

Strategy & Coordination Committee

Personnel & Organization Committee

Investment & Credit Committee

Policy Review Committee

Corporate Planning Office

Internal Audit Dept.

Corporate Communications Dept.

Environmental Affairs Dept.

Philanthropy Dept.

General Affairs Dept.

Legal Dept.

Personnel Dept.

Personnel Benefits & Compensation Dept.

International Human Resources Development Office

Coordination Dept.

International Coordination Dept. A (Americas, Europe, Middle East, Africa)

International Coordination Dept. B (China)

International Coordination Dept. C (Asia & Oceania)

DaimlerBenz Project Dept.

Information & Services Group

Electronics Business Div.

Telecommunications & Broadcasting

Business Div.

Aerospace Div.

Fuels Group

Petroleum Supply & Trading Div.

Petroleum Marketing Div.

LNG Business Div.

Carbon Div.

Metals Group

Steel Div. A

Steel Div. B

Steel Div. C

Ferrous Raw Materials Div.

Non-Ferrous Metals Div.

Continued on next page

Continued from previous page

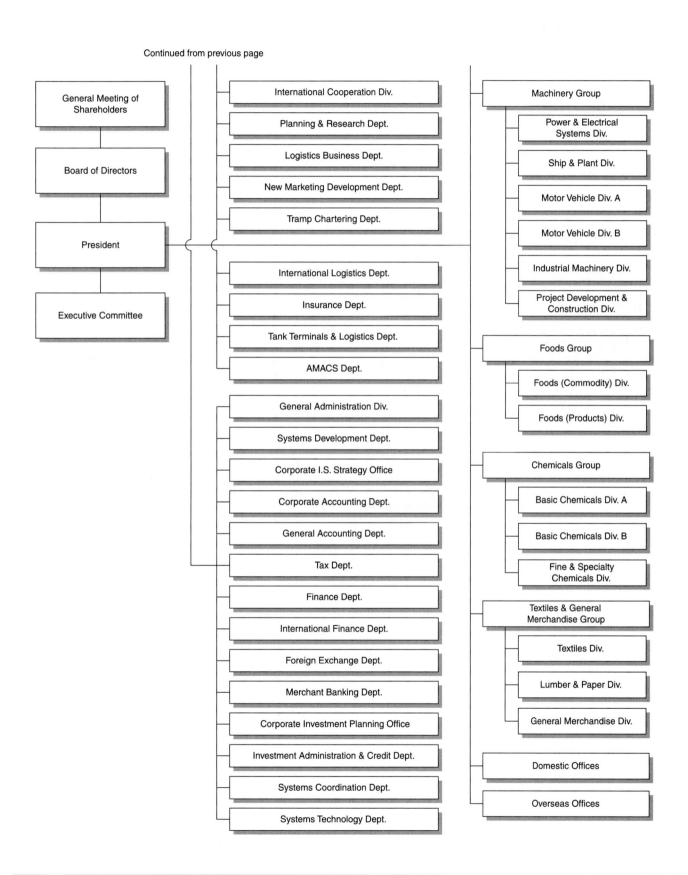

General Meeting of Shareholders

Board of Directors

President

Executive Committee

International Cooperation Div.

Planning & Research Dept.

Logistics Business Dept.

New Marketing Development Dept.

Tramp Chartering Dept.

International Logistics Dept.

Insurance Dept.

Tank Terminals & Logistics Dept.

AMACS Dept.

General Administration Div.

Systems Development Dept.

Corporate I.S. Strategy Office

Corporate Accounting Dept.

General Accounting Dept.

Tax Dept.

Finance Dept.

International Finance Dept.

Foreign Exchange Dept.

Merchant Banking Dept.

Corporate Investment Planning Office

Investment Administration & Credit Dept.

Systems Coordination Dept.

Systems Technology Dept.

Machinery Group
- Power & Electrical Systems Div.
- Ship & Plant Div.
- Motor Vehicle Div. A
- Motor Vehicle Div. B
- Industrial Machinery Div.
- Project Development & Construction Div.

Foods Group
- Foods (Commodity) Div.
- Foods (Products) Div.

Chemicals Group
- Basic Chemicals Div. A
- Basic Chemicals Div. B
- Fine & Specialty Chemicals Div.

Textiles & General Merchandise Group
- Textiles Div.
- Lumber & Paper Div.
- General Merchandise Div.

Domestic Offices

Overseas Offices

REORGANIZATION Part 2 (1999)
For additional details on the restructuring
see profiles starting on page 331

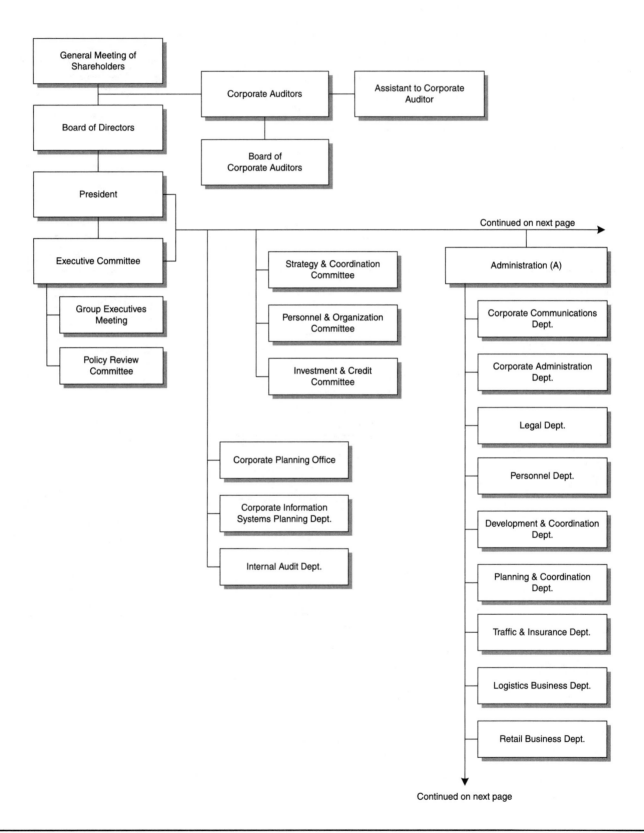

General Meeting of Shareholders

Corporate Auditors

Assistant to Corporate Auditor

Board of Directors

Board of Corporate Auditors

President

Continued on next page

Executive Committee

Strategy & Coordination Committee

Administration (A)

Group Executives Meeting

Personnel & Organization Committee

Corporate Communications Dept.

Policy Review Committee

Investment & Credit Committee

Corporate Administration Dept.

Legal Dept.

Personnel Dept.

Corporate Planning Office

Development & Coordination Dept.

Corporate Information Systems Planning Dept.

Planning & Coordination Dept.

Internal Audit Dept.

Traffic & Insurance Dept.

Logistics Business Dept.

Retail Business Dept.

Continued on next page

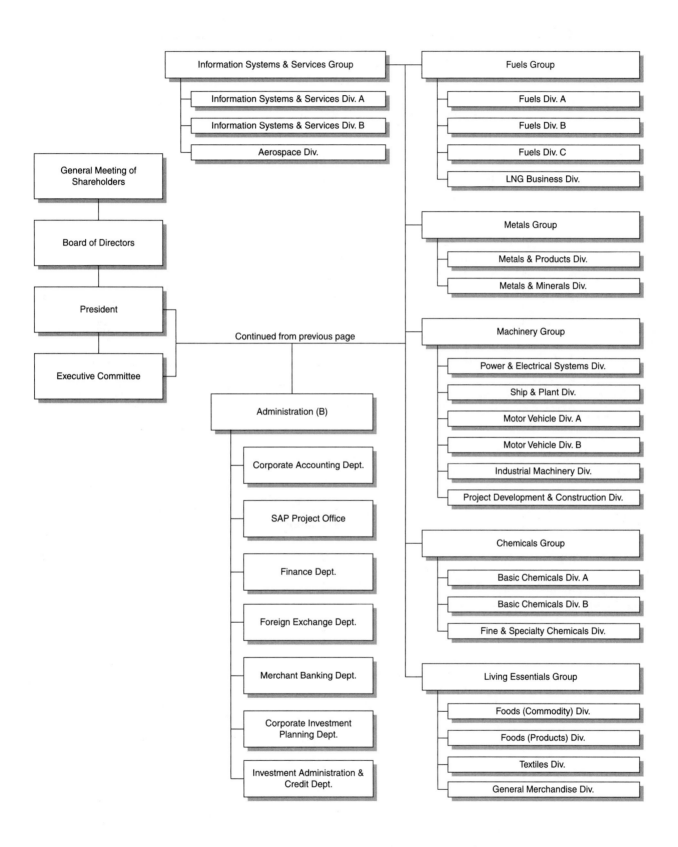

Mitsubishi Rayon Company, Limited

The fibers and resins operating company of the Mitsubishi group

6-41, Konan 1-chome
Minato-ku, Tokyo 108-8506, Japan
Phone: +81 03 5495-3100 **Fax:** +81 03 5495-3184
Web: www.mrc.co.jp **E-mail:** koho@post.mrc.co.jp

Primary SIC: 2823—Cellulosic
Manmade Fibers
Primary NAICS: 325211—Plastics
Material & Resins Mfg

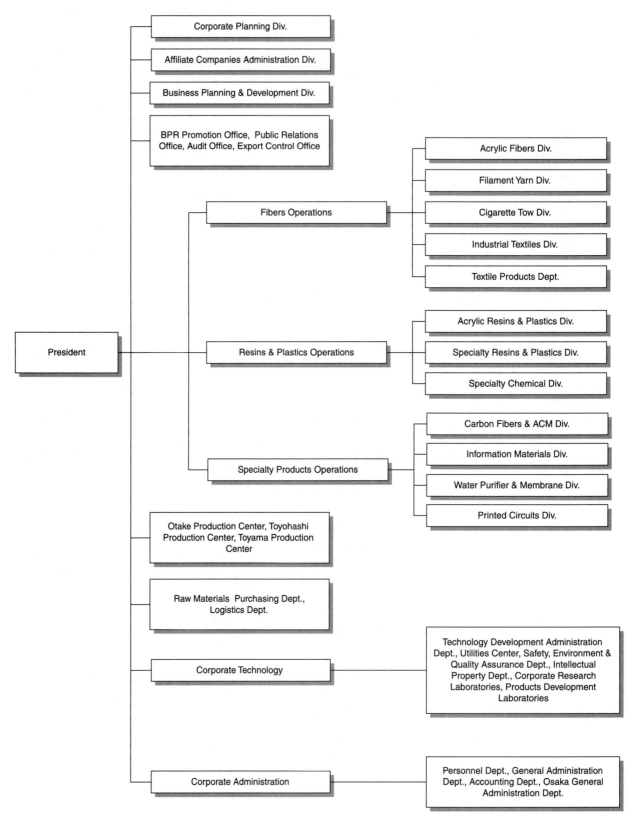

Source: Annual report, 1998

Mitsui & Co., Ltd.

This major trading company's operations span from machinery to energy to metals, among many other product lines

2-1 Ohtemachi 1-chome
Chiyoda-ku, Tokyo 100, Japan
Phone: +81 3 3285-1111 **Fax:** +81 3 3285-9800
Web: www.mitsui.co.jp

Primary SIC: 5084—Industrial Machinery & Equipment
Primary NAICS: 42183—Industrial Machinery & Equipment Whsle

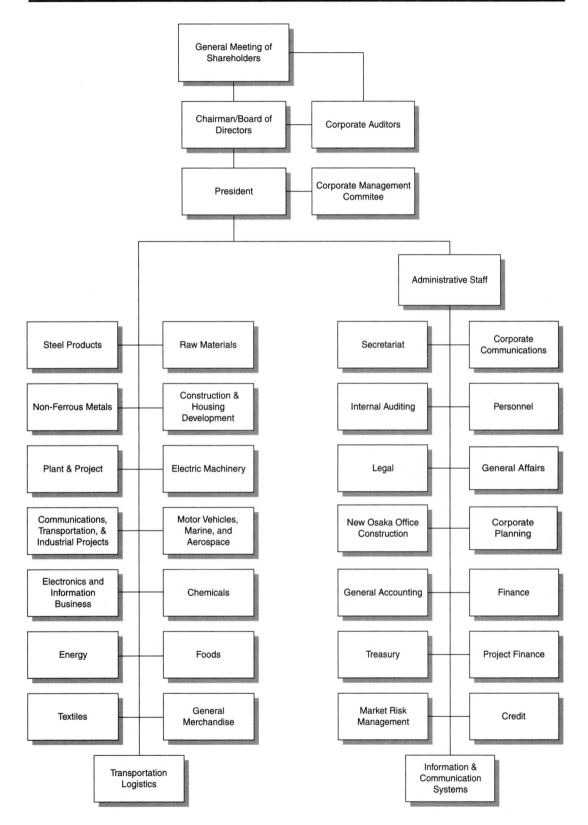

Source: Company web site, 1998

Mitsui Fudosan Co., Ltd.

An owner, developer, lessor, and broker of real estate. Mitsui Fudosan is Japan's market leader in that industry

1-1, Nihonbashi-Muromachi 2-chome
Chuo-ku, Tokyo 103-0022, Japan
Phone: +81 3-3246-3065
Web: www.mitsuifudosan.co.jp

Primary SIC: 6531—Real Estate Agents & Managers
Primary NAICS: 53121—Offices of Real Estate
Agents & Brokers

Board of Directors

Chairman of the Board, President & CEO
Executive Vice President, Senior Managing Director
Managing Directors

Executive Committee

Special Committees

General Managers Committee

Construction Planning Department

Mitsui Fudosan Group Planning Dept.

Space and Environment Institute

Information Systems Department

Corporate Planning & Research Department

Management Planning Department

Mitsui Fudosan Group Planning Division

Subsidiaries and Affiliates Support Dept.

New Business Promotion Dept.

Real Estate Service Division
- Appraisal Department
- Asset Sales Department
- Real Estate Consulting Dept.
- Real Estate Development Dept. (I)
- Real Estate Development Dept. (II)

Oita Branch

Fukoka Branch

Hiroshima Branch

Nagoya Branch

Yokohama Branch

International Department

Residential Development Div.
- Consulting Group
- Suburban Development Department
- Housing Development Department
- Urban Development Department

Continued on next page

Source: Company web site, 1999

Mitsui Fudosan Co., Ltd. (cont.)

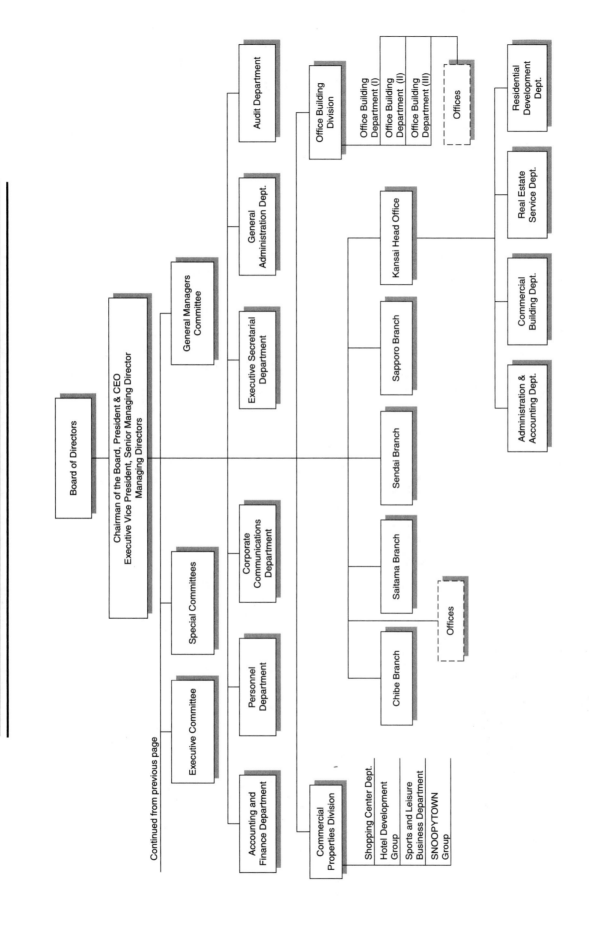

Continued from previous page

Motorola Inc.

Major producer of communications devices for the consumer and commercial markets

1303 E. Algonquin Rd.
Schaumburg, IL 60196
Phone: (847) 576-5000
Web: www.motorola.com

Primary SIC: 3663—Radio & Television
Broadcasting & Communications Equipment
Primary NAICS: 33422—Radio/TV
Broadcast & Wireless Comm Equip Mfg

▶ **REORGANIZATION Part 1 (1996)**
For additional details on the restructuring
see profiles starting on page 331

- Chairman of the Board
- Board of Directors
- Secretary
- Chairman of the Executive Committee
- Chief Executive Officer
- President & COO

- Sr. VP, President, & GM, Land Mobile Products Sector
- Executive VP, President, & GM, Messaging, Information, & Media Sector
- Executive VP & Director, Human Resources
- Executive VP, President, & GM, Semiconductor Products Sector
- Executive VP & CFO
- Executive VP, President, & GM, Cellular Networks & Space Sector
- Sr. VP & General Counsel
- Executive VP, President, & GM, Cellular Subscriber Sector
- Executive VP & President, Americas
- Executive VP, President, & GM, Automotive, Energy, & Components Sector
- Executive VP & Corp. Exec. Director, Asia/Pacific
- Corp. VP & GM, Computer Group
- Executive VP & President, Europe, Middle East, & Africa
- Executive VP & GM, Japan Group

Source: Company and revisions by the editors, 1999

Motorola Inc. (cont.)

REORGANIZATION Part 2 (1999)

For additional details on the restructuring
see profiles starting on page 331

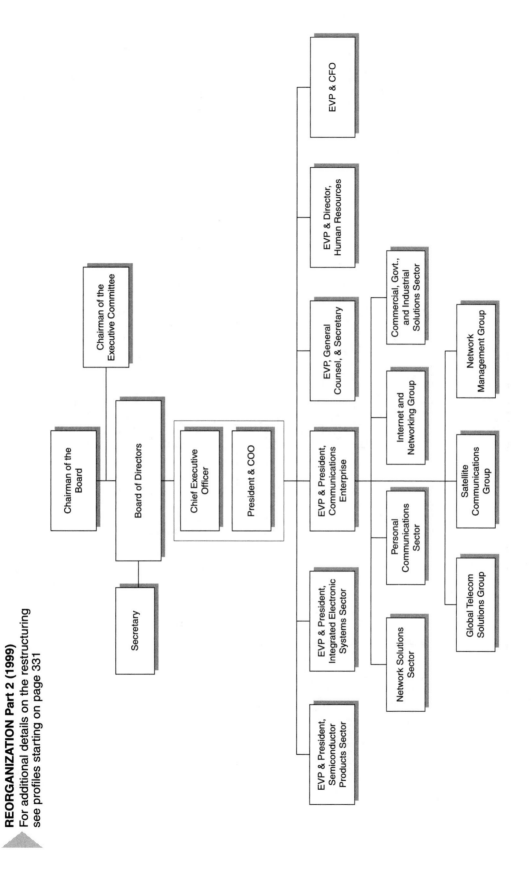

MP Steel Corporation

This privately held regional firm performs heat treatment of steel castings from outside foundries for a variety of end uses

100 N. Fairbanks Ave.
P.O. 3059, Holland, MI 49422
Phone: (616) 392-7017 **Fax:** (616) 392-1352

Primary SIC: 3398—Metal Heat Treating
Primary NAICS: 332811—Metal Heat Treating

President
- Executive Vice President
- General Manager

Chief Financial Officer
- Accounting Department
  - Accounting Manager
  - Accounts Coordinator

Production Department
- Personnel Director
- Scheduler
- Production Manager
  - Prod. Supervisor
  - Production Hourly

Maintenance Department
- Maintenance Manager
- Maintenance Hourly

Traffic Department
- Materials & Distribution Manager
  - Traffic
  - Traffic Hourly

Sales Department
- Sales Manager
- Outside Sales

QA Manager

Quality Department
- Quality Manager
  - Administrative Assistant
  - Quality Hourly

Source: Company, 1999

MPRI

A defense consulting and training company made up principally of former military officers

1201 East Abingdon Drive, Ste. 425
Alexandria, VA 22314
Phone: (703) 684-0853 **Fax:** (703) 684-3528
Web: www.mpri.com

Primary SIC: 8742—Management Consulting Services
Primary NAICS: 541611—Admin & Gen
Management Consulting Services

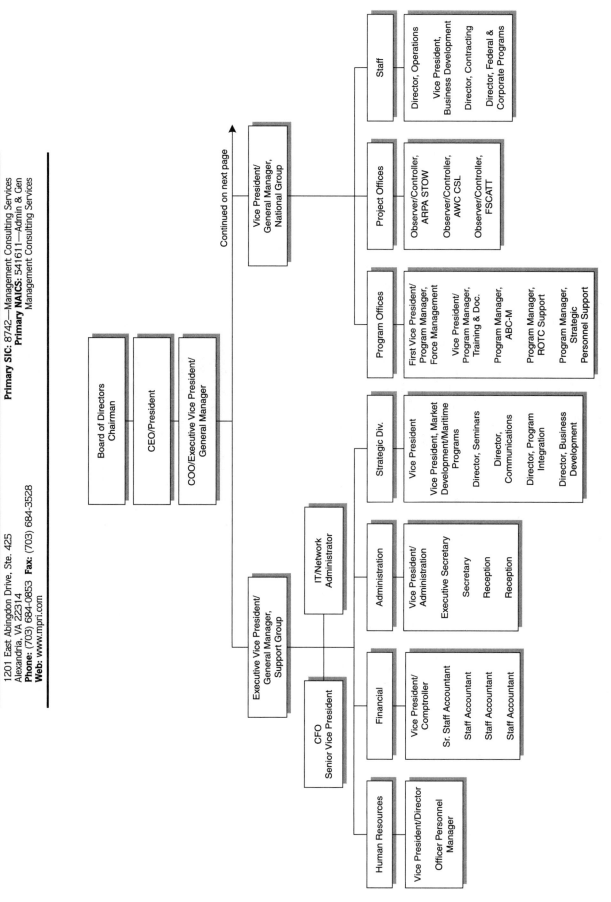

Continued on next page

Board of Directors
Chairman

CEO/President

COO/Executive Vice President/
General Manager

Executive Vice President/
General Manager,
Support Group

CFO
Senior Vice President

IT/Network
Administrator

Human Resources

Vice President/Director

Officer Personnel
Manager

Financial

Vice President/
Comptroller

Sr. Staff Accountant

Staff Accountant

Staff Accountant

Staff Accountant

Administration

Vice President/
Administration

Executive Secretary

Secretary

Reception

Reception

Strategic Div.

Vice President

Vice President, Market
Development/Maritime
Programs

Director, Seminars

Director,
Communications

Director, Program
Integration

Director, Business
Development

Vice President/
General Manager,
National Group

Program Offices

First Vice President/
Program Manager,
Force Management

Vice President/
Program Manager,
Training & Doc.

Program Manager,
ABC-M

Program Manager,
ROTC Support

Program Manager,
Strategic
Personnel Support

Project Offices

Observer/Controller,
ARPA STOW

Observer/Controller,
AWC CSL

Observer/Controller,
FSCATT

Staff

Director, Operations

Vice President,
Business Development

Director, Contracting

Director, Federal &
Corporate Programs

Source: Company web site, 1999

MPRI (cont.)

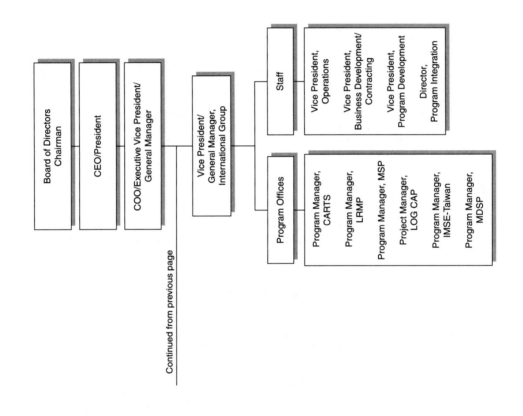

Board of Directors
Chairman

CEO/President

COO/Executive Vice President/
General Manager

Continued from previous page

Vice President/
General Manager,
International Group

Staff

Vice President,
Operations

Vice President,
Business Development/
Contracting

Vice President,
Program Development

Director,
Program Integration

Program Offices

Program Manager,
CARTS

Program Manager,
LRMP

Program Manager, MSP

Project Manager,
LOG CAP

Program Manager,
IMSE-Taiwan

Program Manager,
MDSP

National Association of Securities Dealers, Inc.

The private self-regulatory association of the securities trading industry and parent to the Nasdaq market

1735 K St. NW
Washington, DC 20006-1500
Phone: (202) 728-8000 **Fax:** (202) 293-6260
Web: www.nasd.com

Primary SIC: 8611—Business Associations
Primary NAICS: 81391—Business Associations

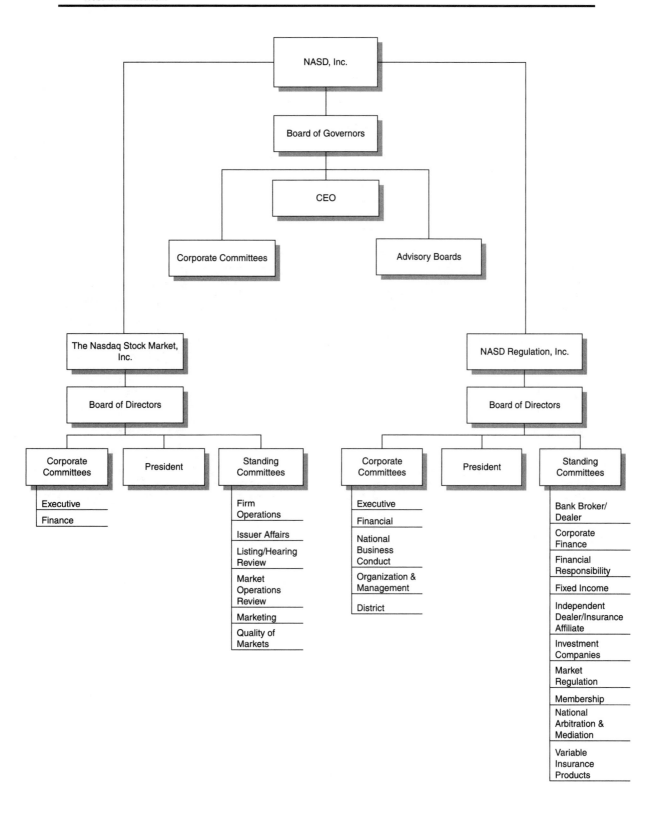

Source: Company web site, 1999

A unit of the Schomac Group, Inc., NSS operates 50 self-storage centers primarily in the southwest

17 W. Wetmore Rd., Ste. 302
Tucson, AZ 85705
Phone: (520) 577-9777 **Fax:** (520) 577-0824
Web: www.nationalselfstorage.com

Primary SIC: 4225—General Warehousing & Storage
Primary NAICS: 53113—Lessors of Miniwarehouse
& Self Storage Units

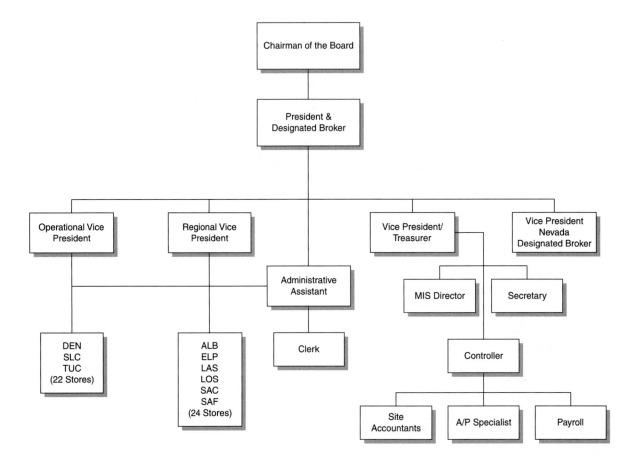

Source: Company web site, 1999

NEC Corporation

This electronics giant makes computers, industrial electronics, communications hardware, and related technology.

7-1 Shiba 5-chome
Minato-ku, Tokyo 108, Japan
Phone: +81 03 3454111 **Fax:** +81 03 37981510
Web: www.nec-global.com

Primary SIC: 3571—Electronic Computers
Primary NAICS: 334111—Electronic Computer Mfg

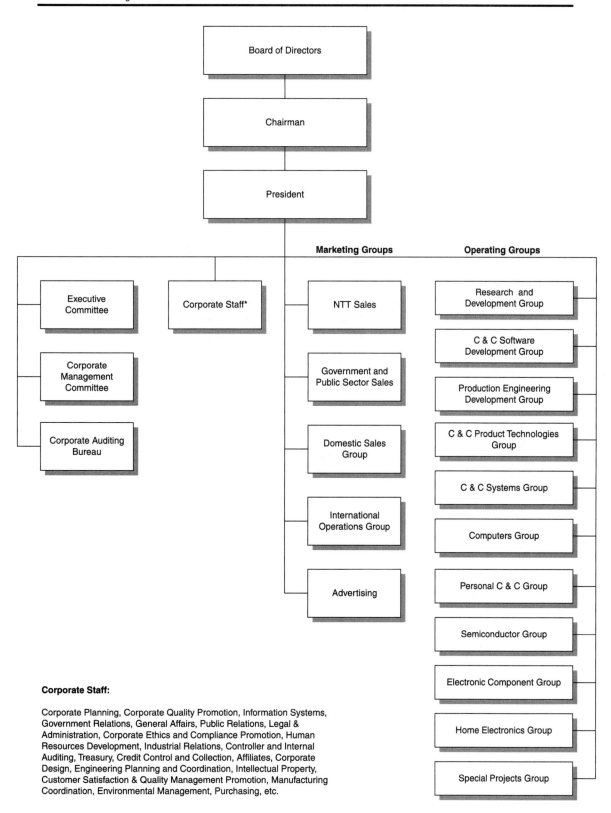

Marketing Groups

- NTT Sales
- Government and Public Sector Sales
- Domestic Sales Group
- International Operations Group
- Advertising

Operating Groups

- Research and Development Group
- C & C Software Development Group
- Production Engineering Development Group
- C & C Product Technologies Group
- C & C Systems Group
- Computers Group
- Personal C & C Group
- Semiconductor Group
- Electronic Component Group
- Home Electronics Group
- Special Projects Group

Board of Directors → Chairman → President

- Executive Committee
- Corporate Staff*
- Corporate Management Committee
- Corporate Auditing Bureau

Corporate Staff:

Corporate Planning, Corporate Quality Promotion, Information Systems, Government Relations, General Affairs, Public Relations, Legal & Administration, Corporate Ethics and Compliance Promotion, Human Resources Development, Industrial Relations, Controller and Internal Auditing, Treasury, Credit Control and Collection, Affiliates, Corporate Design, Engineering Planning and Coordination, Intellectual Property, Customer Satisfaction & Quality Management Promotion, Manufacturing Coordination, Environmental Management, Purchasing, etc.

Source: Company web site, 1998

This holding of Japan's NEC Corp. specializes in producing rechargeable lithium ion batteries

2-5-5, Shinyokohama, Kouhoku-ku
Yokohama-shi, Kanagawa 222-0033, Japan
Phone: +81 045-476-0865 **Fax:** +81 045-476-0864
Web: www.necmolienergy.co.jp

Primary SIC: 3692—Primary Batteries, Dry & Wet
Primary NAICS: 335912—Primary Battery Mfg

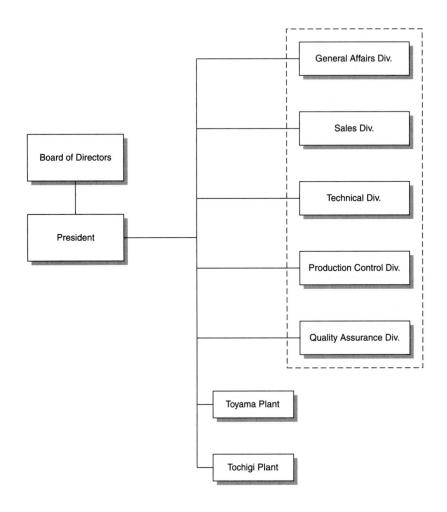

Source: Company web site, 1999

Nestlé SA

By a slim margin coffee is Nestlé's largest line, but it also is a major producer of many other food and beverage products

Ave. Nestlé 55
CH-1800 Vevey, Switzerland
Phone: +41 21 924-2111 **Fax:** +41 21 922-6334
Web: www.nestle.com

Primary SIC: 2095—Roasted Coffee
Primary NAICS: 31192—Coffee & Tea Mfg

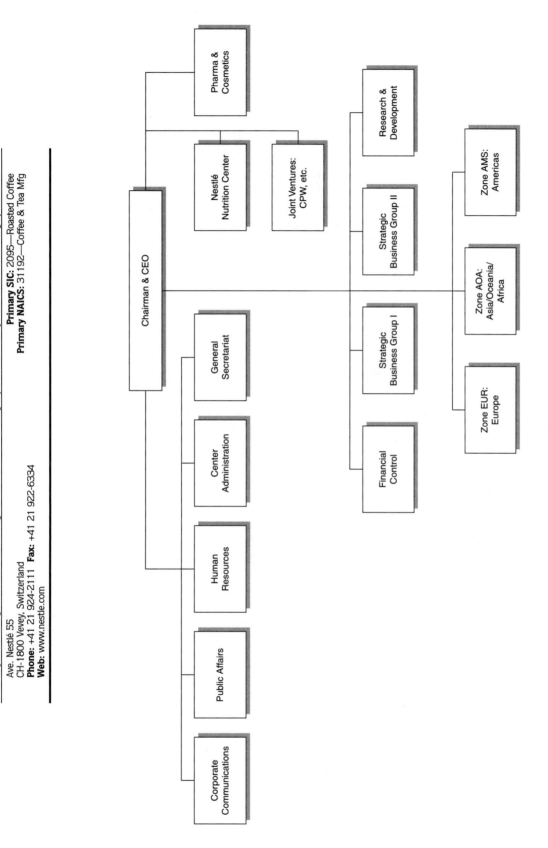

New York City

The world's 4th-largest city is home to more than 16 million people

City Hall
New York, NY 10007
Phone: (212) 788-2958
Web: www.ci.nyc.ny.us

Primary SIC: 9111—Executive Offices
Primary NAICS: 92111—Executive Offices

The Voters of the City of New York

District Attorneys

Office of Special Narcotics

The Council
51 Members:

Manhattan	10
The Bronx	8
Brooklyn	16
Queens	14
Staten Island	3

City Clerk

Public Advocate

Mayor

Comptroller

Payroll Administration

Financial Information Services

Procurement Policy Board

Borough Presidents

Manhattan
The Bronx
Brooklyn
Queens
Staten Island

Community Boards

Borough Boards

Deputy Mayor for Operations

Deputy Mayor for Education & Human Services

Deputy Mayor for Economic Development, Planning, and Administration

Deputy Mayor for Community Development and Business Services

Chief of Staff

Senior Advisor

Corporation Counsel

Law Department

Mayor's Counsel

Office of Management & Budget

– – – – Budgeting Approval

Source: Organization web site, 1999

The Nikko Securities Co., Ltd.

Japan's 3rd-largest securities brokerage. Nikko also has operations throughout the world

3-1, Marunouchi 3-chome
Chiyoda-ku, Tokyo 100-8325, Japan
Phone: +81-3-5644-4362 **Fax:** +81-3-5644-4329
Web: www.nikko.co.jp

Primary SIC: 6211—Security Brokers, Dealers, & Flotation Companies
Primary NAICS: 52312—Securities Brokerage

Board of Directors

Management Committee

Board of Corporate Auditors

COMPLIANCE GROUP
- Compliance & Internal Inspection Div.
- Legal Div.
- Trading Supervisory Div.
- Securities Evaluation Div.
- Security Management Div.
- Personnel Div.
- General Administration Div.
- Public Relations Div.
- Management Office
- Finance & Accounting Div.
- Fund Planning & Operation Div.
- (Nikko Global Holdings)
- Risk Management Div.
- (Risk Management Div.-Europe)
- (Risk Management Div. -Asia & Oceania)
- Operations & System Planning Div.
- Operating Div. for Investment Services
- Proprietary Unit
- Institute of Investment Technology
- Products Planning

RETAIL PRODUCTS GROUP
- Retail Sales Support Div.
- Research & Strategy Div. -Retails

INVESTMENT TRUST GROUP
- Investment Trust Div.
- Retail Business Planning Div.

REGIONAL RETAIL SERVICES GROUP
- 3 Groups, 127 Offices

EXECUTIVE SERVICES, PRIVATE BANKING, MEDIA MARKETING GROUP
- Executive Services Div.
- Private Banking Div.
- Media Marketing Div.

INVESTMENT BANKING GROUP
- Investment Banking Business Planning Div.
- Corporate Services Support Div.
- Corporate Consulting Div.
- M&A Div.
- Corporate Finance Unit
- Initial Public Offering Unit
- Institutional Business Planning Div.

CORPORATE SERVICES GROUP -FINANCIAL INSTITUTIONS -PUBLIC INSTITUTIONS -ASSET MANAGEMENT MKTG.
- Corporate Services Div. I & II -Financial Institutions
- Public Institutions Div.
- Asset Management Marketing Div.

CORPORATE SERVICES GROUP -REGIONAL (Tobu) COMPANIES
- Corporate Services Div. -Regional (Tobu) Companies

CORPORATE SERVICES GROUP -REGIONAL (Shutoken) COMPANIES
- Corporate Services Div. -Regional (Shutoken) Companies

CORPORATE SERVICES GROUP -REGIONAL (Kanto Chubu) COMPANIES
- Corporate Services Div. -Regional (Kanto Chubu) Companies

CORPORATE SERVICES GROUP -REGIONAL (Chugoku Kyushu) COMPANIES
- Corporate Services Div. -Regional (Chugoku Kyushu) Companies

CORPORATE SERVICES GROUP -OSAKA
- Osaka Branch General Administration Div.
- Osaka Branch Corporate Services Div. I & II -Public Companies
- Osaka Branch Corporate Services Div. -Private Companies
- Overseas Business Planning Div.

ASIA & OCEANIA GROUP
- Hong Kong
- Singapore
- Sydney
- Jakarta
- Kuala Lumpur
- Seoul
- Taipei

Continued on next page

Source: Annual report, 1998

The Nikko Securities Co., Ltd. (cont.)

Continued from previous page

Board of Directors

Management Committee

Board of Corporate Auditors

CUSTOMER PRODUCTS GROUP

Documentation Div.

(Products Development & Research Div.-Europe)

(Principal Finance Div.-Europe)

Equities Position Unit

Equities Trading Div.

(Equities Div.-America)

(Equities Div.-Europe)

(Equities Div.-Asia & Oceania)

Financial Products Position Unit

Financial Products Trading Div.

(Fixed Income Div.-America)

(Fixed Income Div.-Europe)

(Fixed Income Div. -Asia & Oceania)

Structure & Primary Position Unit

(Syndicate Div.-Europe)

CORPORATE SERVICES GROUP I & II- PUBLIC COMPANIES

Corporate Services Div. I-VI -Public Companies

CORPORATE SERVICES GROUP -PRIVATE COMPANIES

Corporate Services Div. I-IV -Private Companies

INVESTMENT SERVICES GROUP

Investment Services Div. -Institutional Investors

Investment Services Div. -Corporations

CORPORATE SERVICES GROUP -NAGOYA

Nagoya Branch General Administration Div.

Nagoya Branch Corporate Services Div. -Public Companies

Nagoya Branch Corporate Services Div. -Private Companies

CORPORATE SERVICES GROUP -REGIONAL (Tokai Hokuriku) COMPANIES

Corporate Services Div. -Regional (Tokai Hokuriku) Companies

CORPORATE SERVICES GROUP -REGIONAL (Kinki Shikoku) COMPANIES

Corporate Services Div. -Regional (Kinki Shikoku) Companies

ASIA & OCEANIA GROUP (cont.)

Beijing Rep.

Shanghai Rep.

Bangkok Rep.

AMERICAS GROUP

New York

Chicago

Toronto

Mexico Rep.

EUROPE & THE MIDDLE EAST GROUP

London

Zurich

Geneva

Frankfurt

Berlin

Luxembourg

Paris

Amsterdam

Madrid

Milano

The Nikko Bank (UK) plc

The Nippon Fire & Marine Insurance Co., Ltd.

One of Japan's oldest insurers, the firm provides policies on automobiles and other property

2-10, Nihonbashi 2-chome
Chuo-ku, Tokyo 103-8255, Japan
Phone: +81 03 3272-8111 **Fax:** +81 03 5229-3385

Primary SIC: 6331—Fire, Marine, & Casualty Insurance
Primary NAICS: 524126—Direct Property & Casualty Insurance Carriers

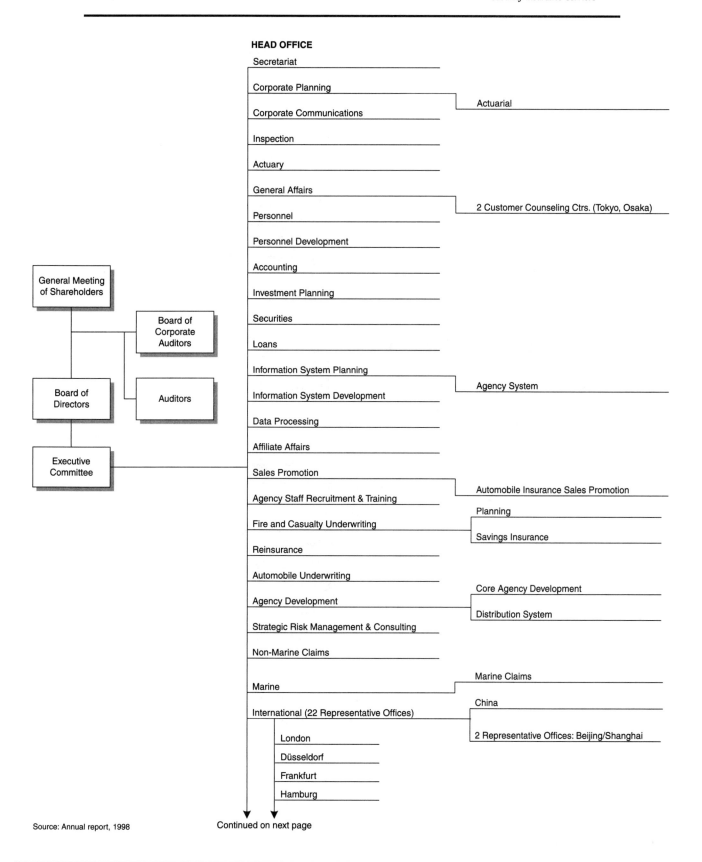

Continued on next page

Source: Annual report, 1998

Continued from previous page

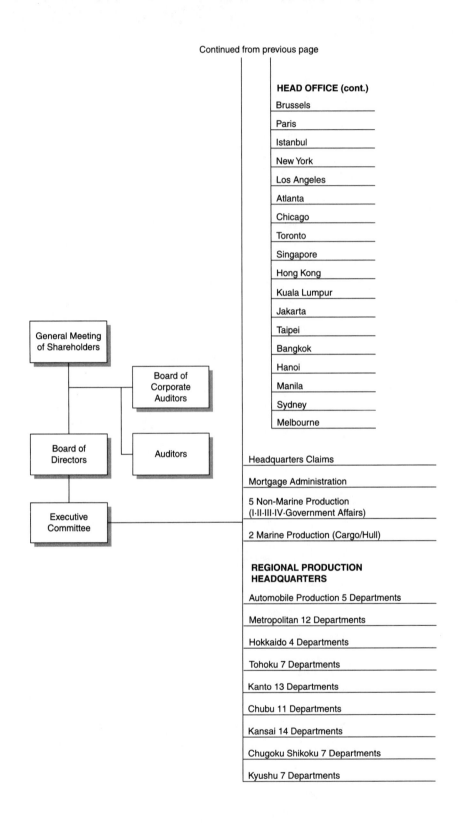

HEAD OFFICE (cont.)

Brussels

Paris

Istanbul

New York

Los Angeles

Atlanta

Chicago

Toronto

Singapore

Hong Kong

Kuala Lumpur

Jakarta

Taipei

Bangkok

Hanoi

Manila

Sydney

Melbourne

General Meeting of Shareholders

Board of Corporate Auditors

Board of Directors

Auditors

Executive Committee

Headquarters Claims

Mortgage Administration

5 Non-Marine Production (I·II·III·IV·Government Affairs)

2 Marine Production (Cargo/Hull)

REGIONAL PRODUCTION HEADQUARTERS

Automobile Production 5 Departments

Metropolitan 12 Departments

Hokkaido 4 Departments

Tohoku 7 Departments

Kanto 13 Departments

Chubu 11 Departments

Kansai 14 Departments

Chugoku Shikoku 7 Departments

Kyushu 7 Departments

Nippon Steel Information & Communication Systems

Better known as ENICOM, this systems integrator is Japan's largest Oracle software supplier

2-20-15 Shinkawa
Chuo-ku, Tokyo 104-8280, Japan
Web: www.enicom.co.jp

Primary SIC: 7373—Computer Integrated Systems Design
Primary NAICS: 541512—Computer Systems
Design Services

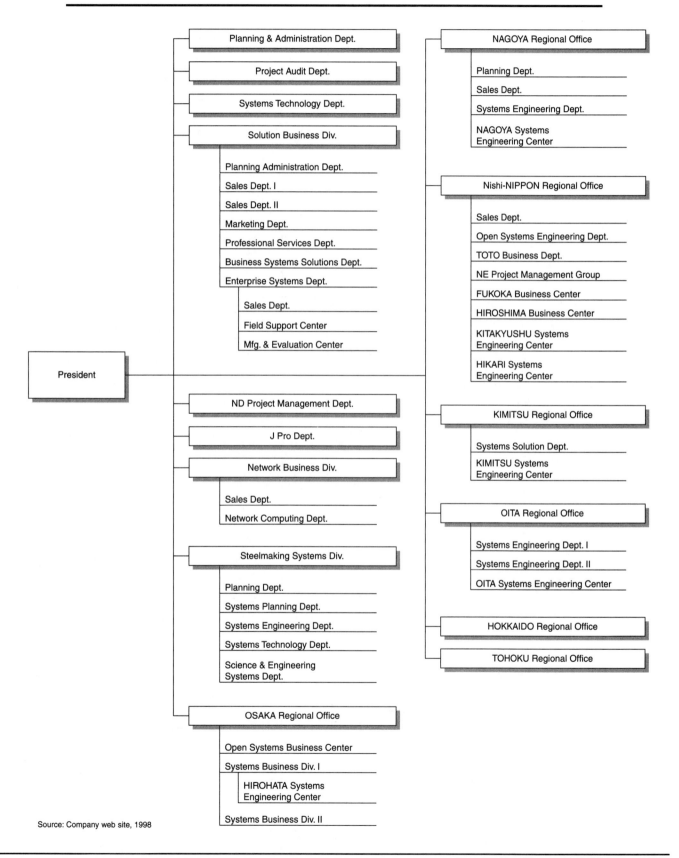

Source: Company web site, 1998

Nippon Telegraph and Telephone Corporation

The dominant player in Japan's telecommunications markets, NTT provides local, long-distance, cellular, & Internet services

2-3-1, Otemachi
Chiyoda-ku, Tokyo 163-8019, Japan
Phone: +81 03 5359-2122
Web: www.ntt.co.jp

Primary SIC: 4813—Telephone Communications,
Except Radiotelephone
Primary NAICS: 51331—Wired
Telecommunications Carriers

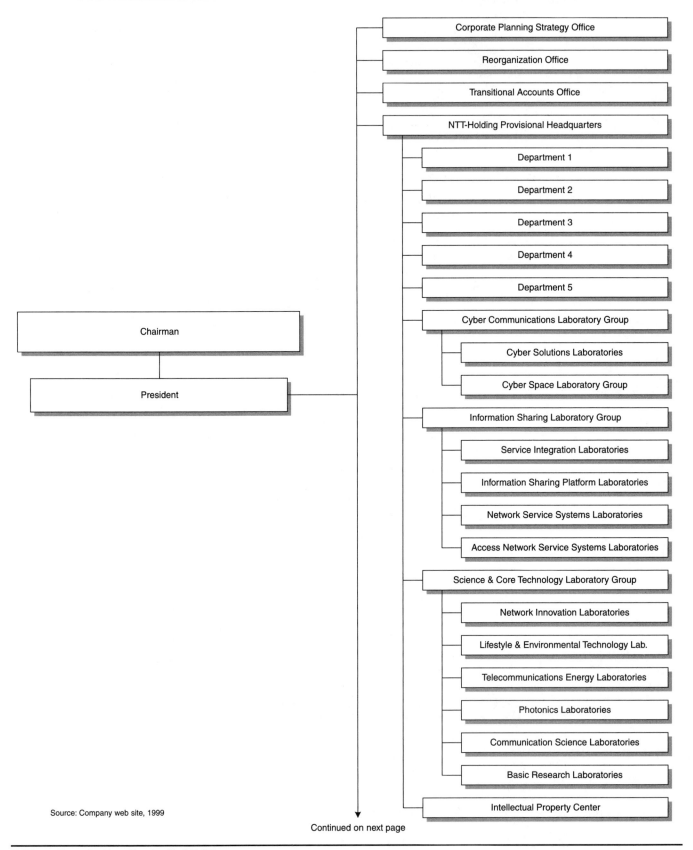

- Chairman
- President

- Corporate Planning Strategy Office
- Reorganization Office
- Transitional Accounts Office
- NTT-Holding Provisional Headquarters
  - Department 1
  - Department 2
  - Department 3
  - Department 4
  - Department 5
  - Cyber Communications Laboratory Group
    - Cyber Solutions Laboratories
    - Cyber Space Laboratory Group
  - Information Sharing Laboratory Group
    - Service Integration Laboratories
    - Information Sharing Platform Laboratories
    - Network Service Systems Laboratories
    - Access Network Service Systems Laboratories
  - Science & Core Technology Laboratory Group
    - Network Innovation Laboratories
    - Lifestyle & Environmental Technology Lab.
    - Telecommunications Energy Laboratories
    - Photonics Laboratories
    - Communication Science Laboratories
    - Basic Research Laboratories
  - Intellectual Property Center

Source: Company web site, 1999

Continued on next page

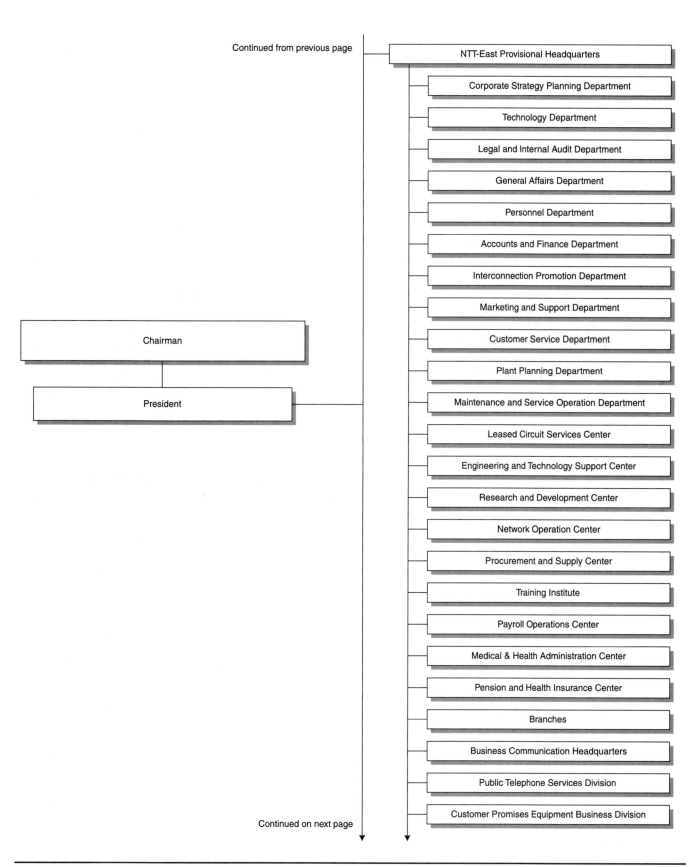

Continued from previous page

NTT-East Provisional Headquarters

Corporate Strategy Planning Department

Technology Department

Legal and Internal Audit Department

General Affairs Department

Personnel Department

Accounts and Finance Department

Interconnection Promotion Department

Marketing and Support Department

Customer Service Department

Plant Planning Department

Maintenance and Service Operation Department

Leased Circuit Services Center

Engineering and Technology Support Center

Research and Development Center

Network Operation Center

Procurement and Supply Center

Training Institute

Payroll Operations Center

Medical & Health Administration Center

Pension and Health Insurance Center

Branches

Business Communication Headquarters

Public Telephone Services Division

Customer Promises Equipment Business Division

Chairman

President

Continued on next page

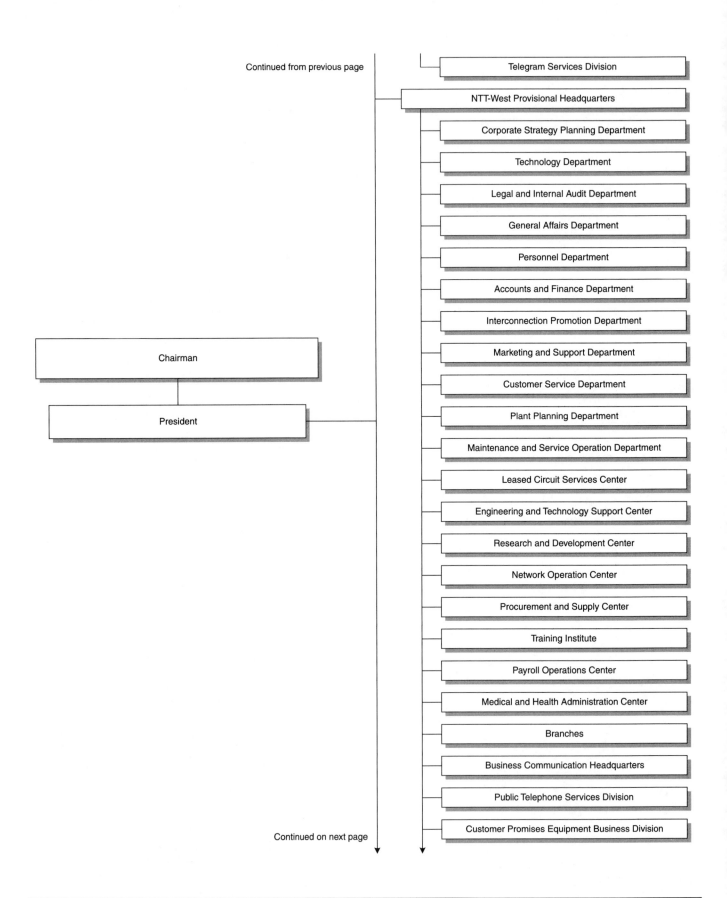

Continued from previous page

Telegram Services Division

NTT-West Provisional Headquarters

Corporate Strategy Planning Department

Technology Department

Legal and Internal Audit Department

General Affairs Department

Personnel Department

Accounts and Finance Department

Interconnection Promotion Department

Marketing and Support Department

Customer Service Department

Plant Planning Department

Maintenance and Service Operation Department

Leased Circuit Services Center

Engineering and Technology Support Center

Research and Development Center

Network Operation Center

Procurement and Supply Center

Training Institute

Payroll Operations Center

Medical and Health Administration Center

Branches

Business Communication Headquarters

Public Telephone Services Division

Customer Promises Equipment Business Division

Chairman

President

Continued on next page

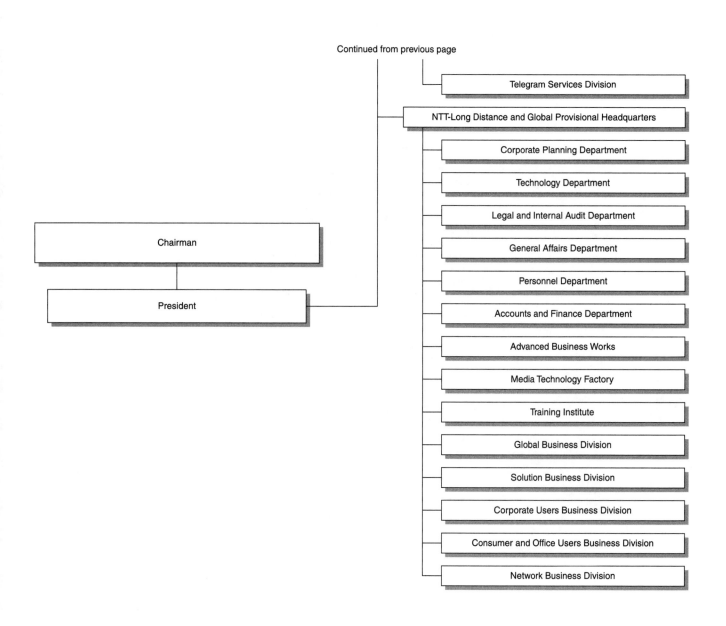

Continued from previous page

Telegram Services Division

NTT-Long Distance and Global Provisional Headquarters

Corporate Planning Department

Technology Department

Legal and Internal Audit Department

General Affairs Department

Personnel Department

Accounts and Finance Department

Advanced Business Works

Media Technology Factory

Training Institute

Global Business Division

Solution Business Division

Corporate Users Business Division

Consumer and Office Users Business Division

Network Business Division

Chairman

President

A major world pharmaceutical and bioscience firm formed through the 1996 merger of Ciba-Geigy and Sandoz Ltd.

Lichtstrasse 35
CH-4002 Basel, Switzerland
Phone: +41 61 324 8000 **Fax:** +41 61 321-0985
Web: www.novartis.com

Primary SIC: 2834—Pharmaceutical Preparations
Primary NAICS: 325412—Pharmaceutical
Preparation Mfg

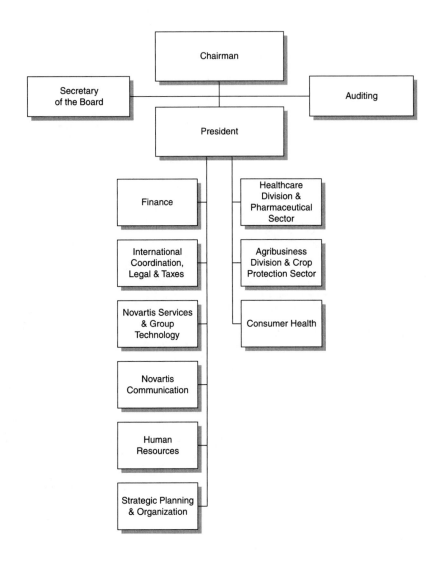

Source: Company web site, 1997

NTT Advanced Technology Corporation

The new technology development arm of Japan's leading telecommunications company

Crystal Park Bldg.
1-1-3 Gotenyama, Musashino-shi
Tokyo 180-8639, Japan
Phone: +81-422-49-1431 **Fax:** +81-422-41-0384

Primary SIC: 8731—Commercial Physical &
Biological Research
Primary NAICS: 54171—R&D in Physical,
Engineering & Life Sciences

Board of Directors

President

Auditors

Corporate Strategy/Planning Headquarters
- Business Management & Planning Dept.
- Business Supervision Dept.
- New Business Planning Dept.
- Corporate Information Systems Section

Sales & Marketing Headquarters
- Planning Dept.
  - Contract Dept.
- Sales Dept. 1
- Sales Dept. 2
- Sales Dept. 3
- Sales Dept. 4
- Sales Dept. 5
- Legal Affairs Dept.
- Big Project Promotion Teams

International Business Promotion Headquarters
- Business Promotion Dept.
- International Cooperation Dept.
- Technology/Export Administration Section
- ECS Test Bed Project Team

Public Relations & Advertising Dept.

Business Administration Headquarters
- Accounting & Finance Dept.
- Credit Assessment Dept.
- Purchasing Administration Dept.
- General Affairs Dept.

Personnel Dept.

Internal Audit Section

TIPS Business Promotion Headquarters
- Technology Transfer Business Division
  - Planning & Sales Dept.
  - Technology Development Dept.
- Intellectual Property Division
  - Planning & Sales Dept.
  - Research & Analysis Dept.
  - Administration Dept.
  - Information Dept.
  - Technology Research Station
- Scientist & Engineer Resource Center
- Scientist & Engineer Temporary Help Center

Multimedia Business Development Headquarters
- Planning Department
- Computer Networks Center
- Traffic Research Center
- HT Center
- Content Business Center
  - Education & Training Center
- Speech & Audio Technology Center
- ERP Business Center
- Mokikios-Business Office
- Cyber Business Product Team
- FEN Center Product Team

West Headquarters
- Planning & Sales Dept.
- Systems Dept.
- Technology Dept.

Continued on next page

Source: Company web site, 1998

Continued from previous page

Board of Directors

President

Auditors

Systems Solutions Business Headquarters
- Business Management & Planning Dept.
- Sales Dept.
- Laboratory Systems Section
- Quality Control Dept.
- Security Service Center

Network Integration Division
- Network & Systems Operations Dept.
- Communications Service Dept.
- Network Technology Dept.

Systems Integration Division
- Systems Integration Dept.
- Business Systems Dept.
- Network Products Dept.

Service Systems Division
- Information Systems Technology Dept.
- Natural Language Processing Technology Dept.

Visual Media Systems Division
- Business Management and Planning Dept.
- Sales Dept.
- Quality Control Dept.
- Image Processing Technology Dept.
- Visual Communications Technology Dept.

Access Networks Business Headquarters

Wireless Communications Division
- Planning and Sales Dept.
- Quality Control Dept.
- Wireless Systems Development Dept.
- Mobile Systems Technology Dept.
- Wireless Multimedia Technology Dept.
- High-Speed Wireless Access Technology Dept.
- Mobile Radio Wave Technology Dept.
- Radio Path Design Technology Dept.
- EMC Center

Access Systems Division
- Planning and Sales Dept.
- Field Systems Technology Dept.
- Management Software Technology Dept.

Core Networks Business Headquarters
- Business Management & Planning Dept.
- Sales Dept.
- Business Solutions Dept.
- Quality Control Dept.

Communications Software Division
- Systems Technology Dept. 1
- Systems Technology Dept. 2
- Systems Technology Dept. 3
- Systems Technology Dept. 4
- Systems Technology Dept. 5

Network Systems Division
- SCN Systems Dept.
- Broadband Communications Systems Dept.
- Node Systems Technology Dept.
- Telecommunications Business Center

Transport Networks Division
- Systems Technology Dept.
- Applied Communications Technology Dept.

Leading-Edge Key Technology Business Headquarters
- Quality Control Dept.

Innovative Technology Business Division
- Planning and Sales Dept.
- Super Repellent Technology Dept.
- Applied Electronics Technology Dept.
- Device Development Support
  - Materials Technology Dept.
  - Device Technology Dept.
- Security Management Service Dept.

Fiber-Optics Division
- Planning and Sales Dept.
- Optical Interconnections Technology Dept.
- Photonic Packaging Technology Dept.

CAD Systems Division
- Sales Dept. 1
- Sales Dept. 2
- Technical Support Dept.
- Marketing Dept.

Precision Technology Division
- Planning and Sales Dept.
- X-ray Mask & Precision Technology Dept.

Materials Development & Analytical Technology Ctr.
- Planning and Sales Dept.
- Materials Analytical Technology Dept.
  - Atsugi Material Analysis Center
- New Materials Development Dept.
- Environmental Safety Technology Dept.

Nuclear Research Centre (SCK CEN)

A major European nonprofit institute for nuclear energy research

Hermann Debrouxlaan 40-42
B-1160 Brussels, Belgium
Phone: +32-14-661-1951 **Fax:** +32-14-661-1958
Web: hades.sckcen.be

Primary SIC: 8733—Noncommercial
Research Organizations
Primary NAICS: 54171—R&D in Physical,
Engineering & Life Sciences

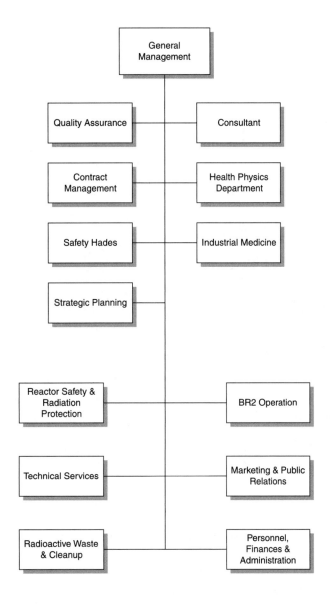

Source: Organization web site, 1999

Oak Ridge National Laboratory

A scientific research facility operated by Lockheed Martin for U.S. Energy Dept. projects

P.O. Box 2008
Oak Ridge, TN 37831-6266
Phone: (423) 574-4163
Web: www.ornl.gov

Primary SIC: 8733—Noncommercial
Research Organizations
Primary NAICS: 54171—R&D in Physical,
Engineering & Life Sciences

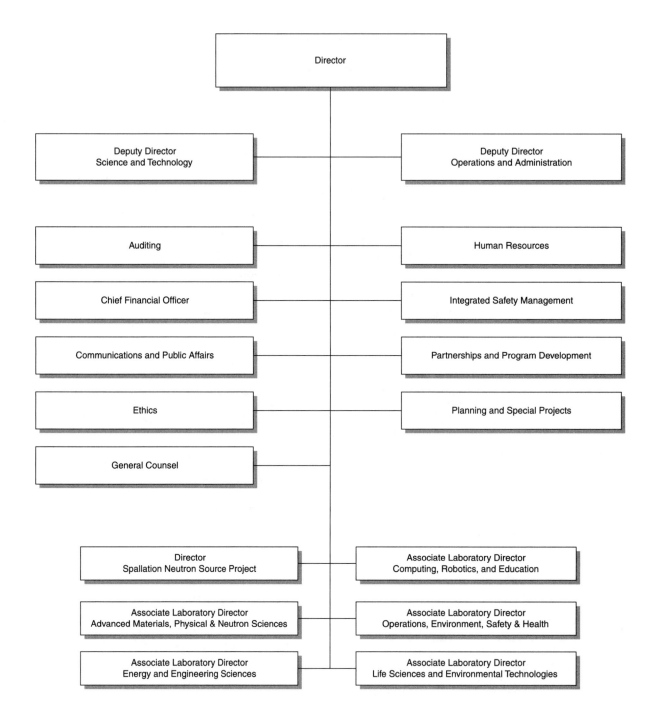

Source: Organization web site, 1999

Online Data Systems, Inc.

A small developer of business niche software for apparel manufacturers and distributors

1621 N. Cedar Crest Blvd., Ste. 101
Allentown, PA 18104-2350
Phone: (610) 433-6511 **Fax:** (610) 433-8040
Web: www.odssoftware.com

Primary SIC: 7371—Computer Programming Services
Primary NAICS: 541511—Custom Computer
Programming Services

Source: Company web site, 1999

Orient Overseas Container Line Ltd.

This container-ship fleet operator is part of publicly traded Orient Overseas Intl. Ltd. of Hong Kong

31/F, Harbour Centre
25 Harbour Road, Wanchai, Hong Kong, China
Phone: (852) 28333888 **Fax:** (852) 25318234
Web: www.oocl.com

Primary SIC: 4412—Deep Sea Foreign
Transportation of Freight
Primary NAICS: 483111—Deep
Sea Freight Transportation

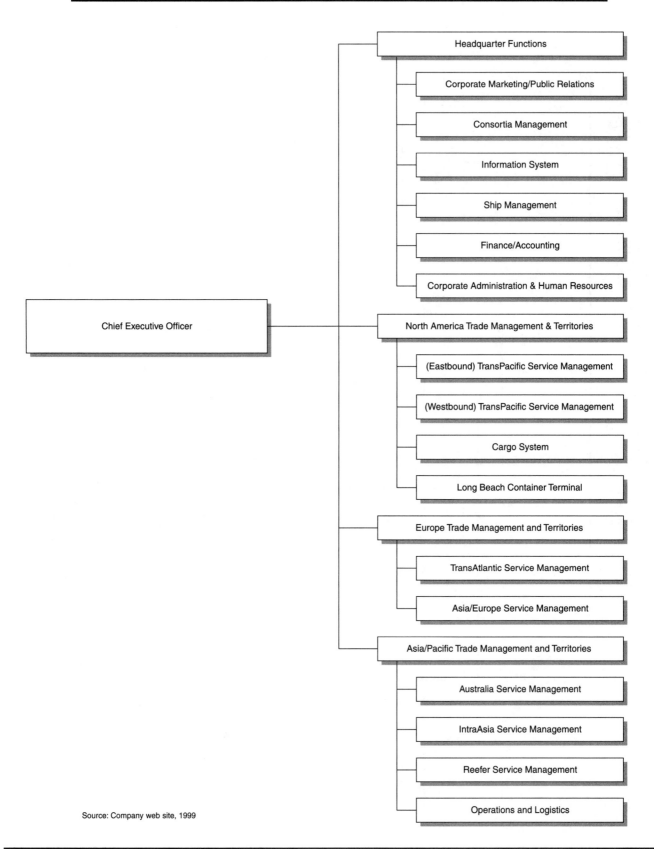

Source: Company web site, 1999

Pediatric AIDS Clinical Trials Group

An internationally recognized research coalition that develops treatments for children with HIV

6101 Executive Blvd., Ste. 350
Rockville, MD 20852
Phone: (301) 230-3150 **Fax:** (301) 770-9276
Web: pactg.s-3.com

Primary SIC: 8733—Noncommercial
Research Organizations
Primary NAICS: 54171—R&D in Physical,
Engineering & Life Sciences

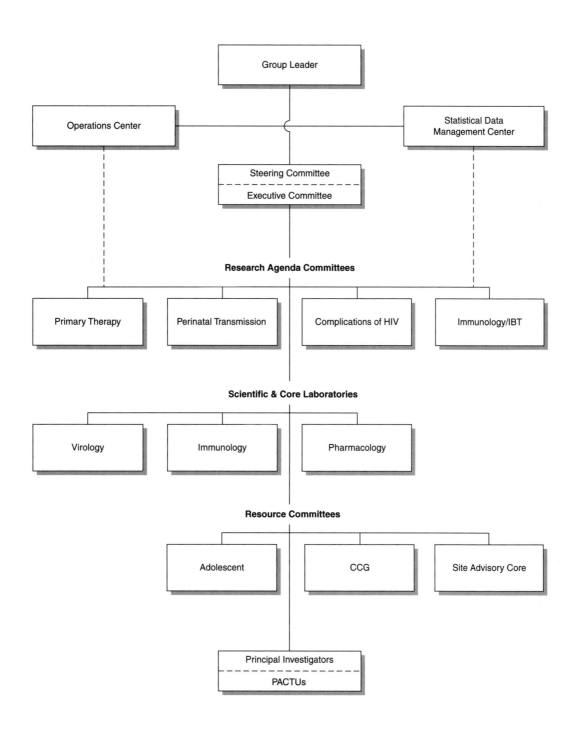

Source: Organization web site, 1999

Pewabic Pottery

A small century-old nonprofit art museum and arts education center

10125 E. Jefferson Ave.
Detroit, MI 48214
Phone: (313) 822-0954 **Fax:** (313) 822-6266
Web: www.pewabic.com

Primary SIC: 8412—Museums & Art Galleries
Primary NAICS: 71211—Museums
E-mail: pewabic@pewabic.com

Board of Trustees

Executive Director

- Museum Archives
- Director, Development/Membership
  - Gallery Sales
  - Gallery Staffing
- Director, Education
  - Studio Assistant
  - **Education & Community Outreach Team**
    - Teachers
    - Outreach
    - Workshops
    - Artist-in-Residence
- Designers
- Director, Business Operations
  - Bookeeper
  - **Customer Service Team**
    - Customer Service Reps.
    - Shipping/Receiving

Director, Operations
- Facility Maintenance
- Management Information Systems
- **Production Team**
  - Floor Supervisor
  - Glazier
  - Kilns/Fabrication
  - Master Mold Maker
  - Vessel Production Supervisor
  - Thrower

Source: Company, 1998

Pfizer Inc.

One of the world's top 5 pharmaceutical makers, Pfizer earns a third of its sales from cardiovascular drugs

235 E. 42nd St.
New York, NY 10017-5755
Phone: (212) 573-2323
Web: www.pfizer.com

Primary SIC: 2834—Pharmaceutical Preparations
Primary NAICS: 325412—Pharmaceutical Preparation Mfg

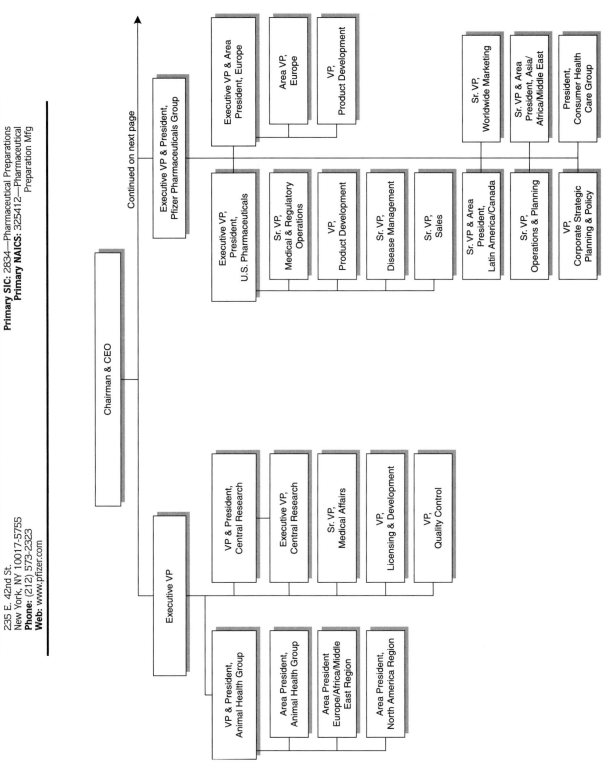

Continued on next page

Source: Company and revisions by the editors, 1998

Pfizer Inc. (cont.)

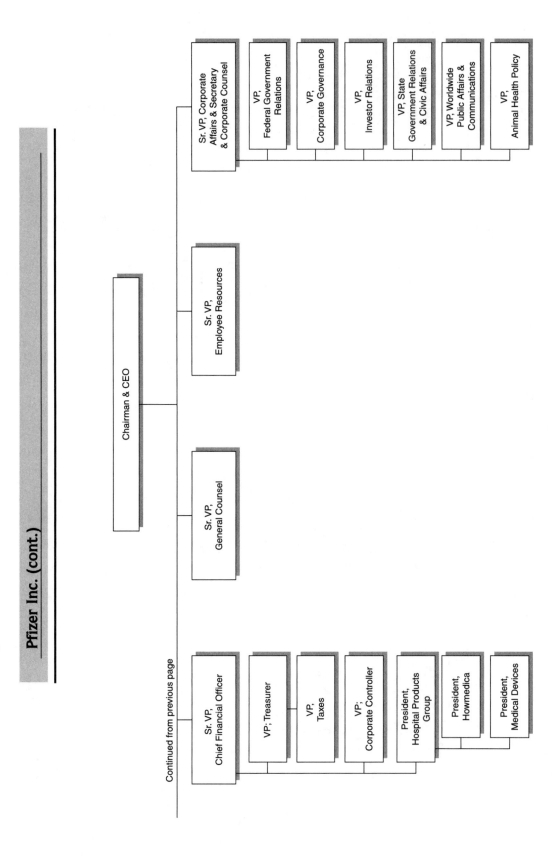

Continued from previous page

Chairman & CEO

Sr. VP, Employee Resources

Sr. VP, General Counsel

Sr. VP, Corporate Affairs & Secretary & Corporate Counsel

VP, Federal Government Relations

VP, Corporate Governance

VP, Investor Relations

VP, State Government Relations & Civic Affairs

VP, Worldwide Public Affairs & Communications

VP, Animal Health Policy

Sr. VP, Chief Financial Officer

VP, Treasurer

VP, Taxes

VP, Corporate Controller

President, Hospital Products Group

President, Howmedica

President, Medical Devices

Pharmaceutical Research & Manufacturers of America

The leading trade group for the U.S. pharmaceutical industry

1100 15th St., N.W.
Washington, DC 20005
Phone: (202) 835-3400
Web: www.phrma.org

Primary SIC: 8611—Business Associations
Primary NAICS: 81391—Business Associations

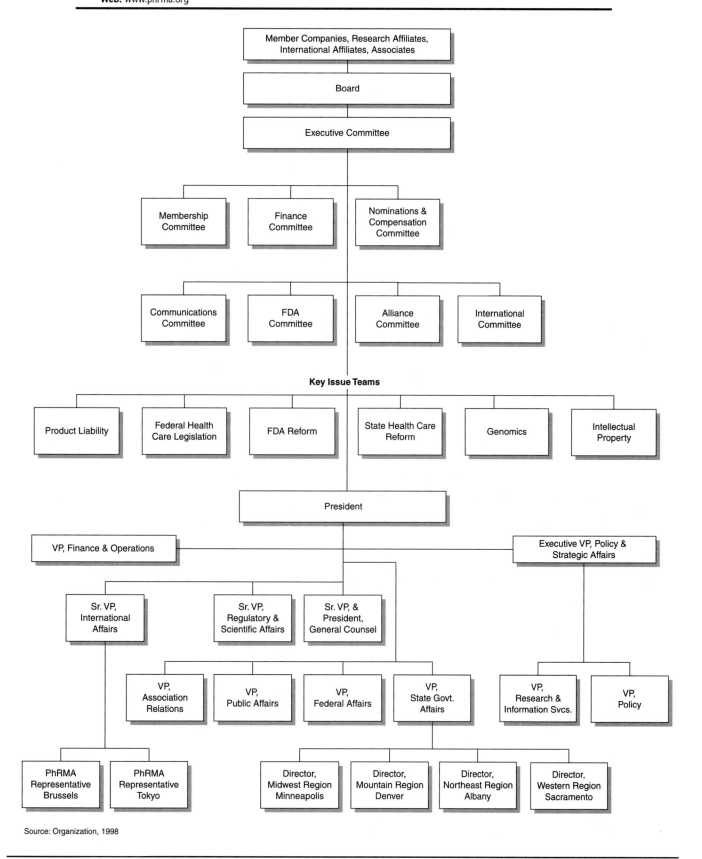

Source: Organization, 1998

Phillips Petroleum Company

This oil and natural gas company is active in all phases of production and marketing, for total sales of $11.8 billion in 1998

6-AI Phillips Bldg.
Bartlesville, OK 74004
Phone: (918) 661-6600 **Fax:** (918) 661-7636
Web: www.phillips66.com

Primary SIC: 2911—Petroleum Refining
Primary NAICS: 32411—Petroleum Refineries

```
                          Chairman & CEO

                          President & COO

    Executive VP, HR,      Executive VP,       Executive VP,
    Capital Budgeting      Upstream            Downstream


Senior VP,        Senior VP,        Senior VP, Upstream                          Senior VP,
Downstream Technology   Gas Processing &   Technology & Project    Senior VP & CFO    Chemicals & Plastics
& Project Development    Marketing         Development

        Senior VP &         VP,                 VP,                 VP,
        General Counsel     Health, Environment &   Strategic Planning   Investor & Public
                            Safety                                   Relations


VP,                               VP,                 VP,
Marketing &       VP & Controller   Exploration & Production   Exploration & Production   VP & Treasurer
Transportation                      Eurasia             Americas

VP,                               VP,                 VP,
Worldwide Exploration   VP,          Specialty Chemicals &    Liquefied Natural Gas,    Secretary
                        Olefins and Polyolefins   Specialty Plastics   Gas & Coal
```

Source: Company, 1999

Plante and Moran, LLP

The 2nd-largest accounting firm in the north-central U.S., Plante and Moran has annual revenues in excess of $100 million

27400 Northwestern Hwy.
P.O. Box 307
Southfield, MI 48037-0307
Phone: (810) 352-2500 **Fax:** (810) 352-0018

Primary SIC: 8721—Accounting, Auditing, & Bookkeeping Services
Primary NAICS: 541211—Offices of Certified Public Accountants

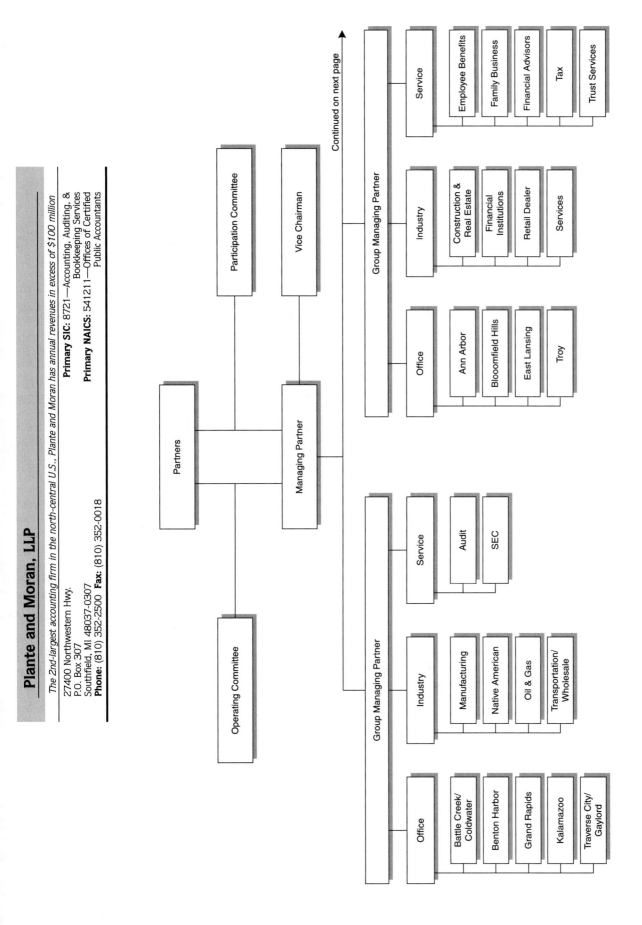

Continued on next page

Source: Company, 1999

Plante and Moran, LLP (cont.)

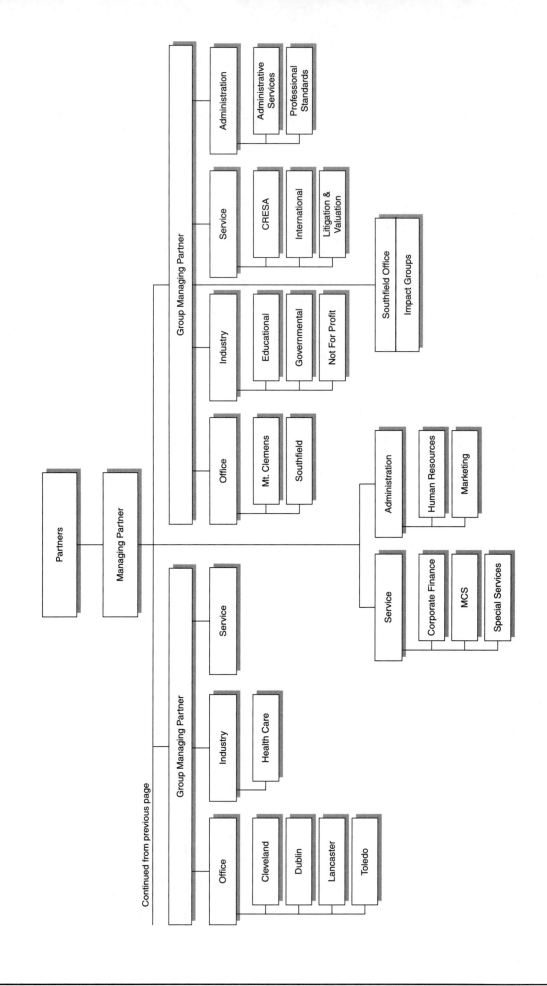

PPA Bank S.A.

A commercial bank offering account services, credit cards, and investment services to businesses and individuals

ul. K. Kordylewskiego 11
PL-31-547 Kraków, Poland
Phone: +48 12 618 3333 **Fax:** +48 12 618 3344
Web: www.ppabank.com.pl

Primary SIC: 6021—National Commercial Banks
Primary NAICS: 52211—Commercial Banking

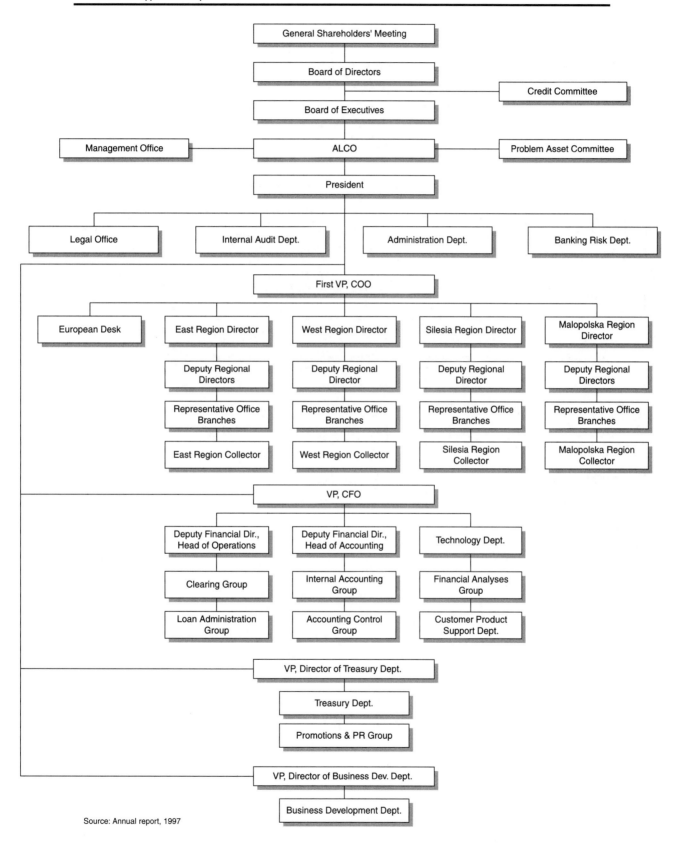

PPG Industries, Inc.

A leader in the paints and coatings industry, PPG still maintains its namesake glass product line

1 PPG Place
Pittsburgh, PA 15272
Phone: (412) 434-3131
Web: www.ppg.com

Primary SIC: 2851—Paints, Varnishes, Lacquers,
Enamels, & Allied Products
Primary NAICS: 32551—Paint & Coating Mfg

REORGANIZATION Part 1 (1996)
For additional details on the restructuring
see profiles starting on page 331

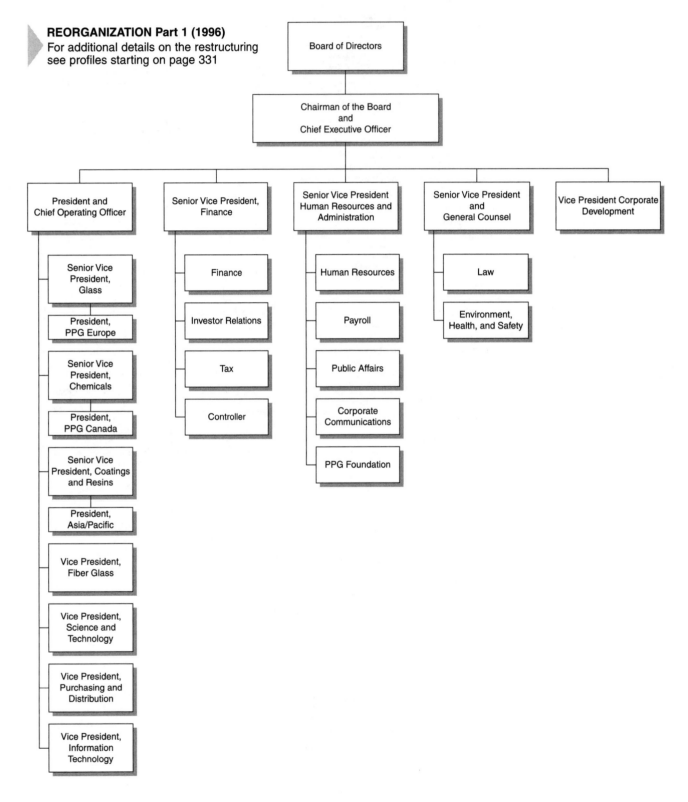

Source: Company, 1999

REORGANIZATION Part 2 (1999)
For additional details on the restructuring
see profiles starting on page 331

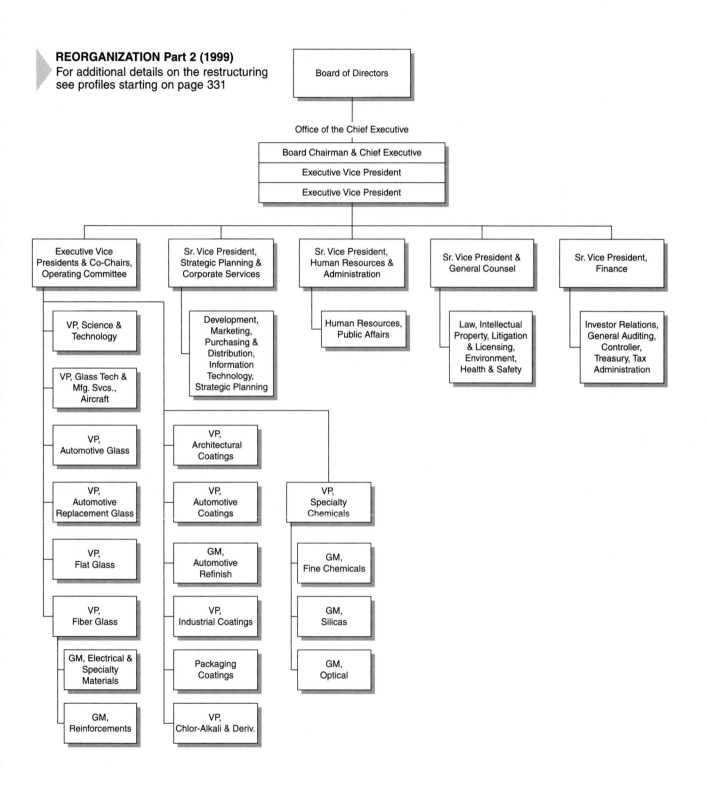

Board of Directors

Office of the Chief Executive

Board Chairman & Chief Executive

Executive Vice President

Executive Vice President

Executive Vice Presidents & Co-Chairs, Operating Committee

Sr. Vice President, Strategic Planning & Corporate Services

Sr. Vice President, Human Resources & Administration

Sr. Vice President & General Counsel

Sr. Vice President, Finance

VP, Science & Technology

VP, Glass Tech & Mfg. Svcs., Aircraft

VP, Automotive Glass

VP, Automotive Replacement Glass

VP, Flat Glass

VP, Fiber Glass

GM, Electrical & Specialty Materials

GM, Reinforcements

Development, Marketing, Purchasing & Distribution, Information Technology, Strategic Planning

VP, Architectural Coatings

VP, Automotive Coatings

GM, Automotive Refinish

VP, Industrial Coatings

Packaging Coatings

VP, Chlor-Alkali & Deriv.

VP, Specialty Chemicals

GM, Fine Chemicals

GM, Silicas

GM, Optical

Human Resources, Public Affairs

Law, Intellectual Property, Litigation & Licensing, Environment, Health & Safety

Investor Relations, General Auditing, Controller, Treasury, Tax Administration

Quality Systems Incorporated

An information systems designer and integrator, QSI is a wholly owned subsidiary of Marconi North America, Inc.

8201 Greensboro Dr., Ste. 1200
McLean, VA 22102
Phone: (703) 847-5820 **Fax:** (703) 847-5880
Web: www.qsi.com

Primary SIC: 7373—Computer Integrated Systems Design
Primary NAICS: 541512—Computer Systems Design Services

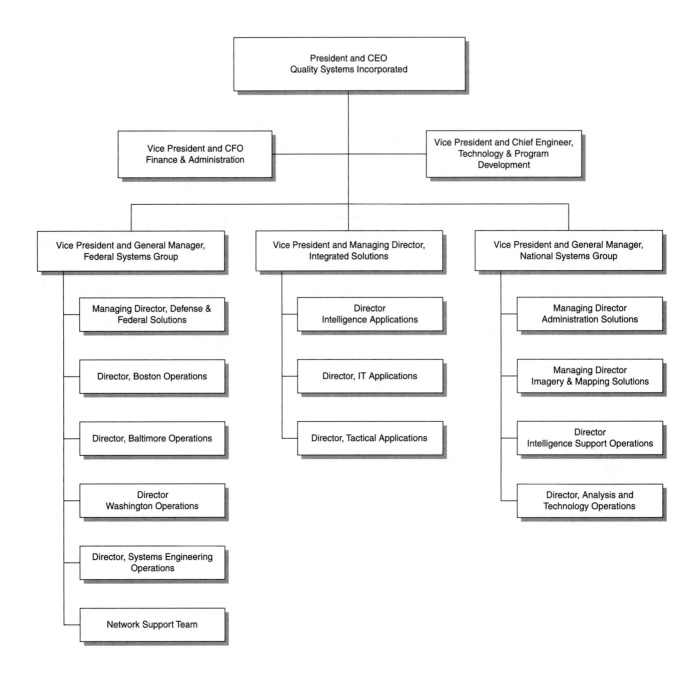

President and CEO
Quality Systems Incorporated

Vice President and CFO
Finance & Administration

Vice President and Chief Engineer,
Technology & Program Development

Vice President and General Manager,
Federal Systems Group

Vice President and Managing Director,
Integrated Solutions

Vice President and General Manager,
National Systems Group

Managing Director, Defense &
Federal Solutions

Director, Boston Operations

Director, Baltimore Operations

Director
Washington Operations

Director, Systems Engineering
Operations

Network Support Team

Director
Intelligence Applications

Director, IT Applications

Director, Tactical Applications

Managing Director
Administration Solutions

Managing Director
Imagery & Mapping Solutions

Director
Intelligence Support Operations

Director, Analysis and
Technology Operations

Source: Company web site, 1997

Quantum Color Graphics, L.L.C.

A mid-size prepress service and printer of corporate brochures, high-end marketing pieces, and other specialty publications

6511 W. Oakton St.
Morton Grove, IL 60053
Phone: (847) 967-3600 **Fax:** (847) 967-3610
Web: www.quantumcolor.com

Primary SIC: 2752—Commercial Printing, Lithographic
Primary NAICS: 323110—Commercial Lithographic Printing
E-mail: info@quantumcolor.com

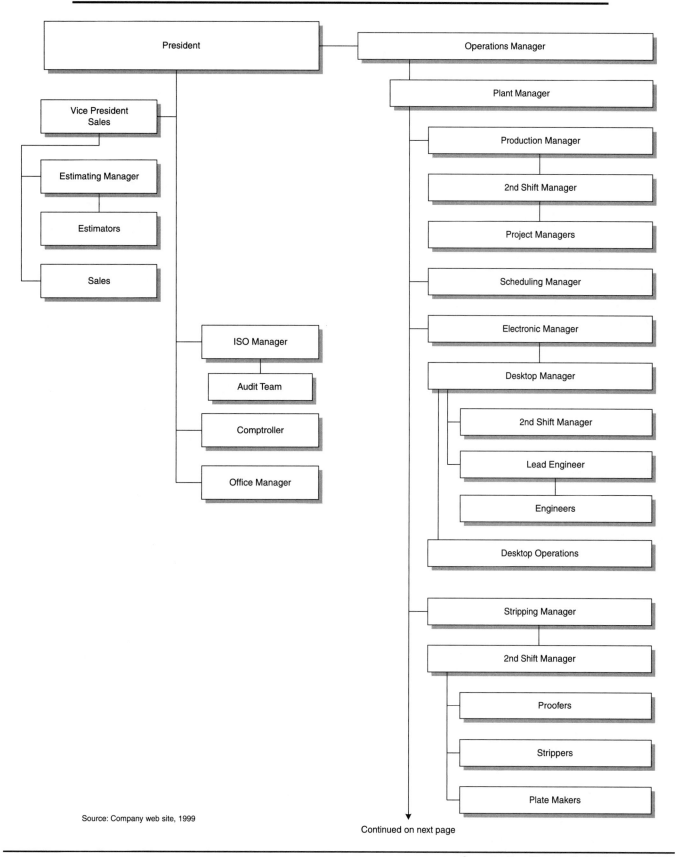

Source: Company web site, 1999

Continued on next page

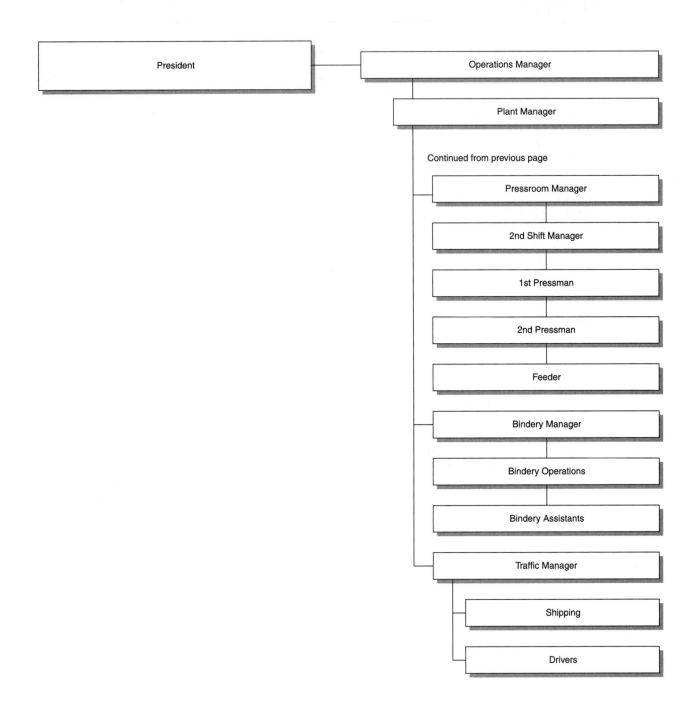

Continued from previous page

Raisio Group plc

This publicly traded Finnish company makes food ingredients, processed foods, and chemicals

P.O. Box 101
FIN-21201 Raisio, Finland
Phone: +358 2 434 2315
Web: www.raisiogroup.com

Primary SIC: 2076—Vegetable Oil Mills,
Except Corn, Cottonseed, & Soybeans
Primary NAICS: 311225—Fats
& Oils Refining & Blending

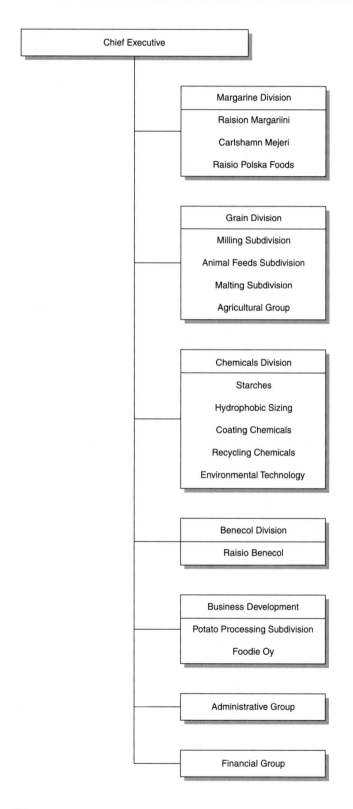

Source: Annual report, 1998

Regia Holdinggesellschaft

With sales above $50 million, Regia is a medium-size printing and packaging vendor for consumer and commercial goods

Dammweg 39
CH-5001 Aarau, Switzerland
Phone: +41-062 834-1300 **Fax:** +41-062 834-1353
Web: www.regia.ch

Primary SIC: 2752—Commercial Printing, Lithographic
Primary NAICS: 323110—Commercial
Lithographic Printing
E-mail: info@regia.ch

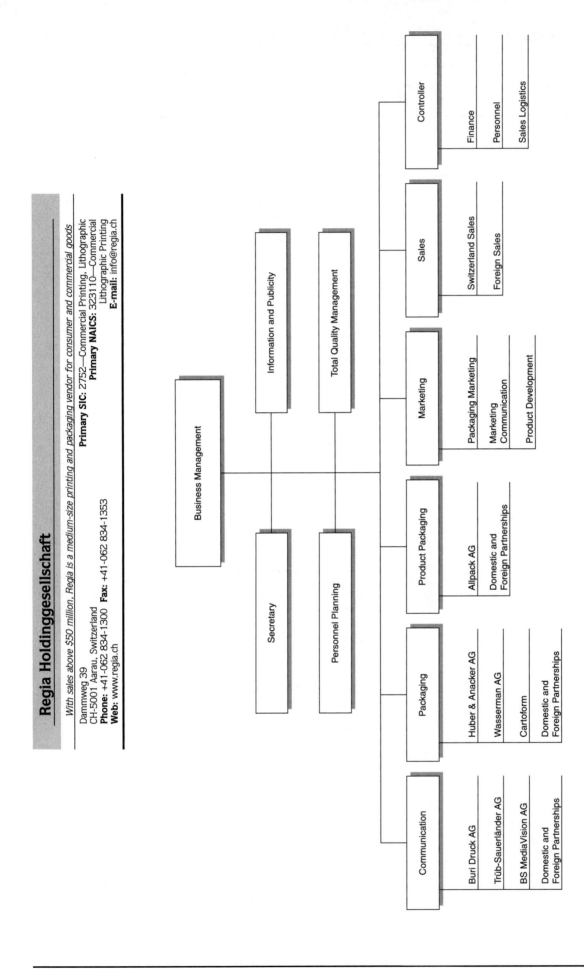

Source: Company web site (translated by the editors), 1999

Republic Parking System

Republic operates 350 parking facilities in the United States and various other countries

Republic Centre, Ste. 2000
Chattanooga, TN 37450
Phone: (423) 756-2771 **Fax:** (423) 265-5728
Web: www.republicparking.com

Primary SIC: 7521—Automobile Parking
Primary NAICS: 81293—Parking Lots & Garages
E-mail: info@republicparking.com

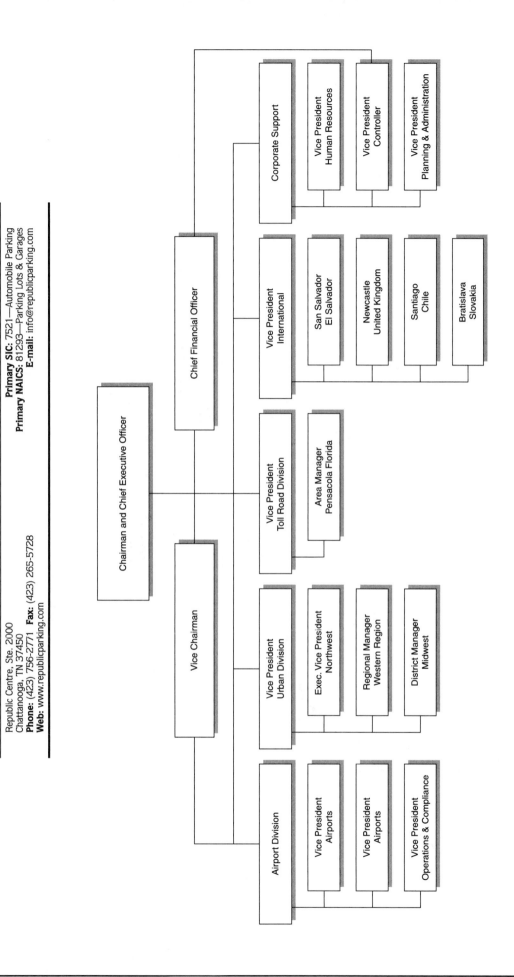

Reuters Group PLC

The world's largest news-gathering organization

85 Fleet St.
London EC4P 4AJ, United Kingdom
Phone: +44 171 250 1122
Web: www.reuters.com

Primary SIC: 7383—News Syndicates
Primary NAICS: 51411—News Syndicates

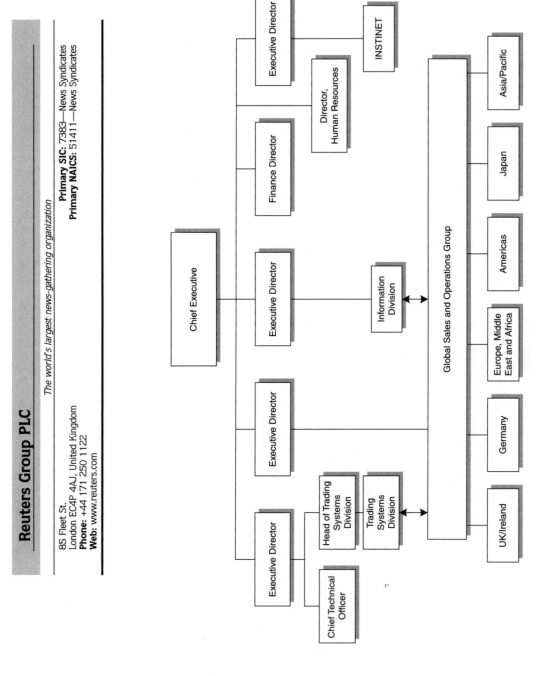

Source: Company web site, 1999

Rhône-Poulenc S.A.

A French chemical giant specializing in pharmaceuticals and life sciences

25, quai Paul-Doumer
F-92408 Courbevoie Cedex, France
Phone: +33 1 47 68 12 34 **Fax:** +33 1 47 68 19 11
Web: www.rhone-poulenc.com

Primary SIC: 2834—Pharmaceutical Preparations
Primary NAICS: 325412—Pharmaceutical
Preparation Mfg

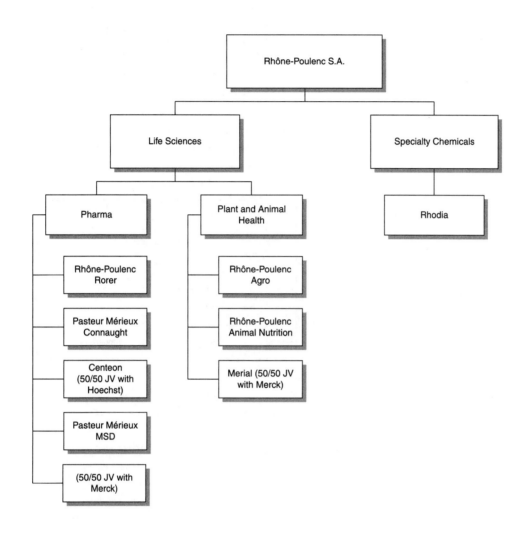

Source: Company web site, 1999

Rohm Co., Ltd.

A large manufacturer of integrated circuits and other electronic components

21, Saiin Mizosaki-cho
Ukyo-ku, Kyoto 615, Japan
Phone: +81 075 311-2121 **Fax:** +81 075 315-0172
Web: www.rohm.co.jp

Primary SIC: 3679—Electronic Components, NEC
Primary NAICS: 334418—Printed Circuit Assembly
(Electronic Assembly) Mfg

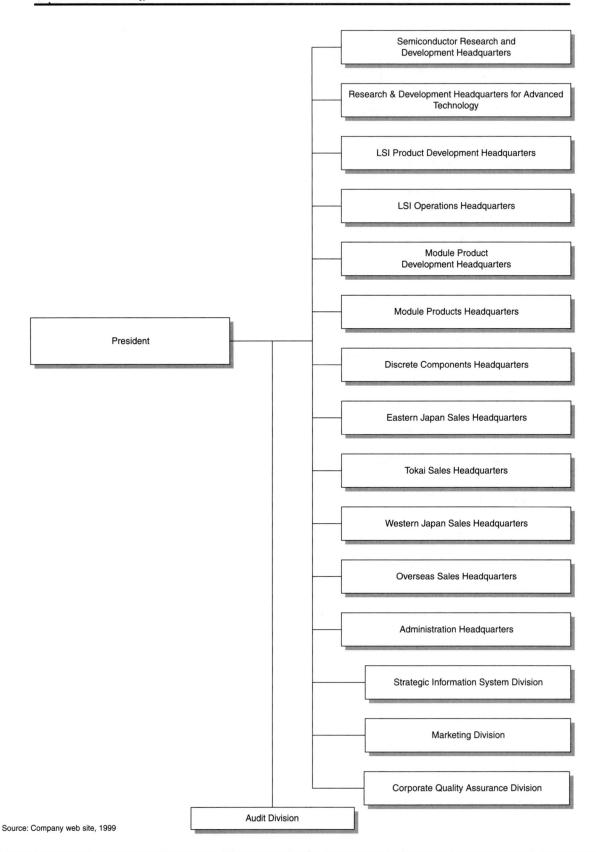

Source: Company web site, 1999

Rohner AG

A mid-size manufacturer of fine chemicals and textile dyes, mostly for export

Gempenstr. 6
CH-4133 Pratteln, Switzerland
Phone: +41 61 825 1111 **Fax:** +41 61 825-1271
Web: www.rohnerag.ch

Primary SIC: 2816—Inorganic Pigments
Primary NAICS: 325131—Inorganic Dye & Pigment Mfg
E-mail: rohner@rohnerag.ch

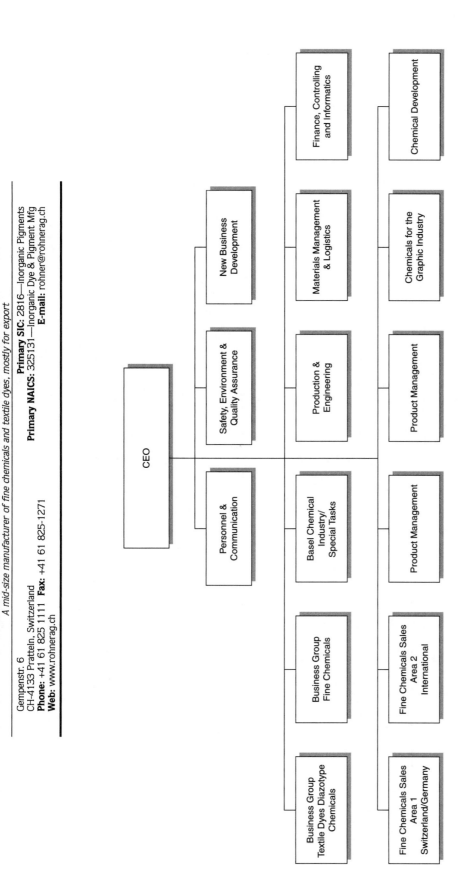

Source: Company web site, 1999

San Miguel Corporation

A leading brewery, San Miguel claims to be southeast Asia's largest food, beverage, and packaging concern

40 San Miguel Ave.
Mandaluyong City 1550, Metro Manila, Philippines
Phone: +63-2-632-3000 **Fax:** +63-2-632-3099
Web: www.sanmiguel.com.ph

Primary SIC: 2082—Malt Beverages
Primary NAICS: 31212—Breweries

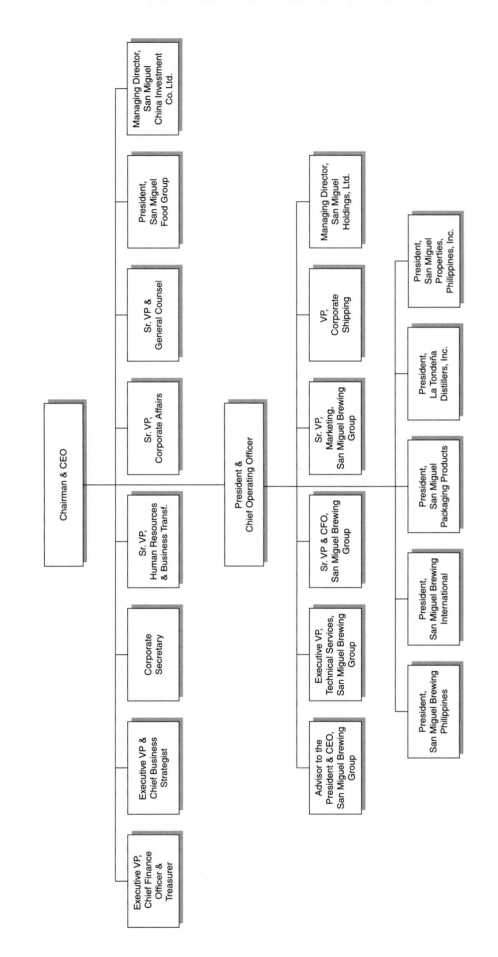

Source: Company and revisions by the editors, 1997

SANYO Electric Co., Ltd.

This electronics manufacturer's products range from audio/video devices to computers and cellular phones

5-5 Keihan Hondori 2-chome
Moriguchi, Osaka 570-8677, Japan
Phone: +81 06 6991-1181 **Fax:** +81 06 6991-6566
Web: www.sanyo.co.jp

Primary SIC: 3651—Household Audio & Video Equipment
Primary NAICS: 33431—Audio & Video Equipment Mfg

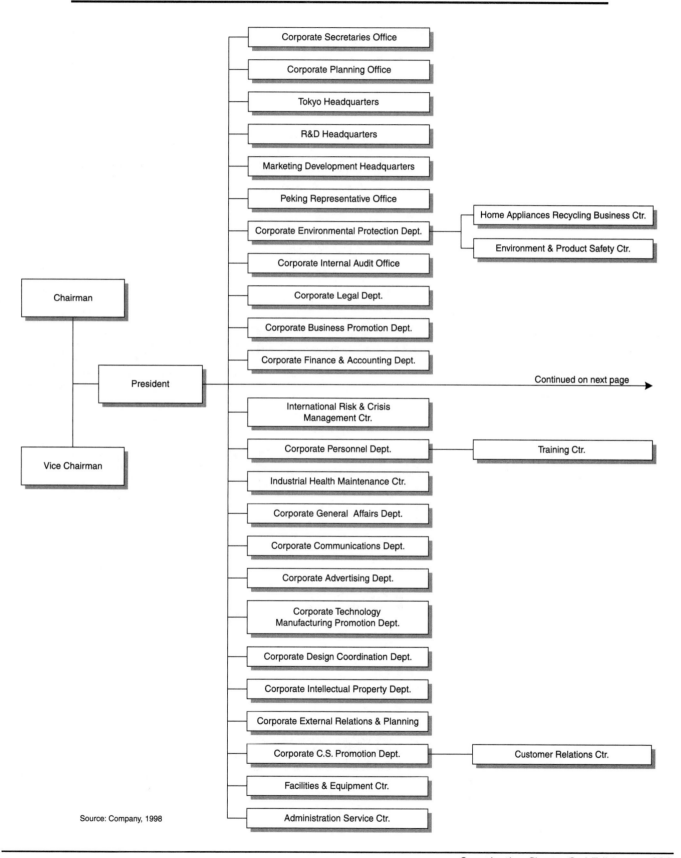

Continued on next page →

Source: Company, 1998

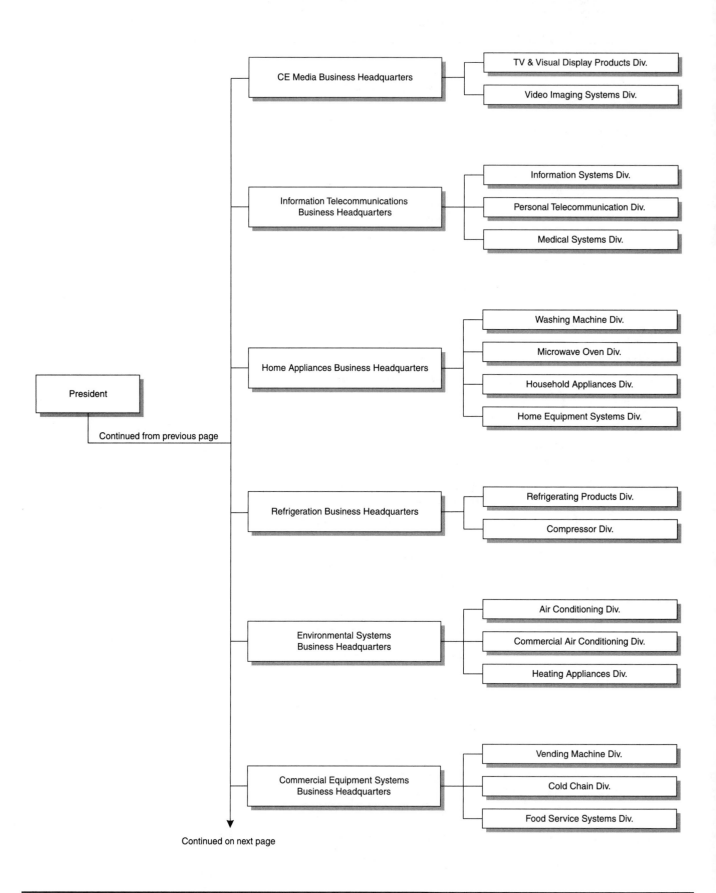

President

Continued from previous page

CE Media Business Headquarters
- TV & Visual Display Products Div.
- Video Imaging Systems Div.

Information Telecommunications Business Headquarters
- Information Systems Div.
- Personal Telecommunication Div.
- Medical Systems Div.

Home Appliances Business Headquarters
- Washing Machine Div.
- Microwave Oven Div.
- Household Appliances Div.
- Home Equipment Systems Div.

Refrigeration Business Headquarters
- Refrigerating Products Div.
- Compressor Div.

Environmental Systems Business Headquarters
- Air Conditioning Div.
- Commercial Air Conditioning Div.
- Heating Appliances Div.

Commercial Equipment Systems Business Headquarters
- Vending Machine Div.
- Cold Chain Div.
- Food Service Systems Div.

Continued on next page

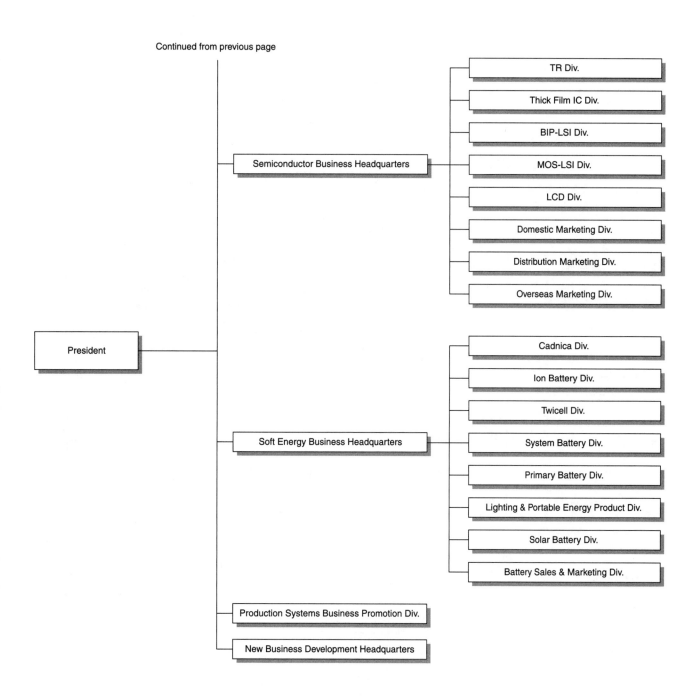

Continued from previous page

President

Semiconductor Business Headquarters
- TR Div.
- Thick Film IC Div.
- BIP-LSI Div.
- MOS-LSI Div.
- LCD Div.
- Domestic Marketing Div.
- Distribution Marketing Div.
- Overseas Marketing Div.

Soft Energy Business Headquarters
- Cadnica Div.
- Ion Battery Div.
- Twicell Div.
- System Battery Div.
- Primary Battery Div.
- Lighting & Portable Energy Product Div.
- Solar Battery Div.
- Battery Sales & Marketing Div.

Production Systems Business Promotion Div.

New Business Development Headquarters

Sanyo Shinpan Finance Co., Ltd.

A regional lender serving primarily Japan's consumer and small business loan markets

1-8, Kamigofuku-machi
Hakata-ku, Fukuoka, Japan
Phone: +81 092-271-3448 **Fax:** +81 092-291-0404
Web: www.sanyo-shinpan.co.jp

Primary SIC: 6162—Mortgage Bankers
Loan Correspondents
Primary NAICS: 522292—Real Estate Credit
E-mail: pubrelat@sanyo-shinpan.co.jp

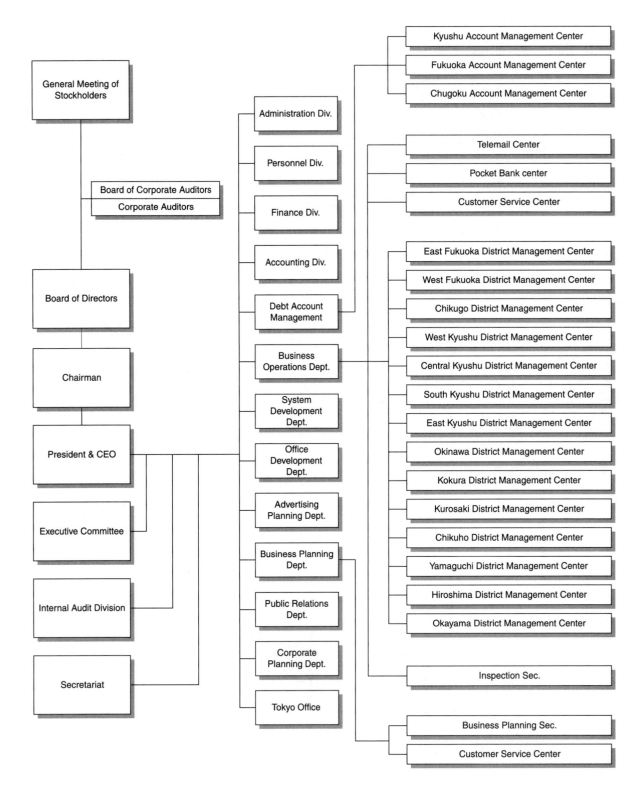

Source: Annual report, 1998

SaskTel International

The international operating subsidiary of Saskatchewan's leading telecommunications carrier

2121 Saskatchewan Drive
Regina, SK S4P 3Y2 Canada
Phone: (306) 777-4509 **Fax:** (306) 359-7475
Web: www.sasktel-international.com

Primary SIC: 4813—Telephone Communications,
Except Radiotelephone
Primary NAICS: 51331—Wired
Telecommunications Carriers

Organizational Chart

- **President, SaskTel International**
  - **Vice President, Marketing & Sales-Systems**
    - Assistant Vice President, Marketing & Sales
    - Authorized Agent
    - Director of Tech Support Systems & Sales
    - Director of Tech Support Systems & Sales
    - Assistant Vice President, Marketing & Sales
    - Assistant Vice President, Marketing & Sales
  - **Vice President, Marketing & Sales**
    - Director of Human Resources
    - Asst. Vice President, Marketing & Sales
    - Director of Telecom Marketing-SE Asia & Pacific Rim
    - Managing Director of Africa
    - Asst. Vice President, Marketing & Sales
  - **Vice President, Finance**
    - Director of Logistics & Administration
    - Director of Operations & Finance
    - Accounting Manager Support
  - **Vice President, Business Operations**
    - Director of Engineering Svcs.
    - Director of Engineering Svcs.
    - Managing Director of Africa
      - Finance Manager, Philippines
        - Administration Philippines
        - Administration Philippines
      - Director of Engineering Svcs., Philippines
        - Field Engineering, Philippines
    - Projects Engineer
      - Projects Director
      - Field Advisor
  - **Executive Vice President, Investments**
    - Administrative Support
    - Chief Technology Officer, Saturn Communications New Zealand
    - Manager of Network Operations, Saturn Communications
    - Manager of Planning & Provisioning, Saturn Communications
  - **Vice President, Software Business Operations**
    - Director of Systems & MICA/SICA Operations
    - Director of Tech Support Systems
    - Director of Tech Support Systems
  - **Administrative Services Manager**
    - Administrative Support
    - Administrative Support
    - Administrative Support

SCHEMA Konsult, Inc.

One of the Philippines' largest engineering and construction consulting firms

7/F JMT Corporate Condominium, ADB Avenue
Ortigas Complex, Pasig City, Philippines
Phone: +63-2-634-5778 **Fax:** +63-2-632-0740
Web: www.schemakon.com

Primary SIC: 8711—Engineering Services
Primary NAICS: 54133—Engineering Services

Board of Directors

President

Vice President,
Cebu Branch

Associate, Sr. Engineers,
Jr. Engineers, CADD Operators,
and Draftsmen

Vice President,
Feasibility Study

Principals/Heads
- Structural Engineering Dept.
- Architectural Dept.
- Electrical Engineering Dept.
- Mechanical Engineering Dept.
- Sanitary & Water
  Resources Engineering Dept.
- Environmental and
  Infrastructure Planning Dept.

Associate, Sr. Engineers,
Jr. Engineers, CADD Operators,
and Draftsmen

Vice President, Project Directorate,
Construction Management & Cost &
Specification Engineering

Principals/Heads
- Project Directorate
- Construction Mgmt. Dept.
- Cost and Specifications Dept.

Associate, Sr. Engineers,
Jr. Engineers, CADD Operators,
and Draftsmen

Vice President,
Business Development, Personnel &
Administration, Administration Finance

Principal/Head,
Business Development Dept.

Business Development
Officers & Staff

Principal/Head,
Personnel & Administration Dept.

Administrative Staff, Secretaries,
Clerks, Computer Operators, Drivers,
Messengers and Utility Personnel

Principal/Head,
Accounting & Finance Dept.

Accountants, Bookeepers, Clerks

Securities and Exchange Commission

The U.S. regulatory agency supervising the issuing, trading, and reporting of stocks, bonds, and mutual funds

450 Fifth St. NW
Washington, DC 20549
Phone: (202) 942-7040   **E-mail:** help@sec.gov
Web: www.sec.gov

Primary SIC: 9651—Regulation, Licensing,
& Inspection of Miscellaneous Commercial Sectors
Primary NAICS: 92615—Reg/License/Inspect
- Misc Commercial Sectors

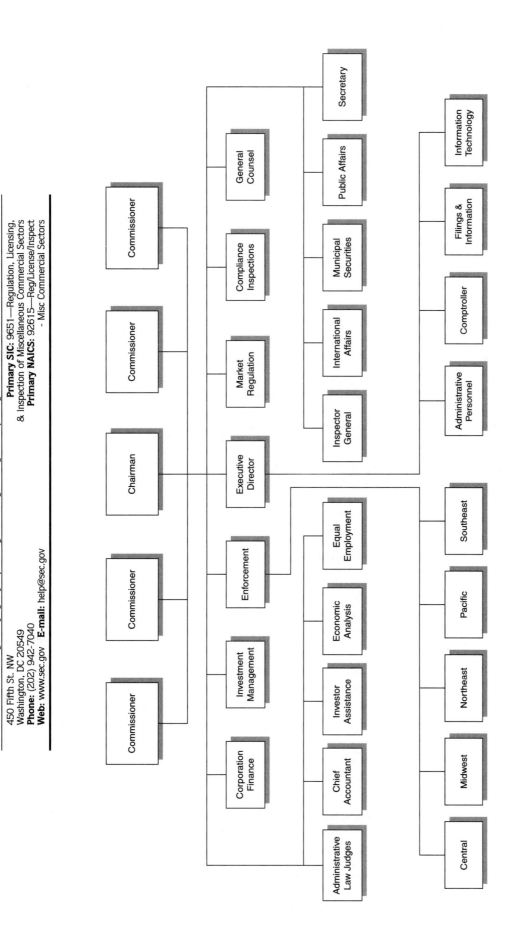

Source: Agency web site, 1999

This large South Korean commercial bank employs over 4,000 people and holds nearly $40 billion in assets

120, 2-ka, Taepyung-ro
Chung-ku, Seoul 100-102, South Korea
Phone: +82 2 774-7674 **Fax:** +82 2 774-7013
Web: www.shinhanbank.com

Primary SIC: 6021—National Commercial Banks
Primary NAICS: 52211—Commercial Banking

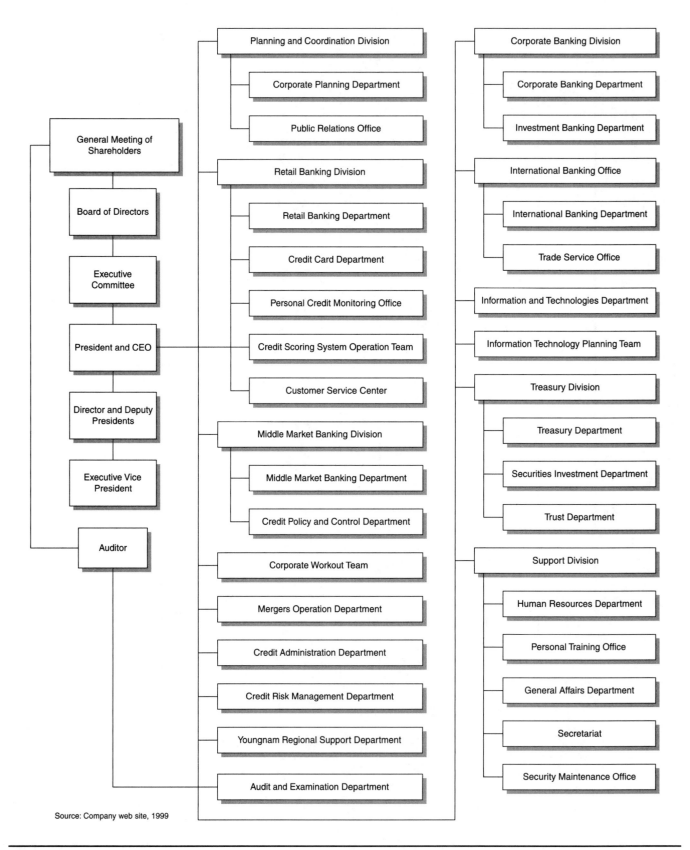

Source: Company web site, 1999

Shokoh Fund & Co., Ltd.

Publicly traded Shoko is a commercial lender targeting small and medium sized businesses

3-2-15 Nihombashi-Muromachi
Chuo-ku, Tokyo 103-0027, Japan
Phone: +81 03 3270-1248 **Fax:** +81 03 3242-3604

Primary SIC: 6159—Miscellaneous
Business Credit Institutions
Primary NAICS: 52211—Commercial Banking

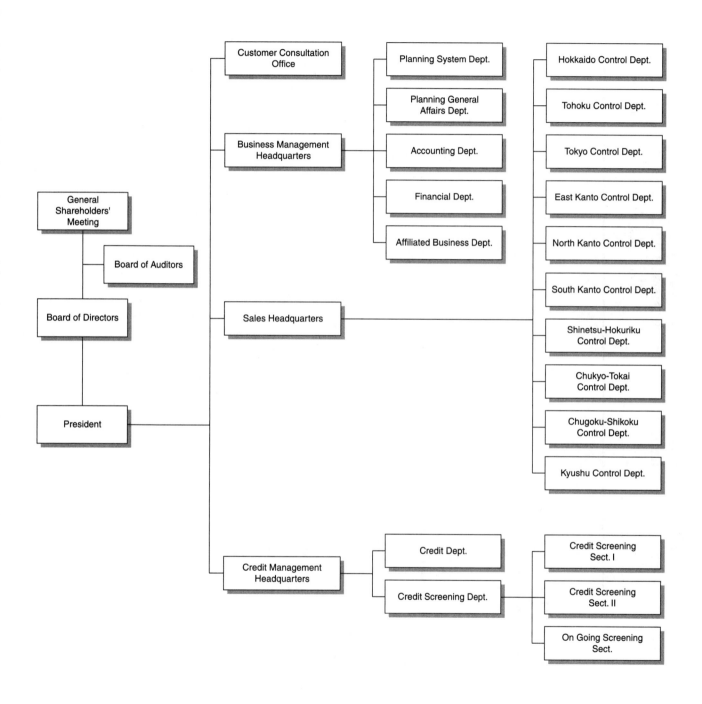

Source: Annual report, 1998

Siemens AG

Employing more than 400,000 workers worldwide. Siemens provides diverse products and services primarily to businesses

Wittelsbacherplatz 2
D-80312 Munich, Germany
Web: www.siemens.de

Primary SIC: 3661—Telephone & Telegraph Apparatus
Primary NAICS: 33421—Telephone Apparatus Mfg

REORGANIZATION Part 1 (1996)
For additional details on the restructuring see profiles starting on page 331

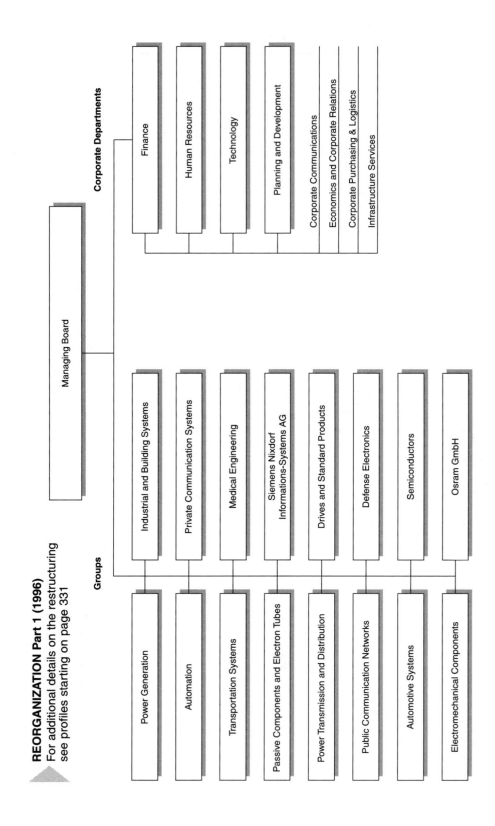

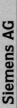

Source: Company web site, 1998

Siemens AG (cont.)

REORGANIZATION Part 2 (1999)
For additional details on the restructuring
see profiles starting on page 331

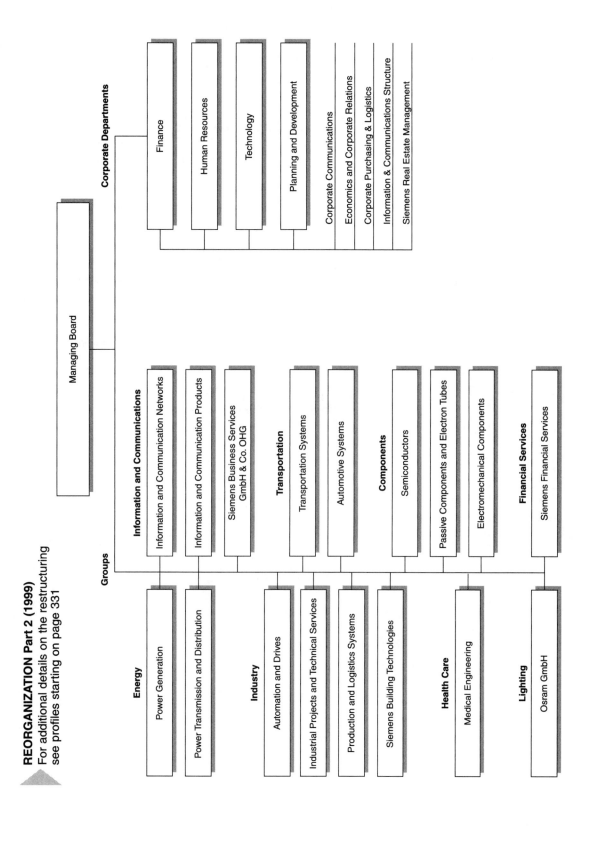

Managing Board

Corporate Departments

- Finance
- Human Resources
- Technology
- Planning and Development
  - Corporate Communications
  - Economics and Corporate Relations
  - Corporate Purchasing & Logistics
  - Information & Communications Structure
  - Siemens Real Estate Management

Groups

Information and Communications
- Information and Communication Networks
- Information and Communication Products
- Siemens Business Services GmbH & Co. OHG

Transportation
- Transportation Systems
- Automotive Systems

Components
- Semiconductors
- Passive Components and Electron Tubes
- Electromechanical Components

Financial Services
- Siemens Financial Services

Energy
- Power Generation
- Power Transmission and Distribution

Industry
- Automation and Drives
- Industrial Projects and Technical Services
- Production and Logistics Systems
- Siemens Building Technologies

Health Care
- Medical Engineering

Lighting
- Osram GmbH

Singapore Airlines Limited

The national airline of this southeast Asian city-state, SIA is also a major international carrier

77 Robinson Rd, SIA Bldg.
Singapore 068896
Web: www.singaporeair.com

Primary SIC: 4512—Air Transportation, Scheduled
Primary NAICS: 481111—Scheduled Passenger Air
Transportation

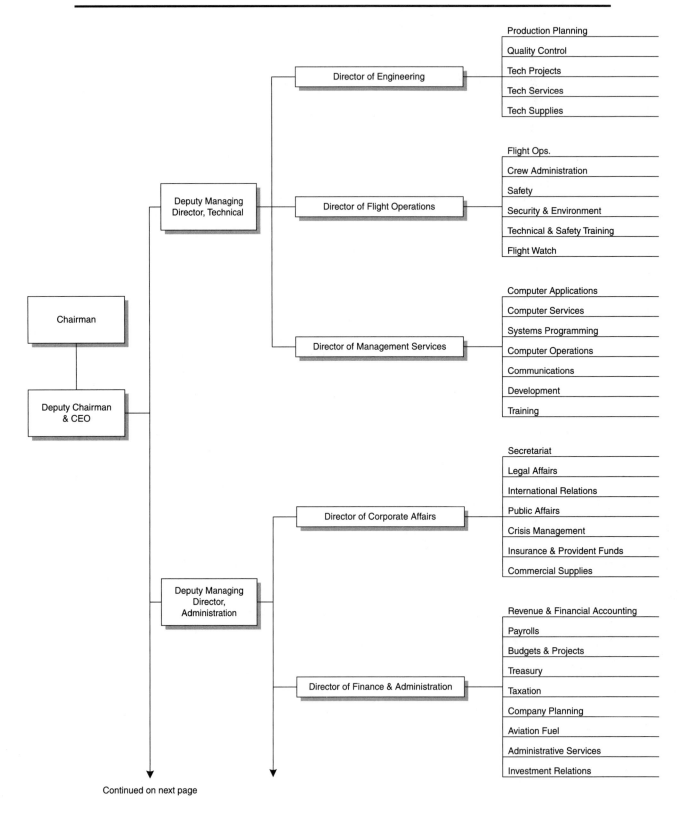

Continued on next page

Source: Company, 1998

Continued from previous page

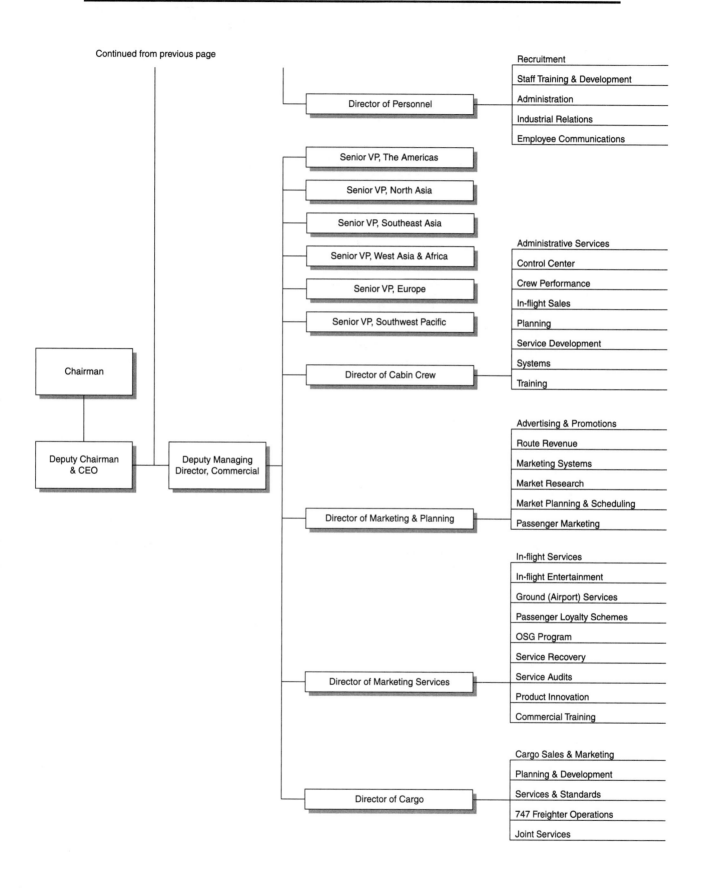

Chairman

Deputy Chairman & CEO

Deputy Managing Director, Commercial

Director of Personnel
- Recruitment
- Staff Training & Development
- Administration
- Industrial Relations
- Employee Communications

Senior VP, The Americas

Senior VP, North Asia

Senior VP, Southeast Asia

Senior VP, West Asia & Africa

Senior VP, Europe

Senior VP, Southwest Pacific

Director of Cabin Crew
- Administrative Services
- Control Center
- Crew Performance
- In-flight Sales
- Planning
- Service Development
- Systems
- Training

Director of Marketing & Planning
- Advertising & Promotions
- Route Revenue
- Marketing Systems
- Market Research
- Market Planning & Scheduling
- Passenger Marketing

Director of Marketing Services
- In-flight Services
- In-flight Entertainment
- Ground (Airport) Services
- Passenger Loyalty Schemes
- OSG Program
- Service Recovery
- Service Audits
- Product Innovation
- Commercial Training

Director of Cargo
- Cargo Sales & Marketing
- Planning & Development
- Services & Standards
- 747 Freighter Operations
- Joint Services

Skyhawk Logistics, Inc.

Provides transportation, warehousing, and logistics support services

1110 Bonifant St., Ste. 501
Silver Spring, MD 20910
Phone: (301) 585-2424
Web: www.skyhawk.com

Primary SIC: 4213—Trucking, Except Local
Primary NAICS: 484122—General Freight
Trucking, Long-Distance, LTL

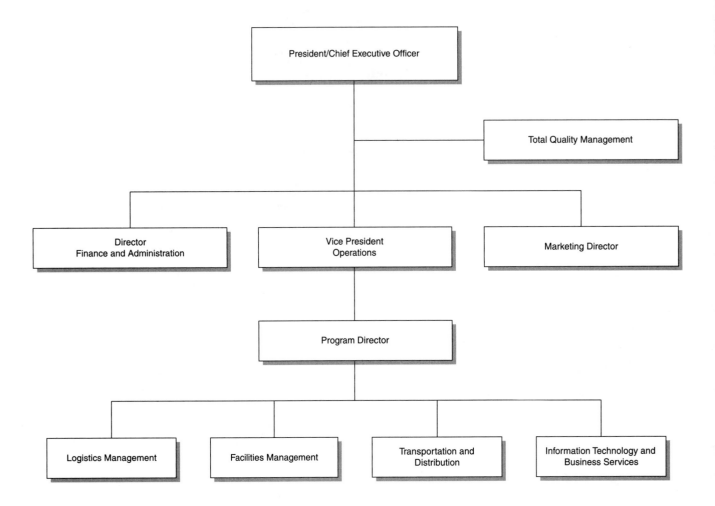

Source: Company web site, 1999

Società Industria Farmaceutica Italiana

Developer and marketer of pharmaceuticals for eye disorders

Palazzo Besso
Largo di Torre Argentina, 11, I-00186 Rome, Italy
Phone: +39 (06) 6896932 **Fax:** +39 (06) 6897128
Web: www.sifi.it

Primary SIC: 2834—Pharmaceutical Preparations
Primary NAICS: 325412—Pharmaceutical Preparation Mfg
E-mail: info@sifi.it

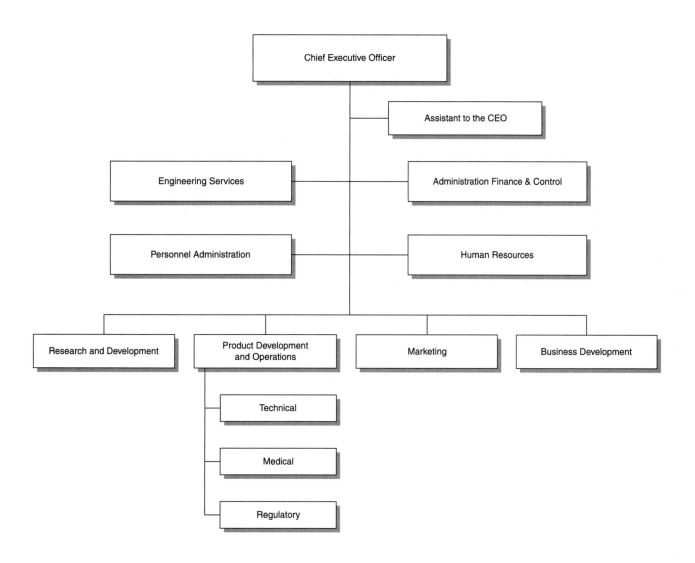

Source: Company web site, 1999

Speedways Heavy Lift Engineering (Pvt.) Ltd.

A Pakistani engineering and construction firm serving primarily the energy and manufacturing sectors

Ibrahim Bldg.
20 W. Wharf Rd., Karachi. 74000 Pakistan
Phone: +92 21 2313685 **Fax:** +92 21 2310422
Web: www.speedwaysgroup.com

Primary SIC: 1629—Heavy Construction, NEC
Primary NAICS: 23492—Pwr/Communication
Transmission Line Construction
E-mail: sabir@speedwaysgroup.com

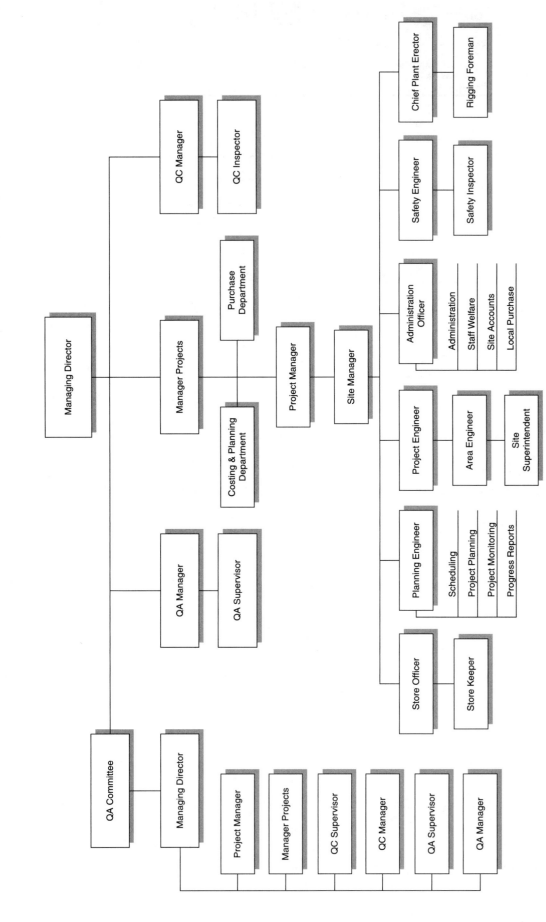

A forest products powerhouse born by the 1998 merger of Sweden's Stora Kopparbergs Bergslags and Finland's Enso Oyj

Kanavaranta 1
FIN-00160 Helsinki, Finland
Phone: +358-2046-131
Web: www.storaenso.com

Primary SIC: 2621—Paper Mills
Primary NAICS: 322121—Paper
(except Newsprint) Mills

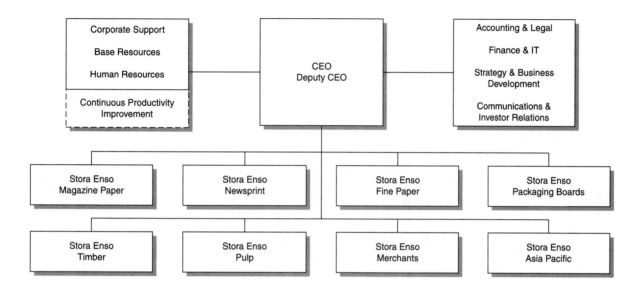

Source: Annual report, 1998

The Sumitomo Bank, Limited

This hundred-year-old bank is Japan's 2nd-largest and one of the global top 5

6-5, Kitahama 4-chome
Chuo-ku, Osaka 541-0041, Japan
Phone: +81 06 227-2111
Web: www.sumitomobank.co.jp

Primary SIC: 6021—National Commercial Banks
Primary NAICS: 52211—Commercial Banking

- Shareholders' Meeting
- Board of Directors
- Executive Committee
- Corporate Auditors
- Board of Corporate Auditors

Secretariat

- Public Affairs Dept.
  - Social Development Dept.
- Corporate Planning Dept.
  - Financial Research Dept.
- Affiliate Administration Dept.
- Personnel Dept.
  - Training Institute
  - Counselor's Office
  - Human Resources Development Dept.
- General Affairs Dept.
- Legal Dept.
- Systems Planning Dept.
- Market Risk Management Dept.
- Credit Policy Dept.
  - Credit Review Dept.
- Audit and Inspection Dept.
  - Treasury Audit Dept.
  - Systems Audit Dept.
- Audit Dept. for the Americas

Branch Banking Group

- Customer Relations Dept.
  - Tokyo Customer Relations Dept.
- Domestic Banking Administration Dept.
  - Operations Supervision Dept.
  - Customer Satisfaction Promotion Dept.
- Operations Supporting Dept.
  - Tokyo Operations Supporting Dept.
- Electronic Commerce Banking Dept.
- Branch Banking Operations Dept.
- International Business Operations Dept.
- Corporate Banking Planning Dept.
- Tokyo International Business Operations Dept.
  - Electronic Banking Dept.
  - Environment Business Dept.
- Middle Market Banking Division-I
  - Domestic Branches in West Japan
  - Public Institutions Business Dept.
  - Middle Market Banking Dept.-I
  - Credit Supervision Dept.-I
- Middle Market Banking Division-II
  - Domestic Branches in East Japan
  - Tokyo Public Institutions Business Dept.
  - Regional Corporate Banking Dept.
  - Middle Market Banking Dept.-II
  - Credit Supervision Dept.-II
- Consumer Banking Division
  - Loan Operations Dept.
  - Tokyo Loan Operations Dept.
  - Telephone Banking Center
  - Consumer Banking Dept.
  - Private Banking Dept.
  - Investment Services Dept.
- Corporate and Institutional Banking Group
  - Business Promotion Dept.
  - Corporate and Institutional Banking Division
  - Tokyo Corporate and Institutional Banking Division
  - Corporate and Institutional Banking Administration Dept.

Continued on next page

Source: Annual report, 1998

The Sumitomo Bank, Limited (cont.)

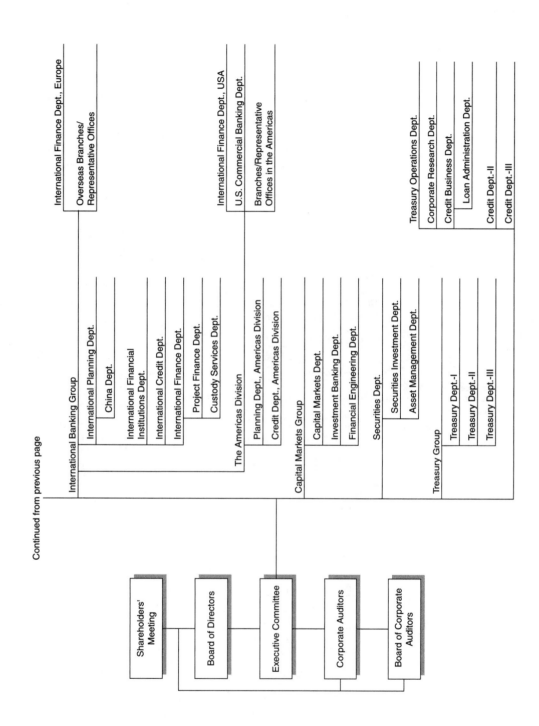

Continued from previous page

Shareholders' Meeting

Board of Directors

Executive Committee

Corporate Auditors

Board of Corporate Auditors

International Banking Group
- International Planning Dept.
  - China Dept.
- International Financial Institutions Dept.
- International Credit Dept.
- International Finance Dept.
- Project Finance Dept.
- Custody Services Dept.
- International Finance Dept., Europe
  - Overseas Branches/Representative Offices

The Americas Division
- Planning Dept., Americas Division
- Credit Dept., Americas Division
- International Finance Dept., USA
  - U.S. Commercial Banking Dept.
  - Branches/Representative Offices in the Americas

Capital Markets Group
- Capital Markets Dept.
- Investment Banking Dept.
- Financial Engineering Dept.
- Securities Dept.
  - Securities Investment Dept.
  - Asset Management Dept.

Treasury Group
- Treasury Dept.-I
- Treasury Dept.-II
- Treasury Dept.-III
- Treasury Operations Dept.
- Corporate Research Dept.
- Credit Business Dept.
  - Loan Administration Dept.
- Credit Dept.-II
- Credit Dept.-III

Sumitomo Chemical Co., Ltd.

A major manufacturer of basic chemicals and petrochemicals supported by an expanding line of specialty chemicals

Tokyo Sumitomo Twin Bldg. (East)
27-1 Shinkawa 2-chome, Chuo-ku
Tokyo 104-8260, Japan
Phone: +81 3-5543-5152 **Fax:** +81 3-5543-5901

Primary SIC: 2812—Alkalies & Chlorine
Primary NAICS: 32511—Petrochemical Mfg
Web: www.sumitomo-chem.co.jp

Chairman

President

Executive Vice Presidents, Senior Managing/ Managing Directors

General Affairs Dept.
Legal Dept.
Personnel Office
Corporate Planning & Coordination Office
Technology & Research Management Office
Intellectual Property Dept.
Environment & Safety Dept.
Quality Assurance Dept.
Finance & Accounting Office
Procurement Dept.
Physical Distribution Dept.
Process & Production Technology Center
Organic Synthesis Research Laboratory
Environmental Health Science Laboratory
Tsukuba Research Laboratory
Biotechnology Laboratory

Basic Chemicals Sector
Planning & Coordination Office
Inorganic & Industrial Chemicals Div.
Methacrylate & Optical Materials Div.
Aluminum Div.
Ehime Works
Basic Chemicals Research Laboratory

Petrochemicals & Plastics Sector
Planning & Coordination Office
Petrochemicals Div.
Plastics Div.
Elastomers Div.
Polymer Products and Market Development Dept.
Chiba Works
Ehime Works (Petrochemicals & Plastics)
Petrochemicals Research Laboratory
Plastics Technical Center

Fine Chemicals Sector
Planning & Coordination Office
Dyestuffs Div.
Specialty Chemicals Div.
Functional Chemicals Div.
Electronic Materials Div.
Osaka Works
Ehime Works (Fine Chemicals)
Chiba Works (Fine Chemicals)
Oita Works (Fine Chemicals)
Fine Chemicals Research Laboratory

Agricultural Chemicals Sector
Planning & Coordination Office
Plant Protection Div.-Domestic
Plant Protection Div.-International
Environmental Health Div.
Farm Chemicals and Materials Div.
Oita Works
Misawa Works
Ehime Works (Agricultural Chemicals)
Agricultural Chemicals Research Laboratory

Nagoya Branch Office
Fukoka Branch Office
Internal Auditors

Source: Company web site, 1998

Sunoco, Inc.

Formerly Sun Company, Sunoco is one of the top independent petroleum refiners and marketers in the U.S.

1801 Market St., 10 Penn Ctr.
Philadelphia, PA 19103-1699
Phone: (215) 977-3000 **Fax:** (215) 977-3409
Web: www.sunocoinc.com

Primary SIC: 2911—Petroleum Refining
Primary NAICS: 32411—Petroleum Refineries

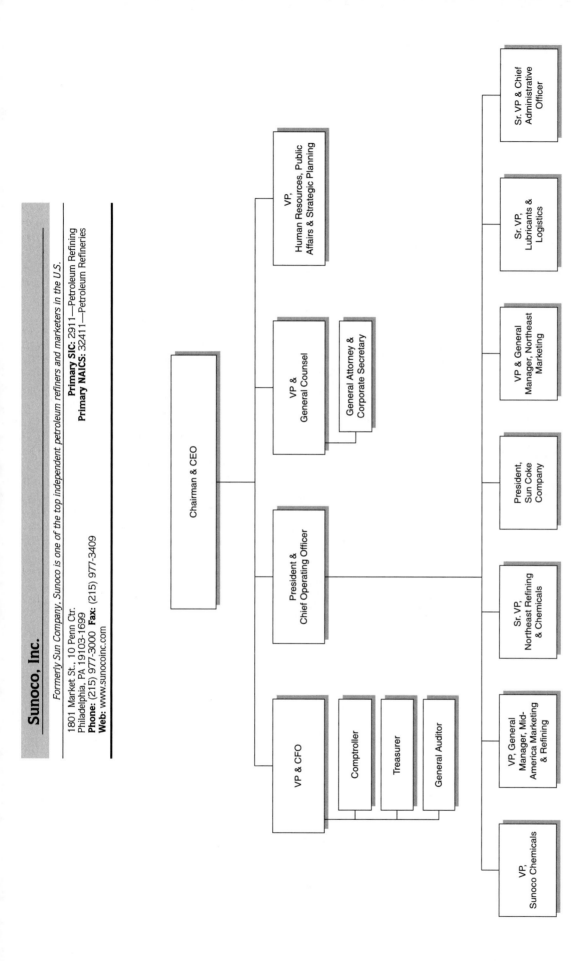

Source: Company and revisions by the editors, 1998

Sweden Post Group

Like many of its European counterparts, Sweden's national post office also provides basic banking services

Mäster Samuelsgatan 70
SE-105 00 Stockholm, Sweden
Phone: +46 8-781 10 00
Web: www.posten.se

Primary SIC: 4311—Postal Service
Primary NAICS: 49111—Postal Service

```
                    Executive Management
                    Group Management
                    
     Postfastigheter AB          Group Staffs
     Postbolagen-Gruppen         Operational Staffs

  Media Och Partners
  Fiansiella Företag
  Offentlig Marknad
  Handel
  Stor-Företag
  Distans-Handel
  International Partners
  Försäljning Företag
  Försäljning Privat

  Posten Brev
  Postgirot
  Posten Logistik
  Posten Utrikes
  Postnet
  Posten Försäljning-Servicenätet
```

Source: Annual report, 1999

Switzerland's largest life insurance carrier, Swiss Life also brings in 40% of its revenue from other countries

General Guisan-Quai 40
CH-8022 Zürich, Switzerland
Phone: +41-1-284-3311 **Fax:** +41-1-281-2080
Web: www.swisslife.com

Primary SIC: 6311—Life Insurance
Primary NAICS: 524113—Direct Life
Insurance Carriers

Chairman of the Supervisory Board

Chairman of the Corporate Executive Board

President

Presidential Functions	Finances	Actuarial Services/ Accounting	Management Services
CEO	Co-President	Co-President	Co-President

Swiss Division	European Division	International Division	La Suisse Division*
Co-President	Co-President	Co-President	Co-President

*Independently operating subsidiary and cross-selling partner in Switzerland

Source: Company web site, 1998

Swisscom AG

Switzerland's leading telecommunications company is also venturing into many foreign markets

Viktoriastrasse 21
CH-3050 Berne, Switzerland
Phone: +41 31 342 2538 **Fax:** +41 31 342-6411
Web: www.swisscom.com

Primary SIC: 4813—Telephone
Communications, Except Radiotelephone
Primary NAICS: 51331—Wired
Telecommunications Carriers

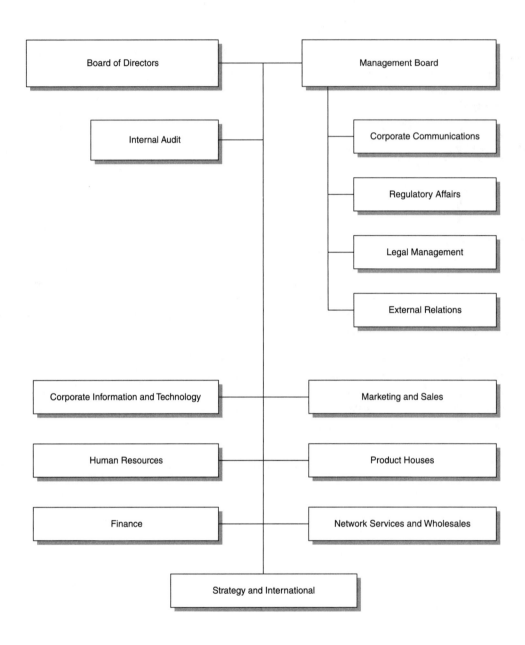

Source: Company web site, 1999

Symetrix Corporation

A research and development firm focusing on materials and architectures for high-performance electronic devices

5055 Mark Dabling Blvd.
Colorado Springs, CO 80918
Phone: (719) 594-6145 **Fax:** (719) 598-3437
Web: www.symetrixcorp.com

Primary SIC: 8731—Commercial Physical &
Biological Research
Primary NAICS: 54171—R&D in Physical,
Engineering & Life Sciences

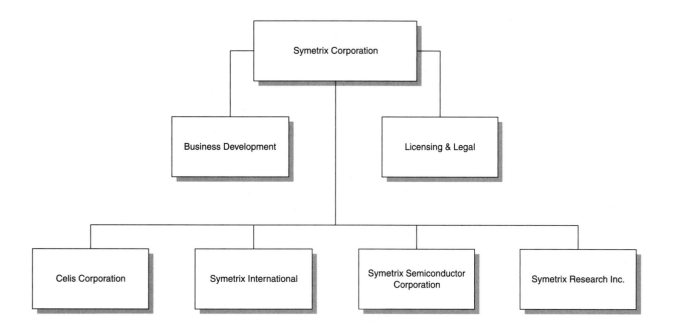

Source: Company web site, 1999

TABAI ESPEC CORP.

This publicly traded company is a market leader in environmental test-chamber manufacturing

3-5-6, Tenjinbashi
Kita-ku, Osaka 530, Japan
Phone: +81 06-358-4741 **Fax:** +81 06-358-5500
Web: www.espec.co.jp

Primary SIC: 3829—Measuring
& Controlling Devices, NEC
Primary NAICS: 334519—Other
Measuring & Controlling Device Mfg

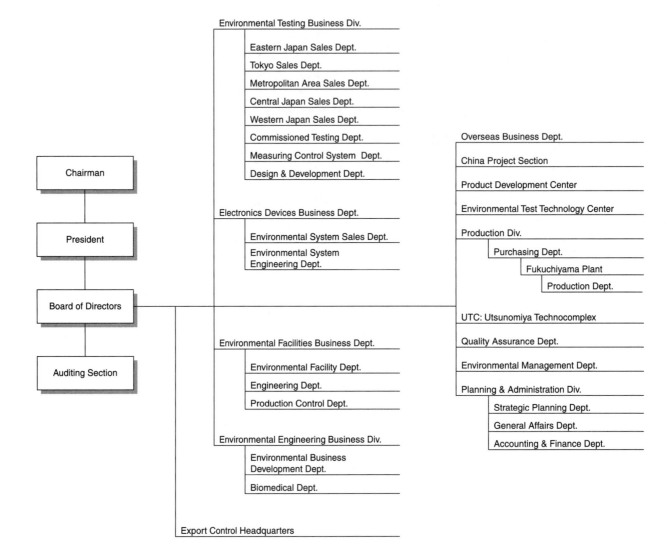

Source: Company web site, 1999

TAISEI Corporation

A 12,000-person engineering, architectural, and contracting firm primarily involved in building construction

1-25-1 Nishi-Shinjuku
Shinjuku-ku, Tokyo 163, Japan
Phone: +81-3-3348-1111 **Fax:** +81-3-3345-0481
Web: www.taisei.co.jp

Primary SIC: 1541—General Contractors-Industrial
Buildings & Warehouses
Primary NAICS: 23331—Mfg & Industrial
Building Construction

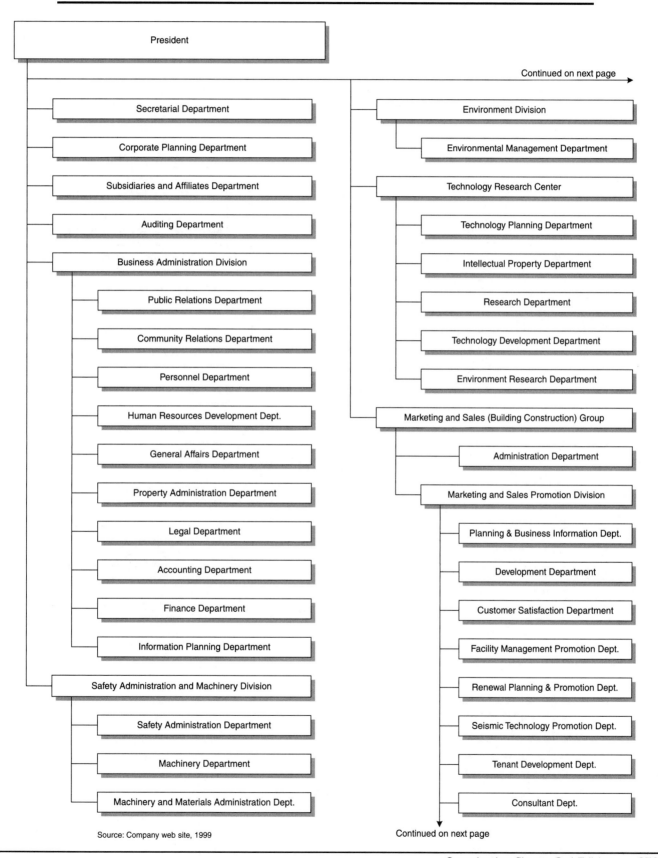

President

- Secretarial Department
- Corporate Planning Department
- Subsidiaries and Affiliates Department
- Auditing Department
- Business Administration Division
  - Public Relations Department
  - Community Relations Department
  - Personnel Department
  - Human Resources Development Dept.
  - General Affairs Department
  - Property Administration Department
  - Legal Department
  - Accounting Department
  - Finance Department
  - Information Planning Department
- Safety Administration and Machinery Division
  - Safety Administration Department
  - Machinery Department
  - Machinery and Materials Administration Dept.

Continued on next page

- Environment Division
  - Environmental Management Department
- Technology Research Center
  - Technology Planning Department
  - Intellectual Property Department
  - Research Department
  - Technology Development Department
  - Environment Research Department
- Marketing and Sales (Building Construction) Group
  - Administration Department
  - Marketing and Sales Promotion Division
    - Planning & Business Information Dept.
    - Development Department
    - Customer Satisfaction Department
    - Facility Management Promotion Dept.
    - Renewal Planning & Promotion Dept.
    - Seismic Technology Promotion Dept.
    - Tenant Development Dept.
    - Consultant Dept.

Continued on next page

Source: Company web site, 1999

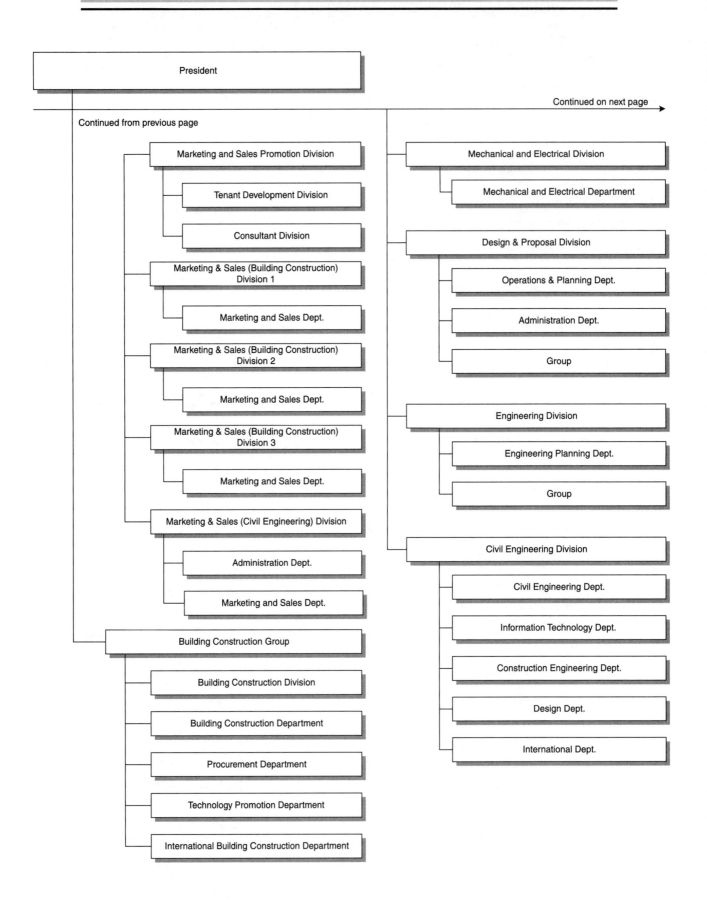

President

Continued on next page

Continued from previous page

Marketing and Sales Promotion Division

Tenant Development Division

Consultant Division

Marketing & Sales (Building Construction) Division 1

Marketing and Sales Dept.

Marketing & Sales (Building Construction) Division 2

Marketing and Sales Dept.

Marketing & Sales (Building Construction) Division 3

Marketing and Sales Dept.

Marketing & Sales (Civil Engineering) Division

Administration Dept.

Marketing and Sales Dept.

Building Construction Group

Building Construction Division

Building Construction Department

Procurement Department

Technology Promotion Department

International Building Construction Department

Mechanical and Electrical Division

Mechanical and Electrical Department

Design & Proposal Division

Operations & Planning Dept.

Administration Dept.

Group

Engineering Division

Engineering Planning Dept.

Group

Civil Engineering Division

Civil Engineering Dept.

Information Technology Dept.

Construction Engineering Dept.

Design Dept.

International Dept.

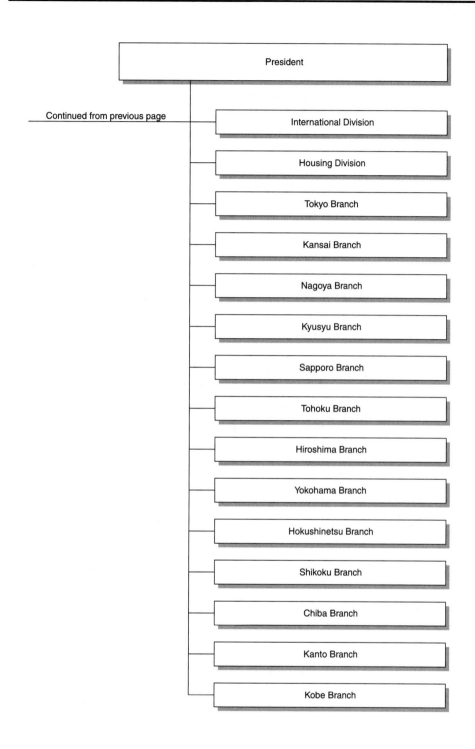

President

Continued from previous page

- International Division
- Housing Division
- Tokyo Branch
- Kansai Branch
- Nagoya Branch
- Kyusyu Branch
- Sapporo Branch
- Tohoku Branch
- Hiroshima Branch
- Yokohama Branch
- Hokushinetsu Branch
- Shikoku Branch
- Chiba Branch
- Kanto Branch
- Kobe Branch

Taiwan Power Co. (Taipower)

Taiwan's state-run electric utility has begun privatization and is beginning to face competition from independent start-ups

242 Roosevelt Rd.
Sec. 3, Taipei 100, Taiwan
Phone: +886 2 365-1234 **Fax:** +886 2 365-0522
Web: www.taipower.com.tw

Primary SIC: 4911—Electric Services
Primary NAICS: 221119—Other
Electric Power Generation

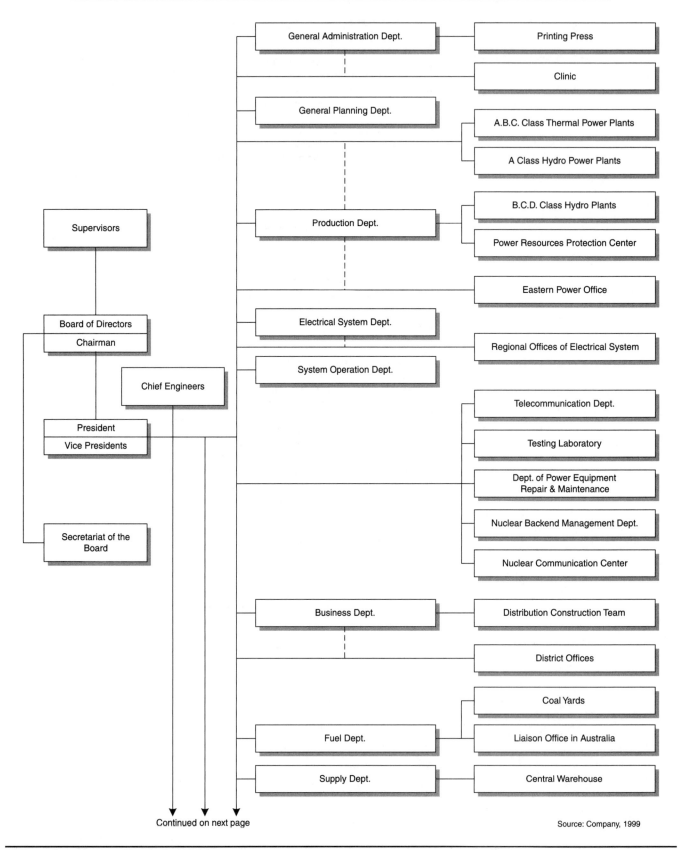

Continued on next page

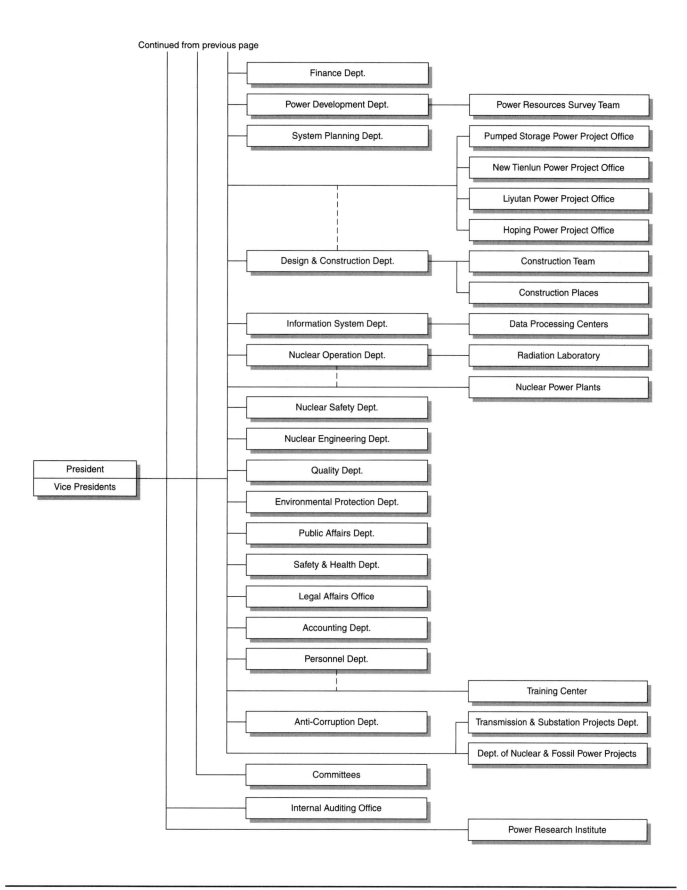

Continued from previous page

President
Vice Presidents

- Finance Dept.
- Power Development Dept. — Power Resources Survey Team
- System Planning Dept.
  - Pumped Storage Power Project Office
  - New Tienlun Power Project Office
  - Liyutan Power Project Office
  - Hoping Power Project Office
- Design & Construction Dept.
  - Construction Team
  - Construction Places
- Information System Dept. — Data Processing Centers
- Nuclear Operation Dept.
  - Radiation Laboratory
  - Nuclear Power Plants
- Nuclear Safety Dept.
- Nuclear Engineering Dept.
- Quality Dept.
- Environmental Protection Dept.
- Public Affairs Dept.
- Safety & Health Dept.
- Legal Affairs Office
- Accounting Dept.
- Personnel Dept.
  - Training Center
- Anti-Corruption Dept.
  - Transmission & Substation Projects Dept.
  - Dept. of Nuclear & Fossil Power Projects
- Committees
- Internal Auditing Office
- Power Research Institute

Takefuji Corporation

A mid-size lender in the consumer market with $11 billion in assets

15-1, Nishi-Shinjuku 8-chome
Shinjuku-ku, Tokyo 163-8654, Japan
Web: www.takefuji.co.jp

Primary SIC: 6141—Personal Credit Institutions
Primary NAICS: 522291—Consumer Lending

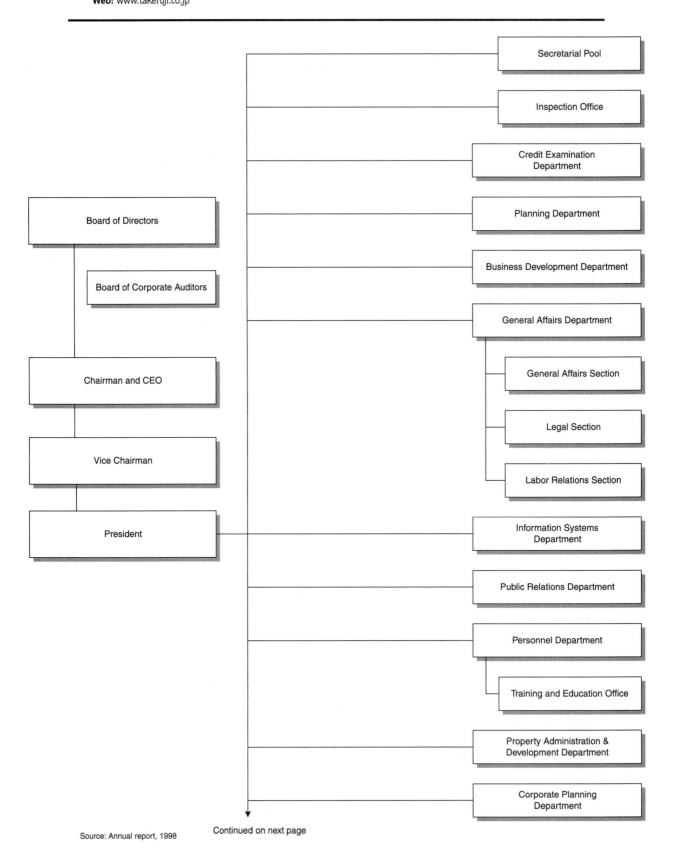

Continued on next page

Source: Annual report, 1998

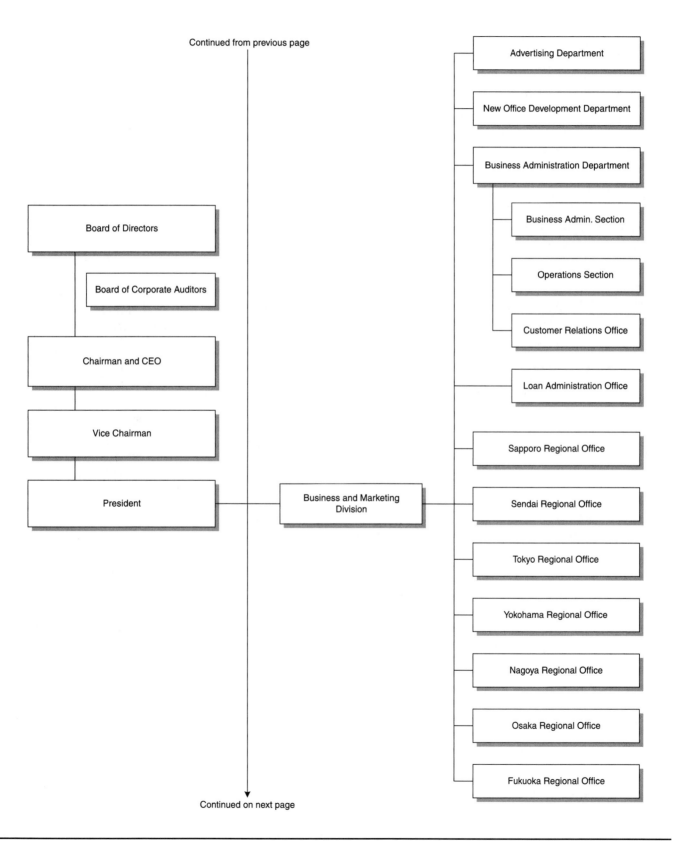

Continued from previous page

Advertising Department

New Office Development Department

Business Administration Department

Business Admin. Section

Operations Section

Customer Relations Office

Board of Directors

Board of Corporate Auditors

Chairman and CEO

Vice Chairman

President

Business and Marketing Division

Loan Administration Office

Sapporo Regional Office

Sendai Regional Office

Tokyo Regional Office

Yokohama Regional Office

Nagoya Regional Office

Osaka Regional Office

Fukuoka Regional Office

Continued on next page

Continued from previous page

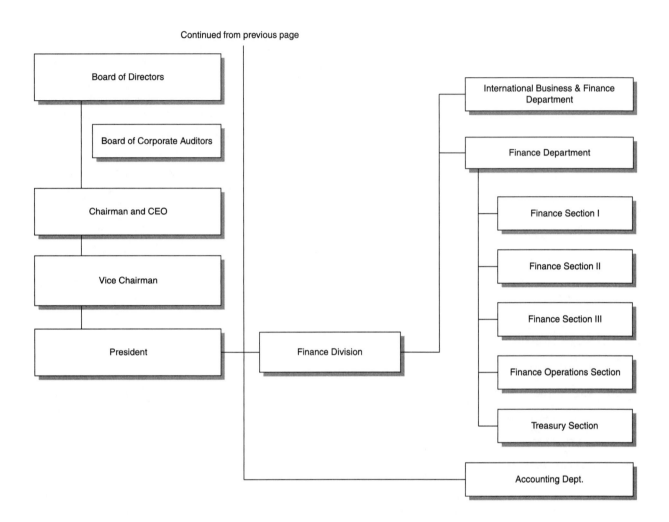

Board of Directors

Board of Corporate Auditors

Chairman and CEO

Vice Chairman

President

Finance Division

International Business & Finance Department

Finance Department

Finance Section I

Finance Section II

Finance Section III

Finance Operations Section

Treasury Section

Accounting Dept.

Tennessee Valley Authority

A government corporation dating to the New Deal era, the TVA is the largest power generating company in the U.S.

400 West Summit Hill Dr.
Knoxville, TN 37902
Phone: (423) 632-2101 **Fax:** (423) 632-6783
Web: www.tva.gov

Primary SIC: 4911—Electric Services
Primary NAICS: 221112—Fossil
Fuel Electric Power Generation

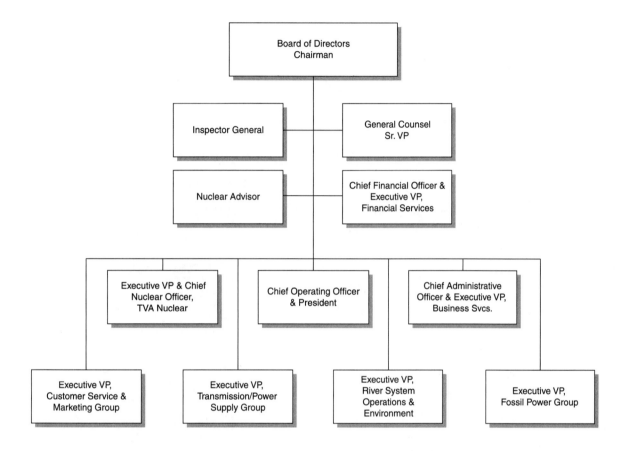

Source: Company and revisions by the editors, 1999

The Tokai Bank, Limited

With more than $250 billion in assets, Tokai has a regional stronghold in Nagoya, Japan's 4th-largest city

21-24 Nishiki 3-chome
Naka-ku, Nagoya 460-8660, Japan
Phone: +81 52-211-1111
Web: www.csweb.co.jp/TBK/

Primary SIC: 6021—National Commercial Banks
Primary NAICS: 52211—Commercial Banking

REORGANIZATION Part 1 (1996)

For additional details on the restructuring see profiles starting on page 331

Executive Committee

Secretariat

Personnel Div.
- Career Services Dept.

Training & Education Div.

Audit Div.

Legal Div.

Premises & General Affairs Div.
- Property Management Dept.

Economic Research Div.

Corporate Planning Group
- Corporate Planning Div.
  - Accounting & Comptroller's Dept.
- ALM Div.
- Public Relations Div.
  - Social Contribution Dept.

Credit Planning Group
- Credit Planning Div.
  - Credit Review & Auditing Dept.
- Credit Division
- Credit Management Div.
- Corporate Research Div.
- Affiliated Business Div.
- Public Relations Div.

Quality Control Group
- Quality Management Div.
- Operation and Administration Div.
  - Nagoya Operations Center
  - Tokyo Operations Center
  - Osaka Operations Center
  - Regional Operations Center
- Systems Development Div.
  - Systems Administration Dept.
- Data Processing Div.

Domestic Business Headquarters

Business Planning Group
- Business Planning Div.
  - Customer Relations Dept.
- Business Development Div.
  - Financial Consultation Dept.
  - Multimedia Dept.
  - Consumer & Housing Loan Operations Center
- Business Information Development Div.
  - New Airport Project Dept.

Business Promotion Group
- Chubu Banking Div.
- Tokyo Banking Div.
- Kansai Banking Div.
- Public Institutions Div., Head Office
- Public Institutions Div., Tokyo
- Head Office
- Tokyo Main Office
- Osaka Branch
- Financial Institutions Div.

International Headquarters
- International Planning Div.
  - Americas Dept.
  - International Systems & Operations Dept.
    - Nagoya International Operations Center
    - Tokyo International Operations Center
    - Osaka International Operations Center
- Foreign Business Promotion Div.
- International Finance Div.
- International Credit Div.
  - International Credit Review & Auditing Dept.

Treasury & Securities Headquarters
- Capital Markets Planning Div.
  - Risk Management Dept.
  - Securities Operations Dept.
- Treasury & Securities Div.
  - Securities Investment Dept.
  - Bond Trading Dept.
  - Treasury Dept.
- Capital Markets & Derivatives Marketing Div.
  - Capital Markets Dept.
  - Derivatives Marketing Dept.
- International Treasury Div.
  - International Trading Dept.

REORGANIZATION Part 2 (1999)
For additional details on the restructuring
see profiles starting on page 331

Executive
Committee

Investment Banking Company
- Overseas Branches & Offices
- International Credit Div.
- Investment Banking Planning Div.
  - Americas Dept.
- Investment Banking Business Development Group
  - International Treasury Div.
    - International Trading Dept.
  - Derivative and Structured Products Div.
  - International Finance Div.

Middle & Retail Banking Company
- Business Planning Div.
  - E-Commerce Dept.
- Credit Div. I
- Customer Service Div.
  - Customer Relations Dept.
  - Tokyo Customer Relations Dept.
  - Osaka Customer Relations Dept.
- Business Promotion Group
  - Domestic Branches
  - Capital Markets Div.
  - Business Information Development Div.
  - Foreign Business Promotion Div.
  - Public Institutions Div., Head Office
  - Public Institutions Div., Tokyo
  - Chubu Banking Div.
  - Tokyo Banking Div.
  - Kansai Banking Div.

Loan Promoting Company
- Credit Div.
  - Credit Management Div.
    - Credit Management Center

Operations Administration Company
- Systems Div.
  - Systems Administration Dept.
- Operations Administration Planning Div.
  - Markets Operations Dept.
  - Nagoya Operations Center
  - Tokyo Operations Center
  - Osaka Operations Center
  - Regional Operations Center
  - Consumer and Housing Loan Operations Center
  - Tokyo Consumer and Housing Loan Operations Center
  - Nagoya International Operations Center
  - Tokyo International Operations Center
  - Osaka International Operations Center

Secretariat

Personnel Div.
- Career Service Dept.
- Training and Education Dept.

Audit Div.
- Overseas Audit Dept.
- Branch Administration Center

Premises & General Affairs Div.
- Property Management Dept.

Economic Research Div.

Legal Div.

New Airport Project Dept.

Credit Planning Div.
- Credit Review Dept.
- Corporate Research Dept.

Operations Planning Div.

ALM Div.
- Securities Investment Dept.
- Treasury Dept.

Public Relations Div.
- Social Contribution Dept.

Risk Management Div.

Affiliated Business Div.

Corporate Planning Div.
- Accounting and Comptroller's Dept.

Retail Banking Company
- Specialist Boutiques
- Consumer Loan Div.
- Retail Banking Planning Div.
  - Private Banking Dept.

Wholesale Banking Company
- Head Office
- Tokyo Main Office
- Osaka Branch
- Credit Div. II
- Financial Institutions Div.
- Wholesale Banking Planning Dept.

Source: Annual report, 1998

Tokyo Electron Limited

A major producer and distributor of semiconductor and LCD panel manufacturing equipment

TBS Broadcast Center
3-6 Akasaka 5-chome, Minato-ku
Tokyo 107-8481, Japan
Phone: +81 03-5561-7000 **Fax:** +81 03-5561-7400

Primary SIC: 3559—Special Industry Machinery, NEC
Primary NAICS: 333295—Semiconductor Machinery Mfg
Web: www.tel.co.jp

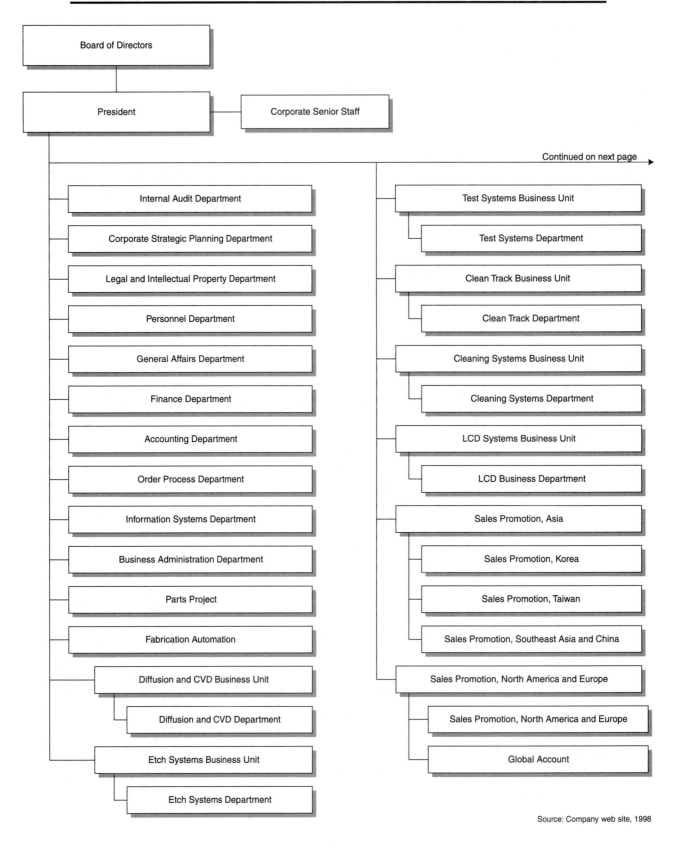

Board of Directors

President

Corporate Senior Staff

Continued on next page ▶

Internal Audit Department

Corporate Strategic Planning Department

Legal and Intellectual Property Department

Personnel Department

General Affairs Department

Finance Department

Accounting Department

Order Process Department

Information Systems Department

Business Administration Department

Parts Project

Fabrication Automation

Diffusion and CVD Business Unit

Diffusion and CVD Department

Etch Systems Business Unit

Etch Systems Department

Test Systems Business Unit

Test Systems Department

Clean Track Business Unit

Clean Track Department

Cleaning Systems Business Unit

Cleaning Systems Department

LCD Systems Business Unit

LCD Business Department

Sales Promotion, Asia

Sales Promotion, Korea

Sales Promotion, Taiwan

Sales Promotion, Southeast Asia and China

Sales Promotion, North America and Europe

Sales Promotion, North America and Europe

Global Account

Source: Company web site, 1998

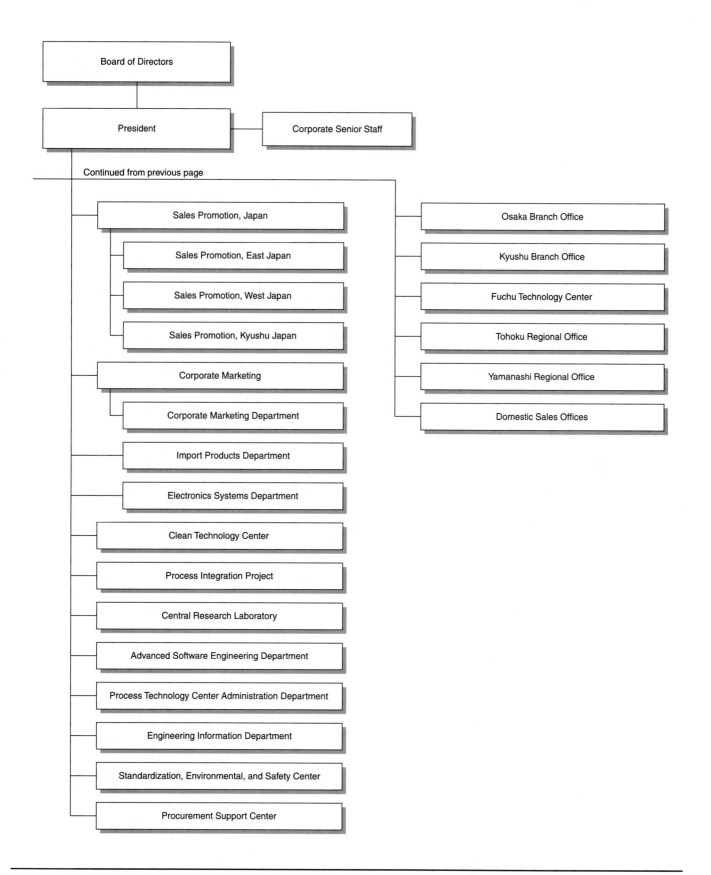

Board of Directors

President

Corporate Senior Staff

Continued from previous page

Sales Promotion, Japan

Sales Promotion, East Japan

Sales Promotion, West Japan

Sales Promotion, Kyushu Japan

Corporate Marketing

Corporate Marketing Department

Import Products Department

Electronics Systems Department

Clean Technology Center

Process Integration Project

Central Research Laboratory

Advanced Software Engineering Department

Process Technology Center Administration Department

Engineering Information Department

Standardization, Environmental, and Safety Center

Procurement Support Center

Osaka Branch Office

Kyushu Branch Office

Fuchu Technology Center

Tohoku Regional Office

Yamanashi Regional Office

Domestic Sales Offices

Tokyo Stock Exchange

Japan's largest stock exchange and a major world market

2-1 Nihombashi-Kabuto-cho
Chuo-ku, Tokyo 103-8220, Japan
Phone: +81 3 3666-0141 **Fax:** +81 3 3663-0625
Web: www.tse.or.jp

Primary SIC: 6231—Security &
Commodity Exchanges
Primary NAICS: 52321—Securities
& Commodity Exchanges

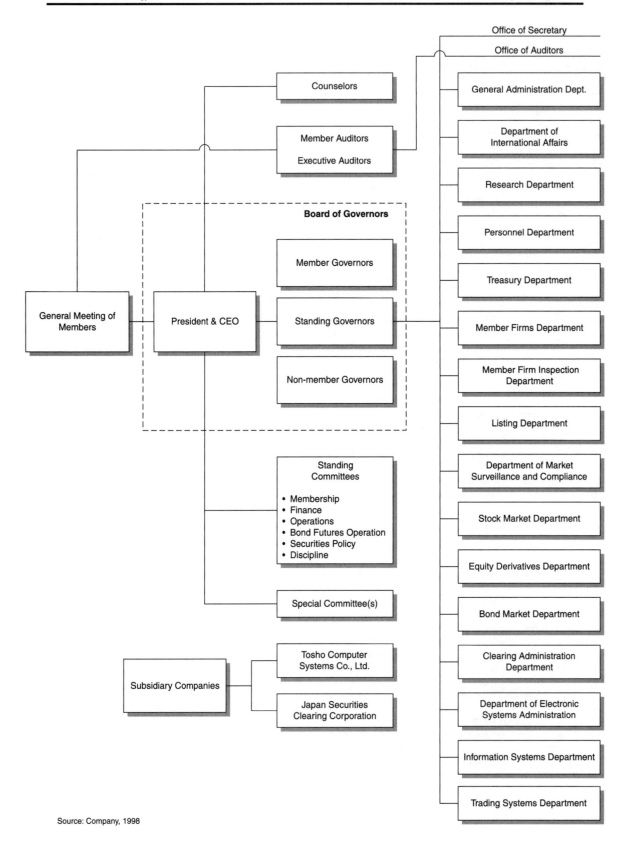

Source: Company, 1998

Tokyu Corporation

Railroads are this sprawling conglomerate's biggest money maker, but it also dabbles in real estate and electrical services

5-6, Nanpeidai-cho
Shibuya-ku, Tokyo 150-8511, Japan
Phone: +81 03 3477-6180 **Fax:** +81 03 3464-6505

Primary SIC: 4011—Railroads, Line-haul Operating
Primary NAICS: 482111—Line-Haul Railroads

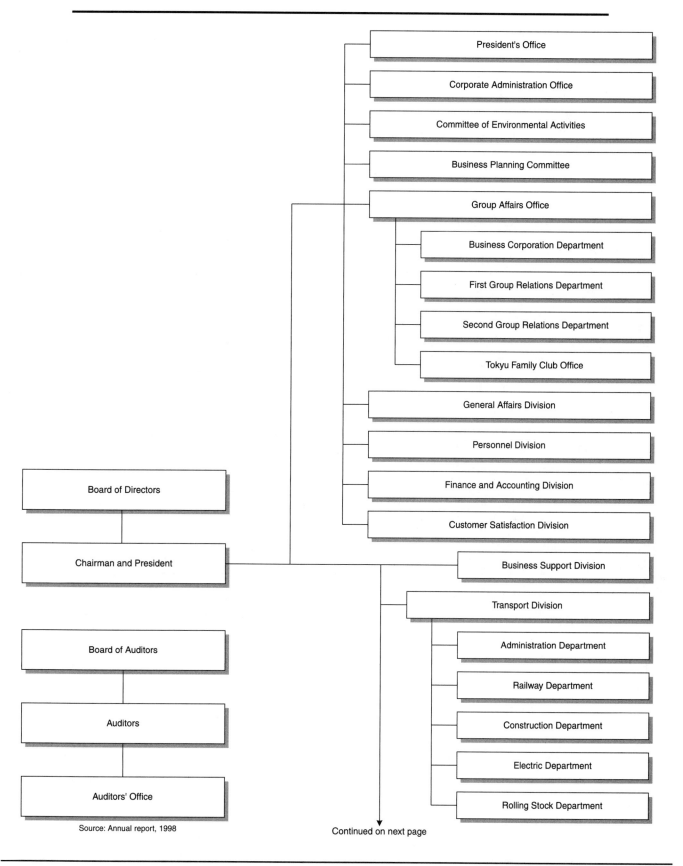

Source: Annual report, 1998

Continued on next page

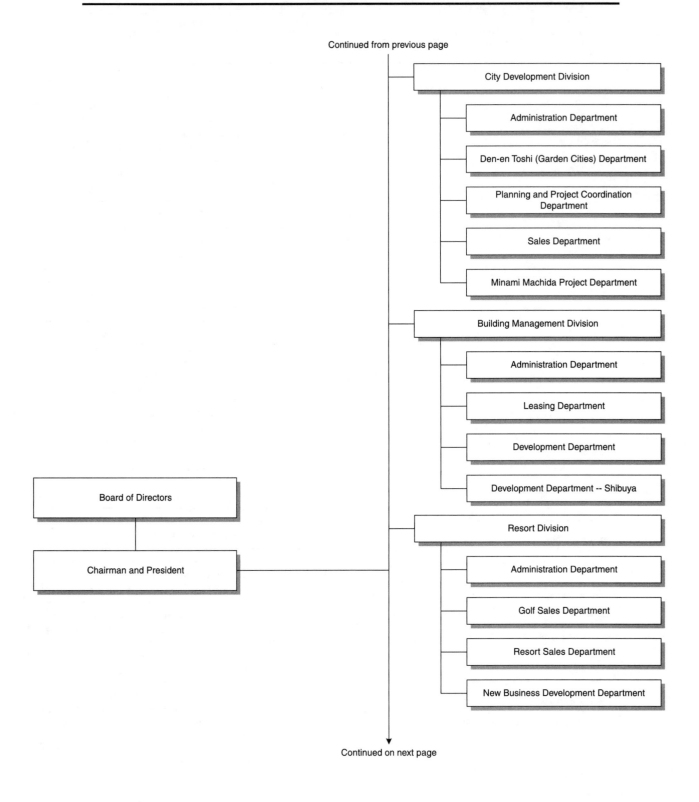

Continued from previous page

City Development Division

Administration Department

Den-en Toshi (Garden Cities) Department

Planning and Project Coordination Department

Sales Department

Minami Machida Project Department

Building Management Division

Administration Department

Leasing Department

Development Department

Development Department -- Shibuya

Board of Directors

Chairman and President

Resort Division

Administration Department

Golf Sales Department

Resort Sales Department

New Business Development Department

Continued on next page

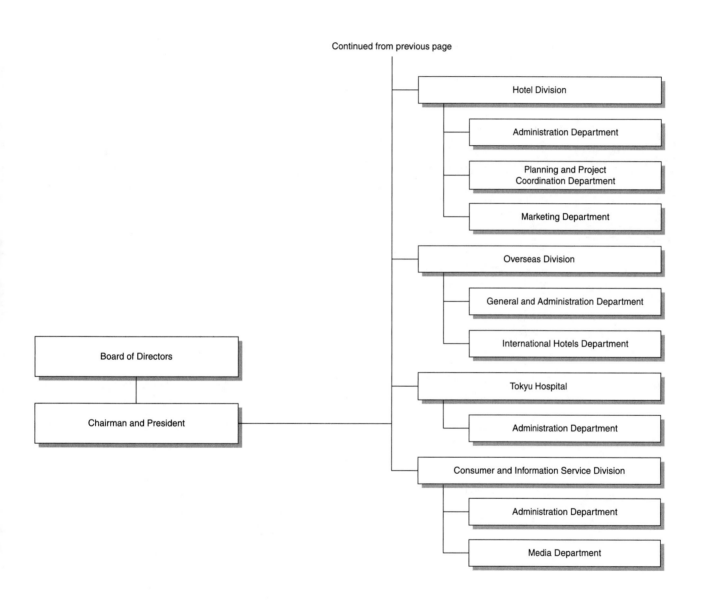

Continued from previous page

Board of Directors

Chairman and President

Hotel Division
- Administration Department
- Planning and Project Coordination Department
- Marketing Department

Overseas Division
- General and Administration Department
- International Hotels Department

Tokyu Hospital
- Administration Department

Consumer and Information Service Division
- Administration Department
- Media Department

Tomen Corporation

A leading Japanese general trading company with offices in over 60 countries

6-7, Kawaramachi 1-chome
Chuo-ku, Osaka 530, Japan
Phone: +81 06-208-2211
Web: www.tomen.co.jp

Primary SIC: 6159—Miscellaneous
Business Credit Institutions
Primary NAICS: 522293—International Trade Financing

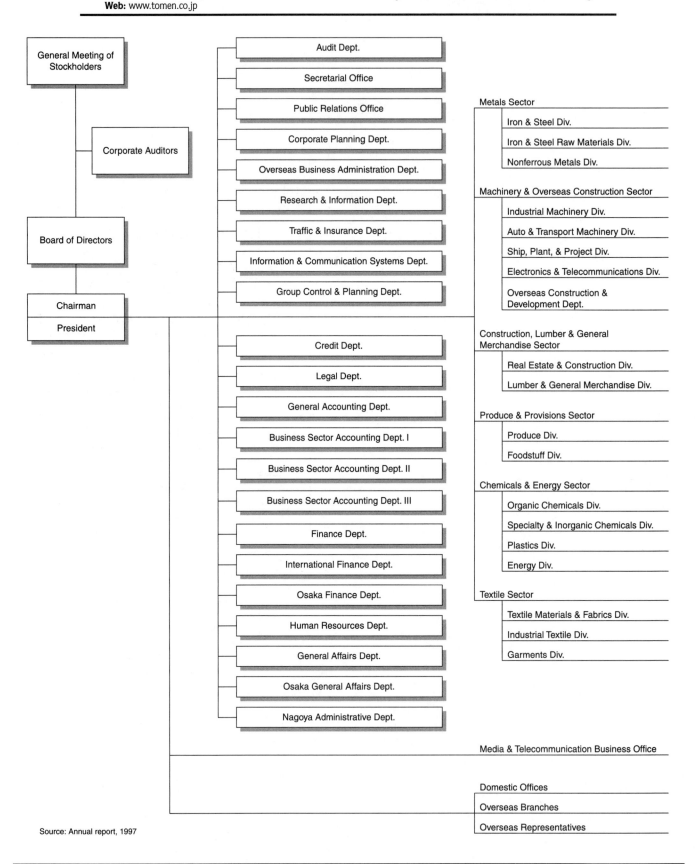

Source: Annual report, 1997

Toray Industries, Inc.

Japan's largest synthetic fiber manufacturer with diverse holdings in textiles, resins, chemicals, and consumer goods

2-1 Nihonbashi-Muromachi 2-chome
Chuo-ku, Tokyo 103-8666, Japan
Phone: +81 03 3245-5111 **Fax:** +81 03 3245-5555
Web: www.toray.co.jp

Primary SIC: 2823—Cellulosic Manmade Fibers
Primary NAICS: 325221—Cellulosic Organic Fiber Mfg

The Toronto-Dominion Bank

With assets approaching C$200 billion, TD is one of Canada's 5 largest banks and offers a range of financial services

Toronto-Dominion Centre
King St. W. and Bay St., Toronto, ON M5K 1A2 Canada
Phone: (416) 982-8222 **Fax:** (416) 982-5671
Web: www.tdbank.ca

Primary SIC: 6021—National Commercial Banks
Primary NAICS: 52211—Commercial Banking
E-mail: tdinfo@tdbank.ca

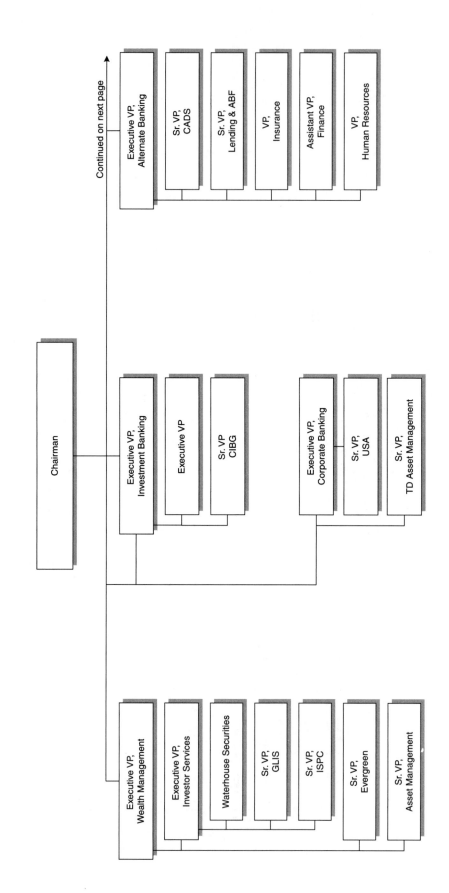

Continued on next page

Source: Company and revisions by the editors, 1997

The Toronto-Dominion Bank (cont.)

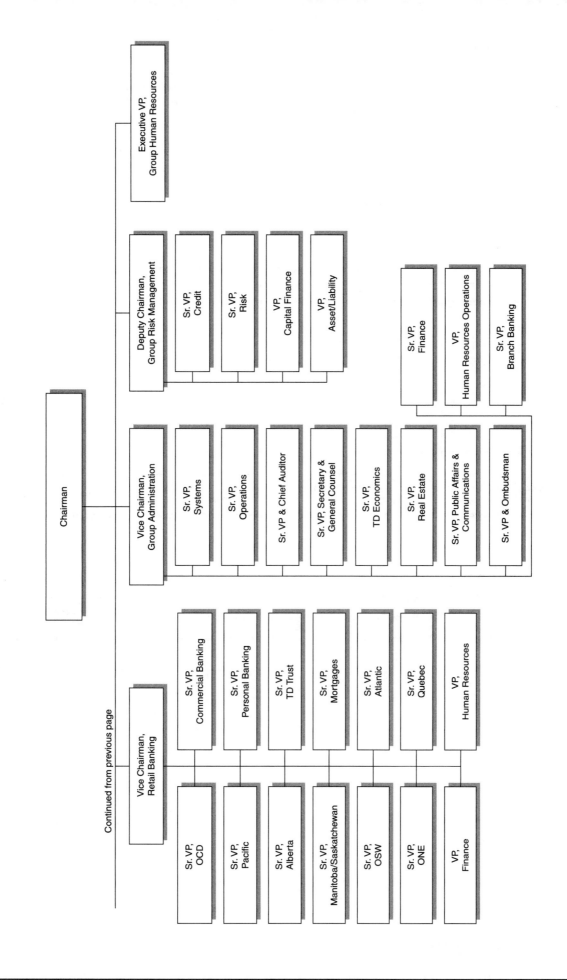

Chairman

- Vice Chairman, Retail Banking
  - Sr. VP, Commercial Banking
  - Sr. VP, Personal Banking
  - Sr. VP, TD Trust
  - Sr. VP, Mortgages
  - Sr. VP, Atlantic
  - Sr. VP, Quebec
  - VP, Human Resources
    - Sr. VP, OCD
    - Sr. VP, Pacific
    - Sr. VP, Alberta
    - Sr. VP, Manitoba/Saskatchewan
    - Sr. VP, OSW
    - Sr. VP, ONE
    - VP, Finance
- Vice Chairman, Group Administration
  - Sr. VP, Systems
  - Sr. VP, Operations
  - Sr. VP & Chief Auditor
  - Sr. VP, Secretary & General Counsel
  - Sr. VP, TD Economics
  - Sr. VP, Real Estate
  - Sr. VP, Public Affairs & Communications
  - Sr. VP & Ombudsman
    - Sr. VP, Finance
    - VP, Human Resources Operations
    - Sr. VP, Branch Banking
- Deputy Chairman, Group Risk Management
  - Sr. VP, Credit
  - Sr. VP, Risk
  - VP, Capital Finance
  - VP, Asset/Liability
- Executive VP, Group Human Resources

Continued from previous page

Toshiba Corporation

A $40 billion international producer of consumer and industrial electronic devices and components

1-1, Shibaura 1-chome
Minato-ku, Tokyo 105-8001, Japan
Phone: +81 03 3457-2096 **Fax:** +81 03 5444-9202
Web: www.toshiba.co.jp

Primary SIC: 3571—Electronic Computers
Primary NAICS: 334111—Electronic Computer Mfg

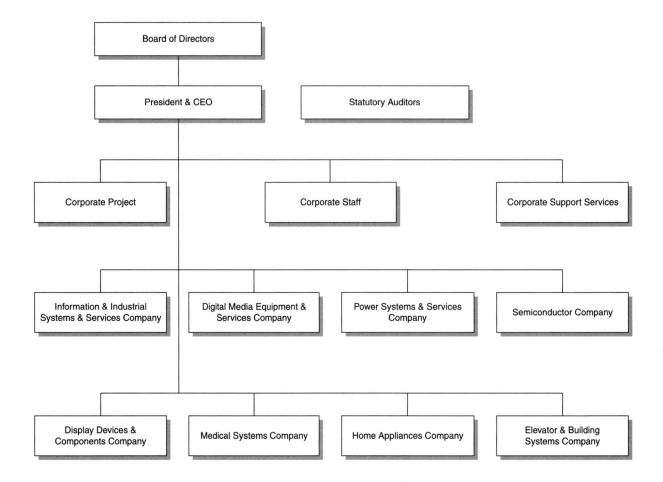

Board of Directors

President & CEO

Statutory Auditors

Corporate Project

Corporate Staff

Corporate Support Services

Information & Industrial Systems & Services Company

Digital Media Equipment & Services Company

Power Systems & Services Company

Semiconductor Company

Display Devices & Components Company

Medical Systems Company

Home Appliances Company

Elevator & Building Systems Company

Source: Company web site, 1999

TOTAL Fina SA

One of France's largest petroleum companies. Total markets its refined products worldwide

Tour TOTAL
24, Cours Michelet
F-92069, Paris La Défense Cedex, France
Phone: +33 1 41 35 40 00 **Fax:** +33 1 41 35 28 27

Primary SIC: 1311—Crude Petroleum & Natural Gas
Primary NAICS: 211111—Crude Petroleum &
Natural Gas Extraction
Web: www.total.com

- Executive Committee
  Management Committee

Continued on next page

- CEO, Vice Chairman
  Executive Committee
  - Special Advisor
  - Special Advisor
  - Strategy and Corporate Planning
  - Information and Telecommunications System
  - Finance
    - Insurance
    - Legal

- Exploration/Production
  - Business Development
  - Exploration/Reservoir
  - Operations
  - Strategy Planning Control
  - USA
  - Africa & Mediterranean
  - Latin America
  - Far East
  - North Sea
  - Russia - CIS

- Gas-Electricity & Other Energies/Trading
  - Gas-Electricity & Other Energies
  - Trading & Shipping

- Refining and Marketing
  - Marketing Europe
  - Asia
  - Overseas
  - USA
  - Refining
  - Specialties
  - Secretary General
  - Strategy

Source: Company web site, 1999

TOTAL Fina SA (cont.)

Continued from previous page

CEO, Vice Chairman Executive Committee

- Head Office Brussels Administration
- Human Resources & Corporate Communications
  - Corporate Communications
- Safety-Environment
- Purchasing

Petrochemical/Paints + USA
- USA
  - Paints Sigma
  - Paints Kalon
  - Strategy & Finance
- Petrochemicals
  - Monomers & Aromatics
  - Polyethylene
  - Polypropylene
  - Styrene & Polystyrene
  - Industrial Activities

Middle East

Chemicals - Hutchinson
- Specialty Chemicals
  - Inks
  - Adhesives
  - Resins
- Hutchinson
  - Automotive Extrusion
  - Automotive Antivibration
  - Automotive Industrial Specialties & Consumer Products

The Toyo Trust and Banking Company, Limited

Toyo's commercial lending, trust administration, and investment activities earned it $2.7 billion in 1998 revenues

4-3, Marunouchi 1-chome
Chiyoda-ku, Tokyo 100-0005, Japan
Phone: +81 81 3-3287-2211 **Fax:** +81 03-3214-0210
Web: www.toyotrustbank.co.jp

Primary SIC: 6021—National Commercial Banks
Primary NAICS: 52211—Commercial Banking

Secretariat
General Planning Dept.
Public Relations Dept.
Personnel Dept.
General Services Dept.
Business Planning Dept.
Research Dept.
Systems Dept.
System Administration Dept.
Operations Planning and Support Dept.
Business Promotion Dept.
Institutions Business Promotion Dept.
Corporate Finance Strategy Dept.
Credit Control Dept. I
Credit Control Dept. II
Consumer Finance Dept.
Financial Institutions Dept.
International Dept.
International Credit Dept.
Treasury Dept.
Trading Dept.
Securities Planning Dept.
Funds Management Dept. I
Funds Management Dept. II

General Meeting of Shareholders

Board of Auditors
Corporate Auditors

Board of Directors

President
Deputy President
Senior Managing Directors
Managing Directors

Executive Committee

Domestic Branches

Overseas Offices

Continued on next page

Source: Annual report, 1998

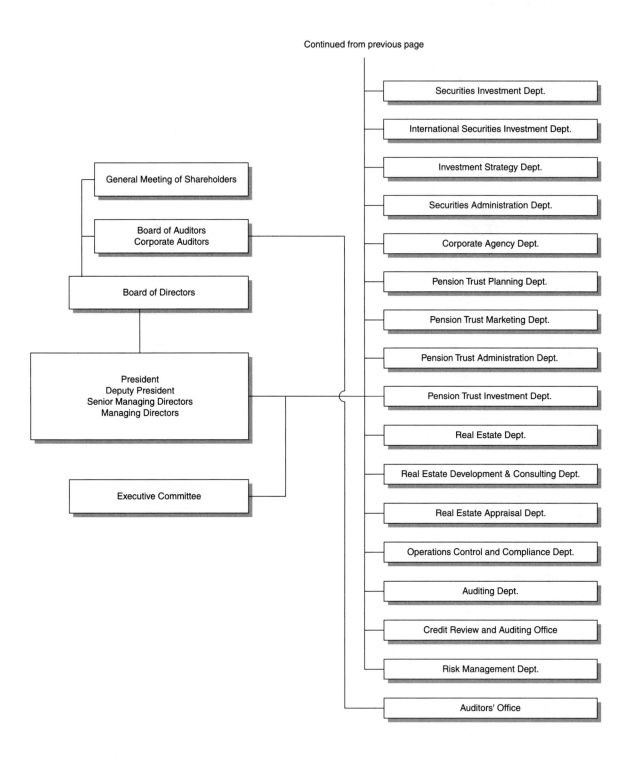

Continued from previous page

General Meeting of Shareholders

Board of Auditors
Corporate Auditors

Board of Directors

President
Deputy President
Senior Managing Directors
Managing Directors

Executive Committee

Securities Investment Dept.

International Securities Investment Dept.

Investment Strategy Dept.

Securities Administration Dept.

Corporate Agency Dept.

Pension Trust Planning Dept.

Pension Trust Marketing Dept.

Pension Trust Administration Dept.

Pension Trust Investment Dept.

Real Estate Dept.

Real Estate Development & Consulting Dept.

Real Estate Appraisal Dept.

Operations Control and Compliance Dept.

Auditing Dept.

Credit Review and Auditing Office

Risk Management Dept.

Auditors' Office

A leading international organization promoting anti-corruption policies in government and business

Otto-Suhr-Allee 97/99
D-10585 Berlin, Germany
Phone: +49 30 343 8200 **Fax:** +49 30 3470 3912
Web: www.transparency.de

Primary SIC: 8399—Social Services, NEC
Primary NAICS: 813319—Other
Social Advocacy Organizations
E-mail: ti@transparency.de

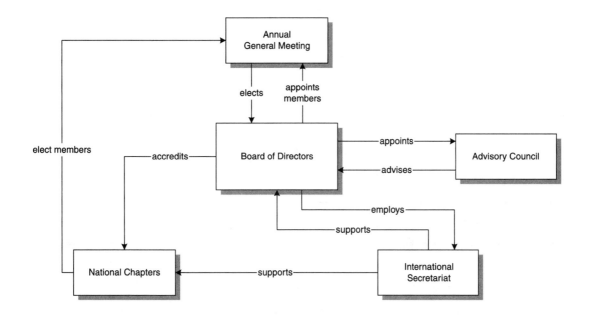

Source: Organization web site, 1998

Operator of a set of travel management agencies in the metropolitan Washington, D.C., area

8484 Georgia Ave.
Silver Spring, MD 20910-5604
Phone: (301) 589-5100 **Fax:** (301) 565-5123
Web: www.tvlon.com

Primary SIC: 4724—Travel Agencies
Primary NAICS: 56151—Travel Agencies

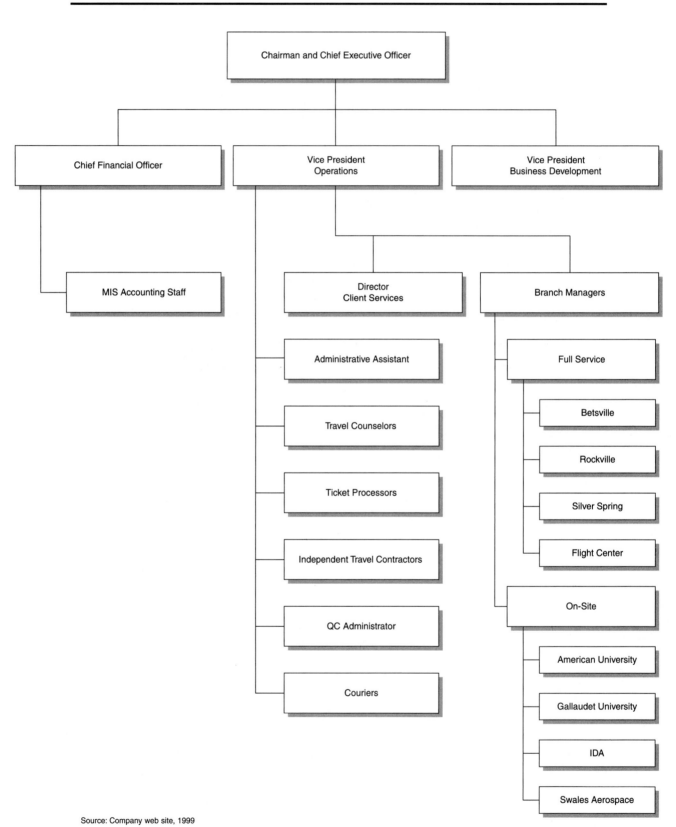

Source: Company web site, 1999

Trident Computer Resources, Inc.

A computer maintenance and software support firm with an emphasis on services for the petroleum industry

151 Industrial Way East
Eatontown, NJ 07724
Phone: (732) 544-9333 **Fax:** (732) 544-1511
Web: www.tridentusa.com

Primary SIC: 7378—Computer
Maintenance & Repair
Primary NAICS: 811212—Computer
& Office Machine R&M

Source: Company web site, 1999

Triton Transport Services, Inc.

A mid-size trucking company with a 450-unit fleet serving primarily the intermodal transportation industry

25651 Detroit Rd., Ste. 301
Westlake, OH 44145-2450
Phone: (800) 366-7623 **Fax:** (440) 808-1010

Primary SIC: 4213—Trucking, Except Local
Primary NAICS: 484121—General Freight
Trucking, Long-Distance, TL

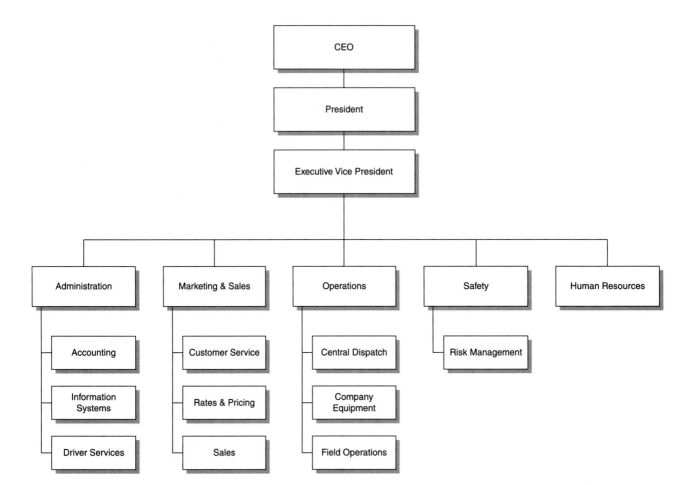

Source: Company web site, 1998

Tulsa Police Department

The department serves a city of 375,000 residents with nearly 800 officers and a support staff of 140

600 Civic Center
Tulsa, OK 74103-3822
Phone: (918) 596-9316
Web: www.tulsapolice.org

Primary SIC: 9221—Police Protection
Primary NAICS: 92212—Police Protection

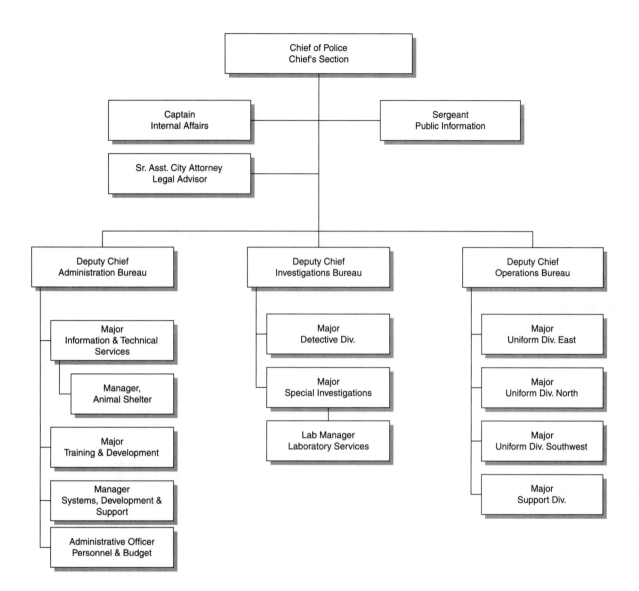

Source: Agency web site, 1998

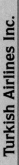

Turkish Airlines Inc.

In transition from a state-owned entity to a private company, the airline is aggressively pursuing European partnerships

Ataturk Havalimani
Yesilkoy, Istanbul, Turkey
Phone: (212) 663 63 00 **Fax:** (212) 663 47 44
Web: www.turkishairlines.com.tr

Primary SIC: 4512—Air Transportation, Scheduled
Primary NAICS: 481111—Scheduled Passenger
Air Transportation

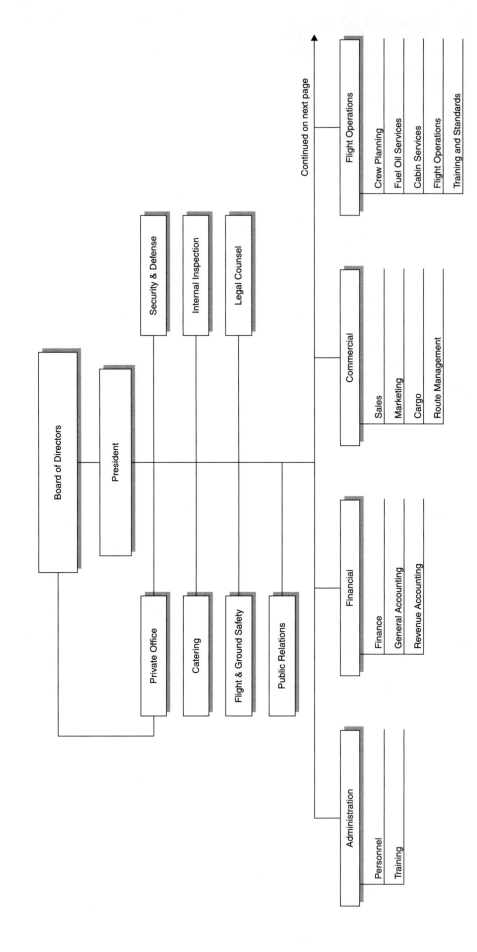

Continued on next page

Source: Company web site, 1999

Turkish Airlines Inc. (cont.)

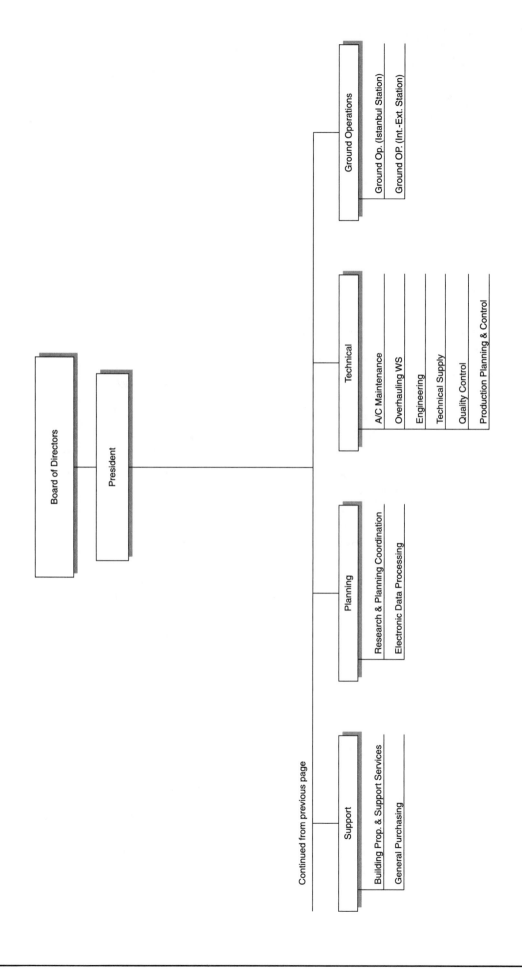

Board of Directors

President

Support
- Building Prop. & Support Services
- General Purchasing

Planning
- Research & Planning Coordination
- Electronic Data Processing

Technical
- A/C Maintenance
- Overhauling WS
- Engineering
- Technical Supply
- Quality Control
- Production Planning & Control

Ground Operations
- Ground Op. (Istanbul Station)
- Ground OP. (Int.-Ext. Station)

Continued from previous page

U S WEST, Inc.

This regional telecom agreed in 1999 to merge with long-distance carrier Qwest Communications

7800 E. Orchard Rd.
Englewood, CO 80111
Phone: (303) 793-6500
Web: www.uswest.com

Primary SIC: 4813—Telephone
Communications, Except Radiotelephone
Primary NAICS: 51331—Wired
Telecommunications Carriers

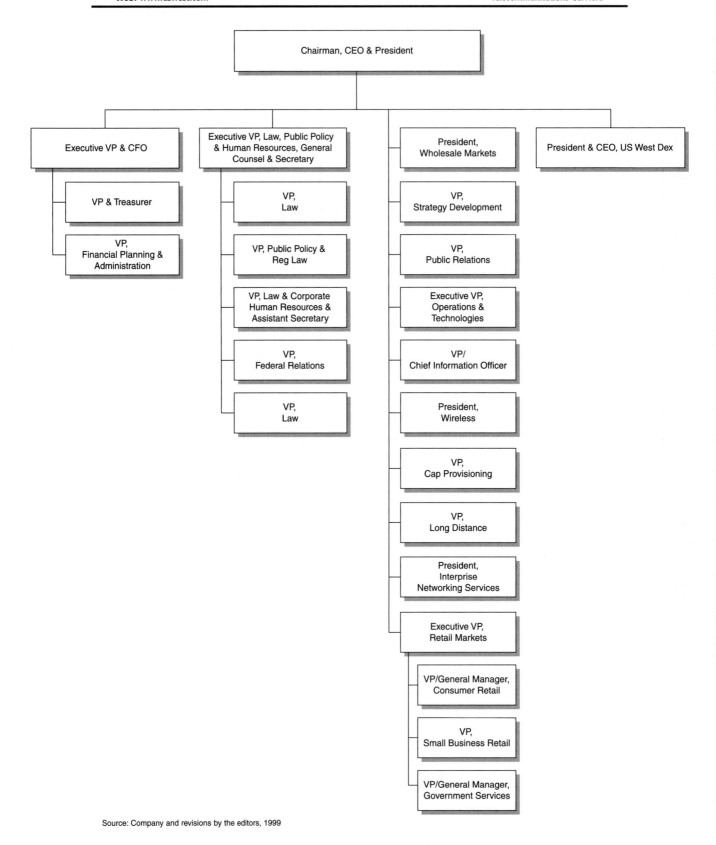

Source: Company and revisions by the editors, 1999

Ube Industries, Ltd.

A multibillion-dollar industrial materials and equipment conglomerate

3-11, Higashi-Shinagawa 2-chome
Shinagawa-ku, Tokyo 140, Japan
Phone: +81 03 5460-3311 **Fax:** +81 03 5460-3388

Primary SIC: 2821—Plastics Material
& Synthetic Resins
Primary NAICS: 325211—Plastics Material
& Resins Mfg

- Auditors
  - Auditors' Office
- Chairman
  - President

- Corporate Planning & Administration Dept.
- Finance Dept.
- Personnel Dept.
- General Affairs Dept.
- Purchasing Dept.

Chemicals & Plastics Div.
- Planning & Control Dept.
- Research & Development Dept.
- Logistics & Purchasing Dept.
- Polyolefins & Synthetic Rubber Div.
- Caprolactam & Engineering Plastics Div.
- Fine Chemicals & Industrial Chemicals Div.
- Specialty Products Div.
- Fertilizer & Agricultural Materials Div.
- Thai Synthetic Rubber Project
- Chiba Petrochemical Factory
- Nishioki Factory
- Sakai Factory
- Chemical Production Center

Construction Materials Div.
- Planning & Control Dept.
- Logistics Dept.
- Technology Development Dept.
- Cement Div.
- Building Materials Div.
- Cement Production Center

- Sapporo Branch
- Tohoku Branch
- Nagoya Branch
- Osaka Branch
- Hiroshima Branch

Continued on next page

Source: Annual report, 1997

Ube Industries, Ltd. (cont.)

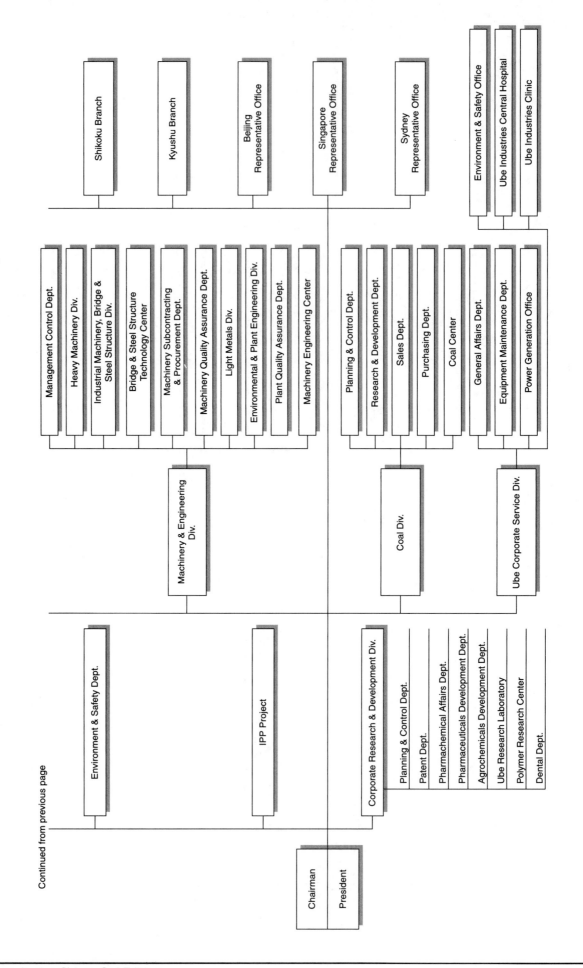

Continued from previous page

- Chairman
- President

- Environment & Safety Dept.
- IPP Project
- Corporate Research & Development Div.
  - Planning & Control Dept.
  - Patent Dept.
  - Pharmachemical Affairs Dept.
  - Pharmaceuticals Development Dept.
  - Agrochemicals Development Dept.
  - Ube Research Laboratory
  - Polymer Research Center
  - Dental Dept.

- Machinery & Engineering Div.
  - Management Control Dept.
  - Heavy Machinery Div.
  - Industrial Machinery, Bridge & Steel Structure Div.
  - Bridge & Steel Structure Technology Center
  - Machinery Subcontracting & Procurement Dept.
  - Machinery Quality Assurance Dept.
  - Light Metals Div.
  - Environmental & Plant Engineering Div.
  - Plant Quality Assurance Dept.
  - Machinery Engineering Center

- Coal Div.
  - Planning & Control Dept.
  - Research & Development Dept.
  - Sales Dept.
  - Purchasing Dept.
  - Coal Center

- Ube Corporate Service Div.
  - General Affairs Dept.
  - Equipment Maintenance Dept.
  - Power Generation Office

- Shikoku Branch
- Kyushu Branch
- Beijing Representative Office
- Singapore Representative Office
- Sydney Representative Office

- Environment & Safety Office
- Ube Industries Central Hospital
- Ube Industries Clinic

UBS AG

A European banking colossus formed by the 1998 merger between Union Bank of Switzerland and Swiss Bank Corporation

Bahnhofstrasse 45
CH-8098 Zürich, Switzerland
Phone: +41-1-234-2602 **Fax:** +41-1-234-3415
Web: www.ubs.com

Primary SIC: 6021—National Commercial Banks
Primary NAICS: 52211—Commercial Banking

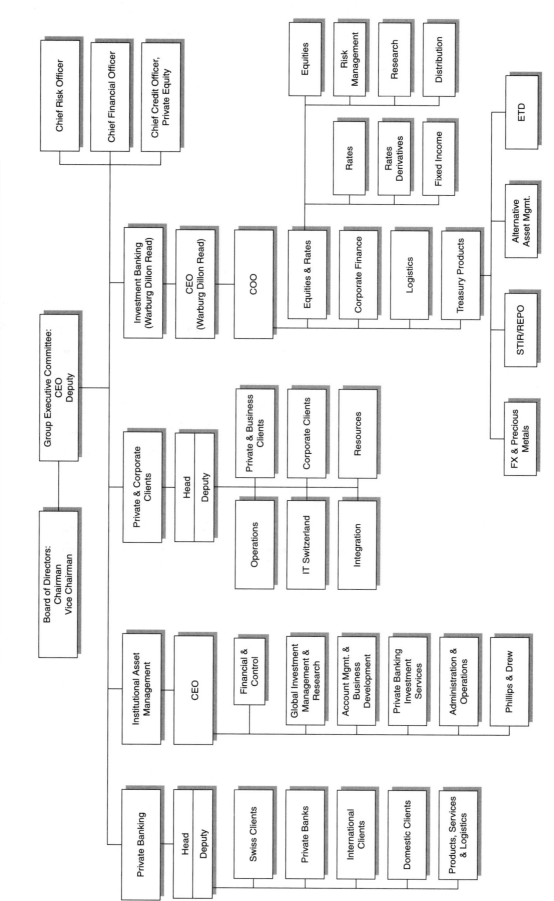

Source: Company web site, 1999

Unilever

With dual headquarters in the UK and the Netherlands, Unilever makes foods, soaps/detergents, and specialty chemicals

Unilever House
Blackfriars, London EC4P 4BQ, United Kingdom
Phone: +44 171 822 6719 **Fax:** +44 171 822 5511
Web: www.unilever.com

Primary SIC: 2841—Soaps & Other
Detergents, Except Speciality Cleaners
Primary NAICS: 325611—Soap
& Other Detergent Mfg

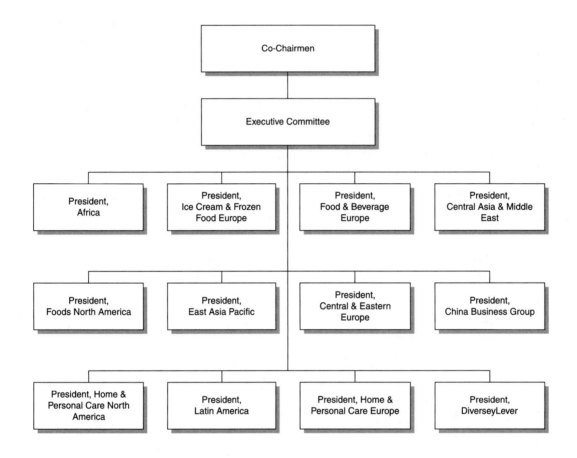

Co-Chairmen

Executive Committee

President, Africa

President, Ice Cream & Frozen Food Europe

President, Food & Beverage Europe

President, Central Asia & Middle East

President, Foods North America

President, East Asia Pacific

President, Central & Eastern Europe

President, China Business Group

President, Home & Personal Care North America

President, Latin America

President, Home & Personal Care Europe

President, DiverseyLever

Source: Company, 1999

The UN system employs over 50,000 people worldwide and has around $20 billion a year in operating expenses

New York, NY 10017
Phone: (212) 963-4475
Web: www.un.org

Primary SIC: 9721—International Affairs
Primary NAICS: 92812—International Affairs

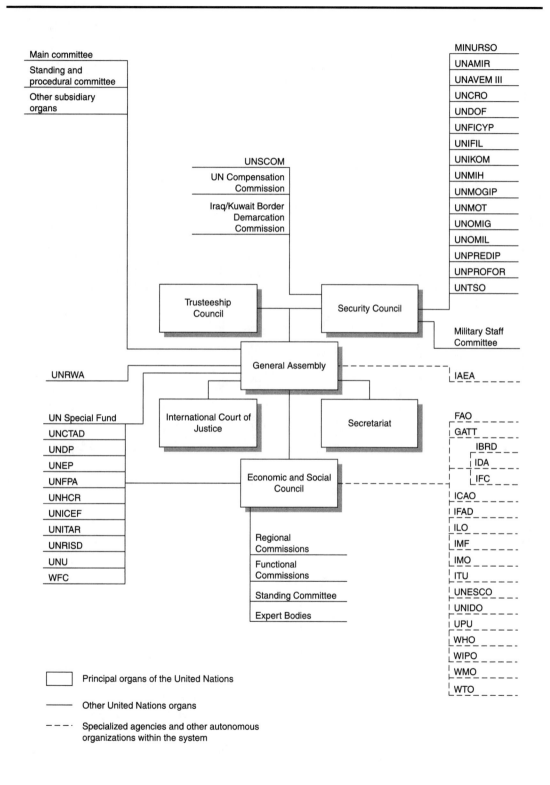

Main committee

Standing and procedural committee

Other subsidiary organs

UNSCOM
UN Compensation Commission
Iraq/Kuwait Border Demarcation Commission

MINURSO
UNAMIR
UNAVEM III
UNCRO
UNDOF
UNFICYP
UNIFIL
UNIKOM
UNMIH
UNMOGIP
UNMOT
UNOMIG
UNOMIL
UNPREDIP
UNPROFOR
UNTSO

Trusteeship Council

Security Council

Military Staff Committee

General Assembly

UNRWA

IAEA

UN Special Fund
UNCTAD
UNDP
UNEP
UNFPA
UNHCR
UNICEF
UNITAR
UNRISD
UNU
WFC

International Court of Justice

Secretariat

Economic and Social Council

Regional Commissions
Functional Commissions
Standing Committee
Expert Bodies

FAO
GATT
IBRD
IDA
IFC
ICAO
IFAD
ILO
IMF
IMO
ITU
UNESCO
UNIDO
UPU
WHO
WIPO
WMO
WTO

Principal organs of the United Nations

Other United Nations organs

Specialized agencies and other autonomous organizations within the system

Source: Organization web site, 1997

U.S. Bureau of the Census

This unit of the Commerce Department collects and disseminates demographic and economic data

Public Information Office
Room 2705, FB-3, Washington, DC 20233
Phone: (301) 457-4100
Web: www.census.gov

Primary SIC: 9611—Administration
of General Economic Programs
Primary NAICS: 92611—Administration
of General Economic Programs

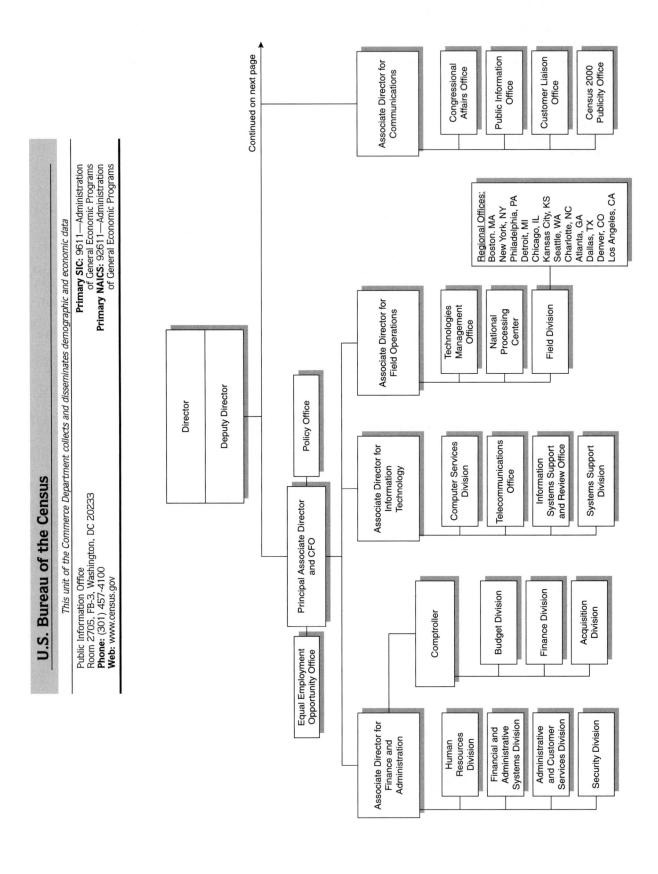

Continued on next page

Director

Deputy Director

Policy Office

Principal Associate Director and CFO

Equal Employment Opportunity Office

Associate Director for Communications
- Congressional Affairs Office
- Public Information Office
- Customer Liaison Office
- Census 2000 Publicity Office

Associate Director for Field Operations
- Technologies Management Office
- National Processing Center
- Field Division

Regional Offices:
Boston. MA
New York, NY
Philadelphia, PA
Detroit, MI
Chicago, IL
Kansas City, KS
Seattle, WA
Charlotte, NC
Atlanta, GA
Dallas, TX
Denver, CO
Los Angeles, CA

Associate Director for Information Technology
- Computer Services Division
- Telecommunications Office
- Information Systems Support and Review Office
- Systems Support Division

Comptroller
- Budget Division
- Finance Division
- Acquisition Division

Associate Director for Finance and Administration
- Human Resources Division
- Financial and Administrative Systems Division
- Administrative and Customer Services Division
- Security Division

Source: Agency web site, 1998

U.S. Bureau of the Census (cont.)

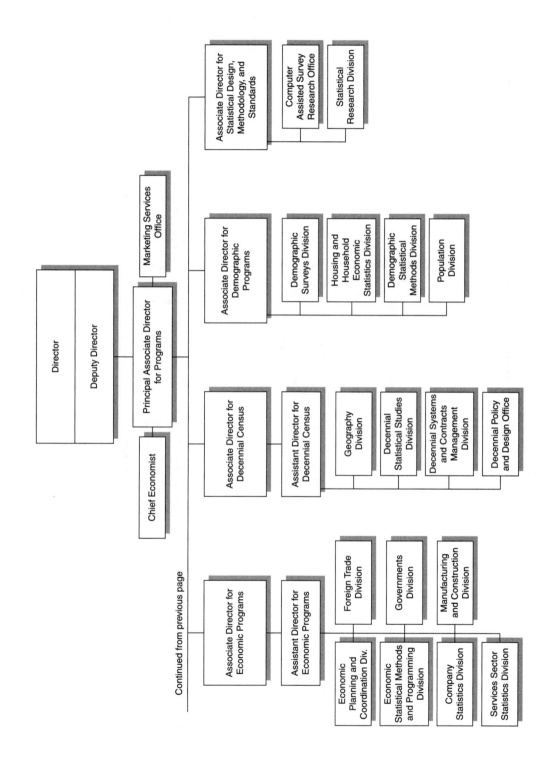

Director

Deputy Director

Chief Economist

Principal Associate Director for Programs

Marketing Services Office

Associate Director for Statistical Design, Methodology, and Standards
- Computer Assisted Survey Research Office
- Statistical Research Division

Associate Director for Demographic Programs
- Demographic Surveys Division
- Housing and Household Economic Statistics Division
- Demographic Statistical Methods Division
- Population Division

Associate Director for Decennial Census

Assistant Director for Decennial Census
- Geography Division
- Decennial Statistical Studies Division
- Decennial Systems and Contracts Management Division
- Decennial Policy and Design Office

Continued from previous page

Associate Director for Economic Programs

Assistant Director for Economic Programs
- Foreign Trade Division
- Economic Planning and Coordination Div.
- Governments Division
- Economic Statistical Methods and Programming Division
- Manufacturing and Construction Division
- Company Statistics Division
- Services Sector Statistics Division

United States Court System

An overview of the major components of the federal court system

Administrative Office of the U.S. Courts
Washington, DC 20544
Phone: (202) 502-2600   **Fax:** (202) 502-2633
Web: www.uscourts.gov

Primary SIC: 9211—Courts
Primary NAICS: 92211—Courts

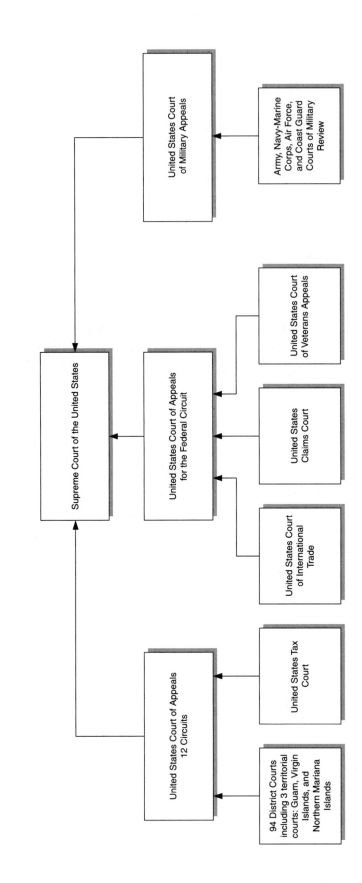

Source: Administrative Office of the U.S. Courts, 1999

United States Executive Branch

Key agencies and departments reporting to the U.S. president

1600 Pennsylvania Ave., N.W.
Washington, DC 20500
Web: www.whitehouse.gov

Primary SIC: 9111—Executive Offices
Primary NAICS: 92111—Executive Offices

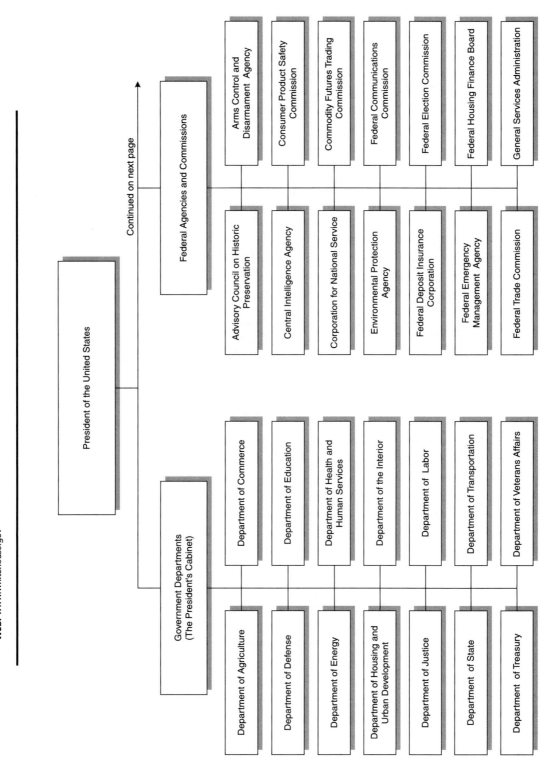

President of the United States

Government Departments
(The President's Cabinet)

Department of Commerce
Department of Education
Department of Health and Human Services
Department of the Interior
Department of Labor
Department of Transportation
Department of Veterans Affairs

Department of Agriculture
Department of Defense
Department of Energy
Department of Housing and Urban Development
Department of Justice
Department of State
Department of Treasury

Federal Agencies and Commissions

Arms Control and Disarmament Agency
Consumer Product Safety Commission
Commodity Futures Trading Commission
Federal Communications Commission
Federal Election Commission
Federal Housing Finance Board
General Services Administration

Advisory Council on Historic Preservation
Central Intelligence Agency
Corporation for National Service
Environmental Protection Agency
Federal Deposit Insurance Corporation
Federal Emergency Management Agency
Federal Trade Commission

Continued on next page

Source: Agency web site, 1998

United States Executive Branch (cont.)

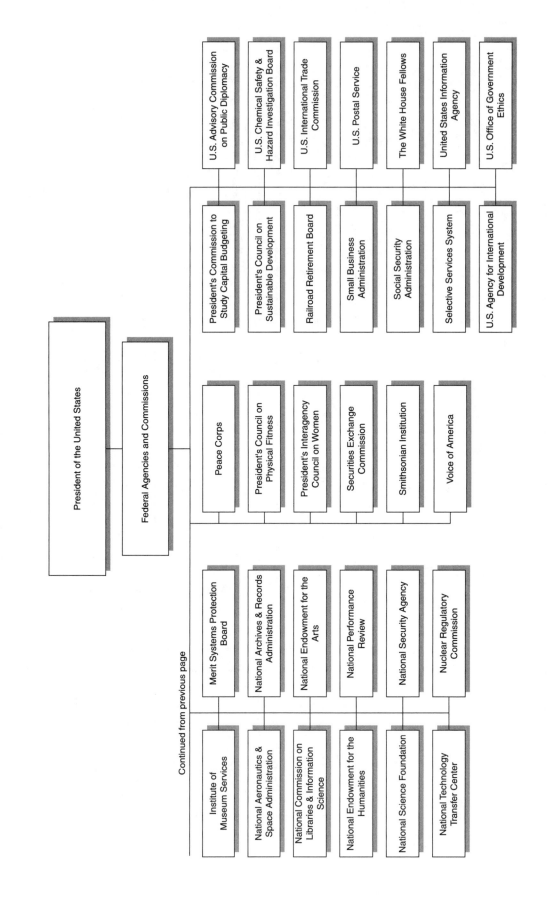

President of the United States

Federal Agencies and Commissions

Continued from previous page

Merit Systems Protection Board

National Archives & Records Administration

National Endowment for the Arts

National Performance Review

National Security Agency

Nuclear Regulatory Commission

Institute of Museum Services

National Aeronautics & Space Administration

National Commission on Libraries & Information Science

National Endowment for the Humanities

National Science Foundation

National Technology Transfer Center

Peace Corps

President's Council on Physical Fitness

President's Interagency Council on Women

Securities Exchange Commission

Smithsonian Institution

Voice of America

President's Commission to Study Capital Budgeting

President's Council on Sustainable Development

Railroad Retirement Board

Small Business Administration

Social Security Administration

Selective Services System

U.S. Agency for International Development

U.S. Advisory Commission on Public Diplomacy

U.S. Chemical Safety & Hazard Investigation Board

U.S. International Trade Commission

U.S. Postal Service

The White House Fellows

United States Information Agency

U.S. Office of Government Ethics

United States Postal Service

This independent agency handles approximately 200 billion pieces of mail a year through 38,000 post offices

475 L'Enfant Plaza, S.W.
Washington, DC 20260-5241
Web: www.usps.gov

Primary SIC: 4311—Postal Service
Primary NAICS: 49111—Postal Service

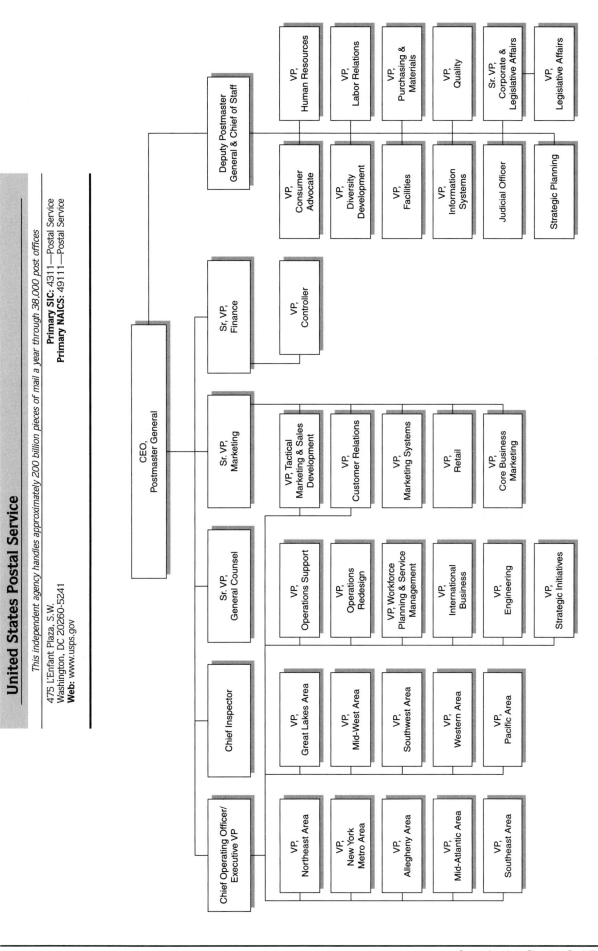

University of California

The 9-campus UC system supports approximately 170,000 undergraduate and graduate students

Office of the President
University Hall, Berkeley, CA 94720
Phone: (510) 642-6000
Web: www.ucop.edu

Primary SIC: 8221—Colleges,
Universities, & Professional Schools
Primary NAICS: 61131—Colleges,
Universities & Professional Schools

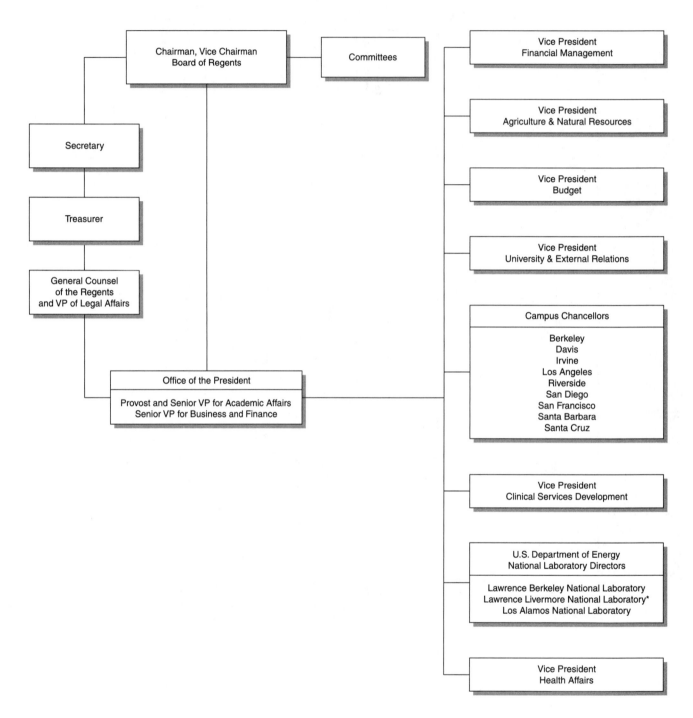

*see separate chart

Source: Organization, 1999

University of California San Diego Libraries

The university library system held nearly 2.6 million volumes as of 1998 and is run by a full-time staff of over 300

Administrative Office, Geisel Library
La Jolla, CA 92093
Web: www.ucsd.edu/libraries/

Primary SIC: 8231—Libraries
Primary NAICS: 51412—Libraries & Archives

University Librarian
Deputy University Librarian

Library Development

Associate University Librarian, Sciences

- Biomedical Library
- Medical Center Library
- Science & Engineering Library
- Center for Magnetic Recording & Research Information Center
- Scripps Institution of Oceanography Library

Associate University Librarian, Social Sciences & Humanities

- Social Sciences & Humanities Library
- Art & Architecture Library
- Music Library
- Mandeville Special Collections Library
- Undergraduate Library
- International Relations & Pacific Studies Library
- User Outreach Office

Assistant University Librarian, Human Resources & Administrative Services

- Administrative Office Management Services Officer
- Business Services Dept.
- Personnel Dept.
- Facilities Dept.
- Staff Training Dept.

Assistant University Librarian, User Support Services

- Acquisitions Dept.
- Catalog Dept.
- Preservation Dept.
- Systems Dept.
- Infopath Services Office

Source: Organization web site, 1997

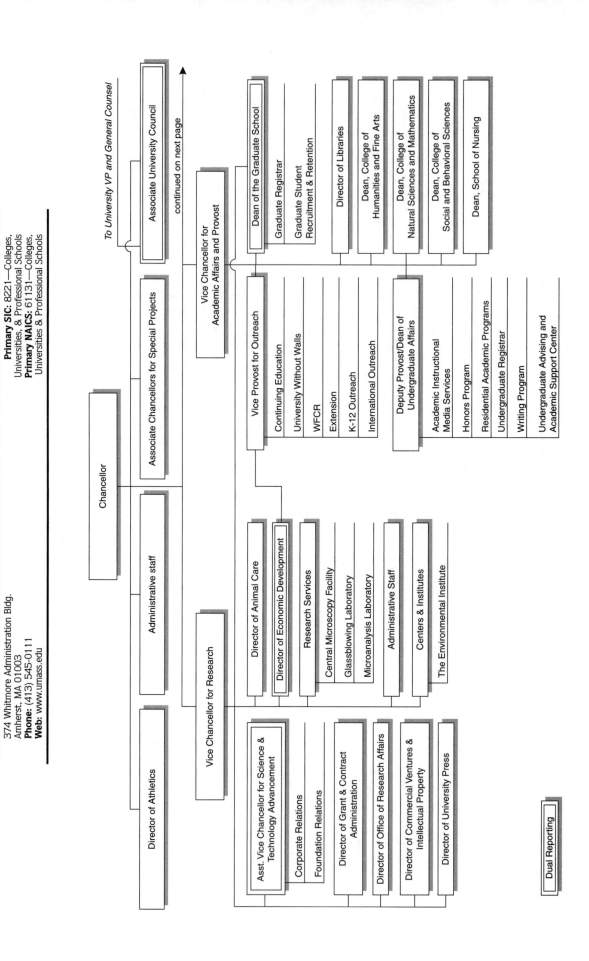

University of Massachusetts Amherst

Amherst is the flagship campus of the University of Massachusetts system

374 Whitmore Administration Bldg.
Amherst, MA 01003
Phone: (413) 545-0111
Web: www.umass.edu

Primary SIC: 8221—Colleges,
Universities, & Professional Schools
Primary NAICS: 61131—Colleges,
Universities & Professional Schools

To University VP and General Counsel

continued on next page

Chancellor

- Associate University Council
- Associate Chancellors for Special Projects
- Administrative staff
- Director of Athletics
- Vice Chancellor for Research
  - Director of Animal Care
  - Director of Economic Development
    - Research Services
    - Central Microscopy Facility
    - Glassblowing Laboratory
    - Microanalysis Laboratory
    - Administrative Staff
    - Centers & Institutes
    - The Environmental Institute
  - Asst. Vice Chancellor for Science & Technology Advancement
    - Corporate Relations
    - Foundation Relations
  - Director of Grant & Contract Administration
  - Director of Office of Research Affairs
  - Director of Commercial Ventures & Intellectual Property
  - Director of University Press
- Vice Chancellor for Academic Affairs and Provost
  - Vice Provost for Outreach
    - Continuing Education
    - University Without Walls
    - WFCR
    - Extension
    - K-12 Outreach
    - International Outreach
  - Deputy Provost/Dean of Undergraduate Affairs
    - Academic Instructional Media Services
    - Honors Program
    - Residential Academic Programs
    - Undergraduate Registrar
    - Writing Program
    - Undergraduate Advising and Academic Support Center
  - Dean of the Graduate School
    - Graduate Registrar
    - Graduate Student Recruitment & Retention
  - Director of Libraries
  - Dean, College of Humanities and Fine Arts
  - Dean, College of Natural Sciences and Mathematics
  - Dean, College of Social and Behavioral Sciences
  - Dean, School of Nursing

Dual Reporting

Source: Organization web site, 1998

University of Massachusetts Amherst (cont.)

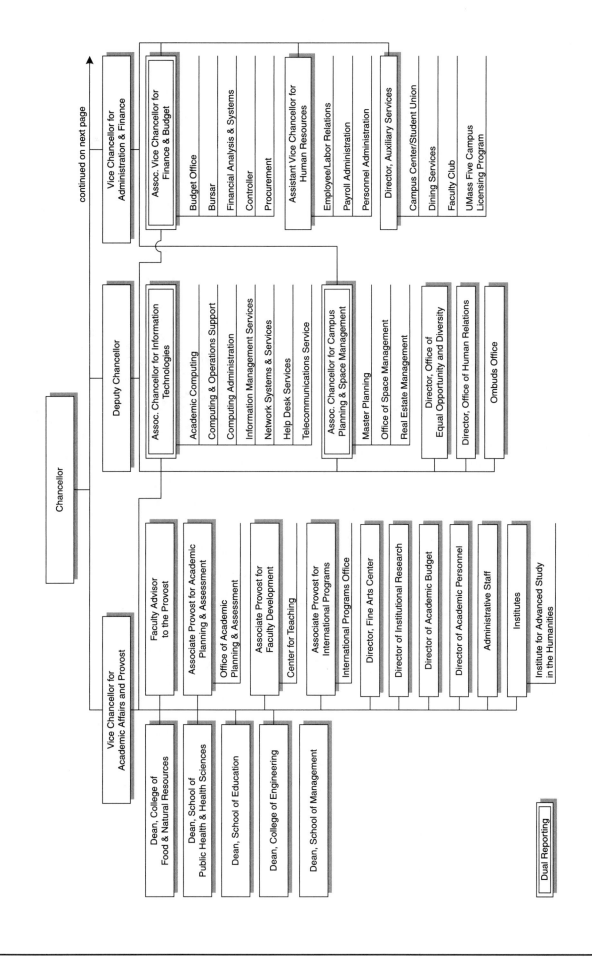

continued on next page

Chancellor

Vice Chancellor for Administration & Finance

Assoc. Vice Chancellor for Finance & Budget
- Budget Office
- Bursar
- Financial Analysis & Systems
- Controller
- Procurement

Assistant Vice Chancellor for Human Resources
- Employee/Labor Relations
- Payroll Administration
- Personnel Administration

Director, Auxiliary Services
- Campus Center/Student Union
- Dining Services
- Faculty Club
- UMass Five Campus Licensing Program

Deputy Chancellor

Assoc. Chancellor for Information Technologies
- Academic Computing
- Computing & Operations Support
- Computing Administration
- Information Management Services
- Network Systems & Services
- Help Desk Services
- Telecommunications Service

Assoc. Chancellor for Campus Planning & Space Management
- Master Planning
- Office of Space Management
- Real Estate Management

Director, Office of Equal Opportunity and Diversity

Director, Office of Human Relations

Ombuds Office

Vice Chancellor for Academic Affairs and Provost

Faculty Advisor to the Provost

Associate Provost for Academic Planning & Assessment
- Office of Academic Planning & Assessment

Associate Provost for Faculty Development
- Center for Teaching

Associate Provost for International Programs
- International Programs Office

Director, Fine Arts Center

Director of Institutional Research

Director of Academic Budget

Director of Academic Personnel

Administrative Staff

Institutes
- Institute for Advanced Study in the Humanities

Dean, College of Food & Natural Resources

Dean, School of Public Health & Health Sciences

Dean, School of Education

Dean, College of Engineering

Dean, School of Management

Dual Reporting

University of Massachusetts Amherst (cont.)

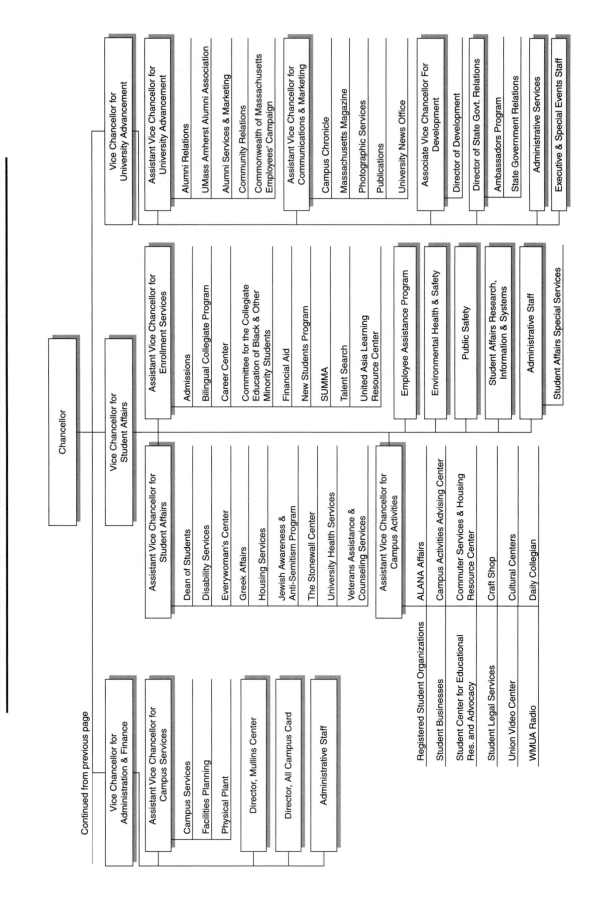

Chancellor

Vice Chancellor for University Advancement
- **Assistant Vice Chancellor for University Advancement**
  - Alumni Relations
  - UMass Amherst Alumni Association
  - Alumni Services & Marketing
  - Community Relations
  - Commonwealth of Massachusetts Employees' Campaign
- **Assistant Vice Chancellor for Communications & Marketing**
  - Campus Chronicle
  - Massachusetts Magazine
  - Photographic Services
  - Publications
  - University News Office
- **Associate Vice Chancellor For Development**
  - Director of Development
  - Director of State Govt. Relations
  - Ambassadors Program
  - State Government Relations
  - Administrative Services
  - Executive & Special Events Staff

Vice Chancellor for Student Affairs
- **Assistant Vice Chancellor for Enrollment Services**
  - Admissions
  - Bilingual Collegiate Program
  - Career Center
  - Committee for the Collegiate Education of Black & Other Minority Students
  - Financial Aid
  - New Students Program
  - SUMMA
  - Talent Search
  - United Asia Learning Resource Center
- Employee Assistance Program
- Environmental Health & Safety
- Public Safety
- Student Affairs Research, Information & Systems
- Administrative Staff
- Student Affairs Special Services
- **Assistant Vice Chancellor for Student Affairs**
  - Dean of Students
  - Disability Services
  - Everywoman's Center
  - Greek Affairs
  - Housing Services
  - Jewish Awareness & Anti-Semitism Program
  - The Stonewall Center
  - University Health Services
  - Veterans Assistance & Counseling Services
- **Assistant Vice Chancellor for Campus Activities**
  - ALANA Affairs
  - Campus Activities Advising Center
  - Commuter Services & Housing Resource Center
  - Craft Shop
  - Cultural Centers
  - Daily Collegian
  - Registered Student Organizations
  - Student Businesses
  - Student Center for Educational Res. and Advocacy
  - Student Legal Services
  - Union Video Center
  - WMUA Radio

Continued from previous page

Vice Chancellor for Administration & Finance
- **Assistant Vice Chancellor for Campus Services**
  - Campus Services
  - Facilities Planning
  - Physical Plant
- Director, Mullins Center
- Director, All Campus Card
- Administrative Staff

University of Toronto

Canada's largest university has some 50,000 full- and part-time students in its undergraduate and graduate programs

Toronto, ON M5S 1A1 Canada
Phone: (416) 978-2011
Web: www.utoronto.ca

Primary SIC: 8221—Colleges,
Universities, & Professional Schools
Primary NAICS: 61131—Colleges,
Universities & Professional Schools

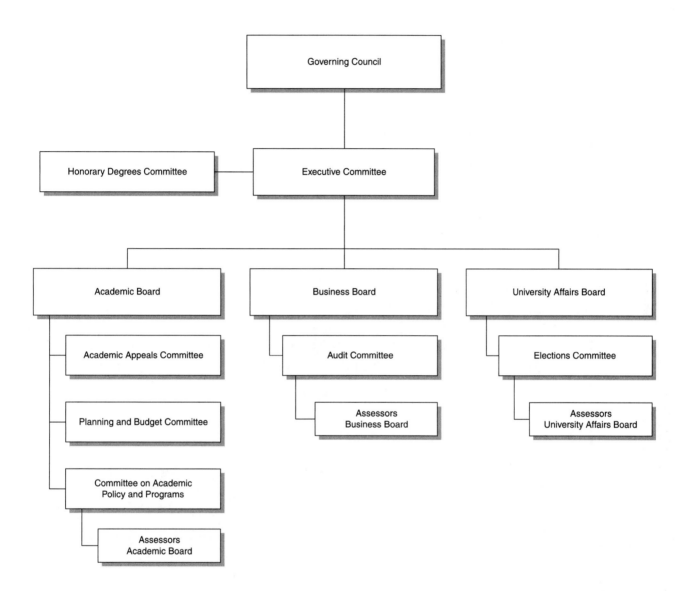

Source: Organization web site, 1998

University System of Georgia

The Georgia state higher education system consists of over 30 colleges and universities and some 200,000 students

270 Washington Street, S.W.
Atlanta, GA 30334
Phone: (404) 656-2512
Web: www.peachnet.edu

Primary SIC: 8221—Colleges,
Universities, & Professional Schools
Primary NAICS: 61131—Colleges,
Universities & Professional Schools

Officers: Chair, Vice
Chair, Chancellor,
Secretary, Treasurer

Members,
Board of Regents

Chancellor

Special Asst.

Secretary to the
Board/Executive
Administrative Asst.

Senior Vice Chancellor
Academic Affairs

Assistant Vice Chancellor
Academic Affairs/Director
of Regents' Testing

Assistant Vice Chancellor
Academic Affairs

Assistant Vice Chancellor
Academic Affairs

Director
Pre-College Programs

Vice Chancellor/CIO
Information & Instructional
Technology

Associate Vice
Chancellor
Information Technology

Asst. Vice Chancellor
Distance Education &
Academic Innovation

Executive Director
Virtual Library,
Customer & Info Svcs.

Vice Chancellor
Student Services

Associate Vice Chancellor
Planning and Policy Analysis

Assistant Vice
Chancellor
Planning

Director
System Policy
Research

Associate Vice Chancellor
Academic Affairs

Director
International Programs &
Services

Senior Vice Chancellor
Capital Resources/
Treasurer

Associate Vice Chancellor
Fiscal Affairs

Budget Director

Director
Business Services

Assistant Vice Chancellor
Internal Audit

Vice Chancellor
Facilities

Assistant Vice
Chancellor
Design & Construction

Assistant Vice
Chancellor
Facilities

Director
Facilities Planning

Director
Environmental Safety

Continued on next page

Source: Organization web site, 1999

University System of Georgia (cont.)

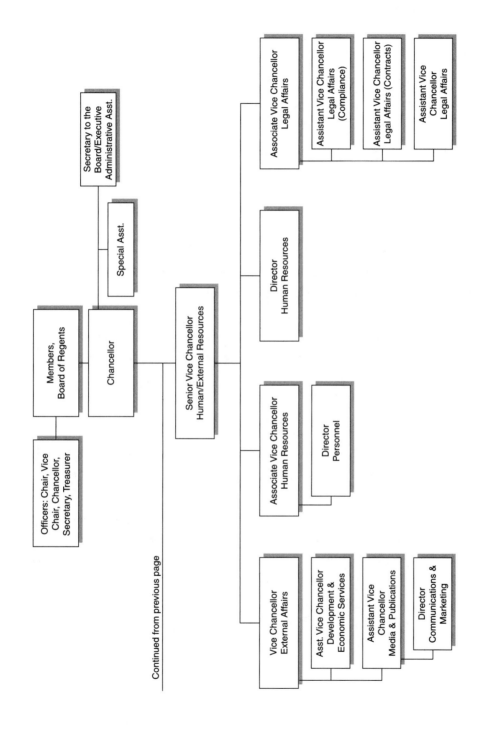

Secretary to the Board/Executive Administrative Asst.

Special Asst.

Members, Board of Regents

Officers: Chair, Vice Chair, Chancellor, Secretary, Treasurer

Chancellor

Senior Vice Chancellor Human/External Resources

Continued from previous page

Associate Vice Chancellor Legal Affairs

Assistant Vice Chancellor Legal Affairs (Compliance)

Assistant Vice Chancellor Legal Affairs (Contracts)

Assistant Vice Chancellor Legal Affairs

Director Human Resources

Associate Vice Chancellor Human Resources

Director Personnel

Vice Chancellor External Affairs

Asst. Vice Chancellor Development & Economic Services

Assistant Vice Chancellor Media & Publications

Director Communications & Marketing

This forest products giant garners most of its sales from printing papers (mostly magazine) & converted paper products

Snellmaninkatu 13, PL 203
FIN-00171 Helsinki, Finland
Web: www.upm-kymmene.com

Primary SIC: 2621—Paper Mills
Primary NAICS: 322121—Paper
(except Newsprint) Mills

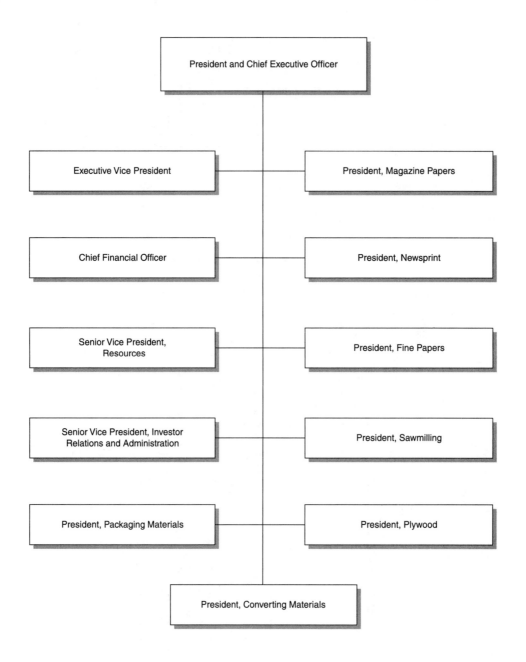

President and Chief Executive Officer

Executive Vice President

President, Magazine Papers

Chief Financial Officer

President, Newsprint

Senior Vice President, Resources

President, Fine Papers

Senior Vice President, Investor Relations and Administration

President, Sawmilling

President, Packaging Materials

President, Plywood

President, Converting Materials

Source: Annual report, 1998

USX Corporation

A holding company for Marathon, a petroleum refiner and marketer, and U.S. Steel, a diversified steel maker

600 Grant St.
Pittsburgh, PA 15219-4776
Phone: (412) 433-1121
Web: www.usx.com

Primary SIC: 2911—Petroleum Refining
Primary NAICS: 32411—Petroleum Refineries

Board Committees

- Audit Committee
- Committee on Financial Policy
- Compensation Committee
- Executive Committee
- Organization & Corporate Governance
- Public Policy Committee

Board of Directors

Chairman of the Board & Chief Executive Officer

President, U.S. Steel Group

VP, Governmental Affairs

VP & Assistant to Chairman

VP, Investor Relations

General Counsel, Secretary & Sr. VP, Human Resources & Public Affairs

Vice Chairman & Chief Financial Officer

VP & Comptroller

VP & Treasurer

VP, Taxes

Vice Chairman, Marathon Group & President, Marathon Oil Co.

Source: Company and revisions by the editors, 1999

VF Corporation

Manufacturer and marketer of popularly priced clothing under brand names such as Wrangler and Lee

678 Green Valley Rd., Ste. 500
Greensboro, NC 27408
Phone: (336) 547-6000 **Fax:** (336) 547-7630
Web: www.vfc.com

Primary SIC: 2325—Men's Trousers & Slacks
Primary NAICS: 315224—Men's/Boys'
Cut & Sew Trouser/Slack/Jean Mfg

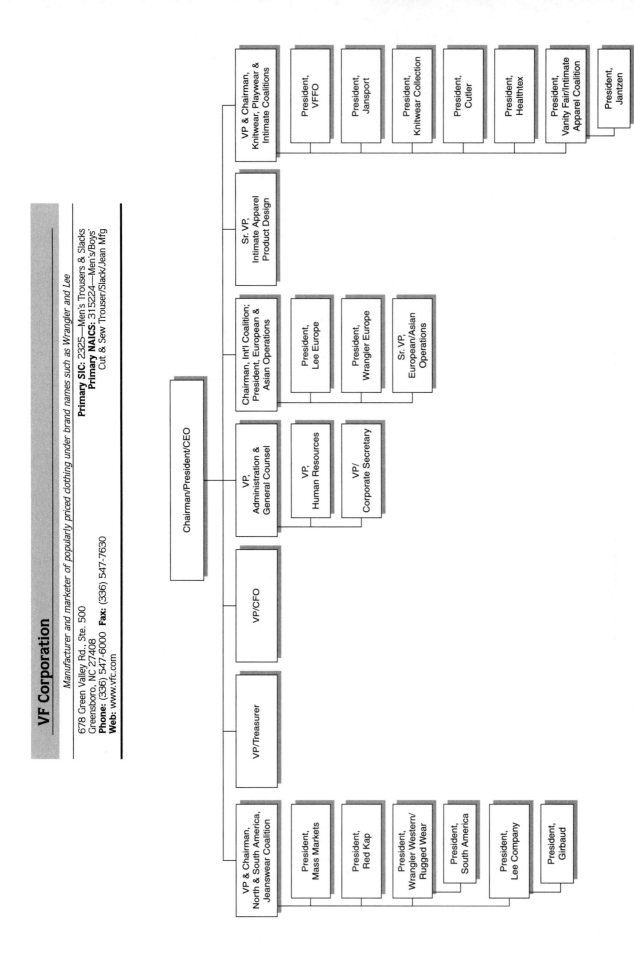

Source: Company and revisions by the editors, 1997

Visteon Automotive Systems

This Ford division is the 2nd-largest auto parts supplier worldwide and is preparing to operate as an independent company

5500 Auto Club Dr.
Dearborn, MI 48126
Phone: (313) 396-5145 **Fax:** (313) 322-9000
Web: www.visteon.com

Primary SIC: 3714—Motor
Vehicle Parts & Accessories
Primary NAICS: 336322—Other Motor
Vehicle Electrical & Electronic Equip Mfg

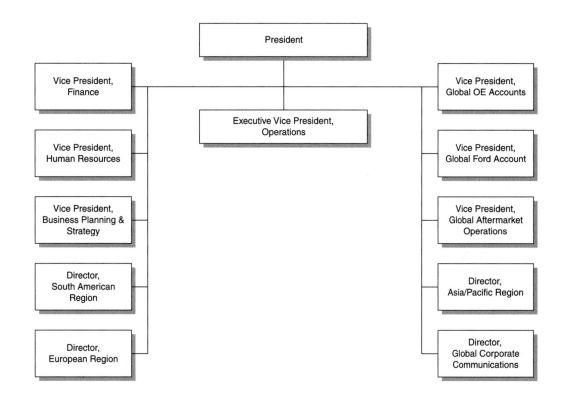

Source: Company web site, 1999

VisualSoft (India) Ltd.

This publicly traded firm supplies contract programming services primarily to clients outside India

1271, Rd.No.1, Jubilee Hills
Hyderabad - 500 033, India
Phone: 91-40-3546714 **Fax:** 91-40-3607637
Web: www.visualsoft-india.com

Primary SIC: 7371—Computer
Programming Services
Primary NAICS: 541511—Custom
Computer Programming Services

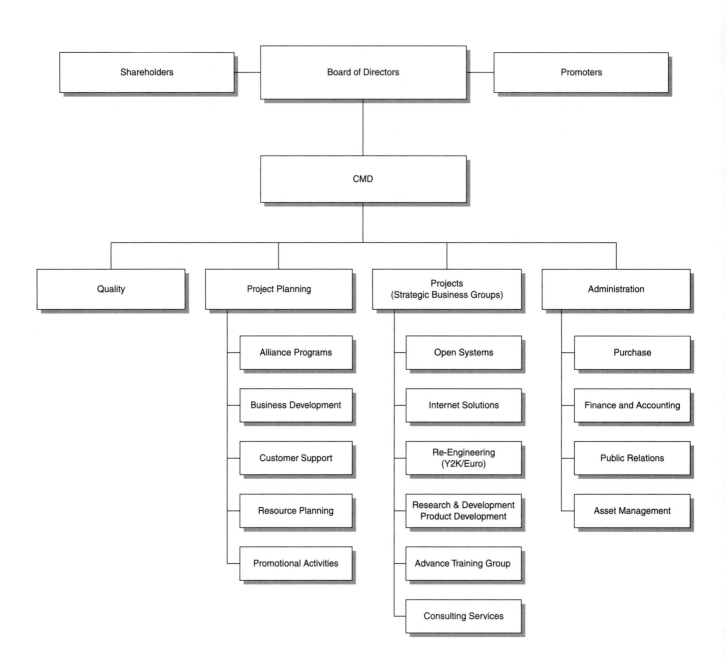

Source: Company web site, 1999

Warner-Lambert Company

This consumer-oriented company makes pharmaceuticals, personal care products, and confectionery

201 Tabor Rd.
Morris Plains, NJ 07950-2693
Phone: (201) 540-2000
Web: www.warner-lambert.com

Primary SIC: 2834—Pharmaceutical Preparations
Primary NAICS: 325412—Pharmaceutical
Preparation Mfg

Pharmaceutical Sector

- Parke-Davis, U.S. & Mexico
- Parke-Davis, Canada
- Parke-Davis, Japan
- Parke-Davis, Australia
- Parke-Davis, South Africa
- Goedecke
- Parke-Davis, France, Benelux
- Parke-Davis, United Kingdom, Eire, Nordic Countries
- Parke-Davis, Italy, Greece
- Parke-Davis, Spain, Portugal
- Parke-Davis Research
- Capsugel

Consumer Healthcare Sector

- Consumer Healthcare, U.S.A.
- Consumer Healthcare, Canada
- Consumer Healthcare, Australia, New Zealand
- Consumer Healthcare, Europe
- Consumer Healthcare, New Mexico
- Consumer Healthcare, Japan
- Consumer Healthcare, South Africa
- Consumer Healthcare, Research & Development

Adams Sector

- Adams, U.S.A.
- Confectionery Products, Europe/Middle East/Africa
- Confectionery Products, Brazil Region
- Confectionery Products, South Africa
- Confectionery Products, Japan
- Confectionery Products, Mexico
- Confectionery Products, Canada
- Confectionery Products, Research & Development

Shaving Products Group

Tetra

- Latin America/Asia Sector

Source: Company web site, 1999

Designer and manufacturer of electronic components for military and commercial communications devices

3601 E. University Dr.
Phoenix, AZ 85034
Phone: (602) 437-1520 **Fax:** (602) 437-9120
Web: www.whiteedc.com

Primary SIC: 3674—Semiconductors
& Related Devices
Primary NAICS: 334413—Semiconductor
& Related Device Mfg

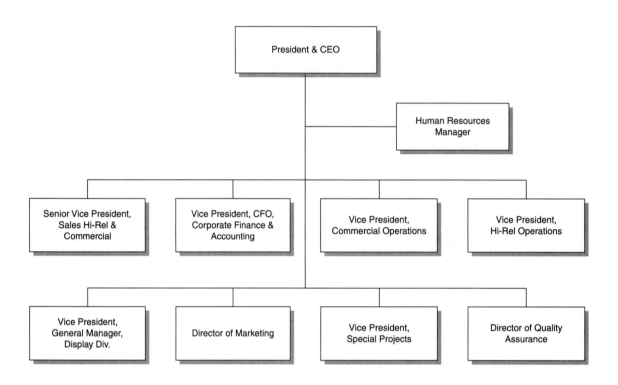

Source: Company web site, 1999

Woodward-Clyde Group, Inc.

Owned by URS Corp., this multinational engineering firm specializes in environmental engineering for urban applications

Stanford Place 3, Ste. 600
4582 S. Ulster St., Denver, CO 80237-2637
Phone: (303) 740-2600 **Fax:** (303) 740-2650
Web: www.wcc.com

Primary SIC: 8711—Engineering Services
Primary NAICS: 54133—Engineering Services

Employee Shareholders

Woodward-Clyde Group, Inc. Board of Directors

Woodward-Clyde Group, Inc. Executive Committee

Montgomery Group Ltd.

Woodward-Clyde Consultants (WCC)

Western Operating Group

Southern Operating Group

Eastern Operating Group

Environmental Practice Group

Waste Practice Group

Geo-Engineering Practice Group

Operations/Practice Matrix

Woodward-Clyde Federal Services (WCFS)

East
North Central
Midwest
Northwest
West
Nevada Project

Woodward-Clyde International (WCI)

Asia-Pacific OG

Europe OG

Mexico OU

Woodward-Constructors (WCO)

Geo-Con, Inc.

Source: Company web site, 1997

The World Bank Group

A UN organization devoted to encouraging and funding economic development in less developed countries

1818 H St., N.W.
Washington, DC 20433
Phone: (202) 477-1234
Web: www.worldbank.org

Primary SIC: 9721—International Affairs
Primary NAICS: 92812—International Affairs

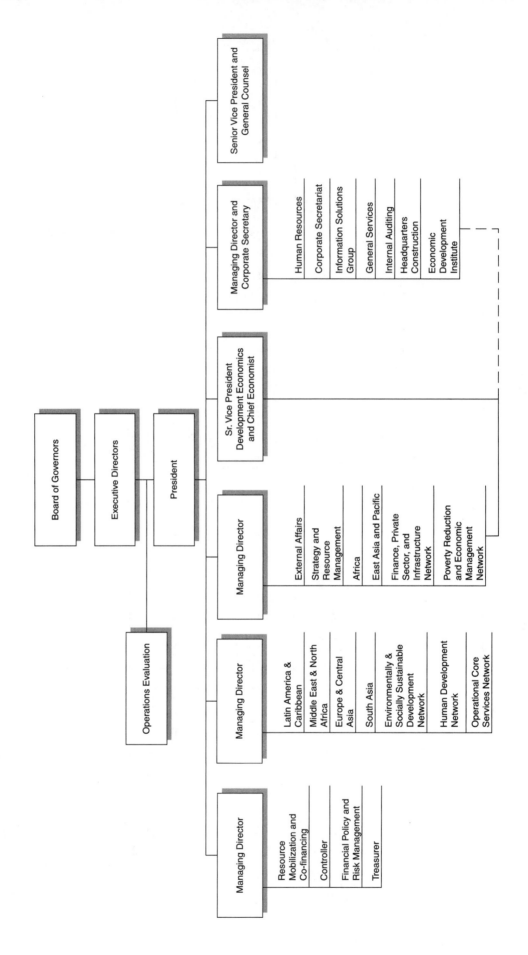

Source: Organization web site, 1998

World Energy Council

A major international cooperative organization for promoting sustainable use and development of energy resources

34 St. James's Street
London SW1A 1HD, United Kingdom
Phone: +44 171 930 3966 **Fax:** +44 171 925 0452
Web: www.wec.co.uk

Primary SIC: 8699—Membership Organizations, NEC
Primary NAICS: 81399—Oth Similar
Org (exc Business/Prof/Labor/Pol)
E-mail: info@wec.co.uk

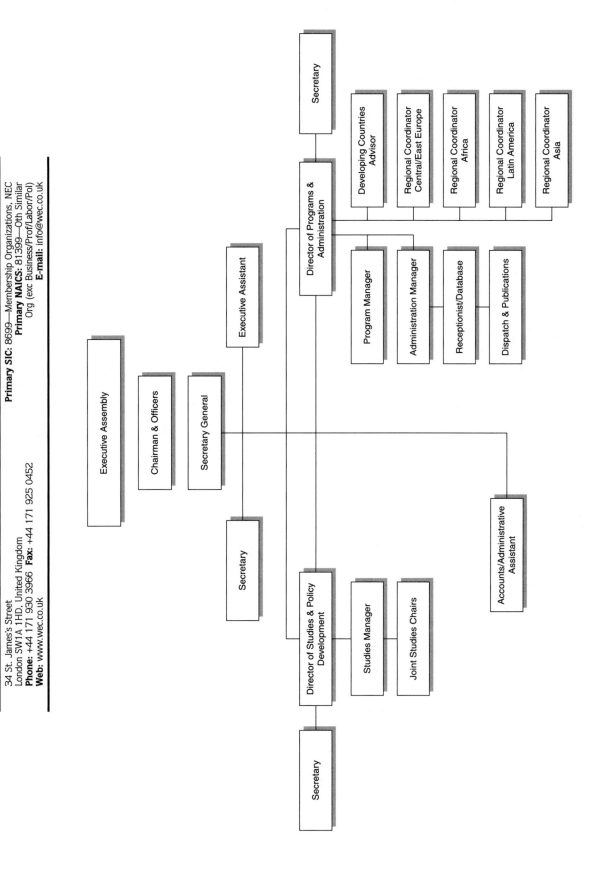

World Trade Organization

The international body responsible for upholding trade agreements and resolving trade disputes

154 rue de Lausanne
CH-1211 Geneva 21, Switzerland
Phone: +41 22 739-5111
Web: www.wto.org

Primary SIC: 9721—International Affairs
Primary NAICS: 92812—International Affairs

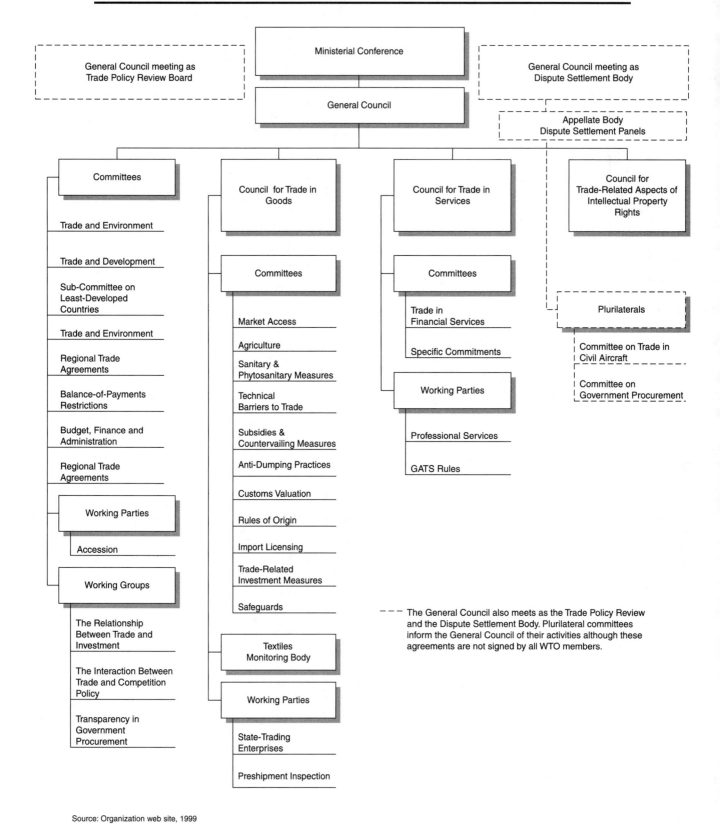

General Council meeting as
Trade Policy Review Board

Ministerial Conference

General Council

General Council meeting as
Dispute Settlement Body

Appellate Body
Dispute Settlement Panels

Committees

Trade and Environment

Trade and Development

Sub-Committee on
Least-Developed
Countries

Trade and Environment

Regional Trade
Agreements

Balance-of-Payments
Restrictions

Budget, Finance and
Administration

Regional Trade
Agreements

Working Parties

Accession

Working Groups

The Relationship
Between Trade and
Investment

The Interaction Between
Trade and Competition
Policy

Transparency in
Government
Procurement

Council for Trade in
Goods

Committees

Market Access

Agriculture

Sanitary &
Phytosanitary Measures

Technical
Barriers to Trade

Subsidies &
Countervailing Measures

Anti-Dumping Practices

Customs Valuation

Rules of Origin

Import Licensing

Trade-Related
Investment Measures

Safeguards

Textiles
Monitoring Body

Working Parties

State-Trading
Enterprises

Preshipment Inspection

Council for Trade in
Services

Committees

Trade in
Financial Services

Specific Commitments

Working Parties

Professional Services

GATS Rules

Council for
Trade-Related Aspects of
Intellectual Property
Rights

Plurilaterals

Committee on Trade in
Civil Aircraft

Committee on
Government Procurement

– – – The General Council also meets as the Trade Policy Review
and the Dispute Settlement Body. Plurilateral committees
inform the General Council of their activities although these
agreements are not signed by all WTO members.

Source: Organization web site, 1999

Xerox Corporation

Maker of copiers, scanners, printers, and related devices, Xerox also obtains a large share of its sales from services

800 Long Ridge Rd.
Stamford, CT 06904
Phone: (203) 968-3000 **Fax:** (203) 968-3572
Web: www.xerox.com

Primary SIC: 3861—Photographic
Equipment & Supplies
Primary NAICS: 333315—Photographic
& Photocopying Equipment Mfg

▶ **REORGANIZATION Part 1 (1996)**
For additional details on the restructuring
see profiles starting on page 331

Continued on next page

CEO

Fuji Xerox

Production Systems Group Pres. & Sr. VP
- Engineering Sys. Div. President
- Printing Unit Sr. VP
- Publishing Unit Sr. VP
- Professional Services Unit VPGM
- Professional Services Unit VPGM
- Group Support

Office Doc. Products Group Pres. & Sr. VP
- Office Network Copying Unit VPGM
- Convenience Copier Unit VPGM
- Strategic Programs VP
- Work Group Copier Unit VPGM
- Network Marketing VP
- Department Copier Unit VPGM
- Group Support
- Color Solutions Unit VPGM

Desktop Products Group Pres. & VP
- Desktop Doc. Sys. Div. President
- Personal Copiers Unit VPGM
- Desktop Printers Unit VPGM
- Channels Operations VP
- Group Support

Customer Operations Executive VP
- U.S. Cust. Ops. Division President
- RX Cust. Ops. Division President
- Americas Cust. Ops. Div. President
- China Cust. Ops. Div. President
- Xerox Bus. Sys. Division President
- Cust. Ops. Staff VP
- Customer Service Director

Corp. Strat. Services Sr. VP
- Manufacturing Support VP
- Int. Supply Chain VP
- Supplies Materials VP
- EH&S Director
- Education & Learning VP

Source: Company web site, 1999

Xerox Corporation (cont.)

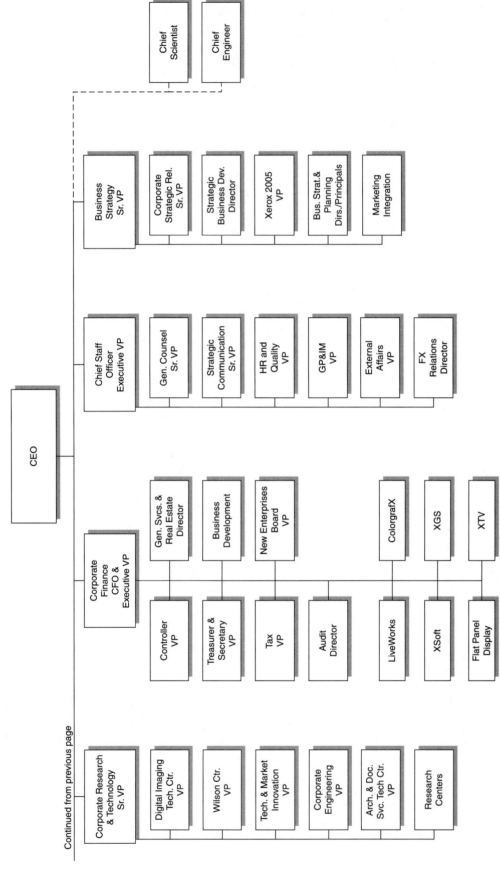

Continued from previous page

Xerox Corporation (cont.)

REORGANIZATION Part 2 (1999)

For additional details on the restructuring see profiles starting on page 331

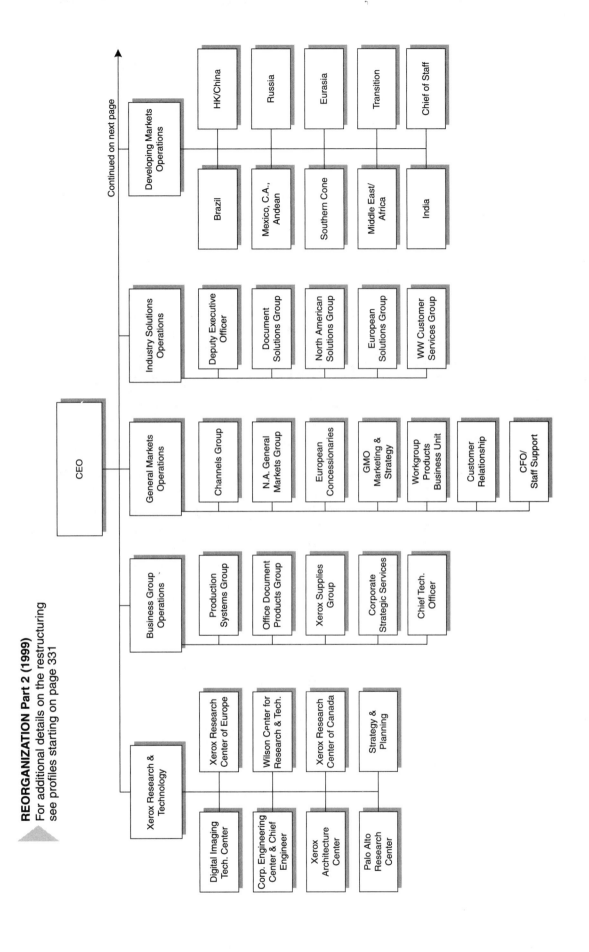

Continued on next page

CEO

Xerox Research & Technology
- Xerox Research Center of Europe
- Wilson Center for Research & Tech.
- Xerox Research Center of Canada
- Strategy & Planning
- Digital Imaging Tech. Center
- Corp. Engineering Center & Chief Engineer
- Xerox Architecture Center
- Palo Alto Research Center

Business Group Operations
- Production Systems Group
- Office Document Products Group
- Xerox Supplies Group
- Corporate Strategic Services
- Chief Tech. Officer

General Markets Operations
- Channels Group
- N.A. General Markets Group
- European Concessionaries
- GMO Marketing & Strategy
- Workgroup Products Business Unit
- Customer Relationship
- CFO/ Staff Support

Industry Solutions Operations
- Deputy Executive Officer
- Document Solutions Group
- North American Solutions Group
- European Solutions Group
- WW Customer Services Group

Developing Markets Operations
- HK/China
- Russia
- Eurasia
- Transition
- Chief of Staff
- Brazil
- Mexico, C.A., Andean
- Southern Cone
- Middle East/ Africa
- India

Xerox Corporation (cont.)

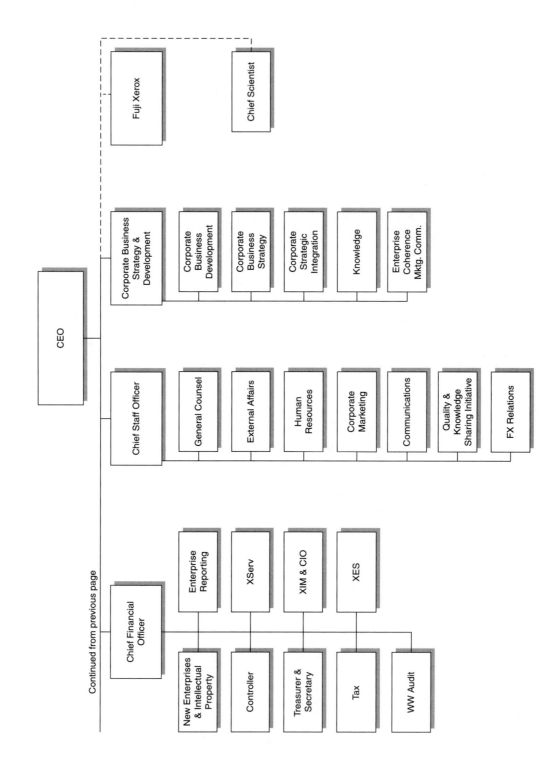

The Yamaguchi Bank, Ltd.

A regional bank serving Japan's Yamaguchi prefecture with more than $35 billion in assets

2-36, 4-chome, Takezaki-cho
Shimonoseki 750-8603, Japan
Phone: +81 832 233411

Primary SIC: 6021—National Commercial Banks
Primary NAICS: 52211—Commercial Banking

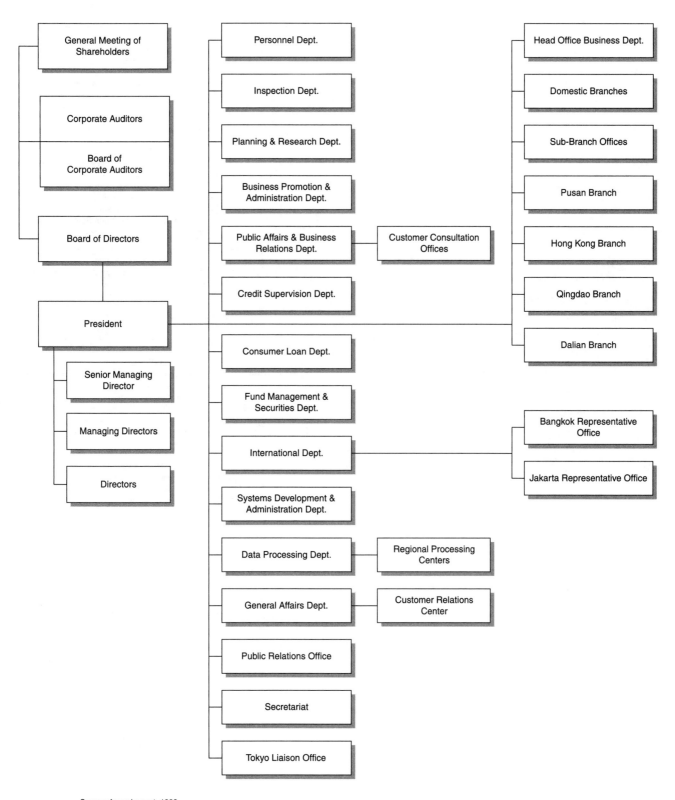

Source: Annual report, 1998

Yudensha Co., Ltd.

Provider of electrical design and construction services

2-8-21 Hatanodai
Shinagawa-ku, Tokyo 142-0064, Japan
Phone: +81 03-3786-1161
Web: www.yudensha.co.jp

Primary SIC: 1731—Electrical Work
Primary NAICS: 23531—Electrical Contractors

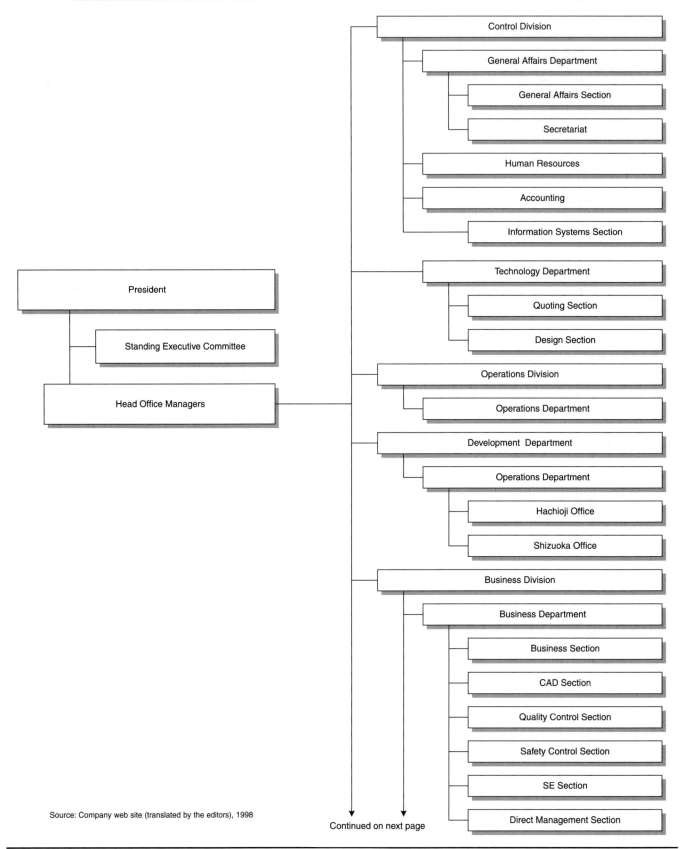

President

Standing Executive Committee

Head Office Managers

Control Division

General Affairs Department

General Affairs Section

Secretariat

Human Resources

Accounting

Information Systems Section

Technology Department

Quoting Section

Design Section

Operations Division

Operations Department

Development Department

Operations Department

Hachioji Office

Shizuoka Office

Business Division

Business Department

Business Section

CAD Section

Quality Control Section

Safety Control Section

SE Section

Direct Management Section

Source: Company web site (translated by the editors), 1998

Continued on next page

Continued from previous page

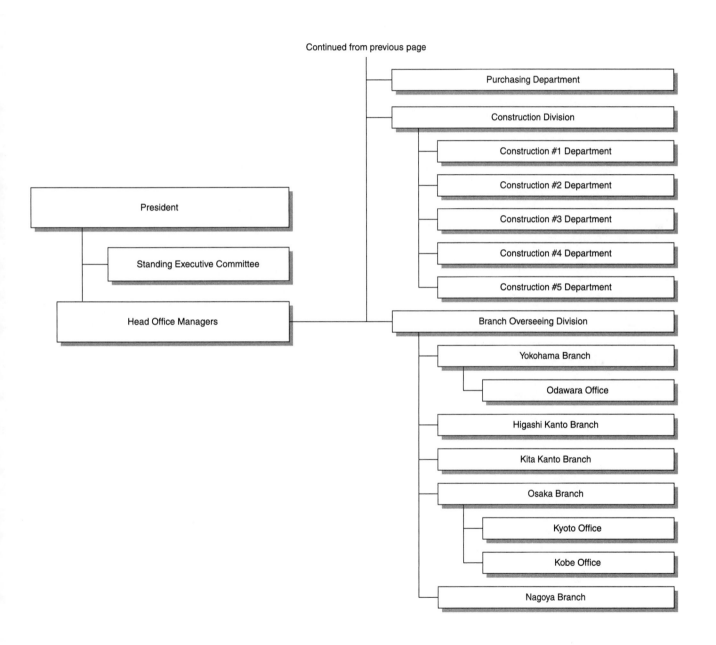

Reorganization Profiles

These notes supplement the series of nine reorganization features throughout the book

DaimlerChrysler AG

The 1998 merger was intended to combine Chrysler's innovative marketing and North American market share with Daimler-Benz's international presence and luxury nameplate. The respective chairmen of the two auto firms became co-chairmen at DaimlerChrysler and together headed an integration council made up of senior officers.

See charts on pages 51-54

The resulting top-level structure blended key elements from both companies. The new management structure reflected an attempt to merge the companies as equals, with similar numbers of top executives being chosen from each company for similar roles in the merged entity. The most sweeping effects of the merger were felt in areas like finance and purchasing, where the management believed it could realize significant gains by pooling those functions between the two firms. On the other hand, marketing and operating units remained largely intact.

General Motors Corporation

This nearly 600,000-person firm, which has gradually been trimming its workforce, undertook a series of restructuring and realignment measures between 1996 and 1998, with some of the most significant occurring in 1998. The firm has perennially been under pressure to cut its cost structure and boost its productivity, both of which have sapped GM's profitability.

Many of the changes were aimed at reducing layers of management and duplication of functions. For example, GM international operating units formerly reported to an international operations president. By 1999, this level had been removed and they were under the direct authority of the GM president and CEO.

See charts on pages 101-108

In other moves, the company integrated the sales and marketing functions for most of its North American car divisions, eliminating the traditional general managers of Chevrolet, Buick, Oldsmobile, and Pontiac. North American car manufacturing operations were likewise consolidated under one executive reporting to the president of GM North America. The company has spun off its Delphi Automotive Systems unit (also featured in this volume) as an independent, publicly traded company, although the bulk of Delphi's contracts are still with GM.

International Business Machines Corporation

Bearing witness to one of the largest and most famous restructurings ever, the charts shown here depict cumulative changes between 1991 and 1998. The most dramatic reworking occurred from 1992 to 1995. In essence, the 1991 chart represents a failing company and the 1998 version represents a thriving one.

Admittedly, all of the changes at IBM over the better part of the decade were not in one direction. In 1991, after one of the firm's worst years ever, then-chairman John Akers embarked on a strategy to divide IBM into a loose federation of companies, a move some dubbed the creation of "Baby Blues," a reference to AT&T's historic break-up in the mid-1980s. Layoffs in the tens of thousands accompanied the plan.

See charts on pages 132-135

However, by spring of 1993 Akers had been replaced by Louis V. Gerstner, an outsider with a vastly different strategy. While Gerstner proceeded with some of the staff cutbacks, his fundamental aim was to keep IBM together and build the business on its market strengths. This included emphasizing integrated computer services under the Global Services umbrella; embracing R&D, which had been slated to be cut sharply under the Akers plan; and emphasizing customer-focused solutions over a narrow product-centric approach.

Under Gerstner, IBM consolidated worldwide manufacturing, refocused its product lines, and reduced excess production capacity. It also built up its intellectual property/licensing business under the stewardship of a new general counsel, decentralized product marketing, and beefed up software offerings with acquisitions of Lotus Development Corp. and Tivoli Systems, Inc. These and other changes were credited with helping restore IBM to record profitability and strong revenue growth by the late 1990s.

Mitsubishi Corporation

Economic strife in its home market has caused Mitsubishi Corp., the flagship trading company of Japan's most famous *keiretsu,* or corporate families, to pursue selective restructuring and increasingly look

See charts on pages 176-179

outside its group of companies for new business opportunities. Typical of many Japanese firms, the rate of change has been gradual, partly due to cultural and political taboos on mass layoffs and abandoning lines of business.

Nonetheless, the company has slowly been consolidating certain operations and distancing itself from less profitable lines of business. For example, in the highly volatile metals trading sector, the company eliminated one of its five divisions in 1997, and consolidated the remaining four into just two as of 1998. Similarly, the trading company merged its foods, textiles, and general merchandise businesses into one group. In the process, the firm has also been trying to shed its traditional compartmentalized internal culture and cultivate new business opportunities outside its corporate family. Among the newer business lines Mitsubishi has been emphasizing are merchant banking and other financial and investment services.

Motorola Inc.

Responding to slow sales growth in 1997 and diminished profits by early 1998, Motorola's leadership in 1998 implemented a massive restructuring to better focus on its primary markets, cut costs, and offer

See charts on pages 184-185

its customers more integrated communications packages. The main thrust of the reforms was consolidating all but two of its main product sectors under one group called the Communications Enterprise. Under this banner went all product lines except semiconductor products and electronic components.

Supporting this effort were a consolidation of manufacturing operations and layoffs of some 15,000 workers worldwide, representing around 10% of Motorola's workforce. There was also considerable management turnover in the process. Motorola also sold off or ceased operations in some

of its underperforming or peripheral businesses, with a goal of being one of the top two players in every market it serves.

PPG Industries, Inc.

With growth in its traditional businesses sluggish and profitability low, PPG embarked on a set of initiatives between 1996 and 1998 to revitalize the company. Among

See charts on pages 220-221

other things, it decentralized its glass and coatings businesses by market segment and acquired a series of coatings companies to bolster its market presence. In one example, PPG entered the packaging coatings business by acquiring part of the Courtaulds line from Akzo Nobel. Altogether, the company made ten acquisitions in a two-year span. Simultaneously, the company sold off some of its European glass and surfactants holdings, and implemented cost reductions and technology upgrades at many existing plants.

Siemens AG

In one of Europe's largest corporate restructurings, Siemens in the late 1990s was in the midst of an aggressive realignment of its operating units. The industrial behemoth organized many of its existing units under new groupings

See charts on pages 242-243

such as energy and industry, while bringing a few new acquisitions into the fold and divesting other holdings. Some of the most extensive restructuring occurred in its new Information and Communications group, which consists network operations and services, network hardware manufacturing, and a business-oriented information technology services unit. Meanwhile, the company was making plans to spin off all of its components and cable manufacturing activities (still shown in the 1999 chart) through sales to other companies or public offerings. The management expected the reorganization to enhance profitability and competitive advantage.

The Tokai Bank, Limited

Between 1996 and 1998 Tokai Bank reorganized its operations into a "company" system of quasi-autonomous profit centers and restructured top management. The changes were intended to make key areas of the business more accountable and efficient. Before the restructuring, Tokai was organized in three main business centers: domestic, international, and investments.

Four of the five new operating companies represent

See charts on pages 268-269

Tokai's main business segments: (1) retail banking with individuals and smaller businesses; (2) wholesale commercial banking with major corporate clients; (3) investment banking and foreign banking; and (4) loan administration and asset collection. The fifth "company" oversees the computer systems used across all units in an effort to pool resources and control administrative costs.

Xerox Corporation

Coming off a widely publicized revamping in the early 1990s, Xerox's organization by the latter half of the 1990s was being massaged to prepare the company for a new strategic focus. The early 1990s restructuring, which was credited with turning the company around from its economic malaise, pushed more decision-making down to the operating areas and reduced staffing.

In 1998, although it was doing fairly well financially, the company announced it was eliminating 10% of its workforce in order to maintain competitive and was focusing increasingly on digital technology and system-level products and services. Top management was keenly aware that Xerox still had a higher employee-to-sales ratio than several key competitors. Outsourcing was picking up some of the slack as the company reduced its head count. In a separate move, the sales organization was redefined with a broader market focus instead of a single-product focus. From these changes Xerox hoped to be better placed to take advantage of new technologies, which it had a history of pioneering but not commercializing effectively.

See charts on pages 323-326

SIC Index

Companies, agencies, and nonprofit organizations are listed by their primary industry codes under the U.S. 1987 Standard Industrial Classification (SIC) system. Diversified firms may also be classified under additional industries.

National Association of Securities Dealers, Inc. 189
Pharmaceutical Research & Manufacturers of America 215

8621 Professional Membership Organizations

American Psychological Association 7-8
Institution of Structural Engineers 130-131
Japan Institute of Energy 148

8661 Religious Organizations

Catholic Diocese of Pittsburgh 30

8699 Membership Organizations, NEC

Japan Automobile Federation 147
World Energy Council 321

8711 Engineering Services

Ekono Energy Ltd. 75
Fuller Company 97
Harbin Power Engineering Company Limited 114
SCHEMA Konsult, Inc. 238
Woodward-Clyde Group, Inc. 319

8721 Accounting, Auditing, & Bookkeeping Services

Plante and Moran, LLP 217-218

8731 Commercial Physical & Biological Research

Fraunhofer Inst. for Interfacial Eng. & Biotech 96
Institut Français du Pétrole 129
Symetrix Corporation 257

8732 Commercial Economic, Sociological, & Educational Research

NTT Advanced Technology Corporation 205-206

8733 Noncommercial Research Organizations

Lawrence Livermore National Laboratory 164
Nuclear Research Centre (SCK CEN) 207
Oak Ridge National Laboratory 208
Pediatric AIDS Clinical Trials Group 211

8741 Management Services

ITD Associates 139

8742 Management Consulting Services

MPRI 187-188

8744 Facilities Support Management Services

Bonneville Pacific Services 24
Micro Craft, Inc. 172

9111 Executive Offices

City of Vancouver 36
Commonwealth of Virginia 38-40
New York City 194
United States Executive Branch 301-302

9131 Executive & Legislative Offices, Combined

Government of Canada 111

9211 Courts

United States Court System 300

9221 Police Protection

Tulsa Police Department 289

9611 Administration of General Economic Programs

U.S. Bureau of the Census 293-294

9631 Regulation & Administration of Communications, Electric, Gas, & Other Utilities

Federal Communications Commission 85

9651 Regulation, Licensing, & Inspection of Miscellaneous Commercial Sectors

Securities and Exchange Commission 239

9721 International Affairs

European Union 84
International Labour Organization 136-137
International Monetary Fund 138
United Nations 299
The World Bank Group 320
World Trade Organization 322

NAICS Index

Companies, agencies, and nonprofit organizations are listed by their primary industry codes under the U.S. 1997 North American Industry Classification System (NAICS). Diversified firms may also be classified under additional industries.

211111 Crude Petroleum & Natural Gas Extraction

Elf Aquitaine 77
Empresa Colombiana de Petróleos (Ecopetrol) 79-80
TOTAL Fina SA 281-282

21221 Iron Ore Mining

Companhia Vale do Rio Doce 41

213112 Oil & Gas Operations Support Activities

Floyd Oil Company 91
J. Ray McDermott S.A. 142, 171

221112 Fossil Fuel Electric Power Generation

Baltimore Gas and Electric Company 15-16
Gener S.A. 99
The Kansai Electric Power Co., Inc. 156-157
Tennessee Valley Authority 267

221119 Other Electric Power Generation

CMP Group, Inc. 37
Taiwan Power Co. (Taipower) 262-263

221122 Electric Power Distribution

DTE Energy Company 66
Edison International 74
Maine Electric Power Company 168

22121 Natural Gas Distribution

El Paso Energy Corporation 76

23331 Manufacturing & Industrial Building Construction

Darma Bajatra Aditunggal, PT 55-56
TAISEI Corporation 259-261

23491 Water, Sewer & Pipeline Construction

CTI Engineering Co., Ltd 46-48
Gasmin Limited 98

23492 Power/Communication Transmission Line Construction

Ingra Engineering and Construction Co. 128
Speedways Heavy Lift Engineering (Pvt.) Ltd. 248

23511 Plumbing, Heating & Air Conditioning Contractor

H.J. Pertzborn Plumbing & Fire Protection Corp. 113

23531 Electrical Contractors

Yudensha Co., Ltd. 329

311225 Fats & Oils Refining & Blending

Raisio Group plc 225
Unilever 298

31134 Nonchocolate Confectionery Manufacturing

Warner-Lambert Company 317

31152 Ice Cream & Frozen Dessert Manufacturing

Nestlé SA 193

31192 Coffee & Tea Manufacturing

Nestlé SA 193

31212 Breweries

Compañía Cervecerías Unidas S.A. 42
Kirin Brewery Co., Ltd. 159
San Miguel Corporation 232

315212 Women's Cut & Sew Apparel Contractors

Desco de Schultess Ltd. 60

315224 Men's/Boys' Cut & Sew Trouser/Slack/Jean Manufacturing

VF Corporation 314

315239 Women's/Girls' Cut & Sew Other Outerwear Manufacturing

VF Corporation 314

321219 Reconstituted Wood Product Manufacturing

Masisa S.A. 169

32211 Pulp Mills

Champion International Corporation 34
Stora Enso Oyj 249

322121 Paper (except Newsprint) Mills

Champion International Corporation 34
Stora Enso Oyj 249
UPM-Kymmene Corporation 312

322122 Newsprint Mills

UPM-Kymmene Corporation 312

323110 Commercial Lithographic Printing

Quantum Color Graphics, L.L.C. 223-224
Regia Holdinggesellschaft 226

336111 Automobile Manufacturing

DaimlerChrysler AG 51-54
Fiat Auto S.p.A. 88
Ford Motor Company 92-94
General Motors Corporation 101-108

336322 Other Motor Vehicle Electrical & Electronic Equipment Manufacturing

DaimlerChrysler AG 51-54
Delphi Automotive Systems Corporation 57, 104, 107, 108
Ford Motor Company 92-94
General Motors Corporation 101-108
Visteon Automotive Systems 93, 315

336399 All Other Motor Vehicle Parts Manufacturing

Autoliv Inc. 12

336412 Aircraft Engine & Engine Parts Manufacturing

General Electric Company 100
Lockheed Martin Corporation 165-167, 208

336413 Other Aircraft Part & Auxiliary Equipment Manufacturing

Composites Atlantic Limited 43

336414 Guided Missile & Space Vehicle Manufacturing

Lockheed Martin Corporation 165-167, 208

339112 Surgical & Medical Instrument Manufacturing

Abbott Laboratories 1
Becton Dickinson and Company 20

42183 Industrial Machinery & Equipment Wholesale

Daiichi Jitsugyo Co., Ltd. 49-50
Mitsubishi Corporation 176-179
Mitsui & Co., Ltd. 181

42272 Petroleum Products Wholesale (Except Bulk Stations/Terminals)

ITOCHU Corporation 140-141

44711 Gasoline Stations with Convenience Stores

Elf Aquitaine 77
Phillips Petroleum Company 216
Sunoco, Inc. 253
TOTAL Fina SA 281-282

481111 Scheduled Passenger Air Transportation

Japan Airlines Company, Ltd. 144-146
Singapore Airlines Limited 244-245
Turkish Airlines Inc. 290-291

482111 Line-Haul Railroads

Tokyu Corporation 273-275

483111 Deep Sea Freight Transportation

Orient Overseas Container Line Ltd. 210

484121 General Freight Trucking, Long-Distance, TL

Triton Transport Services, Inc. 288

484122 General Freight Trucking, Long-Distance, LTL

Skyhawk Logistics, Inc. 246

49111 Postal Service

Sweden Post Group 254
United States Postal Service 303

51113 Book Publishers

Golden Books Children's Publishing Group 109-110

51331 Wired Telecommunications Carriers

France Telecom 95
Japan Telecom Co., Ltd. 149-151
Nippon Telegraph and Telephone Corporation 200-203, 205-206
SaskTel International 237
Swisscom AG 256
U S WEST, Inc. 292

51334 Satellite Telecommunications

COMSAT Corporation 44

51411 News Syndicates

Reuters Group PLC 228

51412 Libraries & Archives

Akron-Summit County Public Library 3
Edinburgh University Library 71-73
University of California San Diego Libraries 305

514191 On-Line Information Services

Nippon Telegraph and Telephone Corporation 200-203, 205-206

51421 Data Processing Services

Bell & Howell Company 21

52111 Monetary Authorities - Central Bank

Bank of England 17
Bank of Japan 18
European Central Bank 82-83
Federal Reserve System 87

52211 Commercial Banking

Citicorp 35
Credit Suisse Group 45
Finance and Trade Bank (FinComBank) 89
Fleet Financial Group Inc. 90
The Hokkaido Takushoku Bank, Limited 119-120
The Industrial Bank of Japan, Limited 125-127
PPA Bank S.A. 219
Shinhan Bank 240
Shokoh Fund & Co., Ltd. 241
The Sumitomo Bank, Limited 250-251
The Tokai Bank, Limited 268-269
The Toronto-Dominion Bank 278-279
The Toyo Trust and Banking Company, Limited 283-284
UBS AG 297
The Yamaguchi Bank, Ltd. 327-328

52221 Credit Card Issuing

Citicorp 35
JACCS Co., Ltd. 143

52222 Sales Financing

General Electric Company 100
Mitsubishi Corporation 176-179

522291 Consumer Lending

Takefuji Corporation 264-266

522292 Real Estate Credit

IFS Financial Corporation 121-122

National Association of Securities Dealers, Inc. 189
Pharmaceutical Research & Manufacturers of America 215

81392 Professional Organizations

American Psychological Association 7-8
Institution of Structural Engineers 130-131
Japan Institute of Energy 148

81399 Other Similar Organizations (Except Business/Professional/Labor/Political)

World Energy Council 321

92111 Executive Offices

City of Vancouver 36
Commonwealth of Virginia 38-40
Government of Canada 111
New York City 194
United States Executive Branch 301-302

92211 Courts

United States Court System 300

92212 Police Protection

Tulsa Police Department 289

92611 Administration of General Economic Programs

U.S. Bureau of the Census 293-294

92613 Regulation & Administration of Utilities

Federal Communications Commission 85

92615 Regulation, Licensing, and Inspection of Miscellaneous Commercial Sectors

Securities and Exchange Commission 239

92812 International Affairs

European Union 84
International Labour Organization 136-137
International Monetary Fund 138
United Nations 299
The World Bank Group 320
World Trade Organization 322

Country Index

General Index